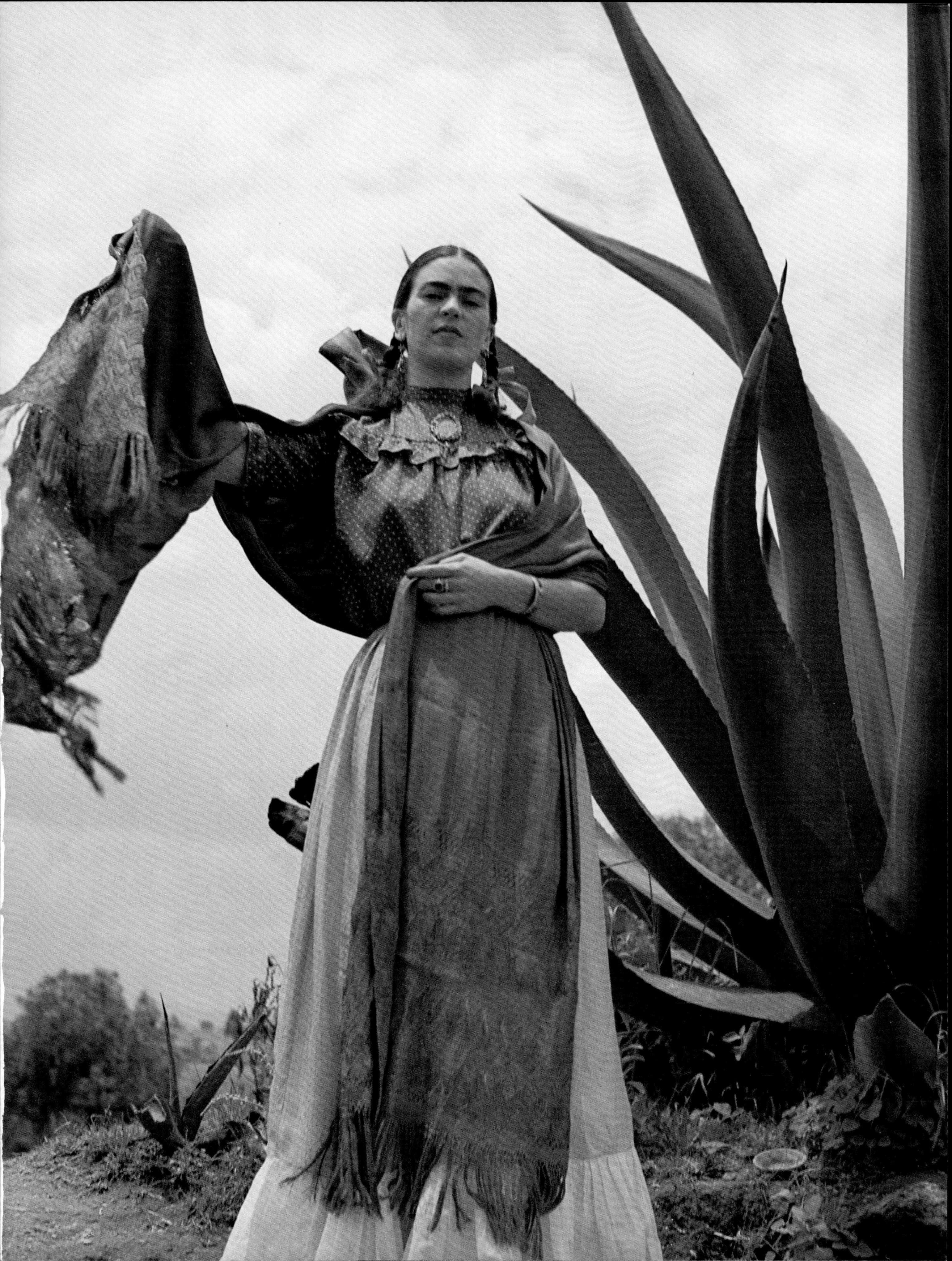

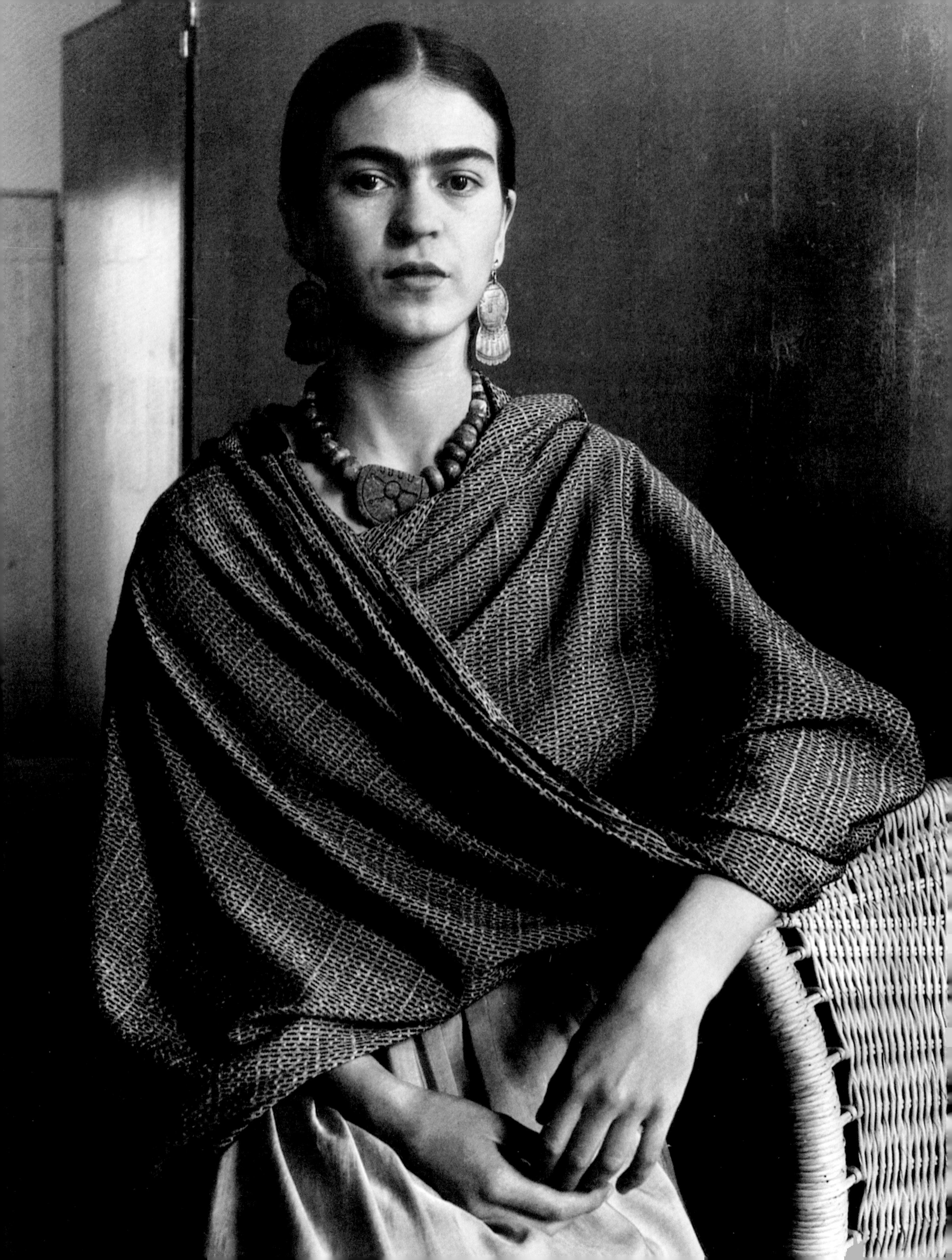

FRIDA KAHLO: MAKING HER SELF UP

Edited by **CLAIRE WILCOX & CIRCE HENESTROSA**

V&A PUBLISHING

Front cover illustration

NICKOLAS MURAY
FRIDA KAHLO IN BLUE SATIN BLOUSE, 1939
Nickolas Muray Photo Archives

Back cover illustration

DANIELA ROCHA
THE BLUE HOUSE, 2017

p. 1

TONI FRISSELL
FRIDA KAHLO, 'SEÑORAS OF MEXICO', US VOGUE, OCTOBER 1937
NITRATE NEGATIVE
Library of Congress Prints and Photographs Division

p. 2

IMOGEN CUNNINGHAM
FRIDA KAHLO, 1931
GELATIN PRINT. 25.4 × 20.32 CM

p. 5

FRIDA KAHLO
SELF-PORTRAIT ON THE BORDERLINE BETWEEN MEXICO AND THE UNITED STATES, 1932
OIL ON METAL. 31 × 35 CM
Modern Art International Foundation. Courtesy María and Manuel Reyero

p. 6

NICKOLAS MURAY
FRIDA KAHLO, 1938
Nickolas Muray Photo Archives

Sponsored by

GROSVENOR

With support from

GROW@ ANNENBERG

First published by V&A Publishing to accompany the exhibition *Frida Kahlo: Making Her Self Up* on view from 16 June until 4 November 2018 at the Victoria and Albert Museum, South Kensington, London SW7 2RL

Distributed in North America by Abrams, an imprint of ABRAMS

ISBN 978 1 85177 960 4

10
2024

A catalogue record for this book is available from the British Library.

Designer: Daniela Rocha
Copy-editor: Rebeka Cohen
Indexer: Hilary Bird

New photography by Javier Hinojosa

Printed by C&C Offset Printing Co. Ltd, China

With thanks to

MUSEO FRIDA KAHLO

MÉXICO GOBIERNO DE LA REPÚBLICA | CULTURA SECRETARÍA DE CULTURA

INBAL INAH

V&A Publishing

Supporting the world's leading museum of art and design, the Victoria and Albert Museum, London

FSC MIX Paper | Supporting responsible forestry FSC® C008047 www.fsc.org

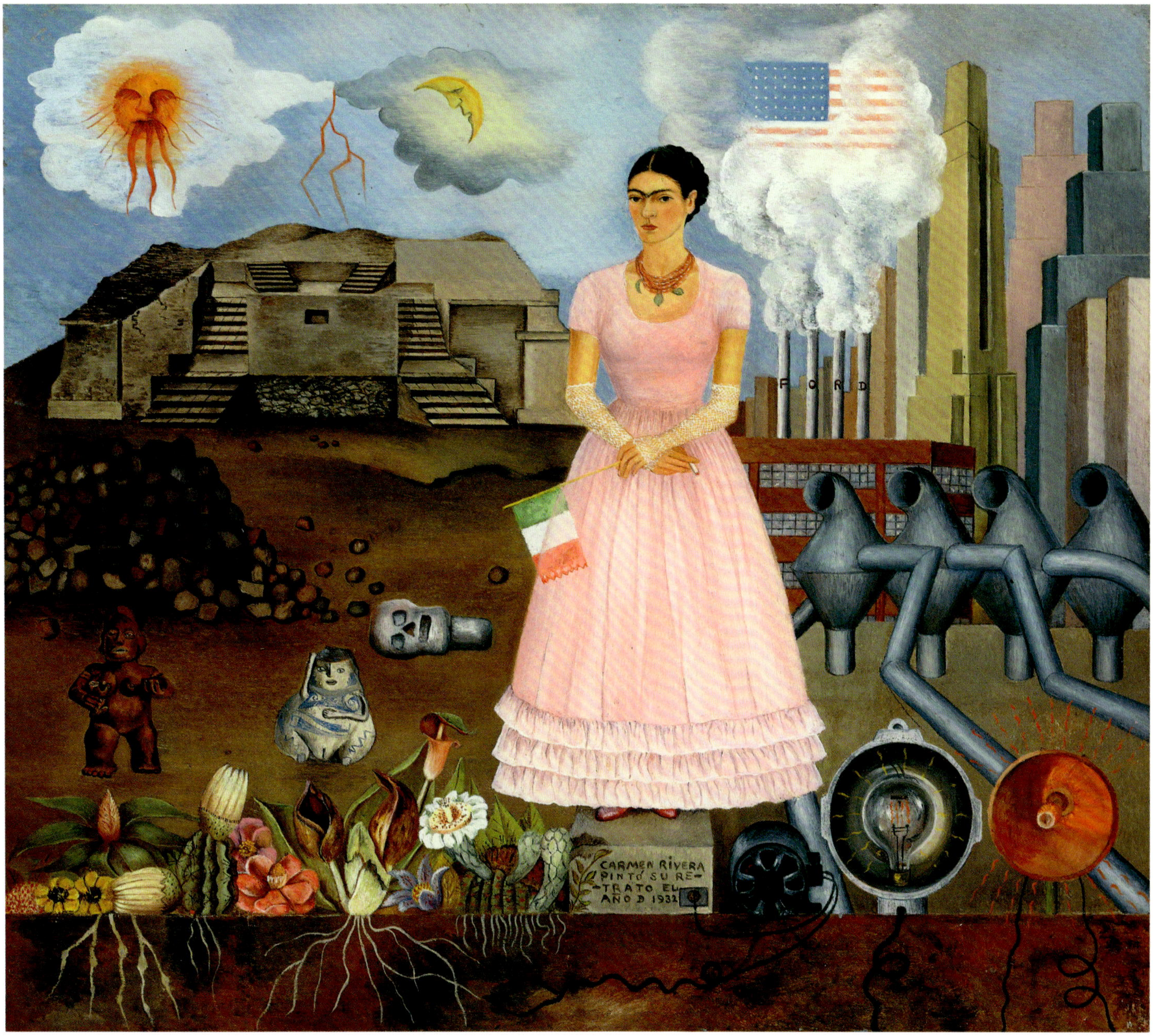
FORD
CARMEN RIVERA
PINTÓ SU RE-
-TRATO EL
AÑO D 1932

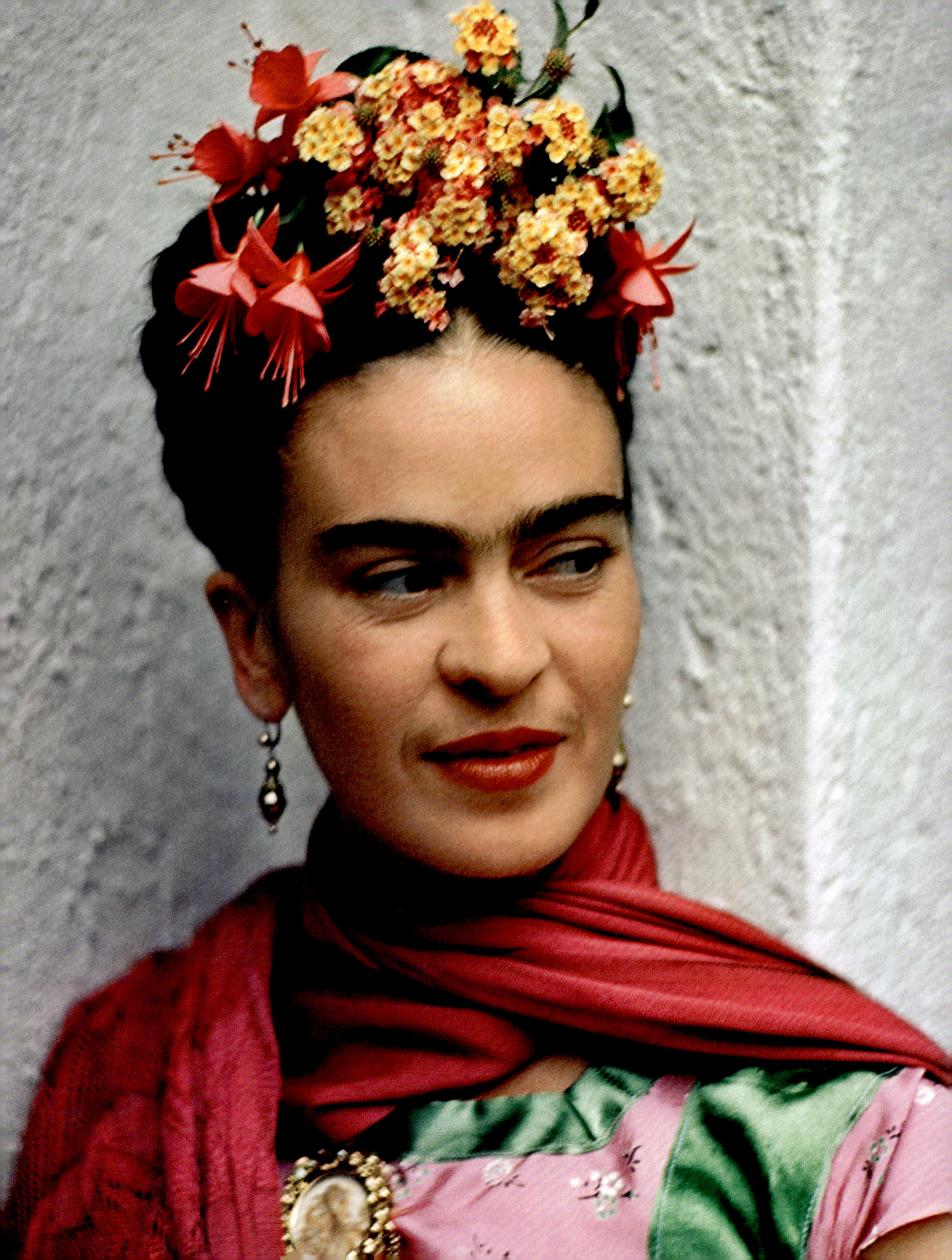

CONTENTS

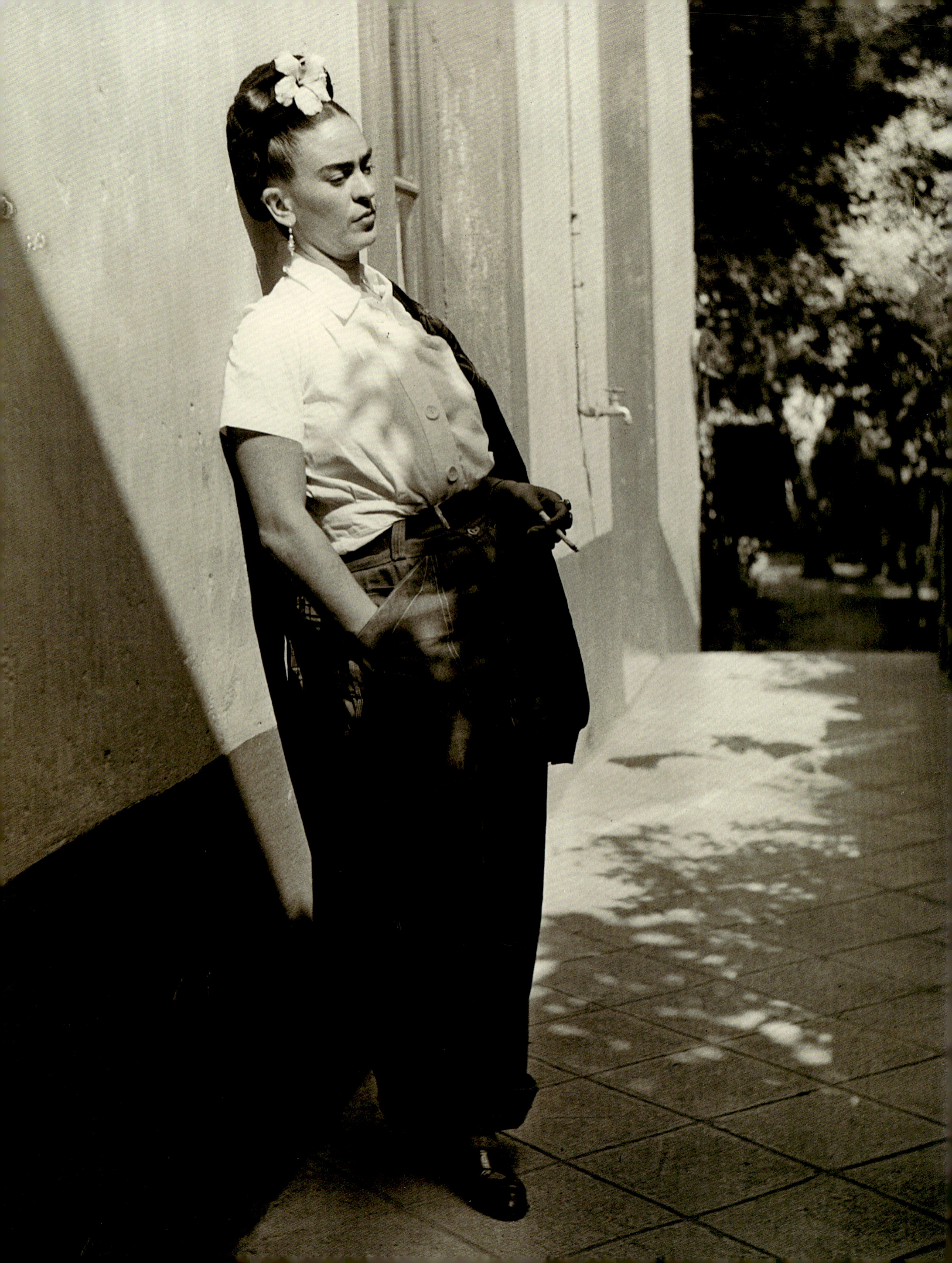

SPONSOR'S FOREWORD

CRAIG McWILLIAM
CEO, Grosvenor Britain & Ireland

The V&A has shed light on artistry and skill for more than 150 years. In its recent exhibitions, the Museum has drawn deeply on its talent for exploring icons through their styling, work and wardrobe – while holding a mirror up to society. In that context, Frida Kahlo is a perfect subject: politically-charged, strikingly original, and unafraid to celebrate herself. Kahlo has been dubbed the original selfie queen. At the same time she is an artist of substance.

We have long believed that the V&A educates and dazzles, elevating everyday handicraft and traditional skills to the status of modern art. Through an exhibition like this, an exceptional individual can help make sense of culture, identity, art and – of course – fashion. Grosvenor Britain & Ireland is delighted to sponsor the exhibition *Frida Kahlo: Making Her Self Up*, and we are proud to partner with the V&A.

We have drawn inspiration from this exhibition to bring a modern echo of Kahlo's impact to our London estate of Mayfair and Belgravia. In 2018, Mayfair and Belgravia's streets will be transformed with floral portraits, events and experiences that celebrate this great artist. We have a vision to make our London estate more active, more open and more integrated – a more popular place that reflects changing needs. Our partnership with the V&A underlines our common passion for the personal experiences that reflect our changing society.

CARLOS PHILLIPS OLMEDO
Director General, Museums Dolores Olmedo, Frida Kahlo y Diego Rivera Anahuacalli

There is art that is so highly personal in nature that it becomes universal. This is true of the art of Frida Kahlo. In constructing her own persona – as if it were a work of art – through a very specific style of clothing and reflecting this in her work, she has become one of the best-known Latin American artists of our time. More than this, she has been transformed into a symbol extending beyond the spheres of culture and art to represent many social movements.

We are proud to be able to participate in the universality of art and, in particular, in the universality of Frida Kahlo. It is our great pleasure to play a part in the combined endeavours of two internationally renowned museums: the Museo Frida Kahlo and the Victoria and Albert Museum.

The works held at the *Casa Azul* (Blue House) were donated to the people of Mexico by Frida Kahlo and her husband Diego Rivera through a trust established with the Bank of Mexico. During 2016 and 2017 more than 150 items were successfully conserved for the exhibition *Frida Kahlo: Making Her Self Up* and the creation of this book. This collection of Frida Kahlo's clothing and possessions is now exhibited at the V&A for the enjoyment and appreciation of a wider audience. The curatorship was a joint undertaking, involving the combined efforts of both museums.

The Frida Kahlo who appears in this new presentation reveals one of her least known aspects: that of an artist who constructs an identity through and by means of her disability. Kahlo customised or made many of the clothes shown in the exhibition and specially photographed for this book. They are clear evidence that she was not only a painter, but a woman of boundless creativity who transformed everything she touched. To Kahlo, writing poetry, designing her own clothes and decorating her corsets with mirrors and oil paint were all one.

We are delighted that the clothes and personal belongings that were such an important element of her persona are being shown in such a prestigious space as the V&A – a world leader in the expression of art through fashion which has hosted so many outstanding exhibitions. I should like to thank Tristram Hunt, Director of the V&A, Linda Lloyd-Jones, Head of Exhibitions and Loans, Claire Wilcox, Senior Curator of Fashion, and all the team at the V&A for making this exhibition and important publication possible.

DIRECTORS' FOREWORDS

TRISTRAM HUNT
Director, Victoria and Albert Museum

Frida Kahlo's powerful and inimitable style is as central to her fame as her paintings, and was constructed with equal care. This remarkable exhibition at the V&A, *Frida Kahlo: Making Her Self Up*, brings together Kahlo's compelling self-portraits and the festive garments and jewellery that she wore throughout her life, for the very first time.

In 2004, arguably one of the most significant discoveries in recent art history took place at the *Casa Azul* (Blue House), Kahlo's lifelong home. Thousands of her personal possessions were rediscovered, including photographs, letters and drawings, medicines and orthopaedic corsets, alongside her distinctive colourful blouses, skirts and shawls. Kahlo's wardrobe is at once sartorial and symbolic in her paintings, and now so familiar from the countless photographs of the artist taken in her lifetime.

International teams of curators, researchers and conservators have helped to preserve this remarkable legacy for future generations. The magnetism of Kahlo's appearance, and the constant multiplication of her image online, reflects the passion that she still inspires. Her rejection of gender orthodoxy and conventional fashion – as an artist who also transcended disability – allowed her to forge a unique identity which spans age, gender and geography in its global appeal.

Frida Kahlo: Making Her Self Up had its genesis in *Appearances Can Be Deceiving: The Dresses of Frida Kahlo* shown at the Museo Frida Kahlo in 2012. I wish to thank its curator, Circe Henestrosa, who is also co-curator of the V&A exhibition, with Claire Wilcox, Senior Curator of Fashion. My deepest thanks are also due to Hilda Trujillo Soto, Director of the Museo Frida Kahlo and Carlos Phillips Olmedo, Director General, Museums Dolores Olmedo, Frida Kahlo y Diego Rivera Anahuacalli for facilitating this very special collaboration.

My gratitude also extends to the Bank of Mexico, which has allowed these fragile artifacts to leave Mexico for the very first time and travel thousands of miles to the V&A, and to the Gelman Collection for the loan of their equally precious paintings. Finally, I would like to thank our sponsor, Grosvenor Britain & Ireland for their support. It is an extraordinary privilege for the V&A to be able to present this landmark exhibition – a fitting tribute to one of the most extraordinary and captivating artists of our time.

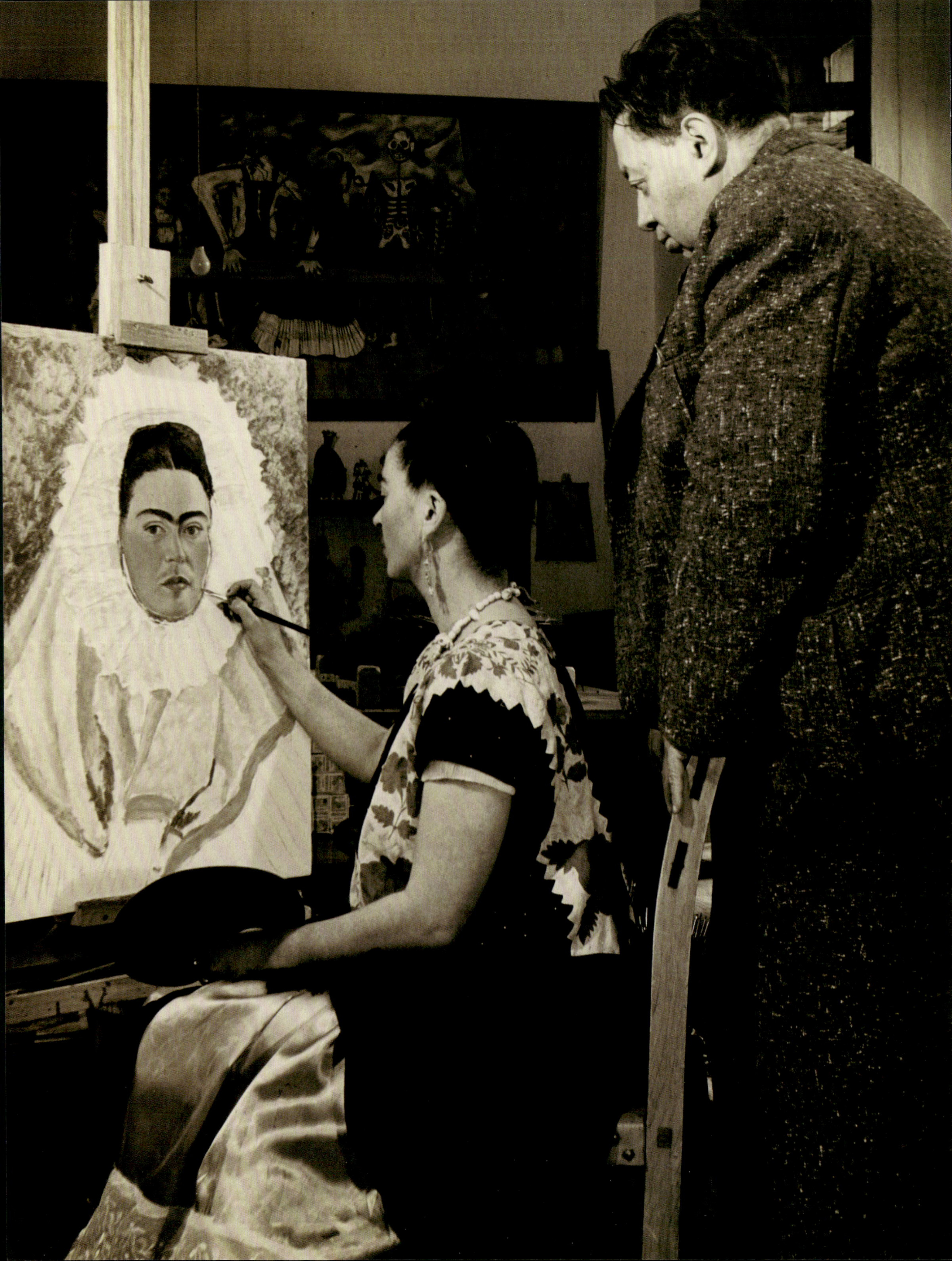

INTRODUCTION: FASHIONING FRIDA

CLAIRE WILCOX & CIRCE HENESTROSA

Frida Kahlo (1907–1954) sits at her easel, fully robed in her Tehuana dress, with brightly embroidered blouse and full skirt billowing to the ground. In her right hand, she holds a fine sable brush, and in her left an artist's palette, which rests on her knee. Kahlo is intent on her unfinished painting, despite the looming presence of Diego Rivera (1886–1957) behind her, watching her paint. Kahlo depicts herself dressed in a *resplandor*, a festive headdress worn at weddings and on saint's days. The starched lace ruff forms an aura around her face, while her watchful eyes meet the viewer's. As with many of Kahlo's art works, the power of the self-portrait lies in its sense of anguish and a tense ambiguity about who is regarding whom.

Self-Portrait as a Tehuana (Diego on My Mind) [88], one of Kahlo's larger works, was not finished until 1943. By then, she had added a force-field of tendrils, adorned her hair with bougainvillea flowers and leaves, and anointed her forehead with Rivera's portrait, thus uniting three of the main preoccupations of her life: her Mexican identity, self-portraiture and her complex relationship with Rivera. Twenty-one years older than Kahlo, Rivera was the leading muralist of his time and together they were at the forefront of Mexico's artistic, cultural and political elite, even accommodating Leon Trotsky in the *Casa Azul* (Blue House) during his exile from Russia in the late 1930s.

The Blue House in Coyoacán, once a village on the outskirts of Mexico City, but now part of the city's suburbs, was the epicentre of Kahlo's life. Here we see her, with habitual cigarette in hand,[1] in the bright sunlit courtyard with her hairless *xoloitzcuintli* dogs[2] and mischievous spider monkeys,[3] or indoors, bejewelled and made up, lying atop carefully arranged bed covers and lace-edged sheets in her four-poster bed. Kahlo's sick bed functioned as both refuge and stage, for following a traumatic accident in 1925 in which she almost died, she spent extended periods encased in immobilizing plaster corsets, writing in January 1950, from hospital: 'Still corseted up and just a f…rigging mess! But I'm not discouraged and I'll try to start painting as soon as I can.'[4] In lieu of access to her easel, the plaster of her corsets became a three-dimensional canvas.

Unlike Rivera and other male artists who asserted their artistic freedom by being depicted in paint-spattered workwear, Kahlo rarely appeared casually dressed, even at her easel, for although underestimated

p.8
EMMY LOU PACKARD
FRIDA KAHLO, 1941
PHOTOGRAPHIC PRINT. 27 × 27 CM
Emmy Lou Packard Papers, Archives of American Art, Smithsonian Institution

p.12
BERNARD SILBERSTEIN
FRIDA KAHLO PAINTING 'SELF-PORTRAIT AS A TEHUANA' WHILST DIEGO RIVERA OBSERVES HER, 1940
PHOTOGRAPHIC PRINT. 24.4 × 20 CM
Library of Congress Prints and Photographs Division

LUCIENNE BLOCH
FRIDA KAHLO AT THE BARBIZON PLAZA HOTEL, NEW YORK, 1933
The Jacques and Natasha Gelman Collection of 20th Century Mexican Art and the Vergel Foundation

as an artist in her lifetime, she was frequently photographed at work. Her charisma and careful regard for the art of dressing offered a photogenic appeal that was at odds with the uncompromising nature of her art; as the founder of Surrealism André Breton observed, her painting was like 'a ribbon around a bomb'. Circe Henestrosa has noted:

> Kahlo's powerful style is as integral to her myth as her paintings. It is her construction of identity through her ethnicity, her disability, her political beliefs and her art that makes her such a compelling and relevant icon today. Her resplendent Tehuana dresses; striking headpieces, hand-painted corsets and prosthetics masterfully masked her physical impairments, but were also a form of self-expression and an extension of her art.[5]

The work of Gannit Ankori and Oriana Baddeley informed Henestrosa's exhibition *Appearances Can Be Deceiving: The Dresses of Frida Kahlo* at the Museo Frida Kahlo in 2012, designed by exhibition-maker Judith Clark, from which the V&A's iteration *Frida Kahlo: Making Her Self Up* evolved. Ankori interrogates the relationship between photographs of Kahlo, her painting and her self-fashioning in her essay *Frida Kahlo: Posing, Composing, Exposing* while Baddeley's essay *Frida Redressed* summarizes Kahlo's remarkable impact on a digital world, which even she could not possibly have imagined. Their texts bookend Henestrosa's essay *Appearances Can Be Deceiving – Frida Kahlo's Construction of Identity: Disability, Ethnicity and Dress* which is informed by her own family roots in the Tehuantapec Isthmus, and the power of its dress.

Today, the Blue House is a museum, but it still feels like a home, overflowing with Kahlo's collections of Mexican popular arts and crafts. The rooms are filled with pre-Columbian sculpture, walls are lined with *ex-votos* (devotional paintings),[6] the kitchen retains its colourful tiles and glass display cases are crowded with pottery figures, dolls and toys. Family photographs still dot the walls, along with heroes of the Russian Revolution, while Kahlo's erudition is reflected in the Spanish, English and German volumes on art, anatomy and political history, and the novels and poetry that line her book shelves.

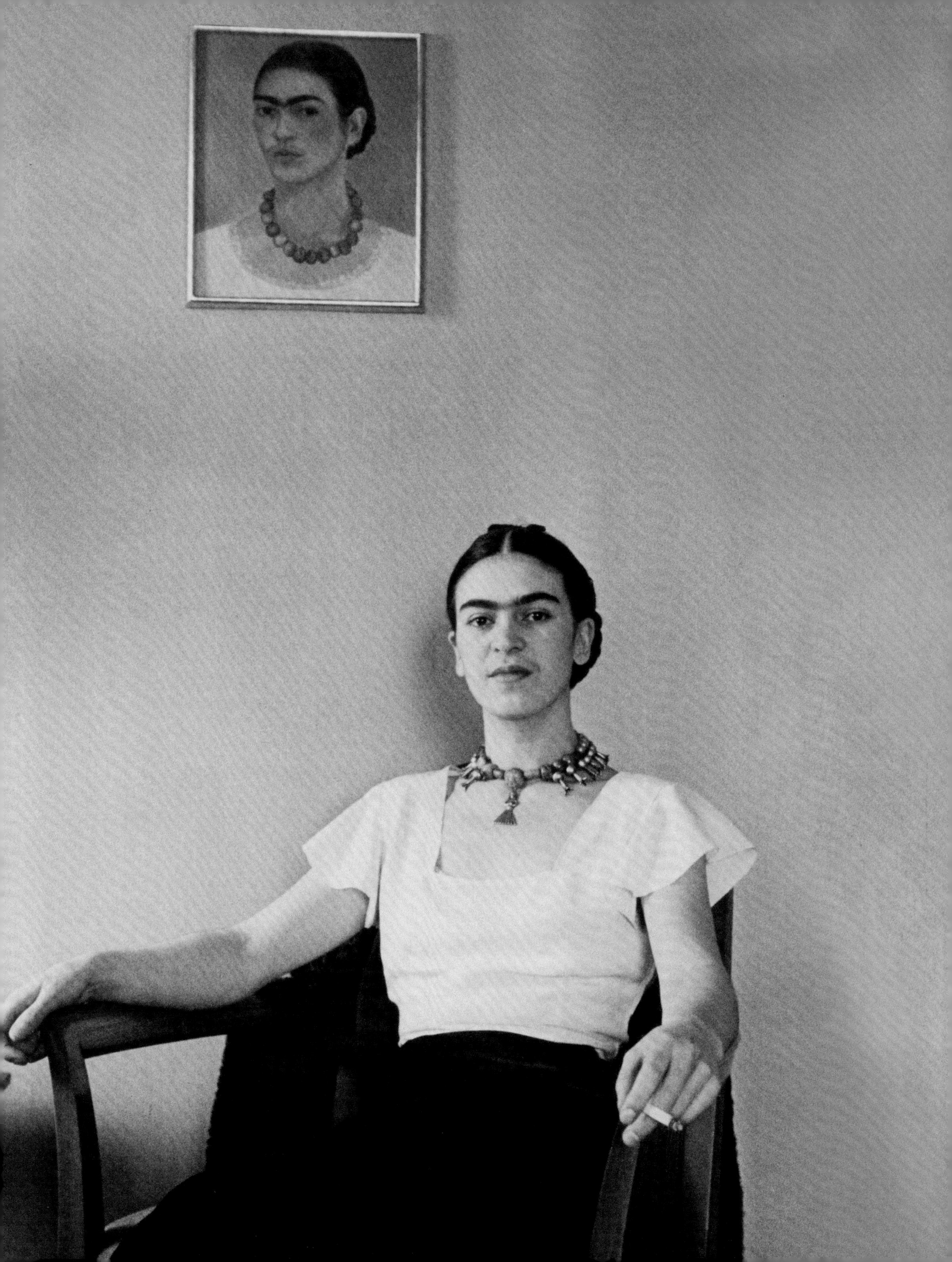

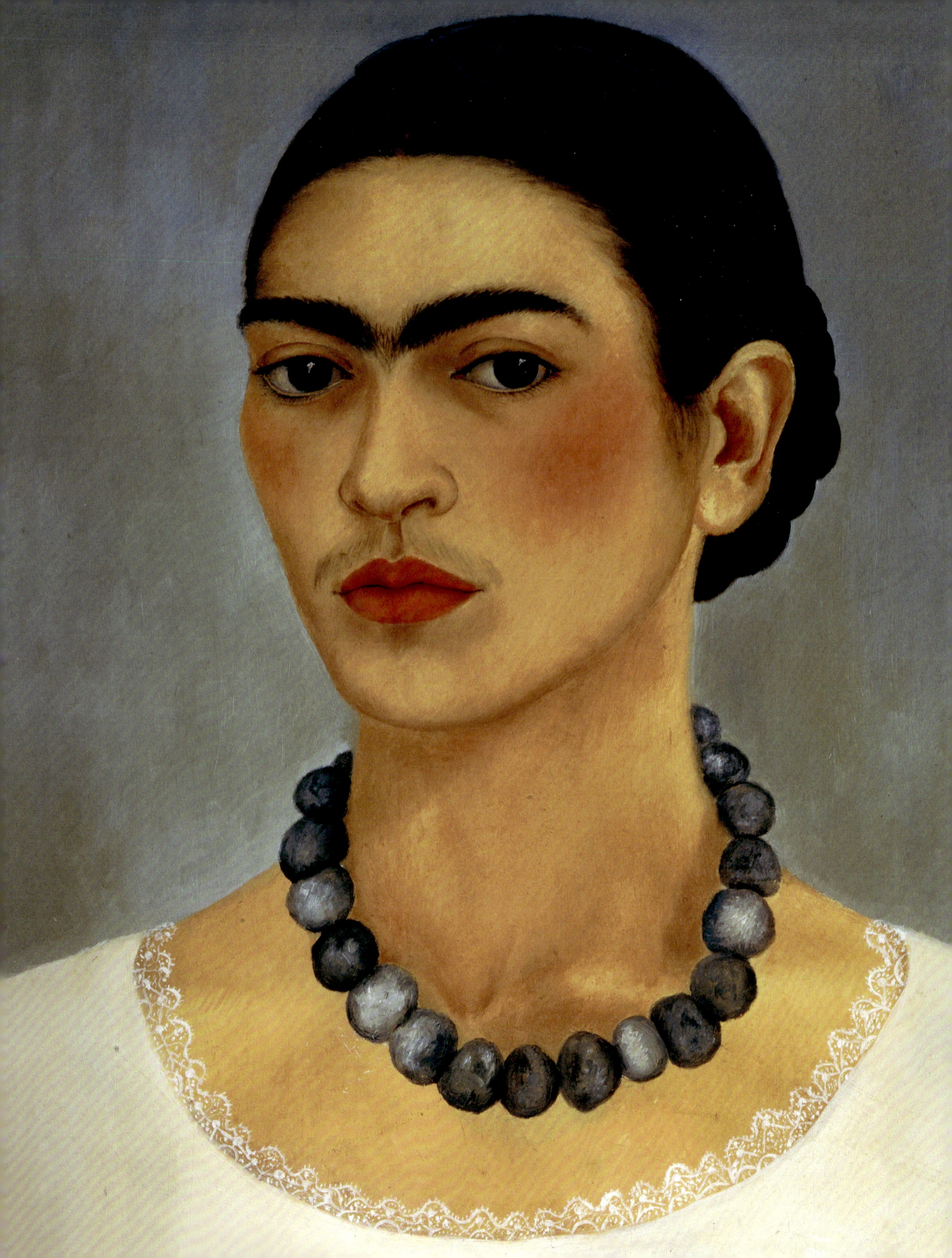

FRIDA KAHLO
SELF-PORTRAIT WITH A NECKLACE, 1933
OIL ON METAL. 35 × 29 CM
The Jacques and Natasha Gelman Collection of 20th Century Mexican Art and the Vergel Foundation

Kahlo and Rivera's lives and art are impossible to comprehend without an understanding of their political ideology following the turmoil of the Mexican Revolution, and the community of artists that was drawn to Mexico during the 1930s. Adrian Locke articulates this in his essay *Quetzalcoatl's Grin: The Changing Face of Art and Culture in Frida Kahlo's Mexico*. Despite her atheism and commitment to Communism, Kahlo's work was imbued with Catholic imagery, which Kirstin Kennedy explores in her essay on the traditions and meanings of the *resplandor*.[7]

Hilda Trujillo Soto's essay *Treasure in the Blue House* tells the remarkable story of the opening of Kahlo's bathroom in 2004, and the discovery of an extraordinary collection of jewellery, surgical corsets, medicines, cosmetics, photographs, letters and, above all, clothing. These objects are so familiar to art historians from her self-portraits and the countless photographs that exist of Kahlo. Locked away by Rivera on her death in 1954, they remained undisturbed until 2004, and the V&A is privileged to be the first to show these priceless artifacts, outside Mexico.

Claire Wilcox's exploration of Kahlo's love of cosmetics, interleaved here with new photography by Javier Hinojosa, offers a unique perspective on how Kahlo faced the world. Clare Phillips also offers new research into the history of Kahlo's eclectic and bold taste in jewellery; ranging from pre-Columbian to modern, it was indelibly associated with her uniquely individual appearance. The inclusion of numerous family photographs of Kahlo has also helped determine the structure of this book which includes six inset booklets containing archive photographs and personal items, while larger pages contain the paintings and newly conserved ensembles, mounted on mannequins.

In November 2017, a team of conservators, mount-makers and curators visited the Blue House to prepare for the exhibition at the V&A which would reunite Kahlo's clothing with some of her self-portraits. Whilst there, they detected many traces of pigment on the skirts upon which Kahlo rested her palette and brushes; some are stained with red paint and small splashes of blue and black ink (Kahlo was an inveterate letter writer), while others have paint embedded in the textile fibres or faint brushstrokes of paint across the surface of the fabric.

Kahlo's commitment to the Tehuana dress of her native Mexico was

DETAIL OF PRE-COLUMBIAN JADE BEADS, PROBABLY EXCAVATED FROM A MAYA SITE AND ASSEMBLED AS A NECKLACE BY FRIDA KAHLO
Museo Frida Kahlo

not for show, or for staged photographs, but an integral part of her daily dress, as the many darns, cigarette burns and stains demonstrate. Perhaps one of the most moving discoveries was the realization that a dash of green paint on one of Kahlo's pre-Columbian necklaces, consisting of jade beads unearthed from archaeological excavations which the artist had strung herself, and which are similar to those featured in her 1933 *Self-Portrait with a Necklace* [p.16], is in fact a deliberately applied brushstroke of green paint. It is tempting to speculate that Kahlo was trying to match the colour of the stones while painting herself.

The symbiotic relationship in Kahlo's life and work between her art and dress cannot be overestimated. Kahlo, as always, forged new ground, meaning that art historians and costume historians have been brought together by the remarkable legacy of both Kahlo's art and wardrobe: the material properties of her clothing bring her paintings to life, while the paintings offer dress in all its symbolic meaning, thus changing the fields of biography, self-portraiture and sartorial expression forever.

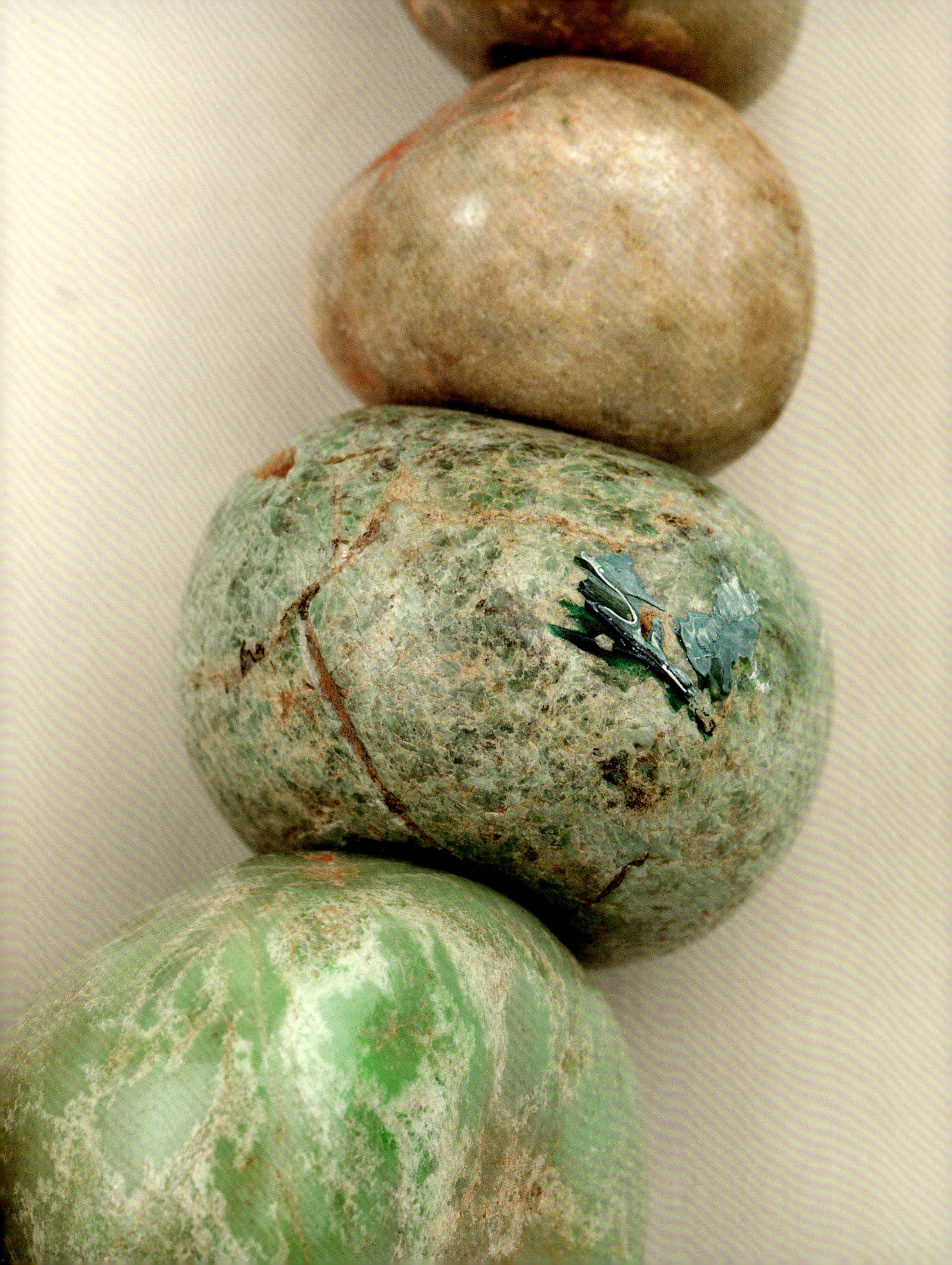

Treasure in the Blue House

HILDA TRUJILLO SOTO

Translated by Ana Baeza Ruiz

There are many detailed studies of Frida Kahlo and Diego Rivera, but these two artists continue to surprise us, almost as if taunting us with new revelations about their life and work. In late 2003, many of their personal possessions were rediscovered at the Museo Frida Kahlo (formerly the *Casa Azul* or Blue House) following 50 years of confinement. This extraordinary collection was made available to the public in 2007, following painstaking conservation, research and curation. It includes over 6,500 photographs, 22 documents and around 300 garments that belonged to Kahlo, as well as many of her personal possessions, drawings and toys. A real treasure trove.

As well as furthering and enriching our knowledge about various aspects of Kahlo and Rivera's lives and work, these archives have opened up new avenues of research. The collection itself is unique, providing us with a broad picture of the cultural and political landscape of Mexico, and further afield, during the first half of the twentieth century – as seen through the creative lens of Kahlo and Rivera.

On 25 September 1957, a few months prior to his death, Rivera left his friend and patron Dolores Olmedo in charge of the Frida Kahlo and Anahuacalli Museums, the terms of which stated that all objects stored in one of the bathrooms in the Blue House should be concealed for a period of 15 years. Another bathroom, a cellar, and several trunks, wardrobes, cupboards and boxes remained sealed up. At that point, the clock stopped ticking.[1]

The bathroom secured by Rivera contained mostly political documents, while the remaining spaces housed letters, photographs and personal – in some cases intimate – possessions. As time passed, it was these more personal items that would come to speak most powerfully of the political passions, dreams and uncertainties of both artists.

In late 2003, the *Comité Técnico del Fideicomiso* and its Director General, Carlos Phillips Olmedo, gave authorization for the sealed rooms in the Blue House to be unlocked and accessed. The main challenge was to carry out this task within a limited budget, given that the Museo Frida Kahlo is, like the Anahuacalli Museum, a non-profit institution (left by Rivera to the people of Mexico), and as such must generate its own income if it is to remain open to the public. In order to meet the challenge

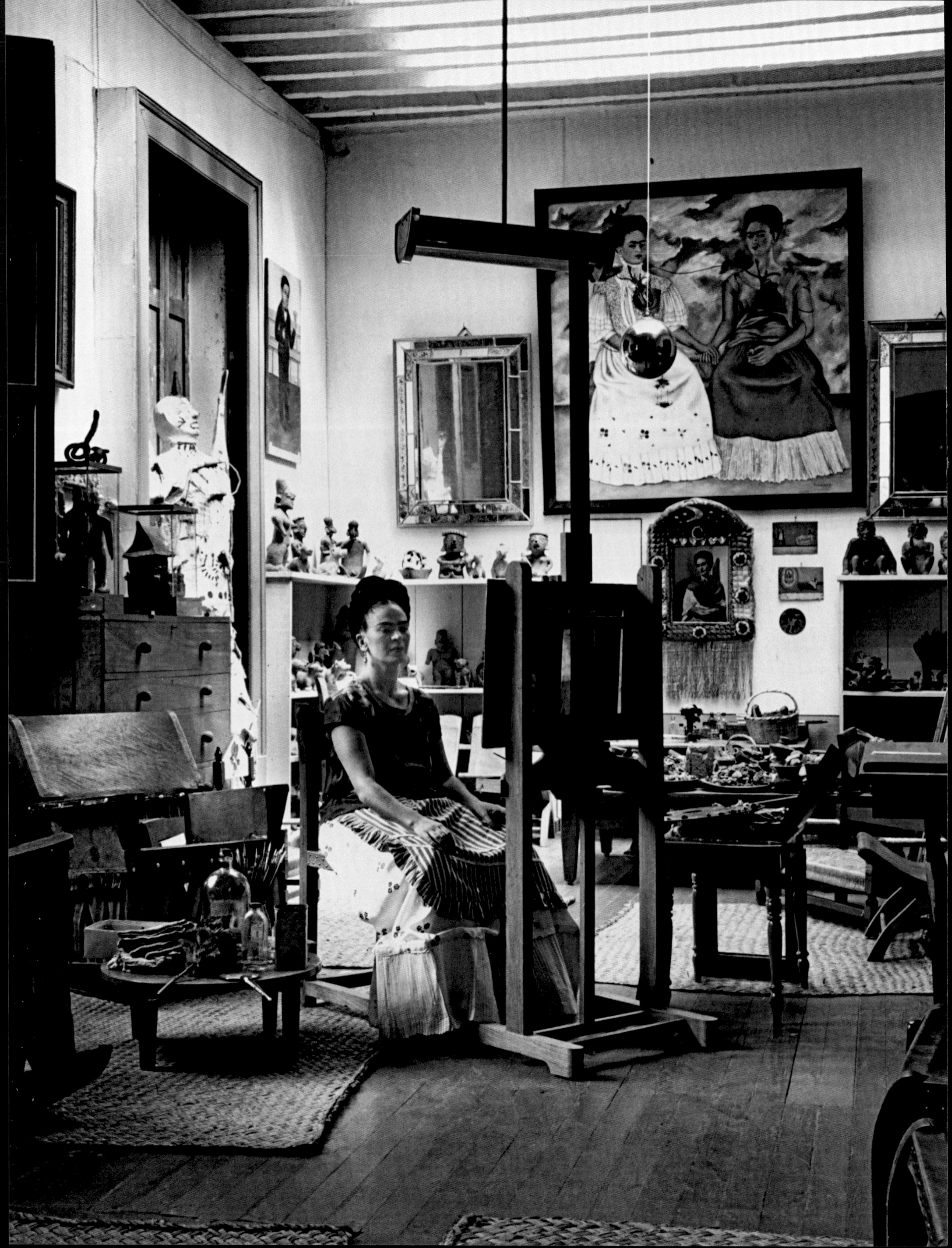

1. FRITZ HENLE
FRIDA KAHLO IN HER STUDIO, C.1943
GELATIN PRINT. 28.75 × 24.77 CM
Fritz Henle Estate

of recovering this important cultural memory, Dr Isabel Grañén Porrúa and Don Alfredo Harp Helú were contacted, via the organization *Apoyo al Desarrollo de Archivos y Bibliotecas de México* (Support for the Development of Archives and Libraries in Mexico).

It took more than four years to catalogue the documents, photographs, art works, books, garments and other objects in the collection. At the same time, textiles and jewellery were cleaned, analyzed and classified along with magazines and newspapers. This has been a huge conservation project that continues to this day, and which has revealed many fascinating narratives along the way. These narratives were the inspiration for this exhibition – *Frida Kahlo: Making Her Self Up*.

Particularly noteworthy stories include the discovery of over 30 drawings by Kahlo, including *Las apariencias engañan (Appearances can be Deceiving)* [38], which were found at the back of one of the wardrobes; another time, a piece of furniture where Kahlo stored her toys was found to contain materials for a Surrealist installation, demonstrating her authorship of this work; similarly, a hand-shaped earring that Picasso presented to Kahlo was found in a plastic box in her desk, until then presumed to contain only her working tools; on a separate occasion, an hitherto unknown oil painting by Rivera was found in an egg carton.[2]

The vast visual archive contains around 6,500 photographs produced in a variety of techniques including works by Edward Weston, Tina Modotti, Man Ray, Manuel Álvarez Bravo, Gisèle Freund, Nickolas Muray, Martin Munkácsi, Imogen Cunningham, Lucienne Bloch, Fritz Henle and Bernard Silberstein, among others, many of whom left only a handful of works in Mexico. Kahlo's clothes, jewellery, accessories and footwear amount to a collection of roughly 300 pieces, and they allow us to document her personal style, which was colourful, texturally rich and imaginative, yet also defiant, irreverent and authentic. The collection of dress and textiles reveals the subtlety and creative richness of Kahlo's personal style, which addressed her gendered identity and helped her confront her disabilities and ill health.[3] Her manner of dress also offered a means of pleasing her husband Rivera, according to some scholars, and of proclaiming her liberal spirit and independence, as well as expressing her pride in her roots. This directly countered accepted fashion

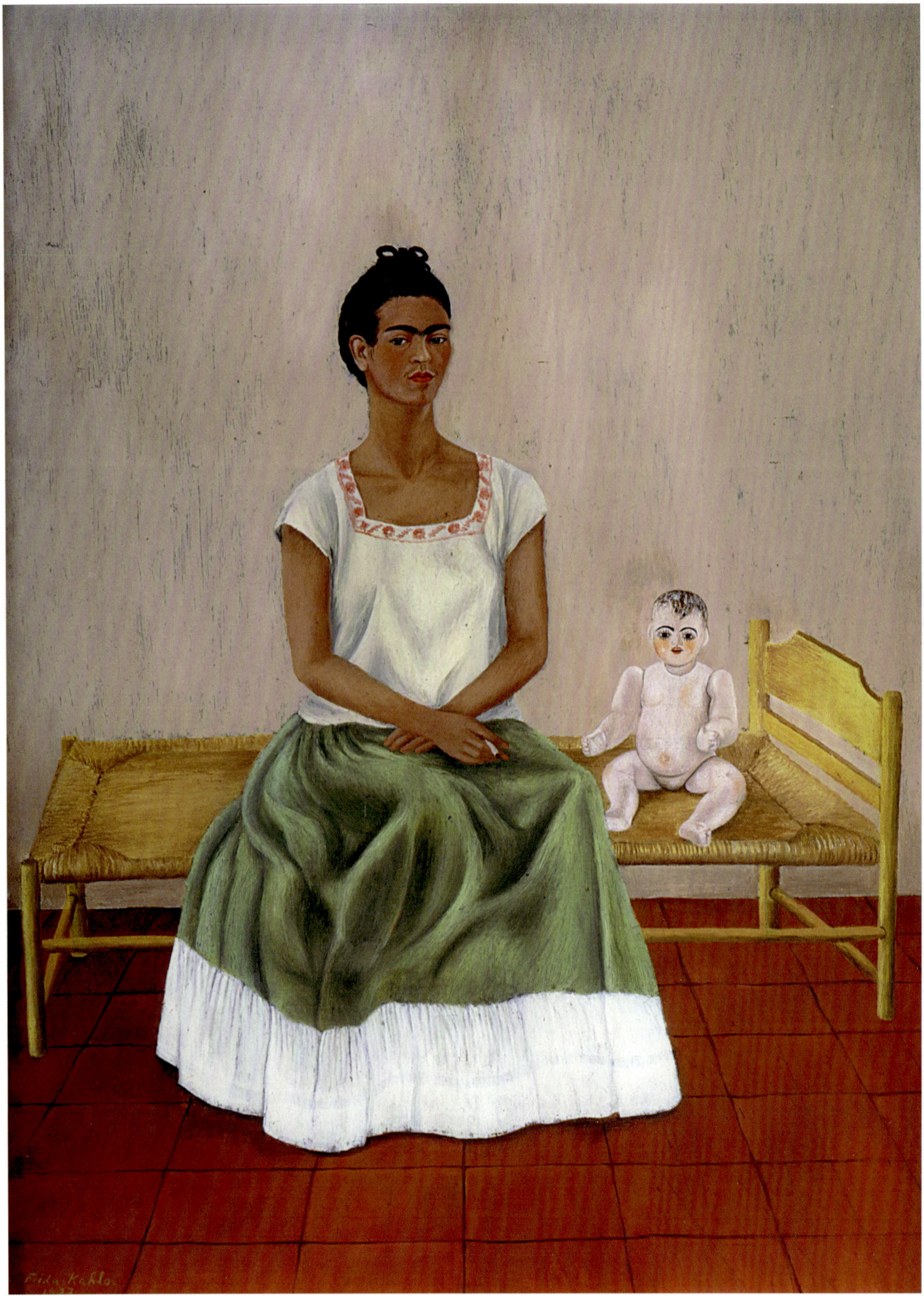

2. FRIDA KAHLO
ME AND MY DOLL, 1937
OIL ON METAL. 40 × 31 CM
The Jacques and Natasha Gelman Collection of 20th Century Mexican Art and the Vergel Foundation

3. GISÈLE FREUND
FRIDA KAHLO IN HER BED, 1952
GELATIN SILVER PRINT. 20 × 19.3 CM
Victoria and Albert Museum. E.85–2003

pp.26–7
4. FRIDA KAHLO
MI CASA AZUL, C.1940
INK AND PENCIL ON PAPER. 20.4 × 27.4 CM
Museo Frida Kahlo

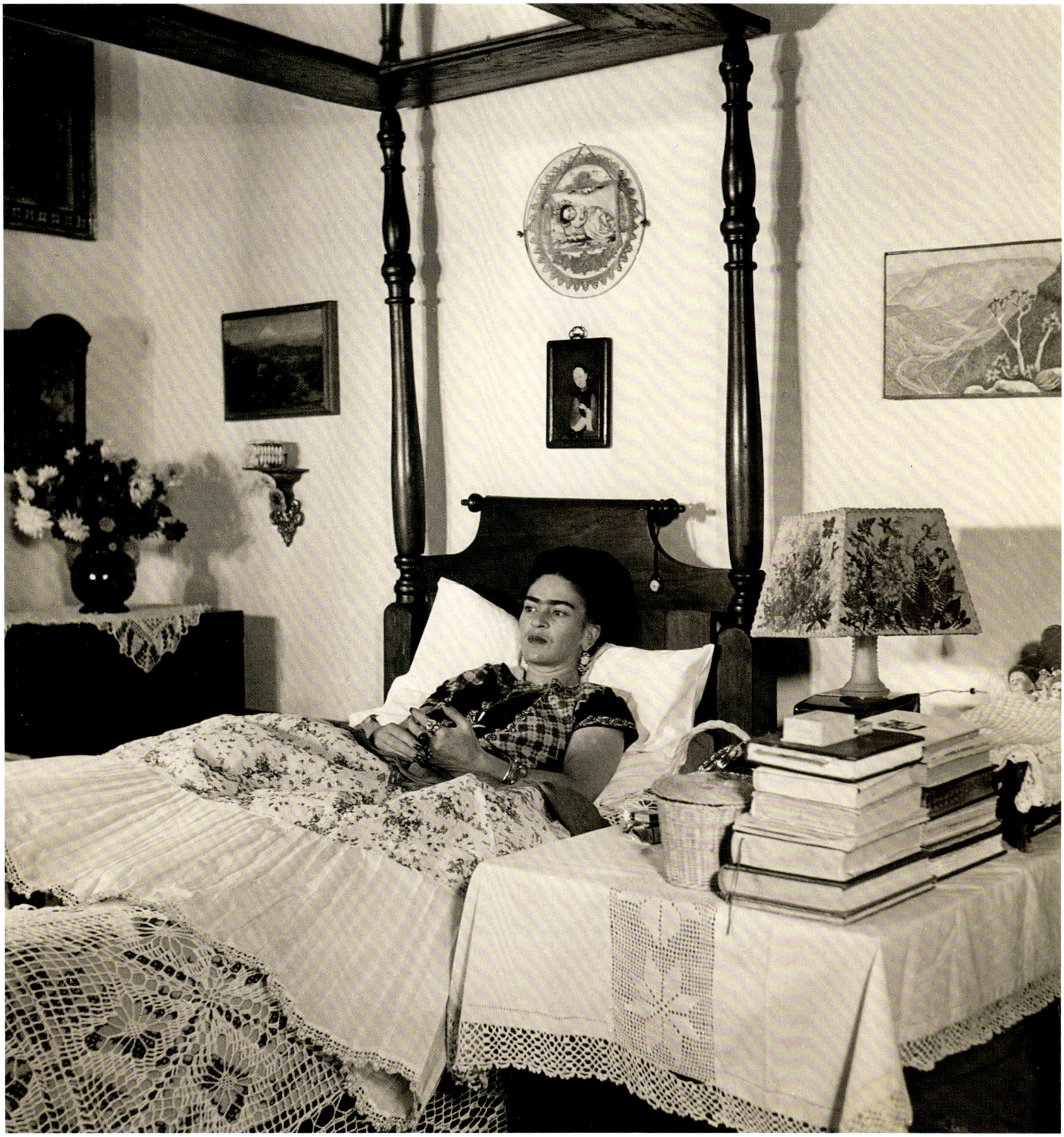

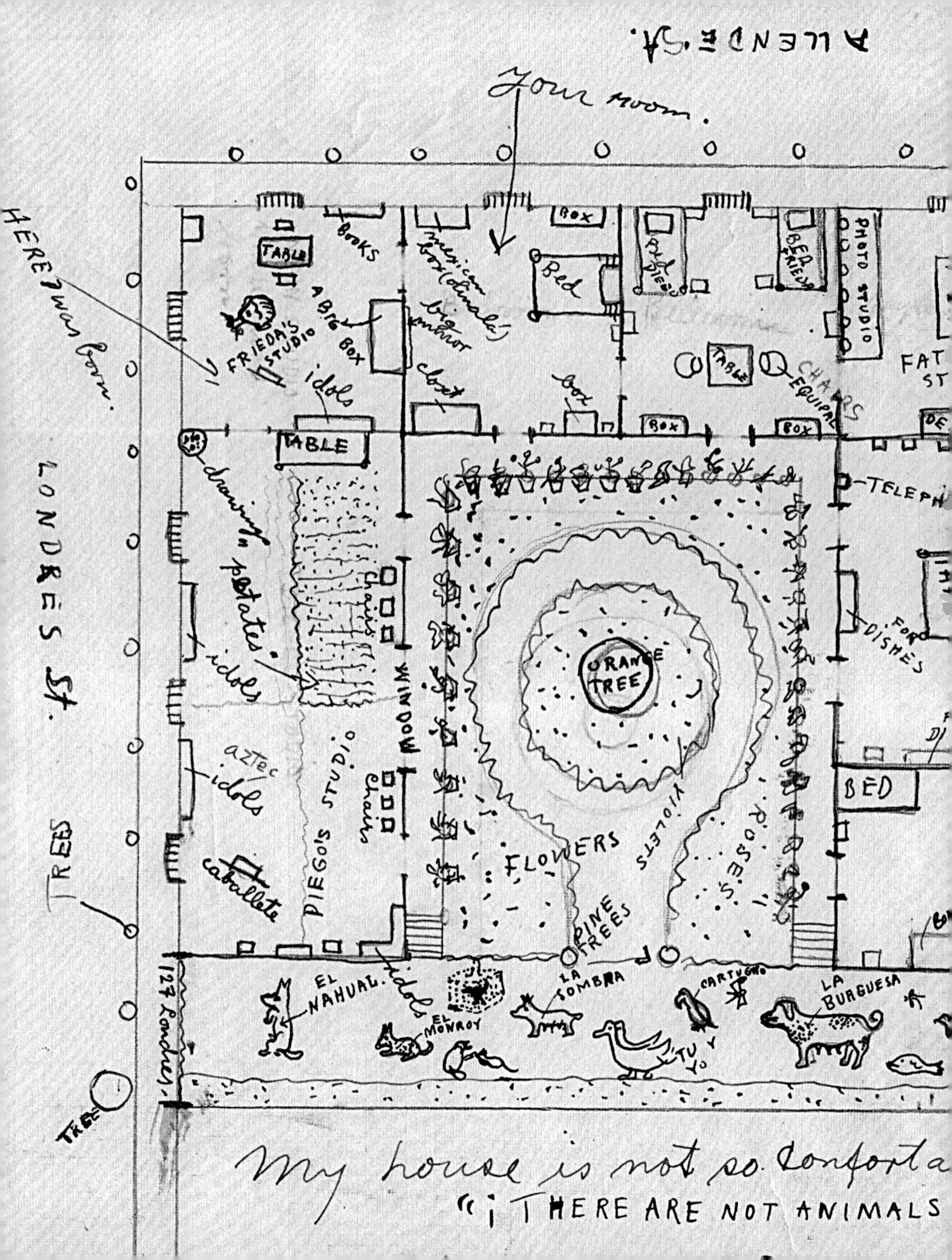
ALLENDE St.
Your room.
HERE I was born.
TABLE
BOOKS
A BIG BOX
big mirror
mexican box (olinalá)
closet
FRIEDA'S STUDIO
idols
TABLE
Bed
box
BOX
BED FRIEDA
PHOTO STUDIO
TABLE
CHAIRS EQUIPAL
FAT
TELEPH
FOR DISHES
BED
LONDRES St.
drawing in potatoes
chairs
WINDOW
idols
aztec idols
DIEGO'S STUDIO
chairs
caballete
ORANGE TREE
FLOWERS
VIOLETS
ROSES
PINE TREES
TREES
127 Londres
EL NAHUAL
EL MONROY
LA SOMBRA
CARTUCHO
LA BURGUESA
TU Y YO
TREE
My house is not so confortable
¡THERE ARE NOT ANIMALS

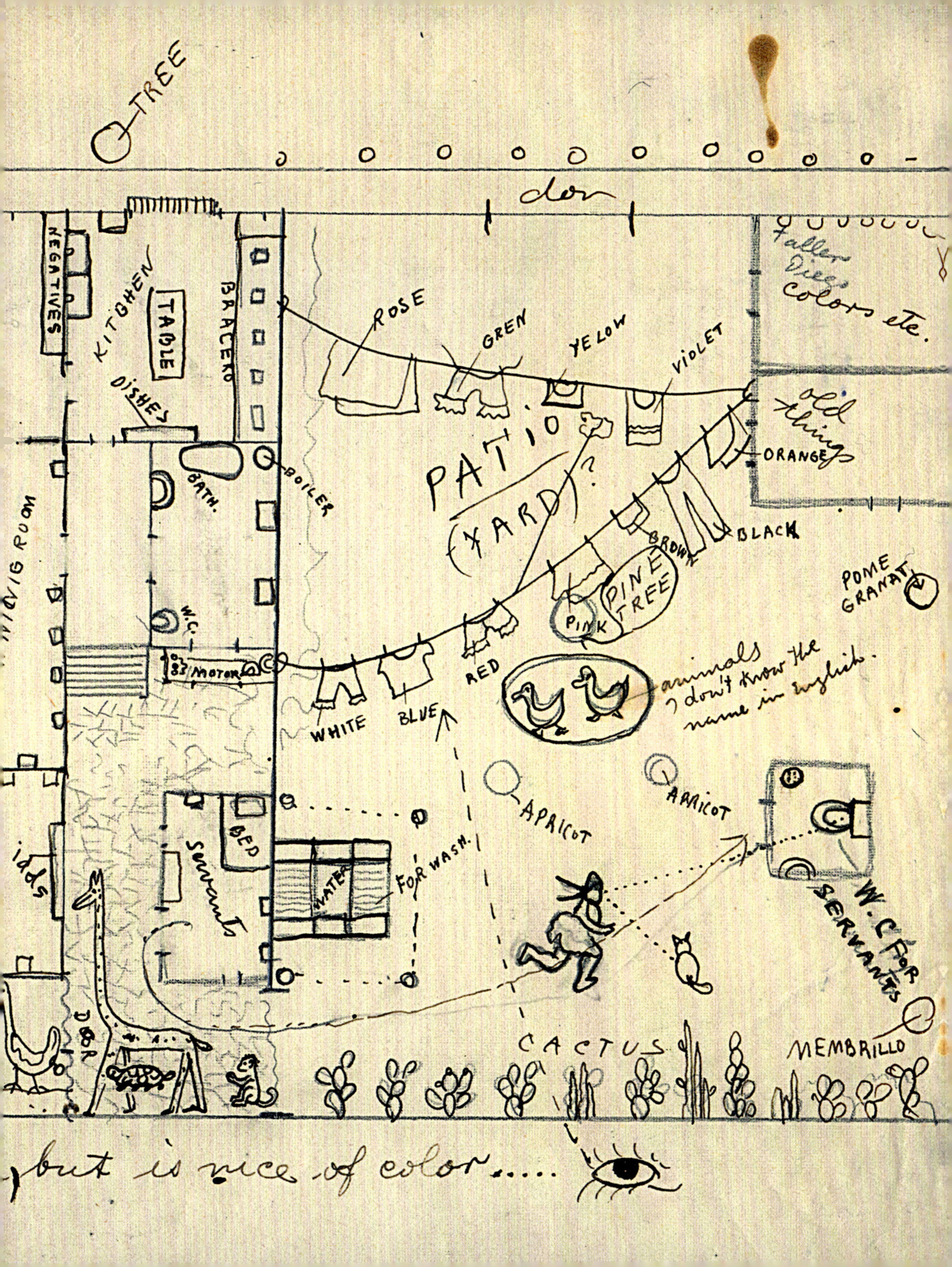
TREE
dor
NEGATIVES
KITCHEN
TABLE
BRACERO
DISHES
BATH.
BOILER
W.C.
83 MOTOR
ROSE
GREN
YELOW
VIOLET
fallen Diego colors etc.
old things
ORANGE
PATIO (YARD)?
BROWN
BLACK
PINK
PINE TREE
POME GRANAT
WHITE
BLUE
RED
animals I don't know the name in english
APRICOT
APRICOT
BED
Servants
WATER
FOR WASH.
W.C FOR SERVANTS
DOOR
CACTUS
MEMBRILLO
but is nice of color.....

5. GISÈLE FREUND
EX-VOTOS, THE BLUE HOUSE, 1951
GELATIN SILVER PRINT. 19.8 × 20 CM
Museo Frida Kahlo

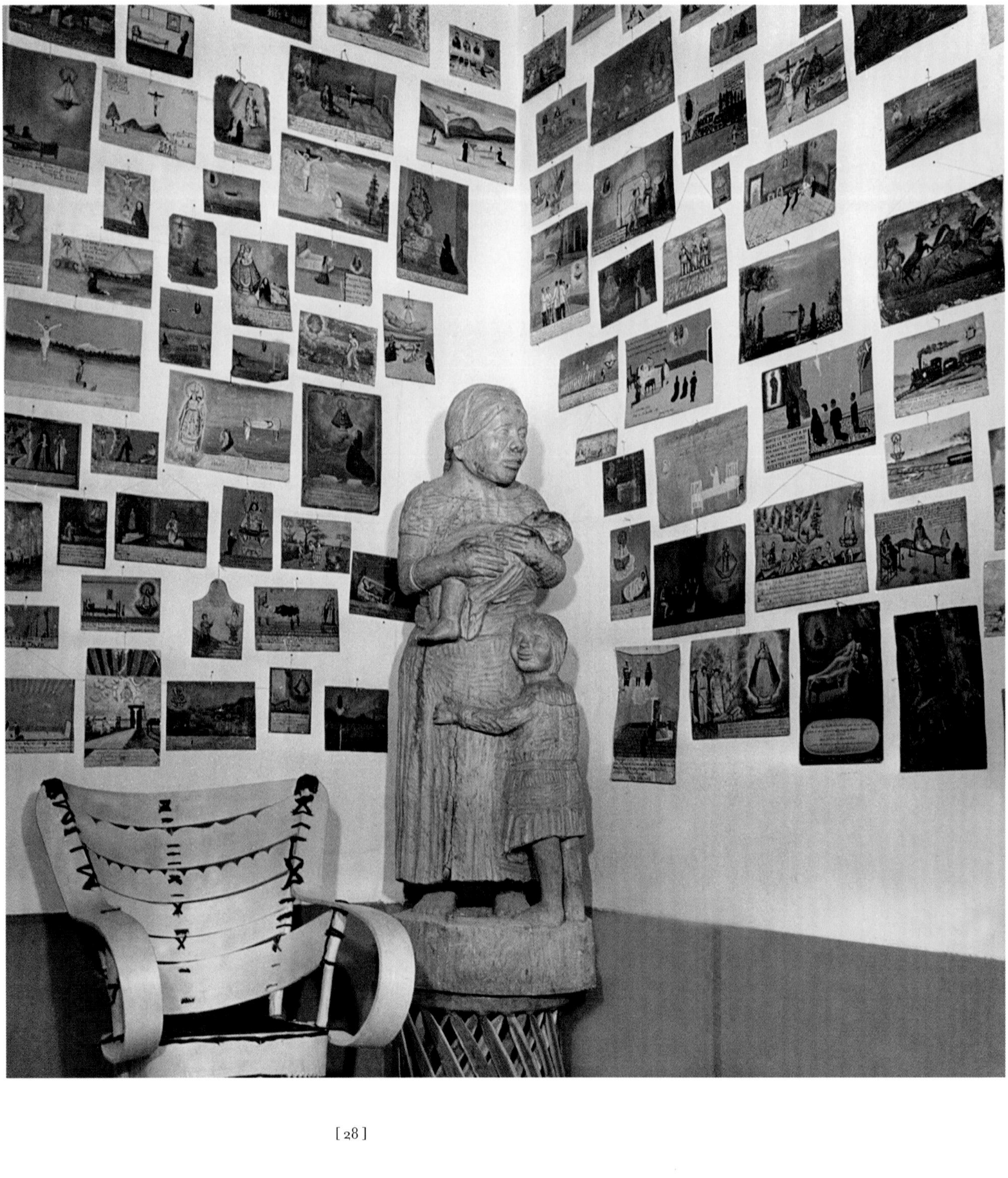

conventions of the time. Kahlo designed her own clothes, embracing them as part of her multifaceted œuvre, and she wore garments from different regions in Mexico with pride. Kahlo turned whatever she found into art.

The art historians Alicia Azuela de la Cueva and Teresa del Conde unearthed many other treasures among the thousands of documents in the archives, including a letter in which Kahlo recounted the creative process behind her 1938 painting *The Suicide of Dorothy Hale* [97]. Further correspondence describes her stay in André Breton's apartment in humorous, yet scathing, terms. Many of Kahlo's books are inscribed with annotations, poems and drawings: it appears that Kahlo made these inscriptions as she read, reclaiming the books and making them part of her life and creative process. She would slip flowers and birds' feathers between the pages to signal the various subjects that inspired her work.

During the early years of her life, Kahlo lived in the tranquil and beautiful Blue House, in the neighbourhood of Coyoacán, to the south of Mexico City. It was built in 1904 in the French architectural style typical of that era. During the Mexican Revolution (1910–20), Kahlo's father, Guillermo Kahlo, a German–Mexican photographer who specialized in taking topographical images of colonial buildings, rented out rooms and mortgaged the house to remedy the difficult financial situation brought about by his unemployment after the overthrow of Porfirio Díaz's dictatorship.

These precarious circumstances were exacerbated by the medical costs associated with the treatment of his daughter's polio, which she contracted aged six, and from the tram accident she suffered when she was 18 on her journey home from the *Escuela Nacional Preparatoria* (National Preparatory School). This tragic incident caused over 20 bone fractures, primarily in Kahlo's spine. Rivera, who became Kahlo's husband in 1929, later repaid these debts, and the Blue House became the property of Mrs 'Frida Kahlo de Rivera'.

After the recovery of the house by Rivera, the couple lived in various locations for long periods, both in Mexico and the United States, and records of these travels – both written and photographic – can be found in the archives. In 1937, Kahlo and Rivera hosted Leon Trotsky at the Blue

6. GISÈLE FREUND
FRIDA KAHLO IN HER GARDEN, 1952
GELATIN SILVER PRINT. 19.7 × 19.1 CM
Victoria and Albert Museum. E.84–2003

pp.32–3
DETAIL OF PRINTED COTTON SKIRT
WITH FLORAL MOTIFS, SEE P.102
Museo Frida Kahlo

House, who was fleeing persecution by Stalin. Eventually, in 1939, Kahlo returned to live in the Blue House. The house's French style, which dated back to the Porfiriato years, was gradually replaced with a pre-Columbian aesthetic, characteristic of the period, using volcanic stone. There are various accounts of this extension in the archives.

The Blue House was where Kahlo's artistic career began: her father encouraged her talents as a painter, providing her with her canvases, brushes and paints. Kahlo endured painful and protracted periods of convalescence confined to her bed, and she underwent more than 30 operations during her lifetime. The photographs taken by Kahlo's lover, Nickolas Muray, are a powerful record of these periods. It was also at the Blue House that Kahlo and Rivera shared their lengthy, loving yet tempestuous relationship. Later, artists, poets, intellectuals and writers gathered there, many of them among the most significant Mexican and international public figures. Their accounts of this time, and the many remarkable events that took place in the house, also form part of the archives.

Although Kahlo paid tribute to the Blue House in her work – she depicted her bed, her studio and other elements of the house in her oil paintings and pencil drawings – she did not make it the central subject of her œuvre. She did, however, create an evocative scale drawing of her home [4]. One of the strongest impressions of the house captured by Kahlo is the painting *My Grandparents, My Parents and I (Family Tree)* (1936) [62], painted three years prior to her return to her birthplace. It is astonishing to be able to compare the photographs that inspired this and other paintings alongside the original art works by Kahlo.

Kahlo and Rivera left an imprint on their home through furnishings, decoration and many other alterations, turning the Blue House into a three-dimensional work of art. Moreover, the archives have shown the ways in which photography, dress and the house itself became creative sources for Kahlo's paintings. What had hitherto been mere intuition is now confirmed fact.

For all these reasons, it is a privilege for the Museo Frida Kahlo and its staff to be part of the ongoing discovery of this treasure, and to be able to help share it abroad through the current exhibition at the V&A.

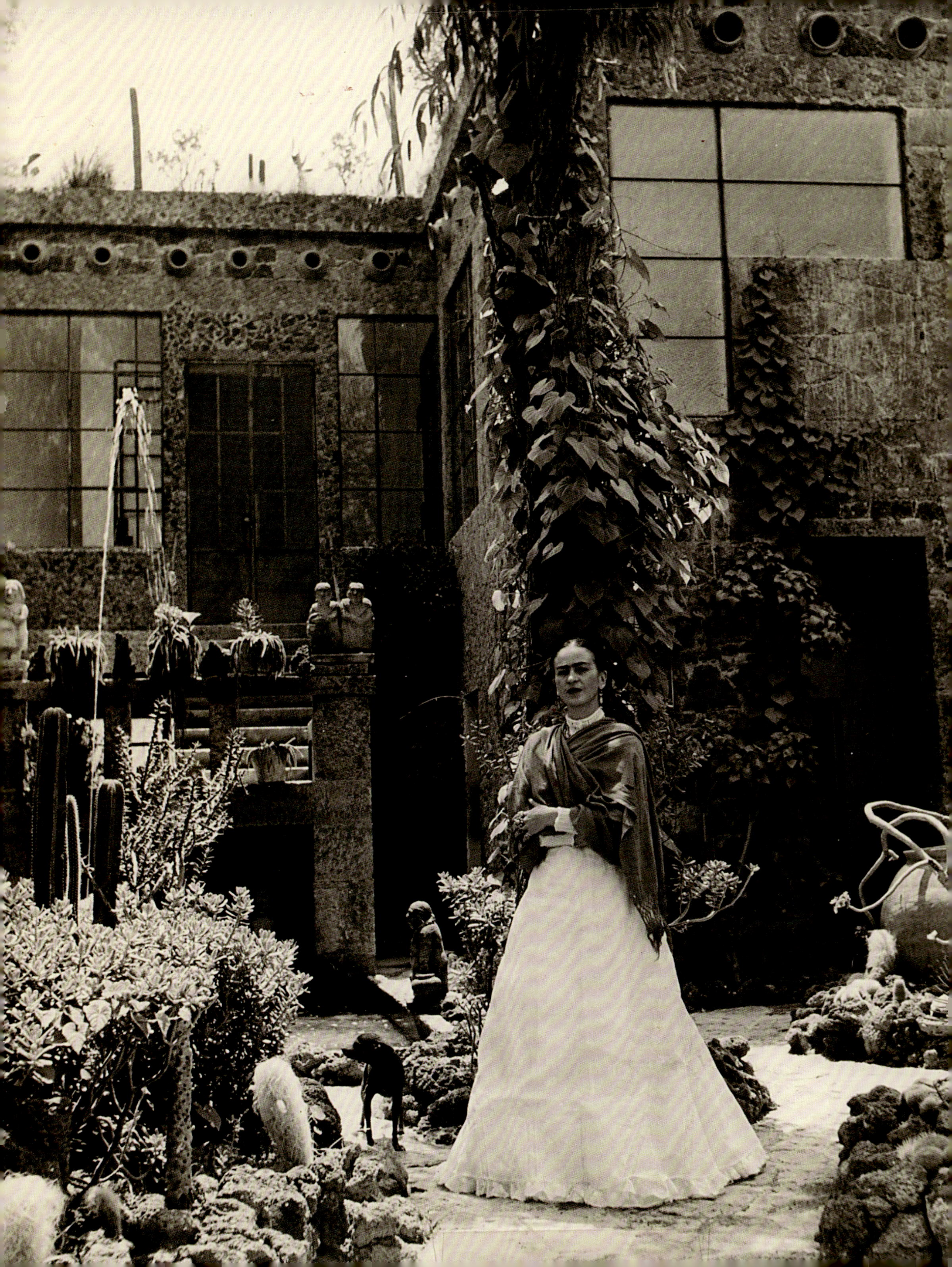

Quetzalcoatl's Grin: The Changing Face of Art and Culture in Frida Kahlo's Mexico[1]

ADRIAN LOCKE

In 1907, the year of Frida Kahlo's birth, few could have predicted how tumultuous the following decades in Mexico would be. When Kahlo died in 1954, aged 47, her short life had been bookended by two violent and destabilizing events. The first was the Mexican Revolution of 1910 during which a dictatorship was overthrown and a hitherto unknown period of social change was ushered in – pessimism was replaced by optimism. The second marked Kahlo's last appearance in public less than two weeks before she died, when she participated in a public demonstration against the coup d'état, covertly supported by the CIA, that deposed the democratically elected president of Guatemala, Jacobo Árbenz – optimism was replaced by pessimism. In many ways, these events mirror Kahlo's life, during which, as in her homeland, hope and despair interchanged, the threat of violence, real and imagined, was never far away and the promise of a stable future remained tantalizingly out of reach. Despite such uncertainty, there was an extraordinary flourishing of the arts, with a distinct international aspect, that few foresaw and in which Kahlo played a central role.

To understand what happened, as well as when and why, we need to take a broader look at Mexico's history. The year 1910 marked the centenary of the first calls for independence made in 1810. Between 1519, when Hernán Cortés claimed the country in the name of the Carlos I, and renamed it *Nueva España* (New Spain), and 1821, when it finally gained its independence, Mexico had been under Spanish colonial rule. After a brief period of imperial rule Mexico entered a democratic period, which ended in 1863 when Napoleon III invaded the country and placed Ferdinand Maximilian, Archduke of Austria, on the throne. This lasted until 1867.

1910 also marked the eightieth birthday of its president, José de la Cruz Porfirio Díaz. The general election of that year duly extended the mandate he had enjoyed for the previous 34 years, a period of rule named after him: the *Porfiriato*. During his tenure, Porfirio Díaz oversaw a system of patronage that ensured political power and national wealth were controlled by an elite made up of landowners, the military and the Catholic church. While American and British investors made huge, virtually tax-free, profits from mining, railways and other industries, most ordinary Mexicans lived in poverty with little or no access to education let alone opportunities for economic or social betterment. In essence, the country was run as a personal fiefdom.

Porfirio Díaz won the election of 1910 amid suspicion of widespread fraud but celebrated his victory regardless. His main challenger was Francisco Madero. A wealthy progressive liberal, Madero advocated political and social reform coupled with a drive to modernize the agricultural, mining and industrial sectors. Following the election Madero was briefly jailed and then exiled to the United States where he reluctantly concluded that the only way to change the status quo in Mexico was by means of force. The subsequent armed uprising, in 1911, led to the fall of Ciudad Juárez, a border town on the Rio Grande, opposite El Paso, Texas. Porfirio Díaz consequently resigned and agreed to go into exile in France reportedly saying 'Madero has unleashed a tiger. Let's see if he can control it'.[2] These were prescient words as Madero's success was indeed short-lived; he was assassinated in office in 1913. What ensued was a tumultuous and violent struggle for power during which he was the first of seven presidents between 1911 and 1920.

After Porfirio Díaz's resignation a popular agrarian uprising started in the provinces and engulfed the countryside before eventually conquering the seat of government in Mexico City.[3] This became known as the Mexican Revolution, a decade-long period marked by violence and instability that shook the country to its foundations and out of which emerged the eponymous heroes Francisco 'Pancho' Villa from the northern state of Chihuahua, leader of the *División del Norte* (Division of the North) whose followers were known as Villistas, and Emiliano Zapata from the southern state of Oaxaca, leader of the *Ejército Libertador del Sur* (Liberation Army of the South) whose followers were known as Zapatistas [7]. By 1923 both were victims of violent deaths but not before they had entered Mexican folklore as men of humble origins who eschewed political power in favour of greater social equality, something they were willing to achieve by force.

By 1920, when Álvaro Obregón assumed the presidency, things had begun to settle and political stability gradually returned. The process of economic, social and political reform promised by the overthrow of

7. JOSÉ CLEMENTE OROZCO
ZAPATISTAS, 1931
OIL ON CANVAS. 114.3 × 139.7 CM
Museum of Modern Art, New York. 470.1937

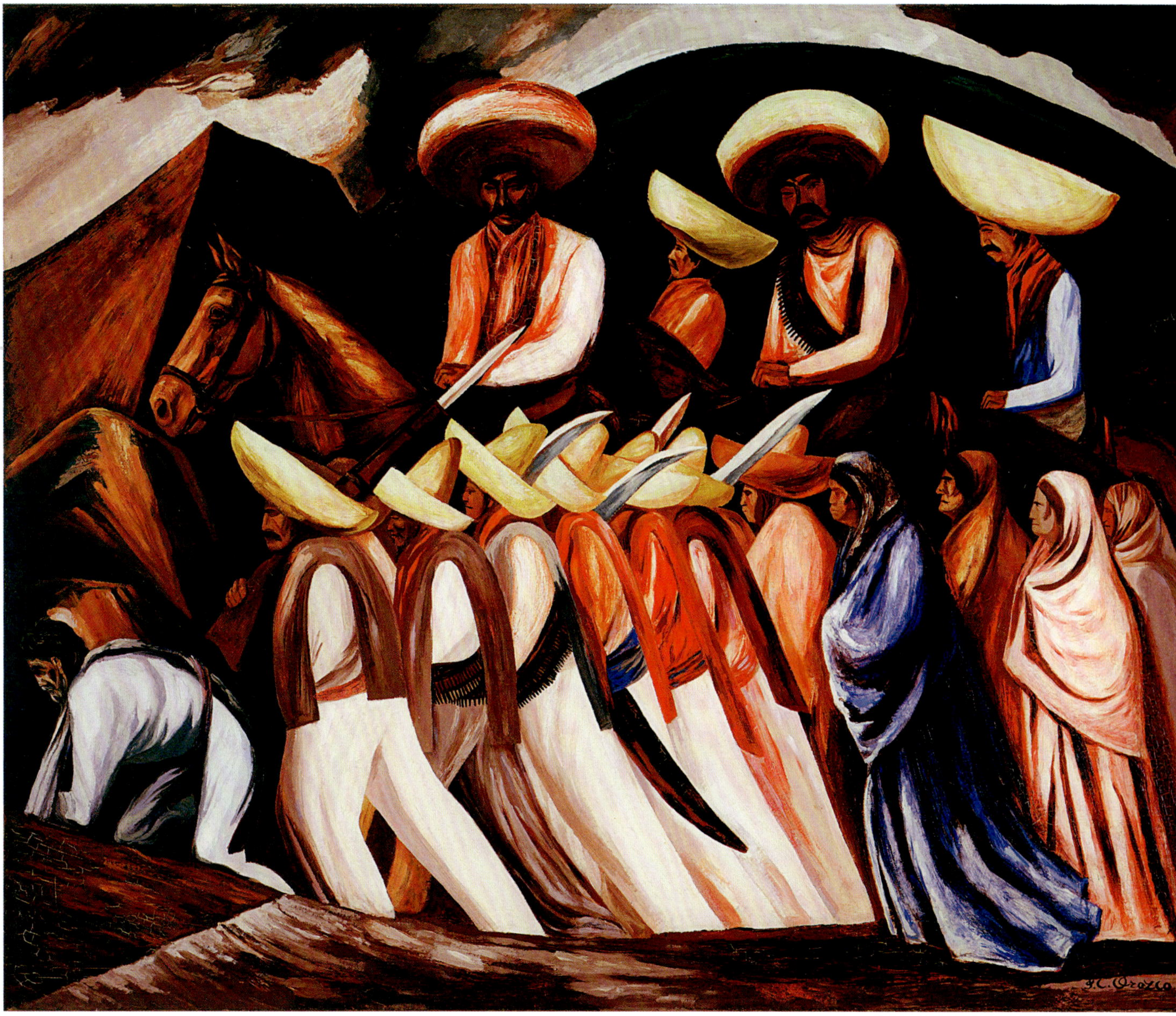

8. SATURNINO HERRÁN
WOMAN FROM TEHUANTEPEC, 1916
OIL ON CANVAS. 150 × 75 CM
Museo de Aguascalientes (INBA), Aguascalientes

9. DIEGO RIVERA
DANCE IN TEHUANTEPEC, 1928
OIL ON CANVAS. 200.7 × 163.8 CM
Museo de Arte Latinoamericano de Buenos Aires

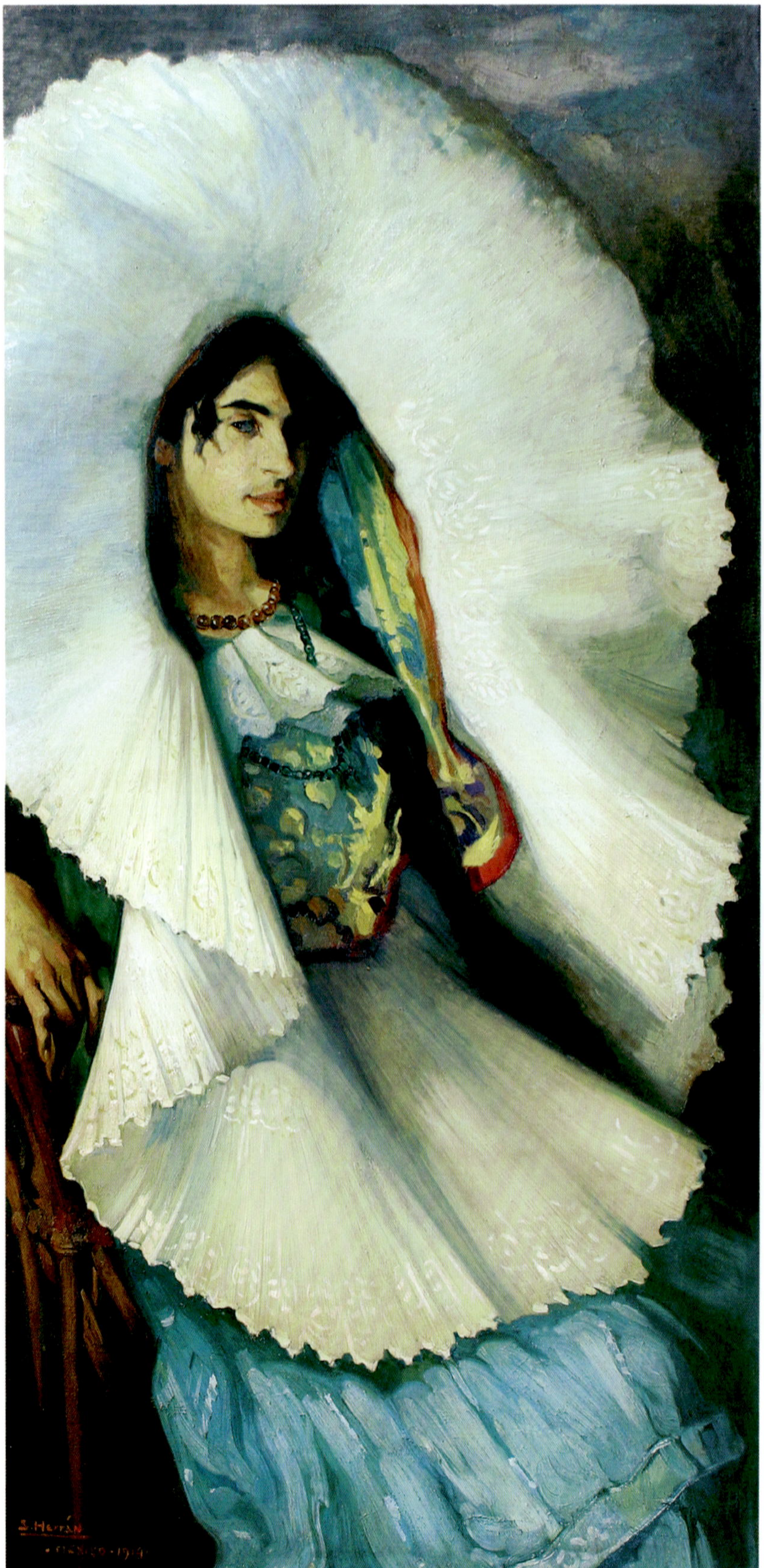

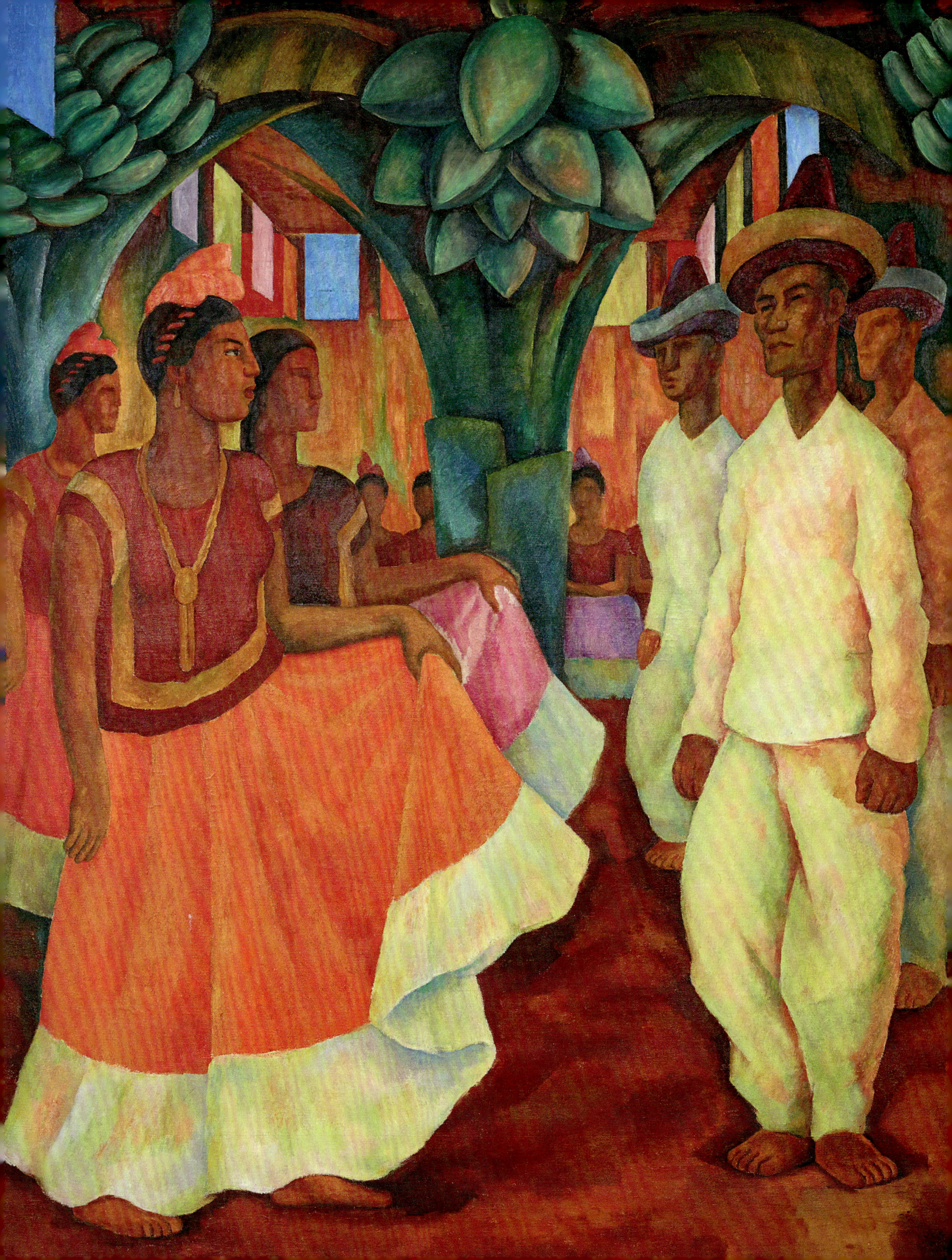

the old elite synonymous with Porfirio Díaz finally began. One of the chief and unexpected beneficiaries of these reforms was the realm of art and culture. It had been, until that point in time, dominated by a very conservative, academic outlook based on traditional subjects such as grand historical allegories, religious images and society portraits. There were, however, two notable exceptions; José-María Velasco, who painted landscapes replete with nationalist symbols, and Saturnino Herrán, who engaged with subjects that celebrated Mexico's rich pre-Columbian (that is, dating from before 1492 when Christopher Columbus 'discovered' the American continent) history and diverse cultural identity [8]. Both Velasco and Herrán would be very influential on the generation of artists, including Dr Atl (Gerardo Murillo) and Diego Rivera, which followed [9, 10].

What did follow was a period of almost unimaginable artistic flowering, one which Anita Brenner, the Mexican-born art critic and journalist, referred to as the 'Mexican Renascence'.[4] Brenner also coined the phrase *los tres grandes* (the three greats) to describe the three main protagonists who came to dominate this period artistically; Rivera, who married Kahlo in 1929, and his great rivals José Clemente Orozco and David Alfaro Siqueiros.[5] This flourishing was the brainchild of José Vasconcelos. As director of the *Secretaría de Educación Pública* (Secretariat of Public Education) Vasconcelos developed and implemented a programme of public art that soon gained momentum and assumed a life of its own that far outgrew the ambitions of its instigator.

A visionary and influential intellectual, Vasconcelos believed that ideas could fundamentally change society, and that education could encourage free-thinking that went beyond ideas of nationhood to embrace much greater ideals. To this end he believed that artists were capable of creating inspiring works that could be used to stimulate profound change. Although he only held office for four years, his scheme would have lasting impact not only in Mexico, but around the world. It influenced the adoption of Socialist Realism as the only permissible art by the Soviet Union in 1932 as well as the Public Works of Art Project, which was part of the New Deal introduced by President Franklin D. Roosevelt in the United States in 1933.

10. DR ATL (GERARDO MURILLO)
VALLEY OF MEXICO FROM THE SOUTH, 1931
Private collection

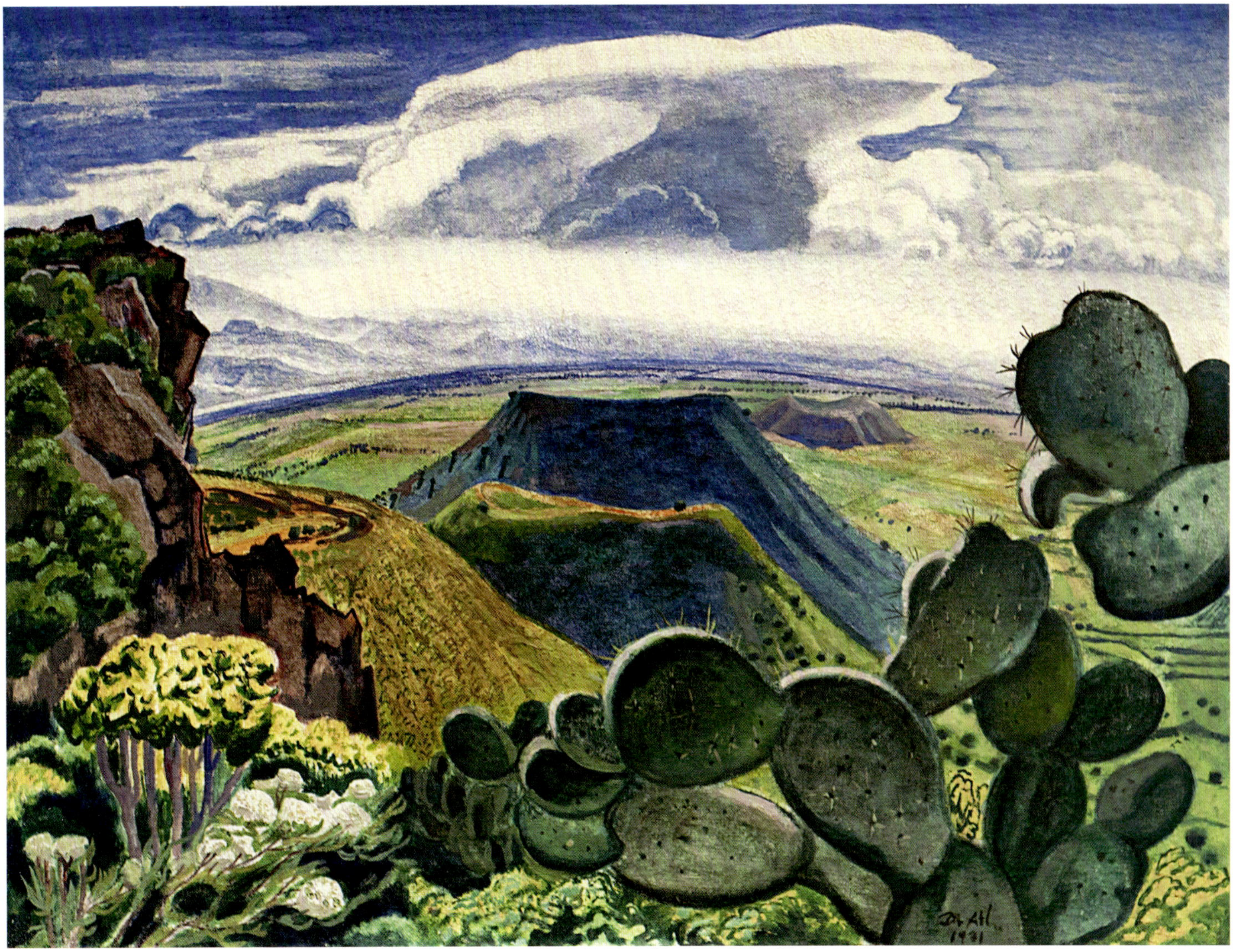

11. DAVID ALFARO SIQUEIROS
ETHNOGRAPHY, 1939
ENAMEL ON COMPOSITION BOARD. 122.2 × 82.2 CM
Museum of Modern Art, New York. 1657.1940

Appropriately, given how Mexico became a fertile ground for home-grown artists, photographers and writers as well as drawing a significant number from across Europe and the United States over the coming years, it was a French-born artist, Jean Charlot, who captured the speed of change that took place. When he first arrived in Mexico in January 1921, the art scene was still dormant. All that changed over the coming months, as he later recalled.[6] By November of that year the art scene in Mexico City was energized and focused. The catalyst for that change was the arrival of Rivera from Paris where he had been living since 1907 forging a very successful career as one of the first exponents of Cubism.[7] Vasconcelos realised that in order for his project to succeed he needed an artist to champion it and who better than the most famous Mexican artist currently working. With a clear plan in mind he enticed Rivera back to Mexico, after first encouraging him to study Renaissance frescoes first-hand in Italy.

Vasconcelos's idea was to utilize the walls of buildings belonging to the government as vast canvases, encouraging artists to decorate them with allegorical images. In a country with high rates of illiteracy this was seen as a convenient way to appeal to ordinary citizens, in a manner not dissimilar to the ways frescoes historically functioned in churches; to lift people, both consciously and subconsciously, and inspire them spiritually. Thus the first mural Rivera painted at the *Escuela Nacional Preparatoria* (National Preparatory School) in Mexico City, 1922–3, symbolized the fusion of native indigenous tradition with the moral imperatives of Judeo–Christian religion and the intellectual standards of Hellenic civilization.[8] Thereafter, Rivera's murals, like those of his contemporaries, became much more focused and polemical in their content: political – those that celebrated the heroes of the revolution such as Villa and Zapata while promulgating the aims of the revolution; historical – celebrating the pre-Columbian cultures of Mexico whilst portraying Spanish colonial rule as barbaric and exploitative and the *Porfiriato*, represented by politicians, bankers, landowners, clergy and military as corrupt; and cultural – celebrating the rich ethnic and ecological diversity of the country as well as the innate creativity of the Mexican people [11, 12].

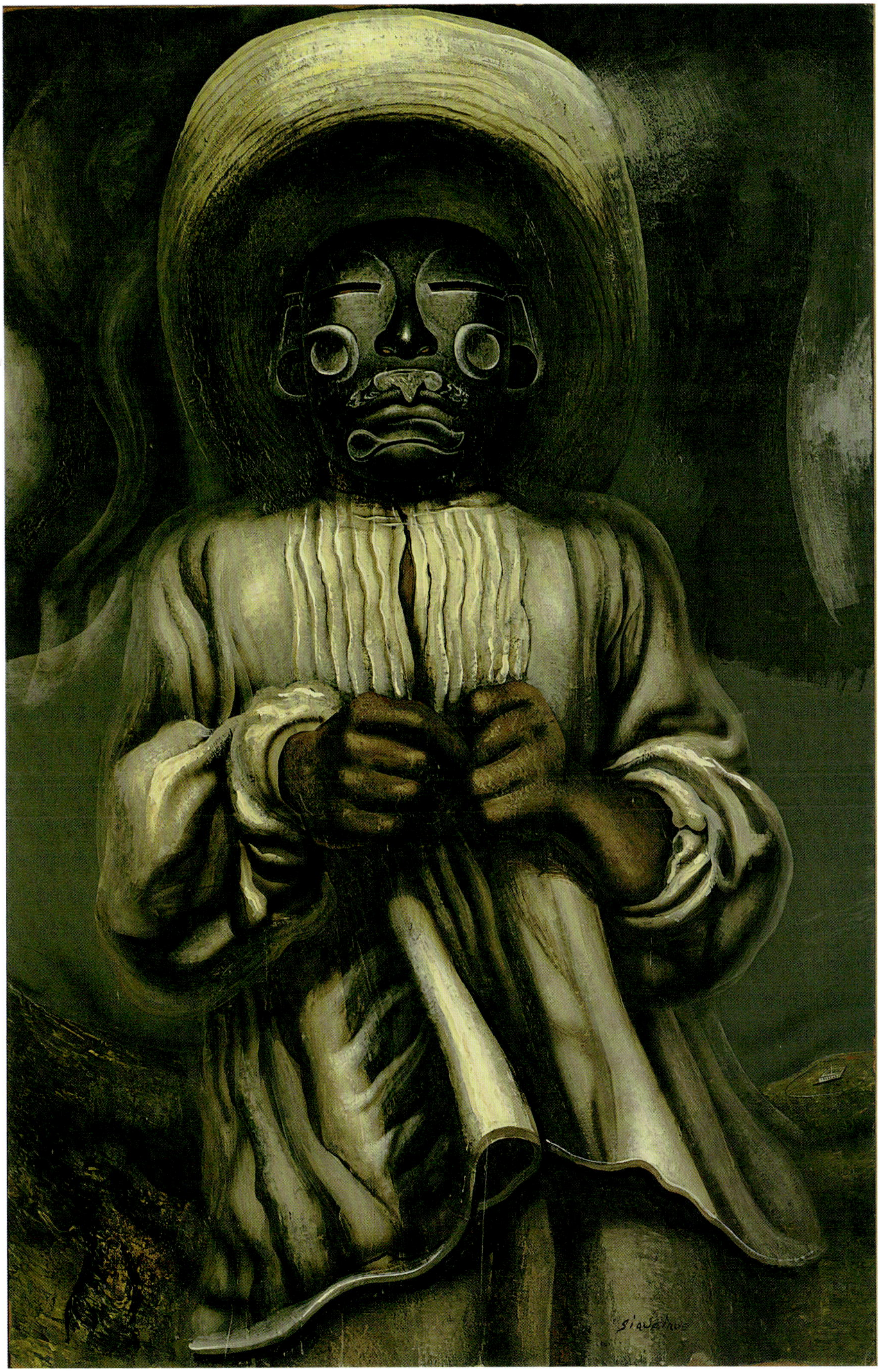

12. RUFINO TAMAYO
LANDSCAPE WITH ROCKS, 1925
OIL ON CANVAS. 49.5 × 39.5 CM
Museo de Arte Moderno (INBA), Mexico City

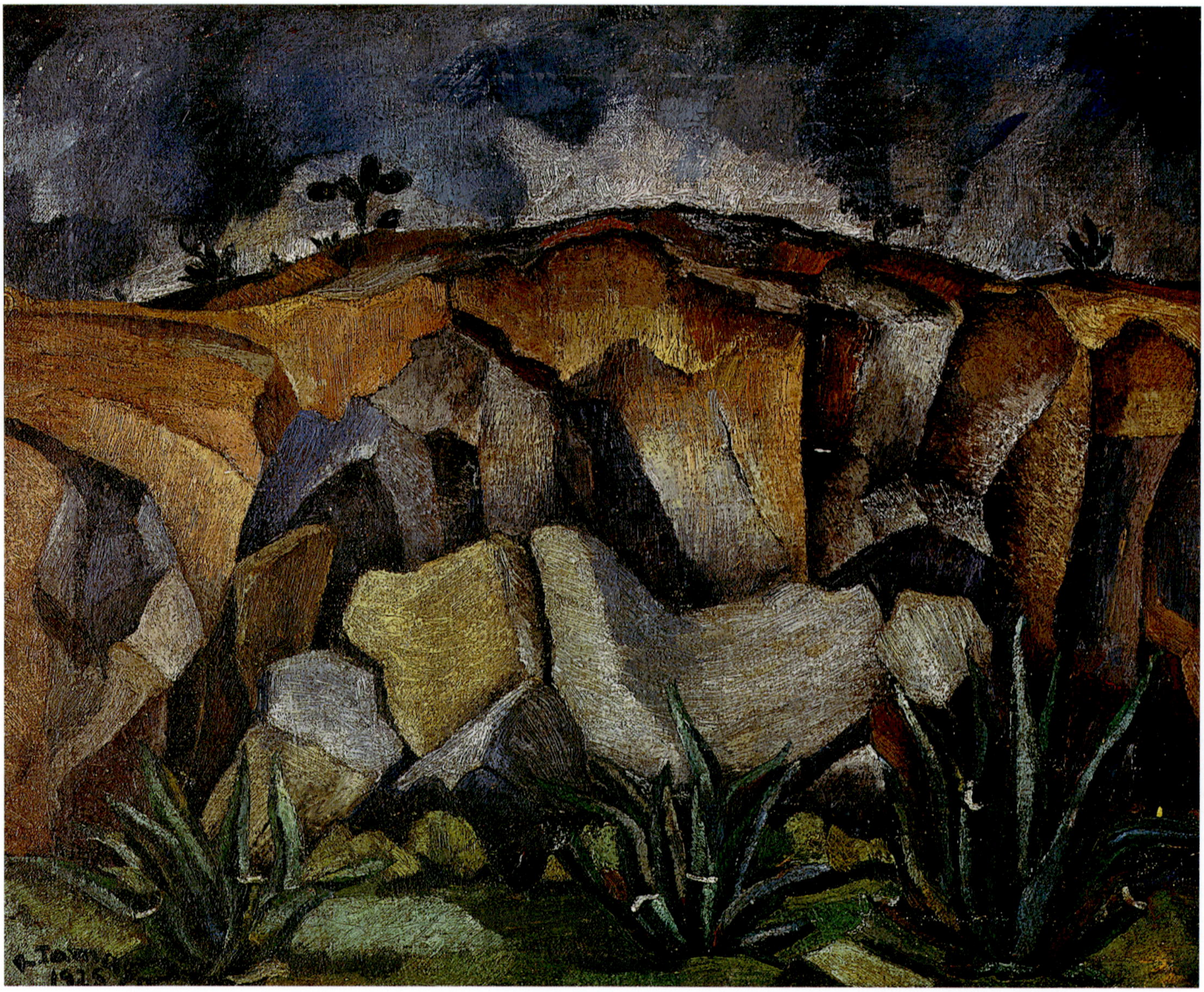

Vasconcelos realised that in order to succeed in his ambition of a unified vision of Mexico, one towards which all Mexicans could work, it was vital to celebrate the history and diversity of the nation. Emphasis was given to archaeological excavations as well as building museums to exhibit their finds alongside anthropological and sociological studies. Whereas once artists had aspired to travel abroad, now their imaginations were fired by their own country. Despite challenging travelling conditions, they began to explore and study the diverse riches the country had to offer. As the Mexican poet and diplomat Octavio Paz stated, 'the Mexican Revolution was the discovery of Mexico by Mexicans'.[9] The Isthmus of Tehuantepec, in the south of Mexico, for instance, was a very popular destination for artists such as Diego Rivera or the painter and caricaturist Miguel Covarrubias. Other destinations included the archaeological sites of Teotihuacan, a vast complex of pyramids and temple platforms, outside Mexico City [14], the Mayan city state of Chichen Itza in the Yucatan and the Zapotec citadel of Monte Alban in Oaxaca. For the first time, ordinary Mexicans became a subject of interest for their fellow citizens. A new, charged national spirit emerged that saw Mexicans embrace and celebrate the diversity of their country. Rather than look outward for cultural stimulation they started to look inward.

By the time Kahlo encountered Rivera in 1928, when he was engaged in one of his most ambitious and successful mural cycles at the *Secretaría de Educación Pública*, Mexico had become a place of real interest for Americans and Europeans. They were drawn to Mexico for numerous reasons and were often closely integrated into the local art scene.[10]

For some artists, it offered the promise of paid work. For American painter and poet Marsden Hartley, on a Guggenheim Fellowship, Mexico provided a cheap and stimulating place to live; there was also a misplaced perception that it had relaxed attitudes towards open relationships, homosexuality, drink and drugs. For others, like dramatists Antonin Artaud and Vladimir Mayakovsky, it was a country that promised authenticity, replete with regional identities, indigenous communities and ways of life that were fast disappearing elsewhere. Some, like the English writer and painter D.H. Lawrence and the Hungarian war photographer and photo journalist Robert Capa for instance, came because their US visas had expired. Others, like the Canadian–American Philip Guston and the American sisters Marion and Grace Greenwood, were politically motivated and were commissioned to paint murals.

André Breton came to visit his political hero Leon Trotsky, who was living in Kahlo's family home in Coyoacán. On arrival, he described Mexico as the Surrealist country *par excellence* and, much to her irritation, Kahlo as a Surrealist artist. The fourth *Exposición internacional del surrealismo* (International Exhibition of Surrealism) took place at the Galería de Arte Mexicano in 1940 curated by the Austrian-born Wolfgang Paalen and Peruvian poet César Moro.

Like many other artists, writers, photographers and film directors, Josef and Anni Albers originally came as German tourists but returned time after time; Mexico was very conveniently located near to the United States and accessible by car. The English novelist Graham Greene came to witness and record the suppression of Catholicism. British sculptor and engraver Leon Underwood was commissioned to illustrate a travel account. The young French photographer Henri Cartier-Bresson came as part of a doomed scientific project. The Soviet film director Sergei Eisenstein came to make a feature film. The American photographer Edward Weston, disillusioned with life in California, came to find himself, persuaded by his lover, Italian–American Tina Modotti, to join her there. Together they revolutionized photography in Mexico inspiring, among others, Manuel Álvarez Bravo, Lola Álvarez Bravo, Agustín Jiménez, Aurora Eugenia Latapí and Emilio Amero.

The reasons were diverse but what was beyond question was the very real interest that Mexico generated. It became a destination for artists that witnessed an explosion of artistic expression. The attraction of Mexico only increased with the rise of Fascism in Europe and the outbreak of the Second World War when travel across the Atlantic became impossible and Mexico was viewed as a safe haven that welcomed refugees. In 1940, the Museum of Modern Art, New York hosted *Twenty Centuries of Mexican Art*, an ambitious exhibition that presented a rich array of pre-Columbian, colonial, republican, modern and popular arts. The state-sponsored exhibition was intended for Paris but was sent to New York instead because of the extreme risk of shipping art works.

13. TINA MODOTTI
WOMAN WITH OLLA, C.1926
GELATIN SILVER PRINT. 18.4 × 23 CM
Museum of Modern Art, New York. 331.1965

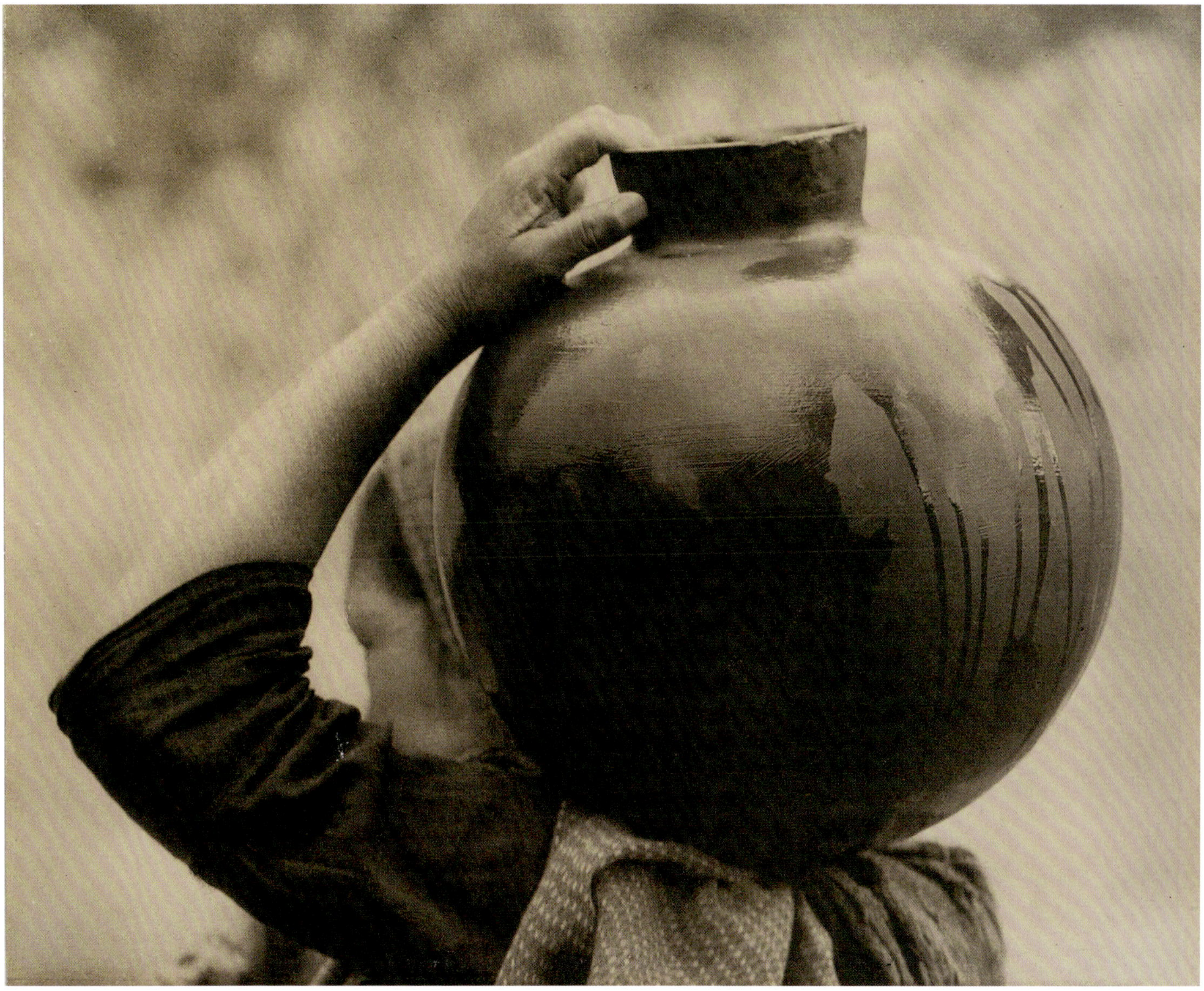

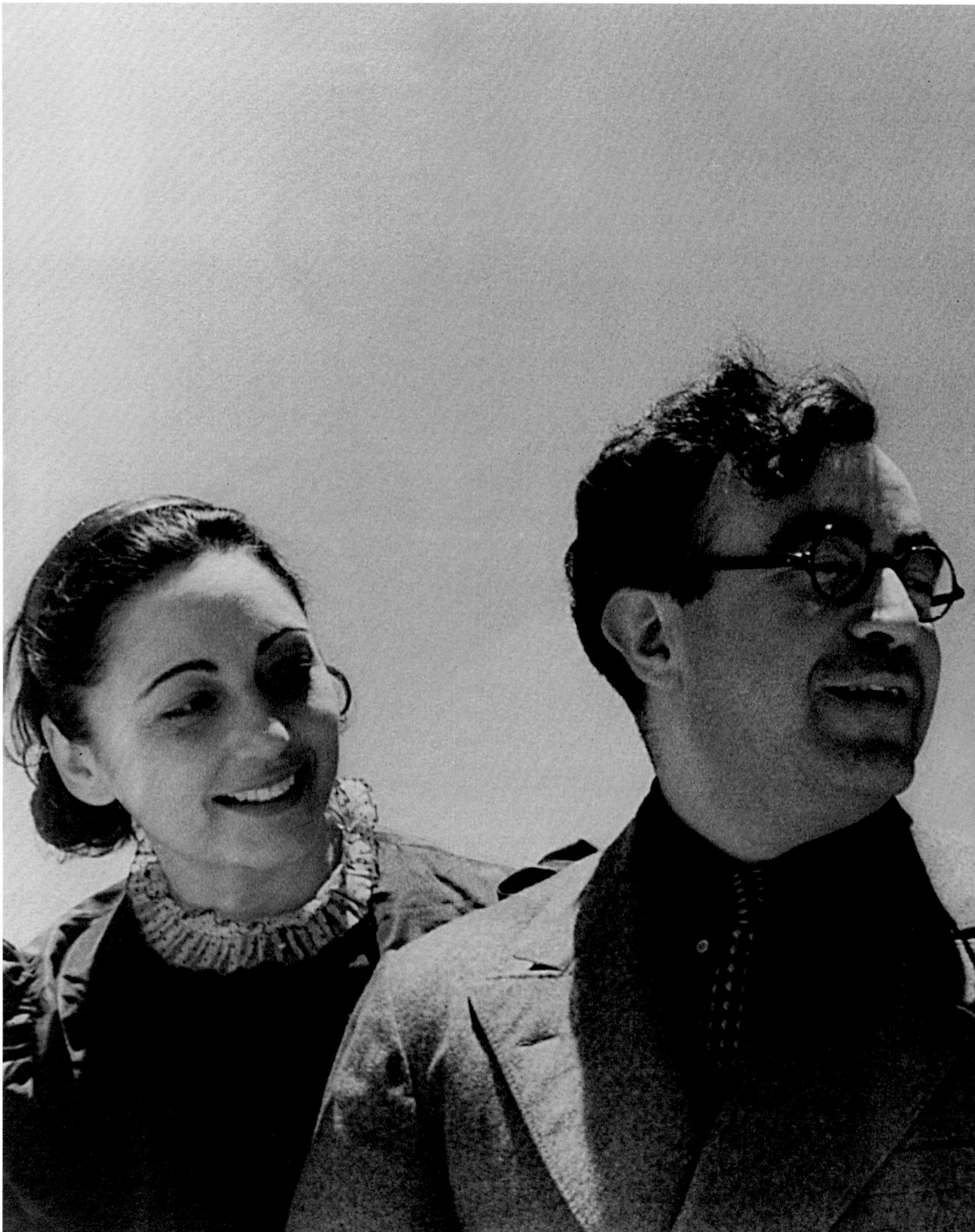

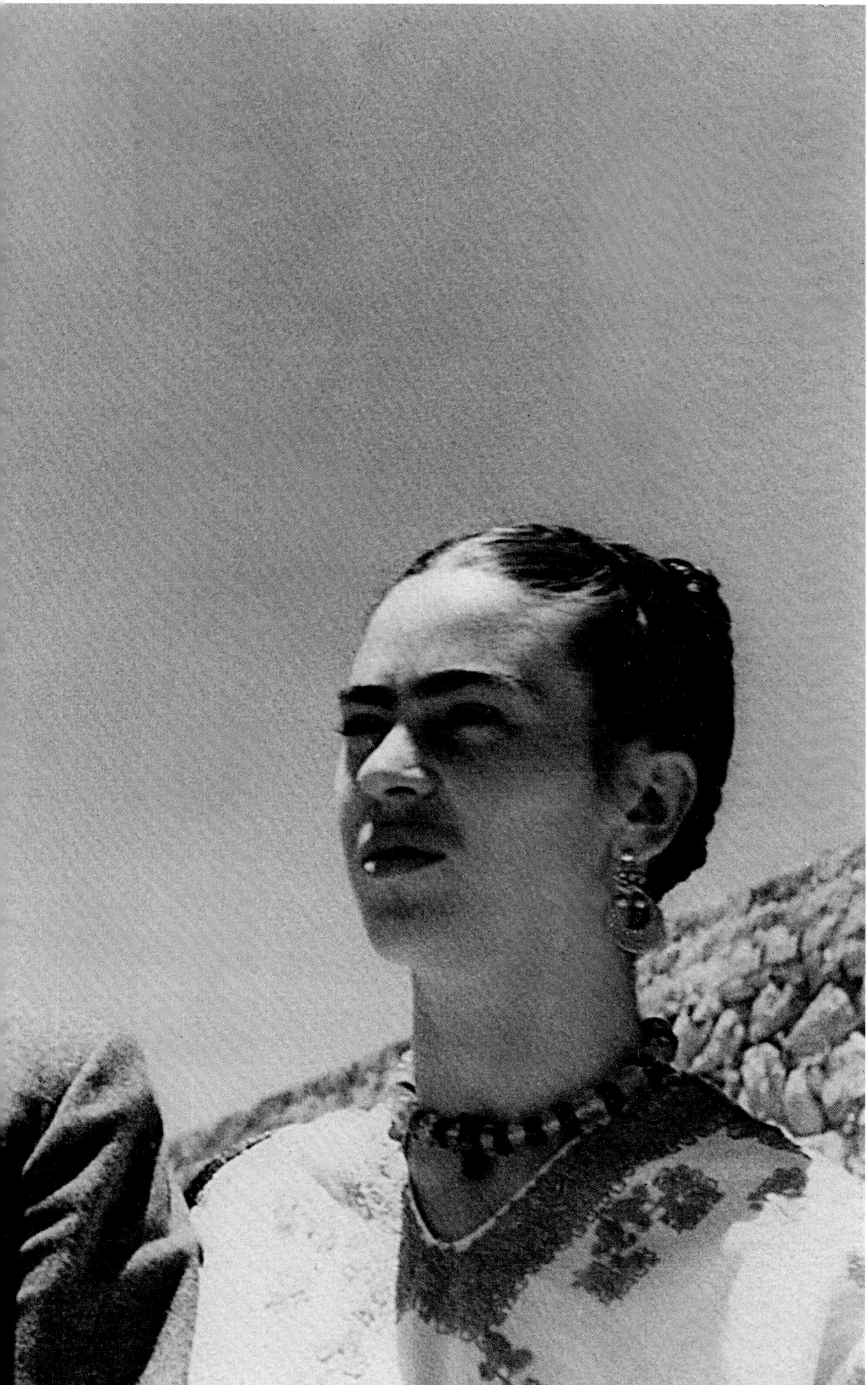

14. PHOTOGRAPHER UNKNOWN
ROSA COVARRUBIAS, CARLOS CHÁVEZ AND FRIDA KAHLO AT THE PYRAMID OF TENAYUCA, C.1945
GELATIN PRINT. 11.5 × 17.5 CM
Archivo Miguel Covarrubias,
Universidad de las Américas Puebla (UDLAP)

15. ROBERTO MONTENEGRO
WOMAN FROM TEHUANTEPEC (THE TEHUANA), 1930
OIL ON CANVAS. 70 × 70 CM
Bank of Mexico Collection

16. MARÍA IZQUIERDO
ALTAR OF OUR LADY OF SORROWS, 1946
OIL ON CANVAS. 74 × 59 CM
Private collection

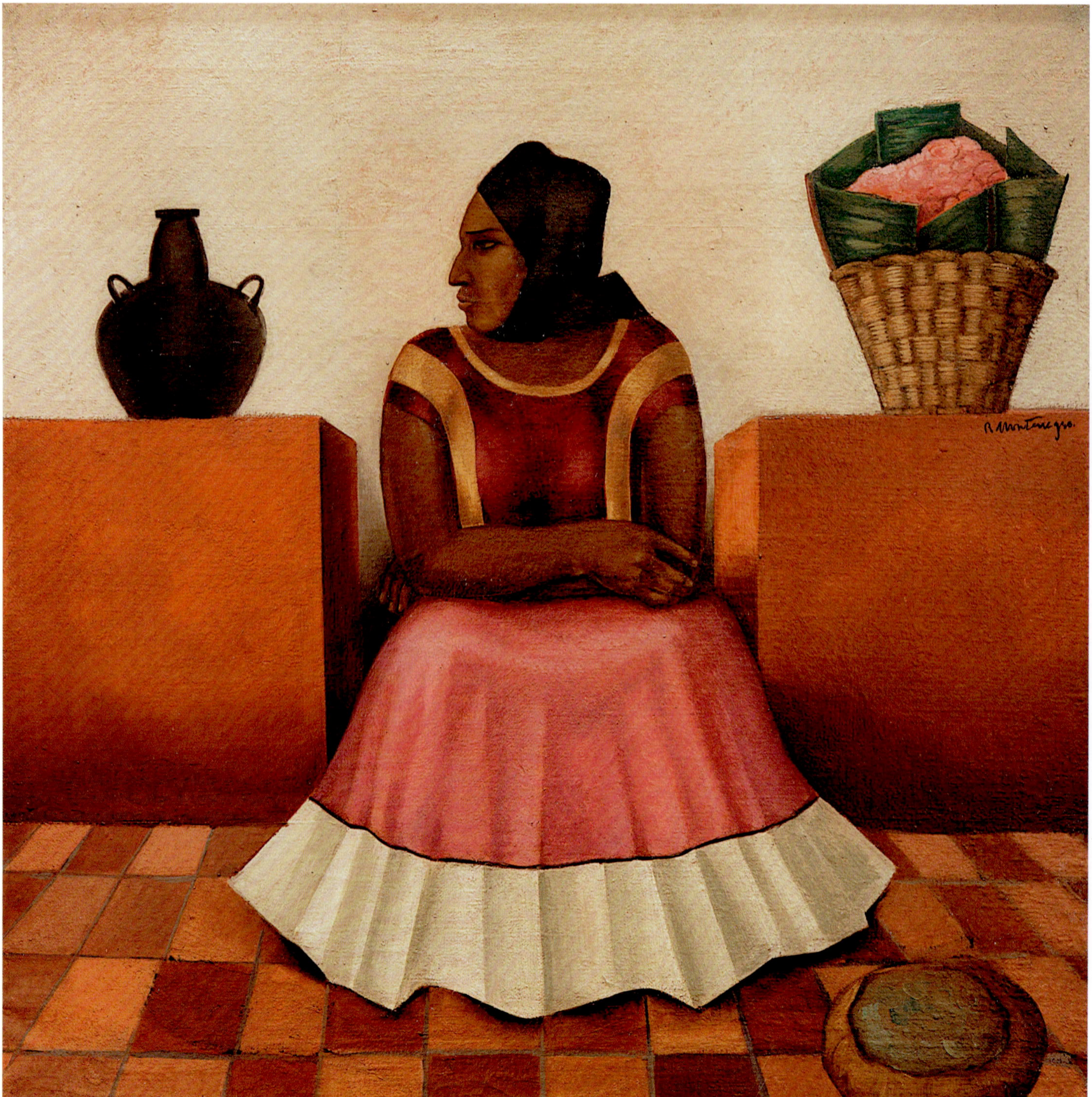

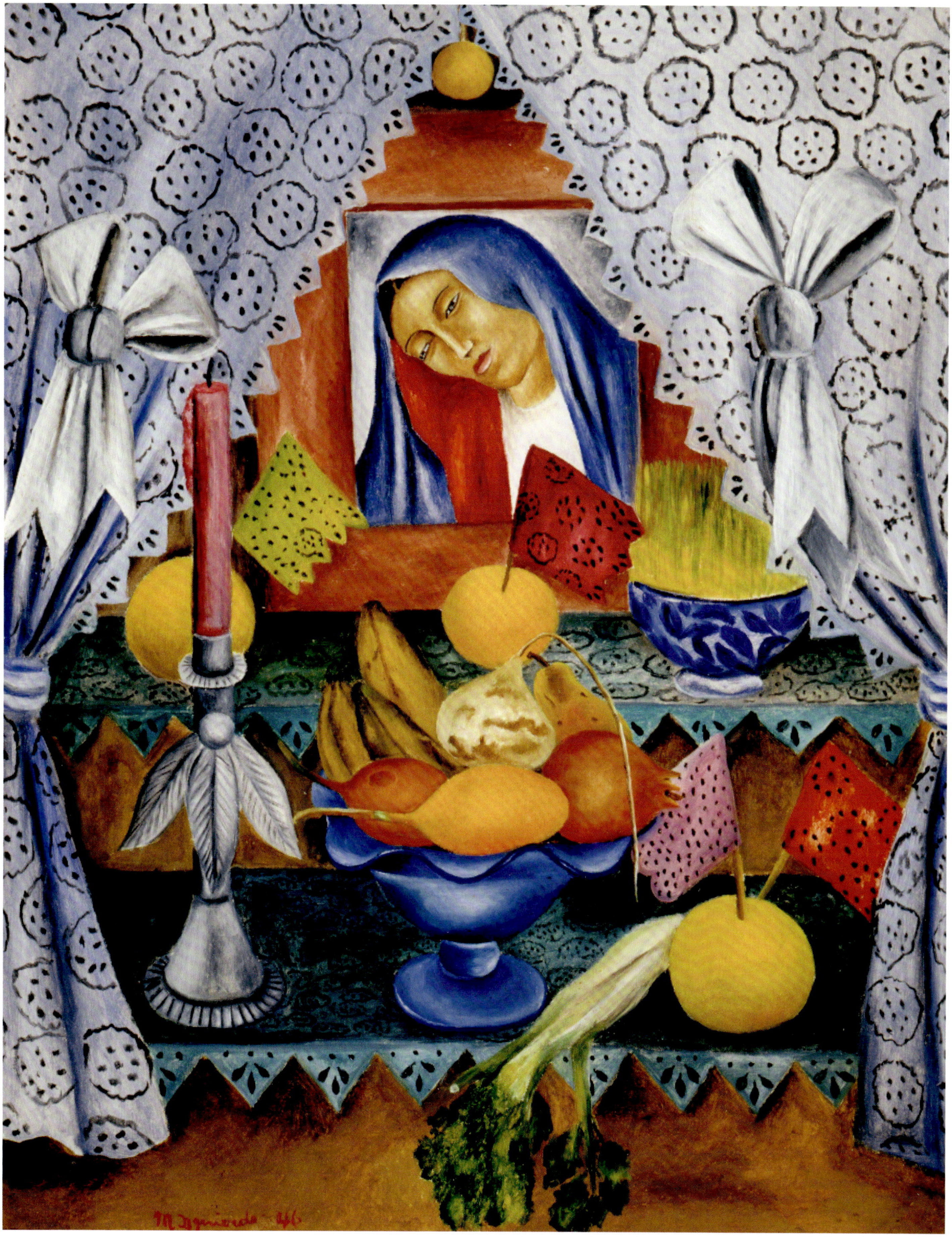

17. JOSÉ GUADALUPE POSADA
CALAVERAS DEL MONTÓN, NÚMERO 1
(CALAVERAS FROM THE HEAP, NUMBER 1), 1910
PAPER, LETTERPRESS. 40.1 × 29.5 CM
Library of Congress Prints and Photographs Division

Art was not only idealized but also politicized. Artists formed a collective, *Sindicato de Obreros Técnicos, Pintores y Escultores* (Union of Technical Workers, Painters and Sculptors) in 1922 to protect their rights; all members were paid the same daily rates. In its manifesto, Siqueiros stated that the artist should abandon the easel, representative of bourgeois taste, in favour of monumental art 'as it is public property'.[11] It was also, significantly, a time when all forms of art were considered equal. A journal established by the American Frances Toor, *Mexican Folkways*, championed the popular arts of Mexico, employing Rivera as its art editor. He designed the covers and photographers including Weston, Modotti and Lola Álvarez Bravo illustrated the great diversity of arts they captured on their travels across the country.[12] In 1926, Brenner commissioned Weston to take photographs for a book project, 'Mexican Decorative Arts' which would later become *Idols Behind Altars*. Weston, who longed to travel within Mexico and needed the money, travelled with Modotti. Together they took over 200 photographs for the project [19, 21, 22, 24].[13] Many of these objects were, along with pre-Columbian art, collected and proudly displayed by artists and intellectuals, often appearing in paintings. Artists like Kahlo and María Izquierdo celebrated the diversity of Mexico by proudly wearing regional clothes and pre-Columbian jewellery [16]. Remarkably, even before Rivera, who had a retrospective at the Museum of Modern Art, New York the following year, Izquierdo was the first Mexican artist to have a solo exhibition in the United States, at the Art Center in New York in 1930, organised by Frances Flynne Paine, who was a passionate supporter of Mexican art.

Charlot rediscovered the preeminent Mexican engraver José Guadalupe Posada who had spent his career producing illustrations for broadsheets and other cheap publications and championed his work [17].[14] Posada would inspire future generations of woodcut and etching artists which led to a highly influential and increasingly politicized collective, the *Taller de Gráfica Popular*, known as the TGP (Popular Graphics Workshop), founded in 1937.[15] The hitherto neglected traditions of woodcut and etching on tin plate were resurrected and elevated to new heights.

It was not, however, all plain sailing. Despite the dramatic increase in art production, artists were not a united collective, nor working towards

NUMERO 1.

CALAVERAS DEL MONTON.

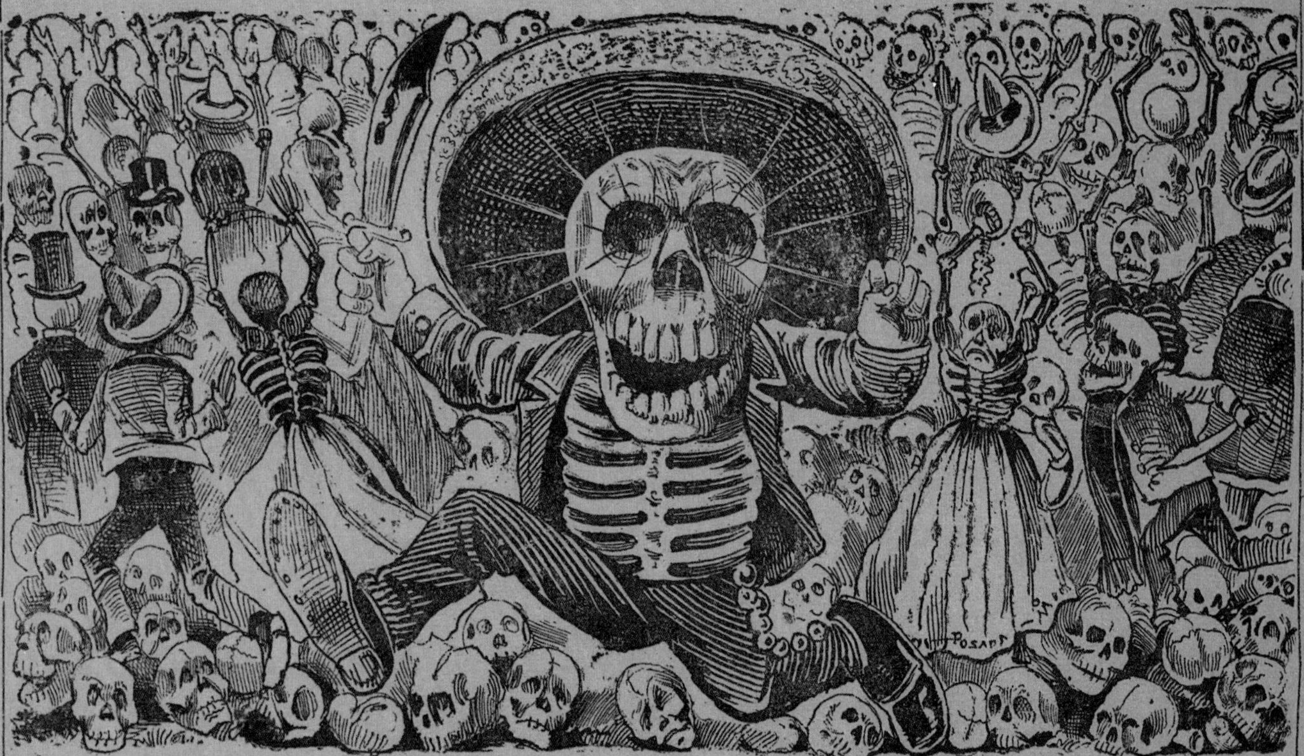

Es la vida pasajera
Y todos pelan el diente,
Aquí está la calavera,
Del que ha sido presidente.
También la de Don Ramón
Y todos sus subalternos
Son como buenos Gobiernos
Calaveras del montón.

No caven ya en el Panteón
Es mucha la guesamenta,
Entre ellas también se cuenta;
La de Landa y Escandón.
Que les prendan sus siriales
A nombre de la Nación
Alcabo que son iguales;
Calaveras del montón.

Las otras son de Oficiales
Sin ninguna distinción,
Coroneles. . . . . Generales
Y jefes de división.
Mayores con charreteras
Capitanes de instrucción,
Toditos son calaveras
Calaveras del montón.

A la vez los ayudantes
Con todito su Escuadrón.
Y siguen los Aspirantes:
Calaveras todos son.
Calavera es el Teniente
Y también la reclusión,
Y lo mismo el subteniente
Calaveras del montón.

Esto si que es un recreo
Nadie de morir se escapa
A las muertes con su capa
Diciendo misa las veo;
Y responsos para el Papa.
Ya le prendieron sus ceras
Y se hayan en oración
Calaveras del montón.

También al fuereño toca
Su partesita en la fiesta,
Que por abrir la boca;
Un eléctrico lo acuesta.
Estas si que son tonteras
El andar en la función,
Toditos son calaveras
Calaveras del montón.

Muchos hicieron corajes
Y sucumbieron de enojo,
Fueron grandes personajes:
E hicieron todo á su antojo.
Como fieles y constantes
De su patria en la Nación;
A hoy los representantes
Calaveras todos son.

Empesamos por el chino
Y vamos viendo despues,
Que al llegar á su destino;
Murió con el Japones.
La china fué la primera
Un representante envió,
Y se quedó calavera;
De tantas cosas que vió.

España un enviado dió
Que fué especial y muy fiel,
Pues al momento cumplió,
Con el encargo del Rey.
Tu persona placentera
Va en mi representación,
Pero quedó calavera
Calavera del montón.

Los valientes tiradores,
Soldados de artillería
Juntos con los zapadores;
Calaveras son en este día
El soldado de primera
Y el cabo de pelotón;
Con su horrible calavera
Espantan en el panteón.

Calaveras por millares
Se van contando por cientos,
Todos fueron militares;
Y pasaron por sargentos
Comandantes de sección
Que se numere la hilera
Que grite la calavera:
Ya estamos en el panteón.

Ya se llenó el panteón
No queda ni un ahujero,
Pues se cuentan por montón;
Calaveras por entero.
Hoy el sepulturero
Escarba como una fiera,
Y busca la calavera;
De Don Francisco Madero.

Que de pezar se murió
Sin encontrar á la suerte;
La muerte se lo llevó
En su lomo como fuerte.
Madero murió inosente
Pero quedó la madera
Por querer ser presidente
Lo volvieron calavera.

Todo charlatán pulquero
Que á mujeres engañó,
Calavera se volvió;
Tan solo por embustero.
Aquél que vendió su quezo
Con la muerte allá en la plaza,
Se ha quedado como tiezo
Calavera de su casa.

El vendedor de las peras
Los saca muelas chorriados,
Se han quedado calaveras;
Y con los dientes pelados.
Y aquellos que se murieron
Enfermos del corazón,
Ya sus velas les prendieron;
Calaveras del montón.

Ya las inditas placeras
No hicieron buena fortuna,
Por andar vendiendo tuna;
Se volvieron calaveras.
Lo mismo el del chicharrón
E todas las enchiladeras;
Son roídas calaveras;
Calaveras del montón.

Imprenta de Antonio Vanegas Arroyo.—2a Calle de Santa Teresa, Número 43.—México año de 1910.

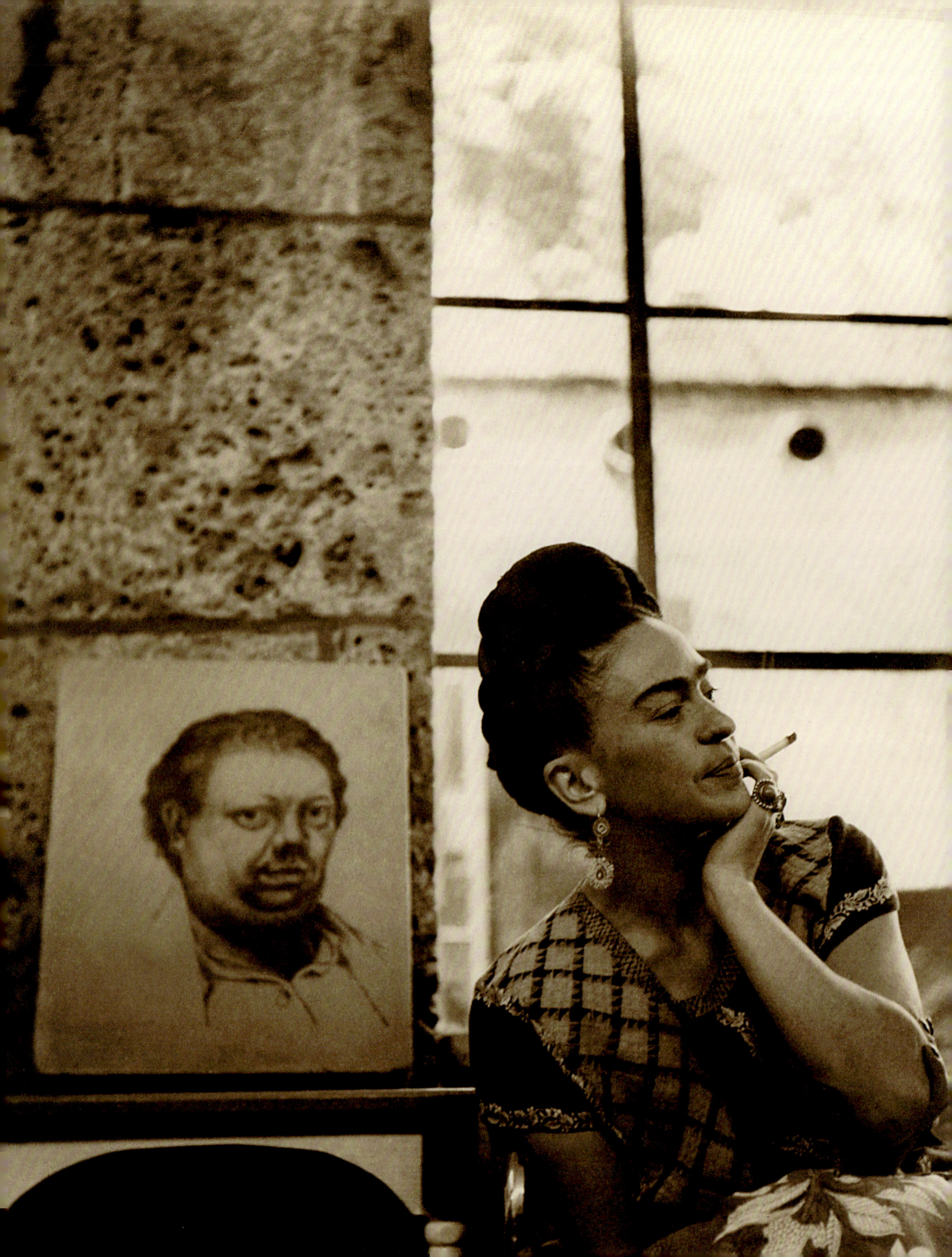

18. LOLA ÁLVAREZ BRAVO
FRIDA KAHLO SEATED ALONGSIDE LITHOGRAPHIC STONE FOR DIEGO RIVERA'S 'SELF-PORTRAIT', 1930, C.1945
Private collection

the same goals. There were artistic and political tensions and rivalries throughout the 1920s and 1930s. Siqueiros was imprisoned for a failed assassination attempt on Trotsky. He and Rivera fell out publically over their Communist beliefs; Rivera supported Trotsky and Siqueiros, Stalin. Izquierdo was prevented from painting murals. The young Oaxacan artist, Rufino Tamayo (at the time Izquierdo's partner), refused to be drawn into producing what he considered Mexican art, questioning the motivation and subject matter of the muralists. He moved to New York to pursue his career there. After being instrumental in establishing the reputation of her husband, Manuel, Lola Álvarez Bravo had to fight to build her reputation as a photographer in her own right after he left her. Modotti was exiled from Mexico on trumped-up political charges. In 1936 Artaud was horrified to discover that indigenous communities were still being marginalized and persecuted by the government and that European cultural influences still dominated.[16] As early as 1925 both Lawrence and Weston criticized the ideology of Rivera's paintings.[17] Charlot, fed up with the infighting among artists in Mexico City, moved to the Yucatan in 1926 to record the archaeological discoveries being made at Chichen Itza. Significant as they are, these issues fail to overshadow the remarkable creativity that continued into the 1940s as artists continued to work in Mexico and were joined by those, such as English-born Leonora Carrington and Gordon Onslow Ford, Spaniard Remedios Varo and Hungarian Kati Horna, fleeing the rise of Fascism in Europe and the Spanish Civil War. Or those artists unable to travel to Europe including Chilean Roberto Matta and Americans Edward Hopper and Robert Motherwell.

Once the country's elite had been interested in showing themselves as sophisticated, sharing an international taste in art, as described by Charlot: 'the rich thrive on alabaster statuettes, Louis XV pianos and telephones in the style of Louis XVI'.[18] Following the Mexican Revolution this was no longer the case. Art was democratized and while the aspiration among artists, to have a more equitable and integrated society, remained, in reality the goals of the revolution, to implement long lasting and far reaching reform, did not last. The new political regime became increasingly conservative, replacing the previous regime's corruption and nepotism with its own system of political patronage. Ironically, as the content of murals became more and more political and increasingly critical of past regimes, colonial or republican, or joyously celebrating the heroes of the revolution like Villa and Zapata, the political arena became narrower and reform dried up. What did not disappear, however, was the newly discovered passion for all things Mexican. The art that was produced in this extraordinary period, and with which Kahlo has become indelibly associated, continues to fascinate and develop. Once the opportunity for Mexicans to express themselves freely arrived, there was to be no stopping it [18].

19. EDWARD WESTON
PALACE II, MITLA – THREE STONE FRIEZES, EACH WITH A DIFFERENT GEOMETRIC PATTERN, 1926
GELATIN SILVER PRINT. 19.2 × 24 CM
Center for Creative Photography, University of Arizona, Tuscon. 82.8.133

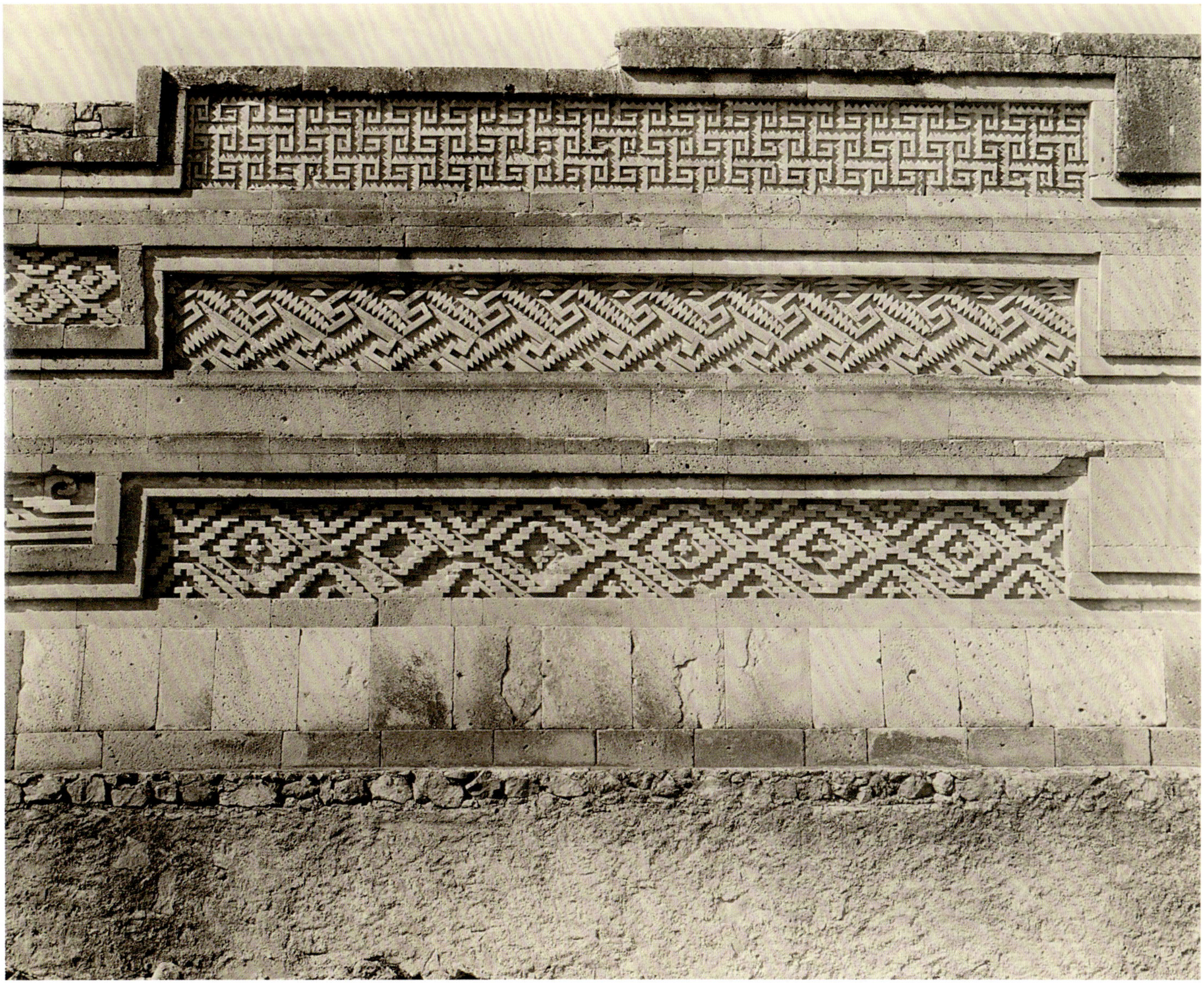

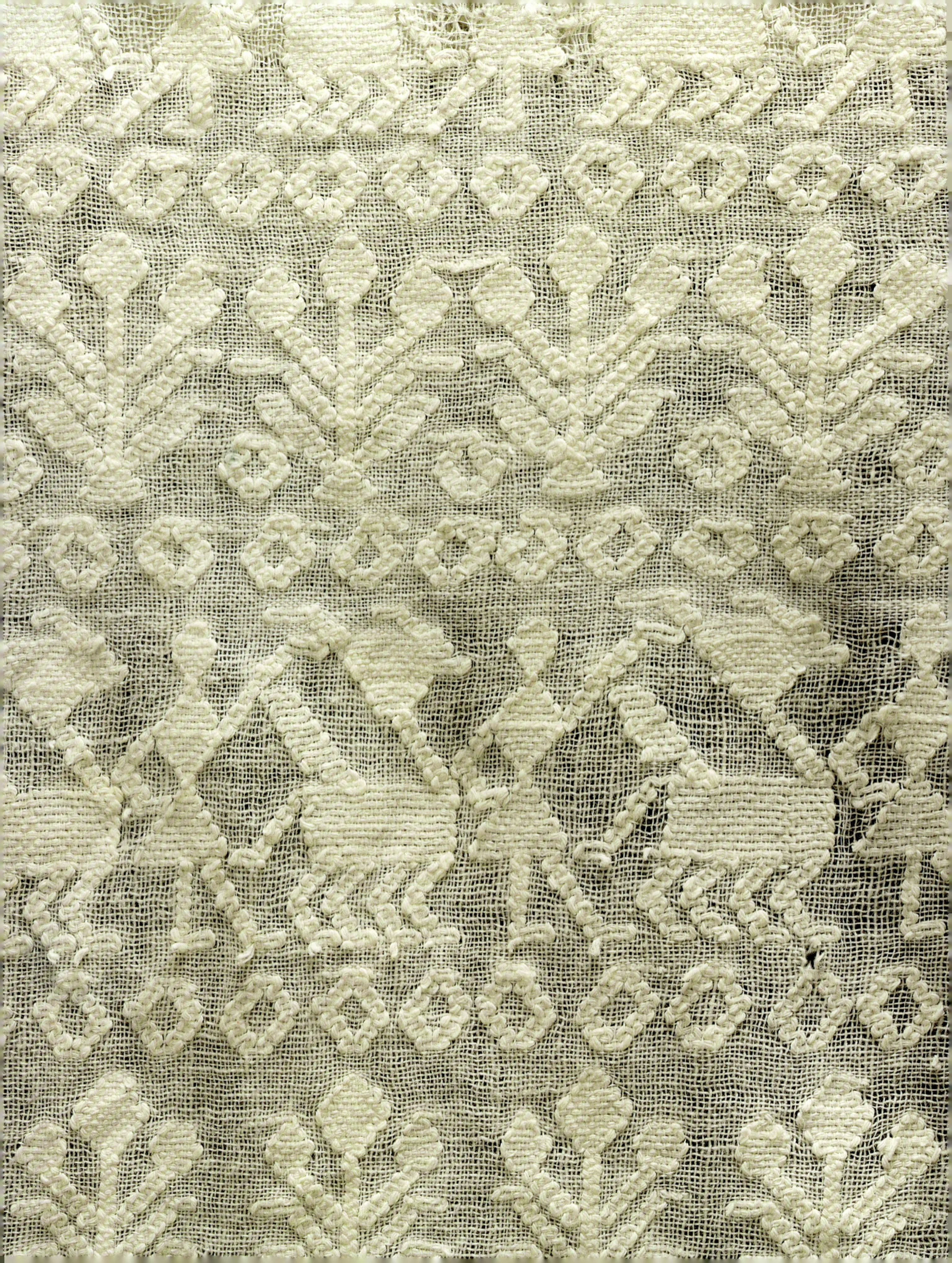

20. DETAIL OF GUATEMALAN COTTON HUIPIL WITH WOVEN DESIGN OF MAIZE-LIKE PLANTS AND HUMAN FIGURES WITH ANIMALS, SEE P.111
Museo Frida Kahlo

21. EDWARD WESTON
ZAPOTEC HUIPIL (TUNIC) FROM TUXTEPEC, WITH GEOMETRIC DESIGNS, 1926
GELATIN SILVER PRINT. 23.5 × 15.6 CM
Center for Creative Photography, University of Arizona, Tuscon. 82.8.108

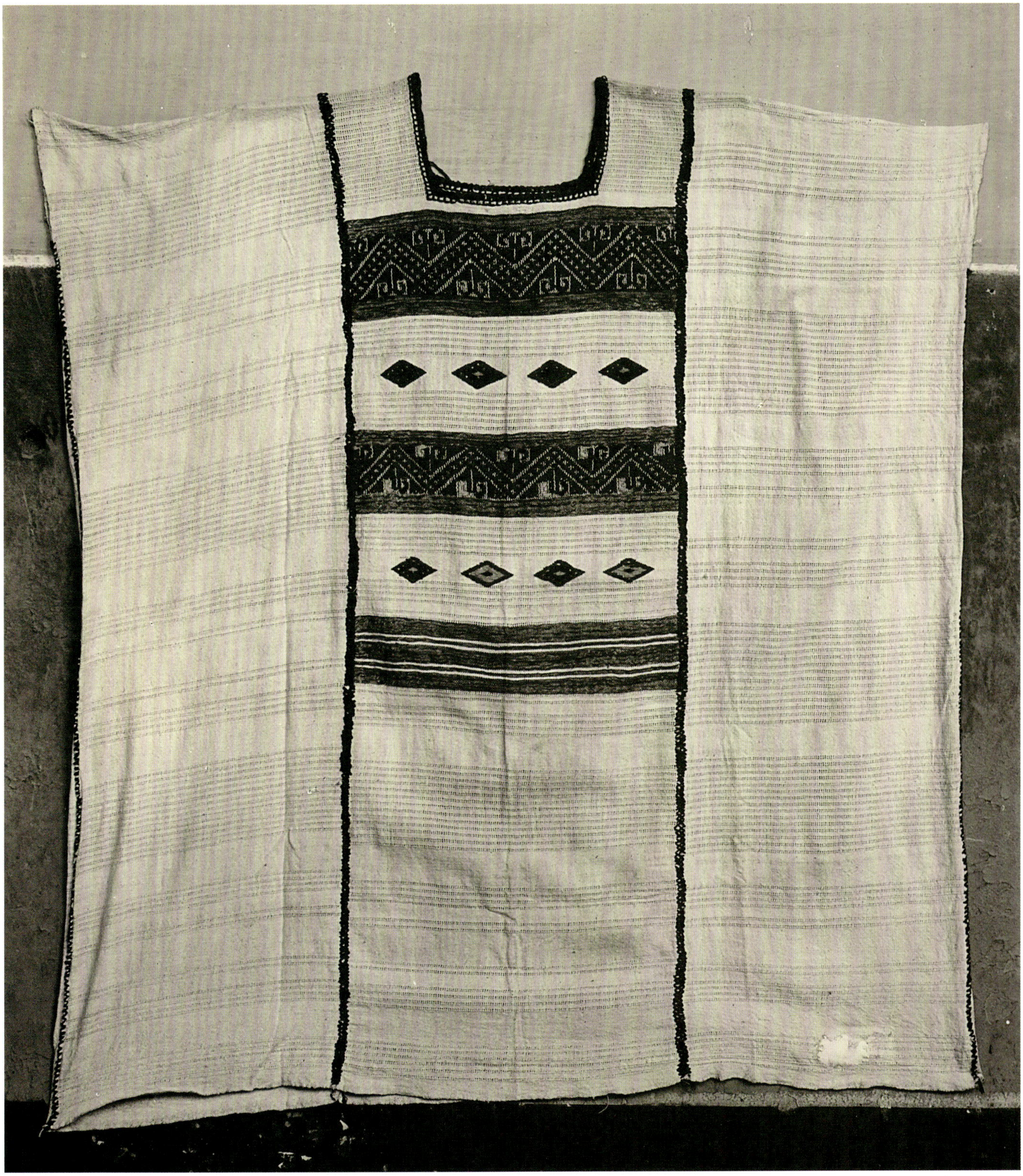

22. EDWARD WESTON
BLOUSE FROM PUEBLA EMBROIDERED
WITH FLOWERS, 1926
GELATIN SILVER PRINT. 23.5 × 15.6 CM
Center for Creative Photography,
University of Arizona, Tuscon. 82.8.109

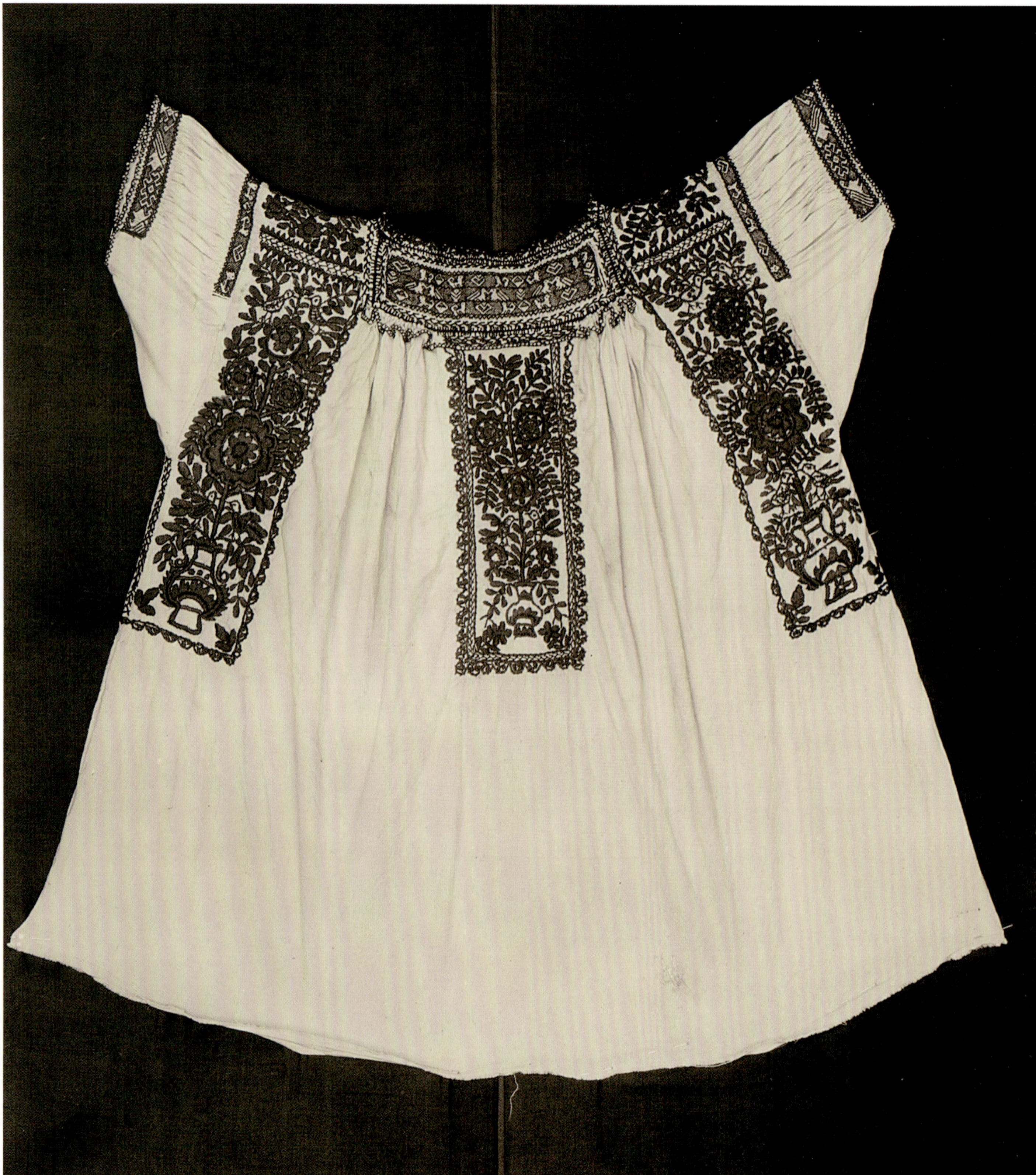

23. EMBROIDERED COTTON BLOUSE FROM COAPA, PUEBLA
Museo Frida Kahlo

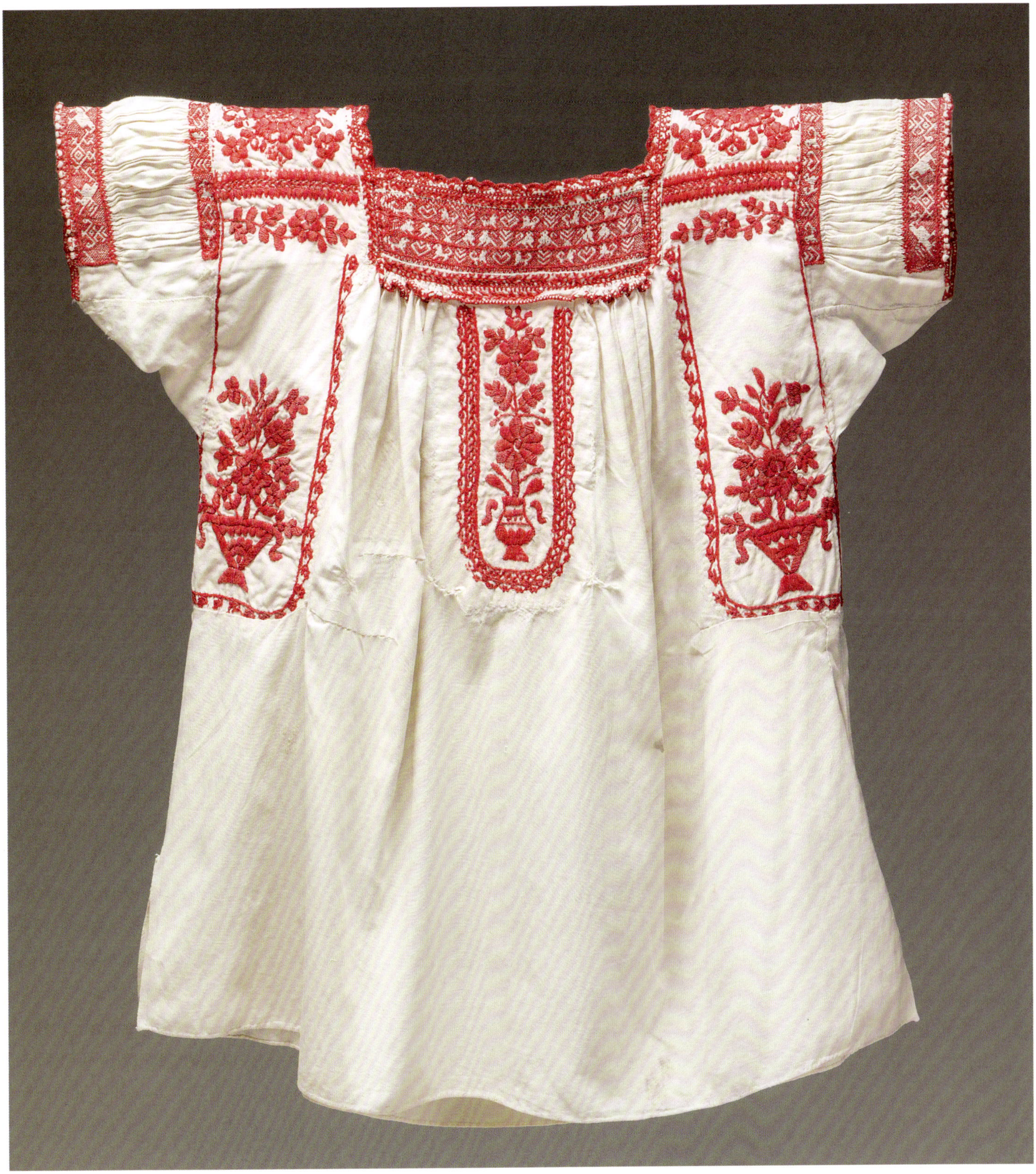

24. EDWARD WESTON
HUICHOL MAN'S CEREMONIAL BELT WITH EMBROIDERED BAGS, 1926
GELATIN SILVER PRINT. 15.6 × 23.5 CM
Center for Creative Photography, University of Arizona, Tuscon. 82.8.270

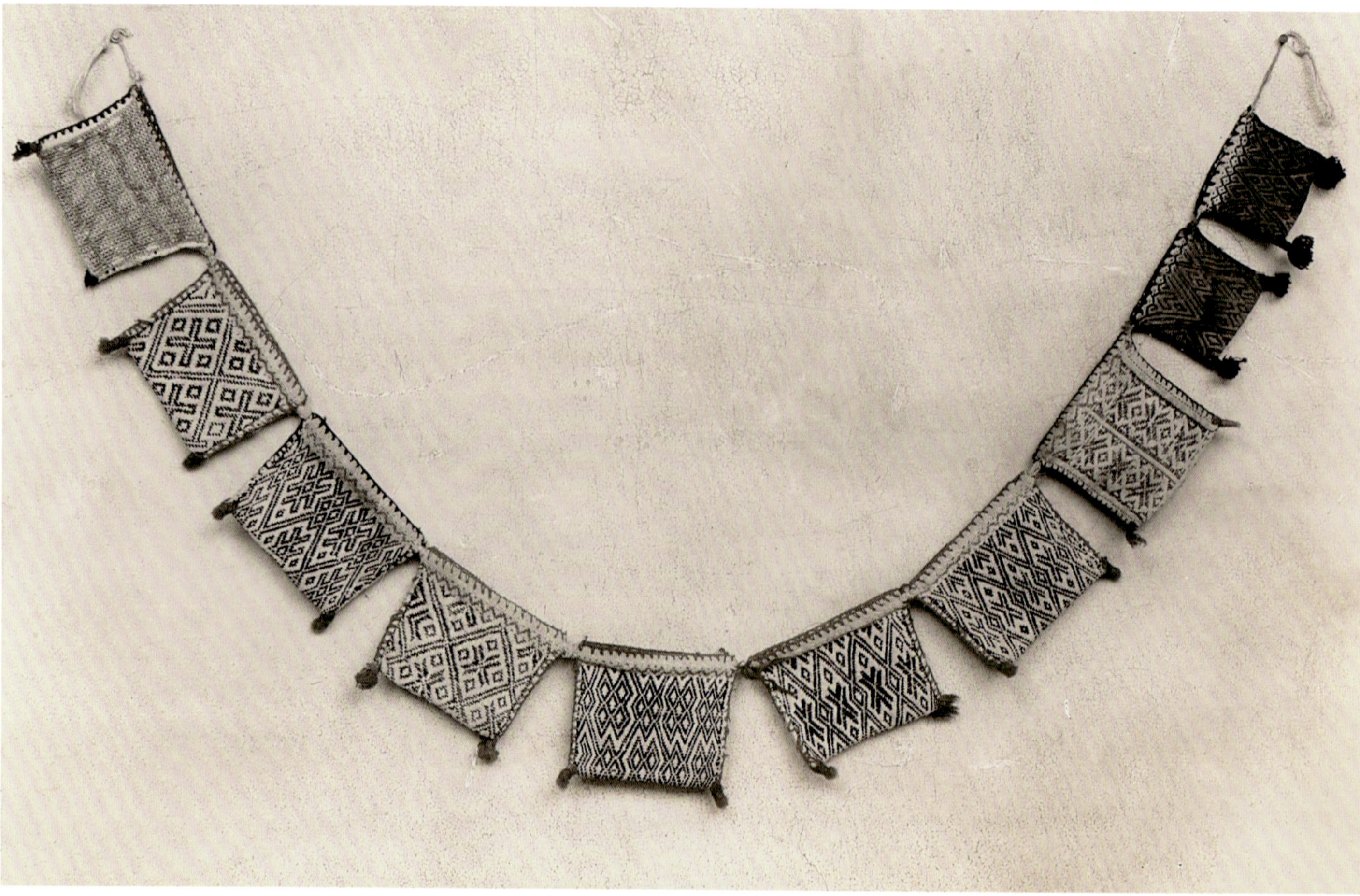

25. WOVEN BAG, PATTERNED ON THE LOOM, WITH TWISTED CARRYING CORD
Museo Frida Kahlo

26. WOVEN BAG, PATTERNED ON THE LOOM, WITH TWISTED CARRYING CORD
Museo Frida Kahlo

pp.64–5
DETAIL OF IKAT-PATTERNED RAYON REBOZO FROM GUANAJUATO
Museo Frida Kahlo

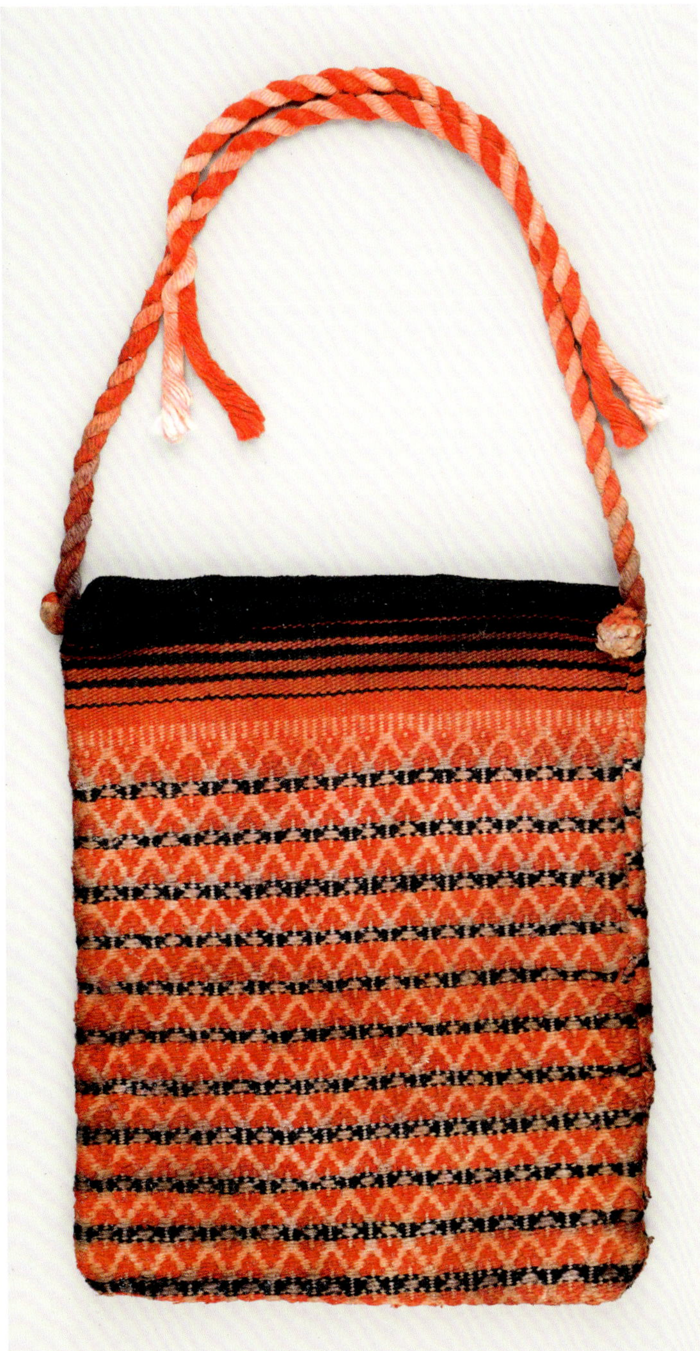

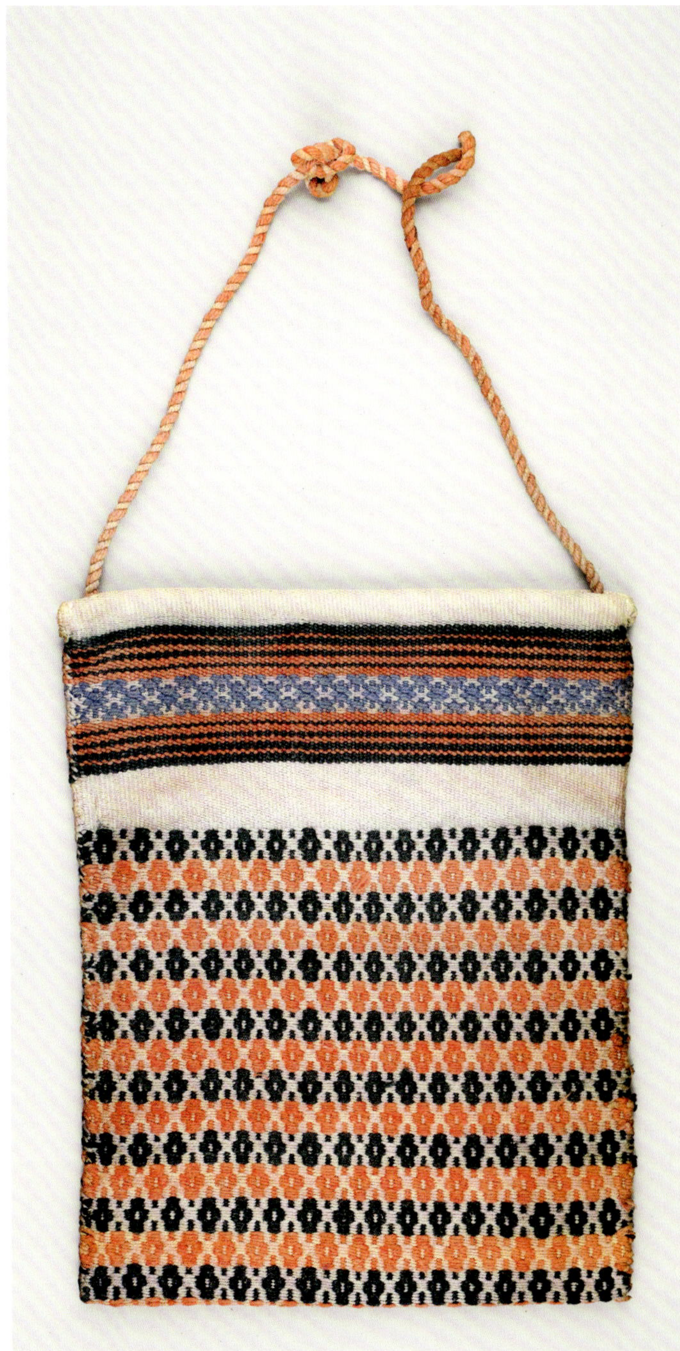

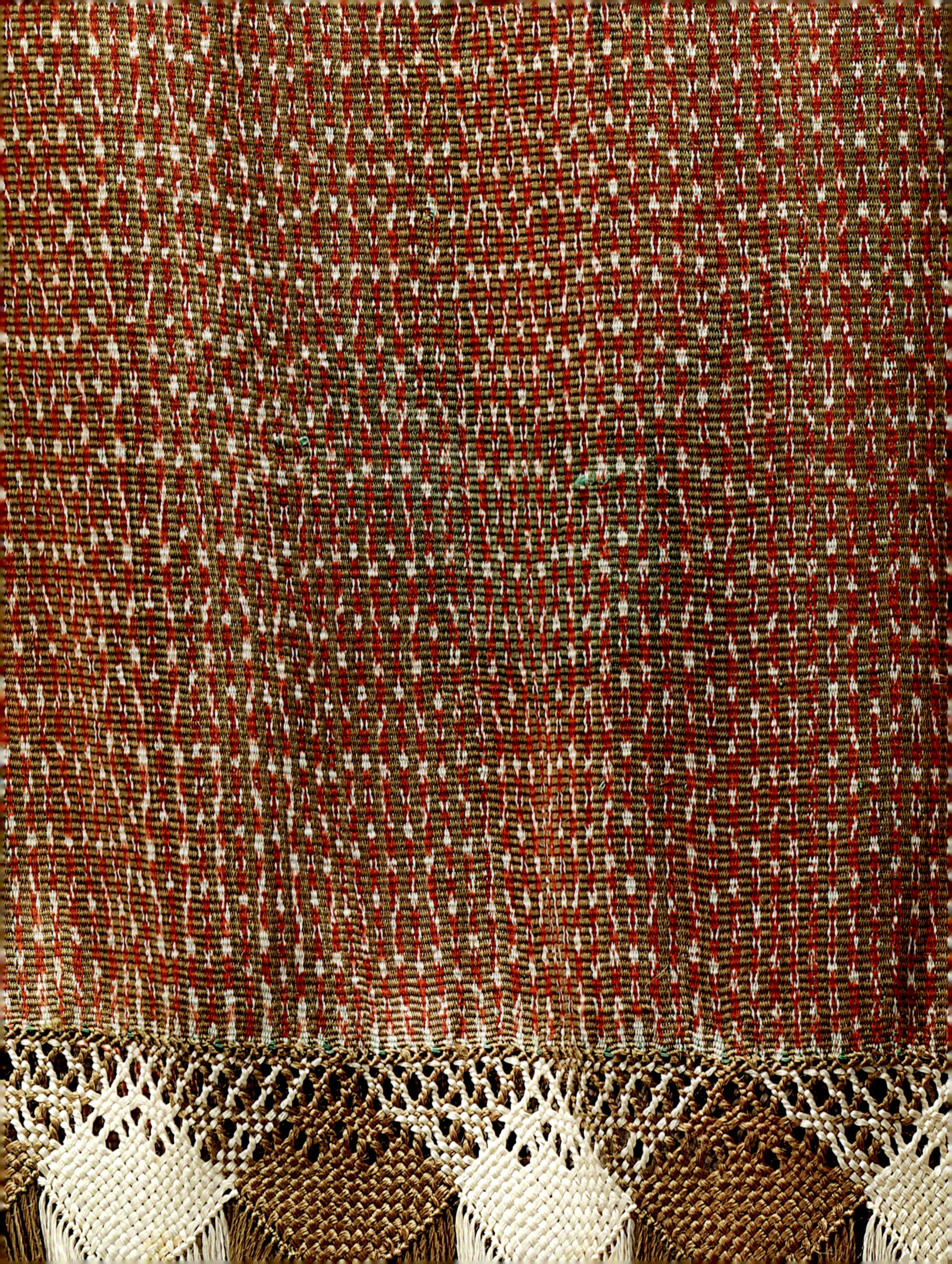

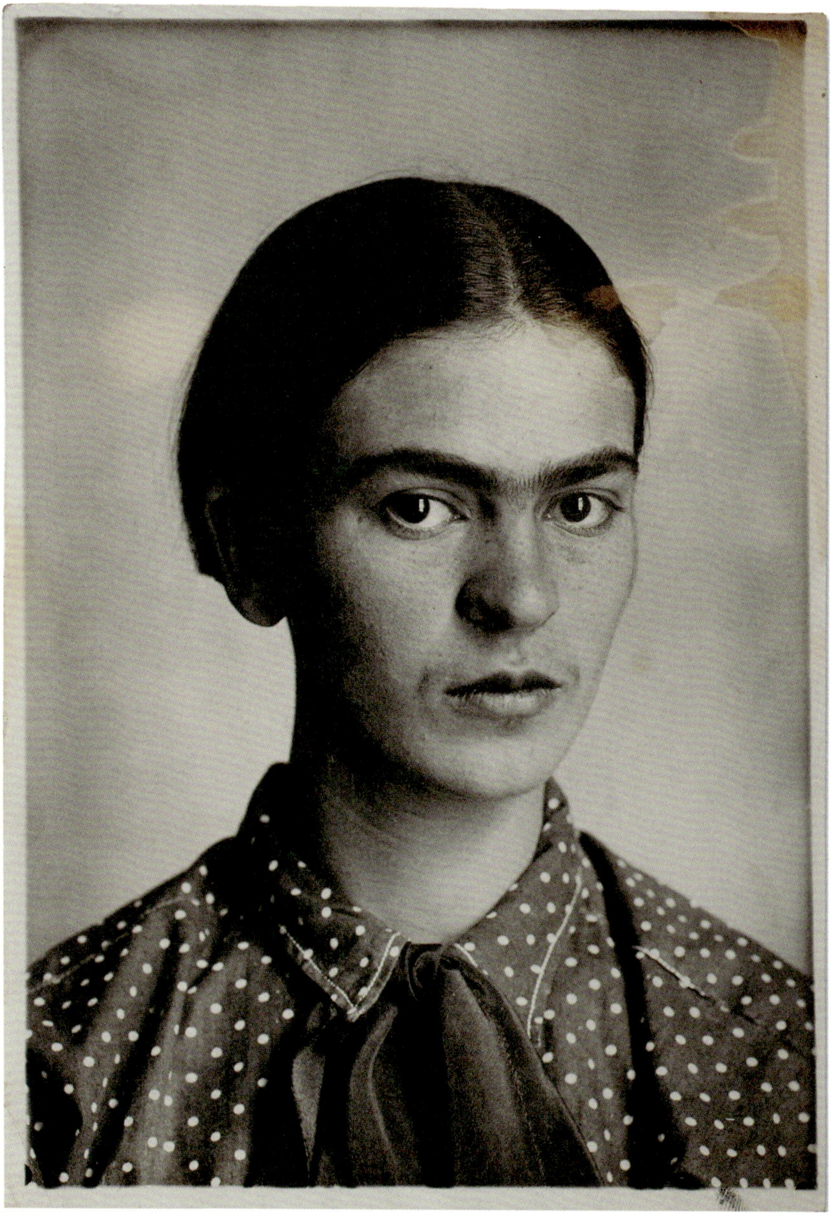

Il. 7

GUILLERMO KAHLO
FRIDA KAHLO, C.1926
ON VERSO: 'APRIL 1929, JULY. TO DIEGO. FRIEDA'
GELATIN SILVER PRINT. 17.2 × 12.2 CM
Museo Frida Kahlo

GUILLERMO KAHLO
FRIDA KAHLO AGED 19, 7 FEBRUARY 1926
Throckmorton Fine Art, Inc., New York

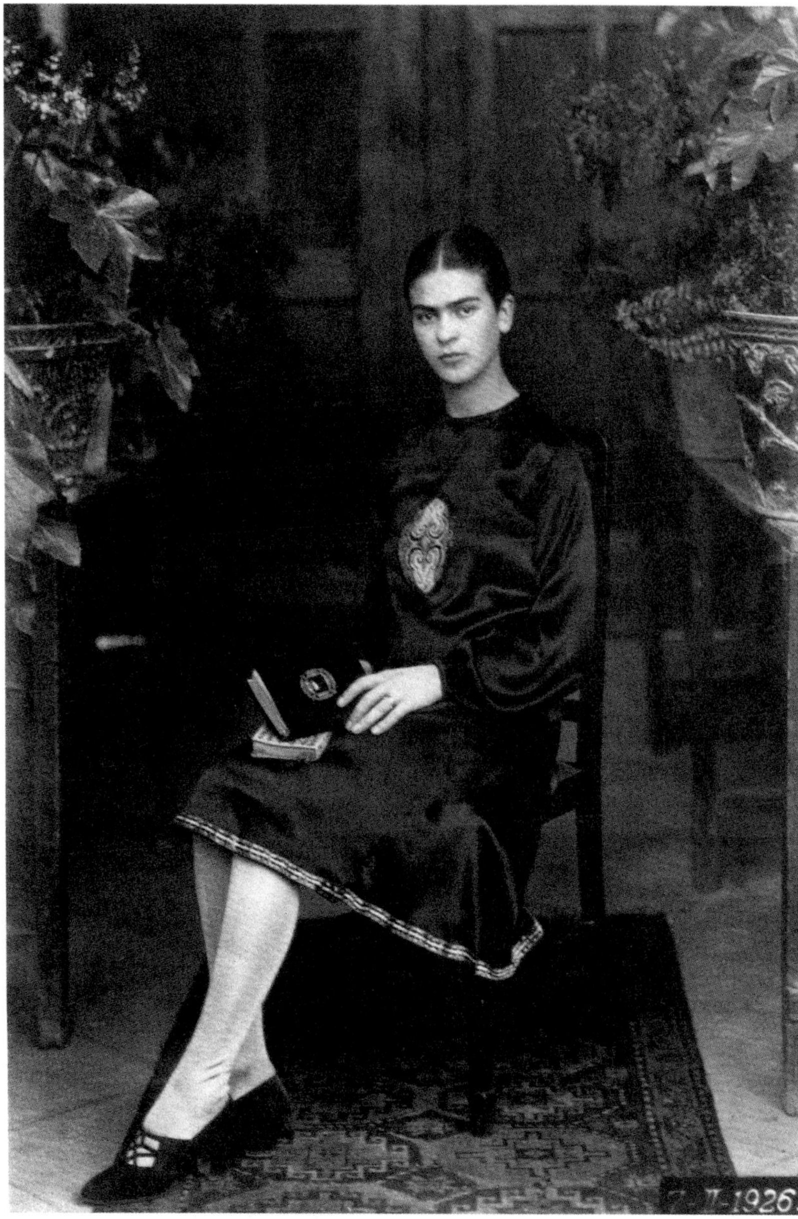

Il. 3

GUILLERMO KAHLO

FRIDA KAHLO AND FAMILY, 7 FEBRUARY 1926

Throckmorton Fine Art, Inc., New York

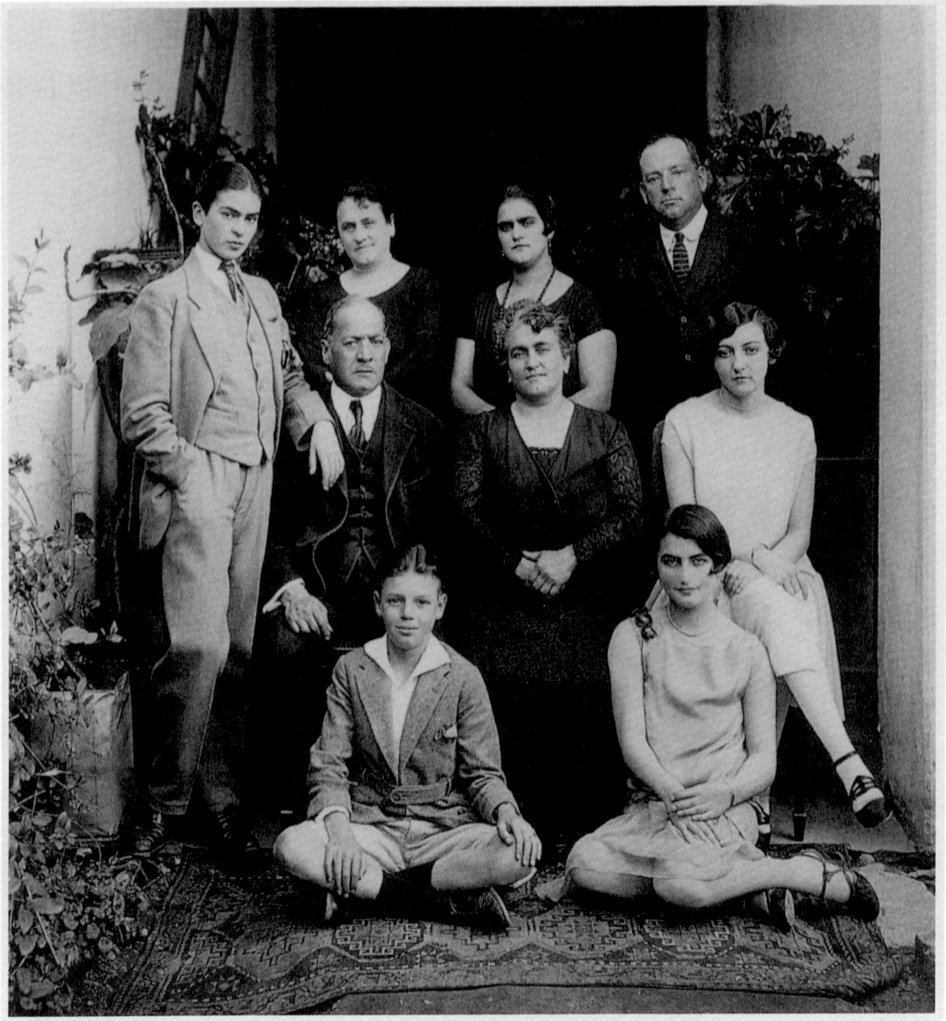

GUILLERMO DÁVILA
FRIDA KAHLO OUTSIDE DIEGO RIVERA'S STUDIO, C.1929
GELATIN PRINT. 15.24 × 10.16 CM
Throckmorton Fine Art, Inc., New York

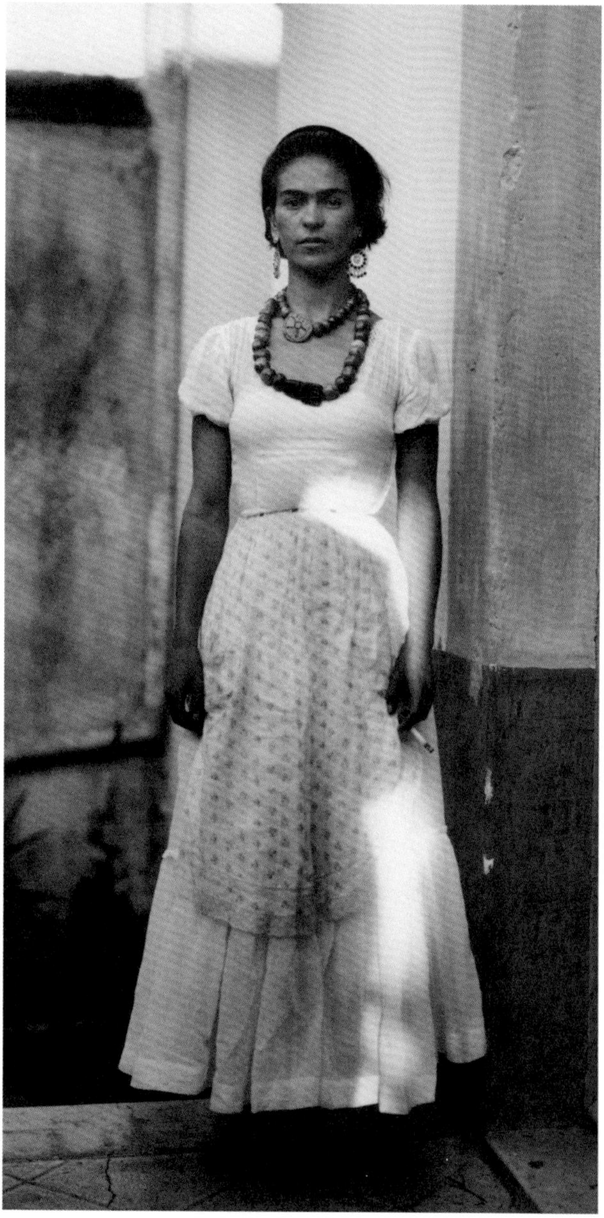

II.5

GUILLERMO KAHLO
FRIDA KAHLO, 16 OCTOBER 1932
GELATIN SILVER PRINT. 17 × 12 CM
Museo Frida Kahlo

PHOTOGRAPHER UNKNOWN
ANTONIO PINEDO KAHLO, CRISTINA KAHLO, ISOLDA PINEDO KAHLO, C.1944
GELATIN SILVER PRINT. 13.8 × 8.7 CM
Museo Frida Kahlo

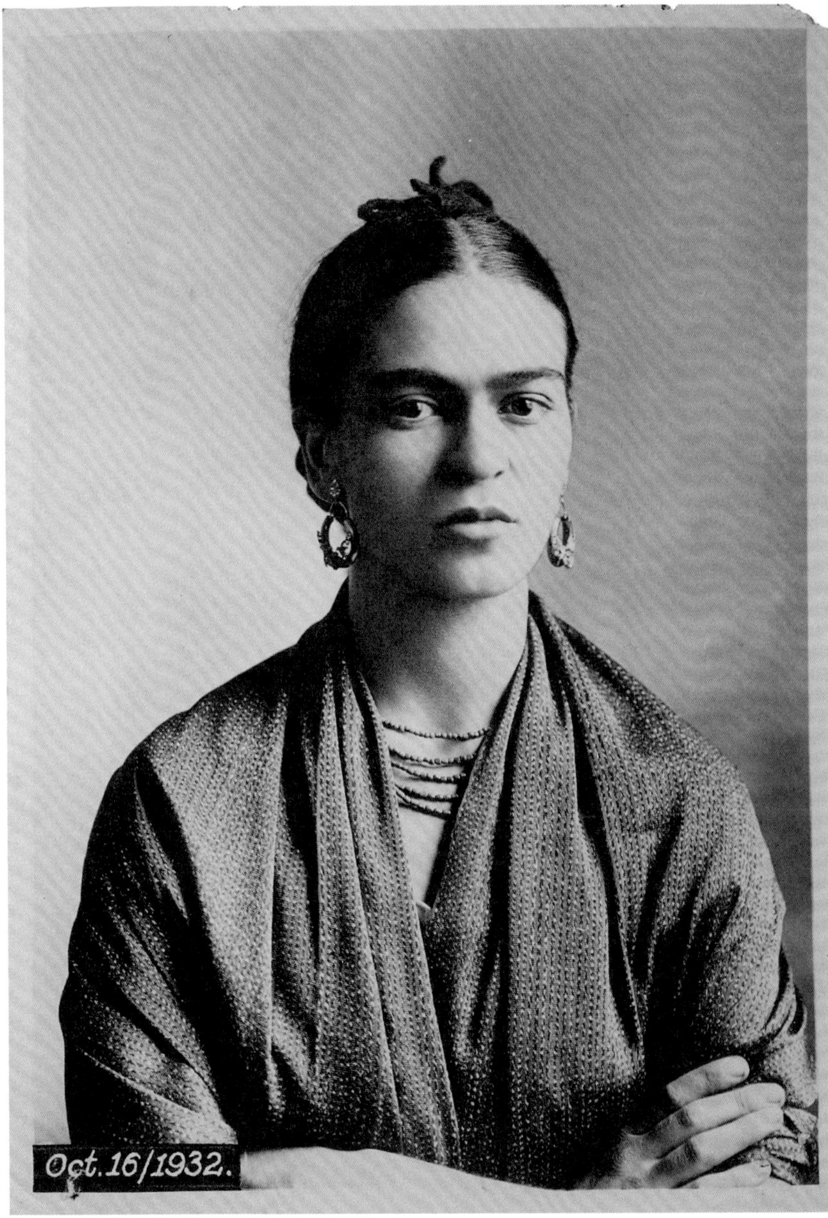

II.7

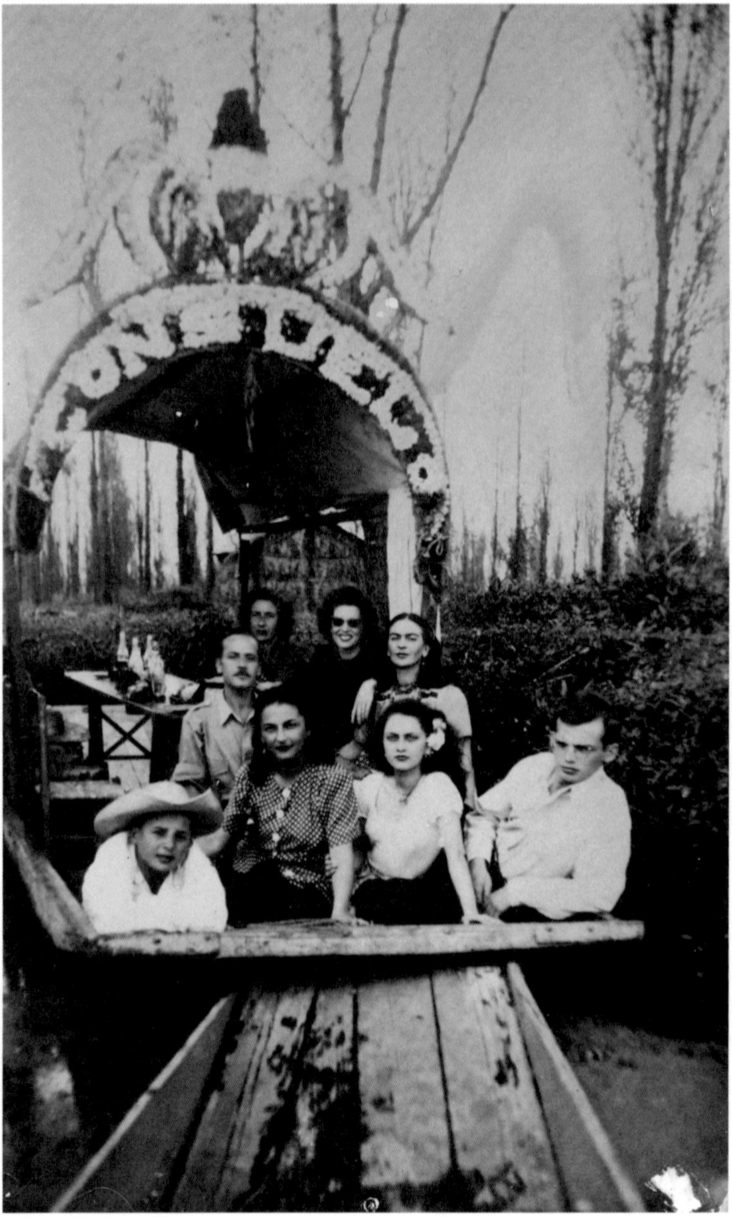

II.*8*

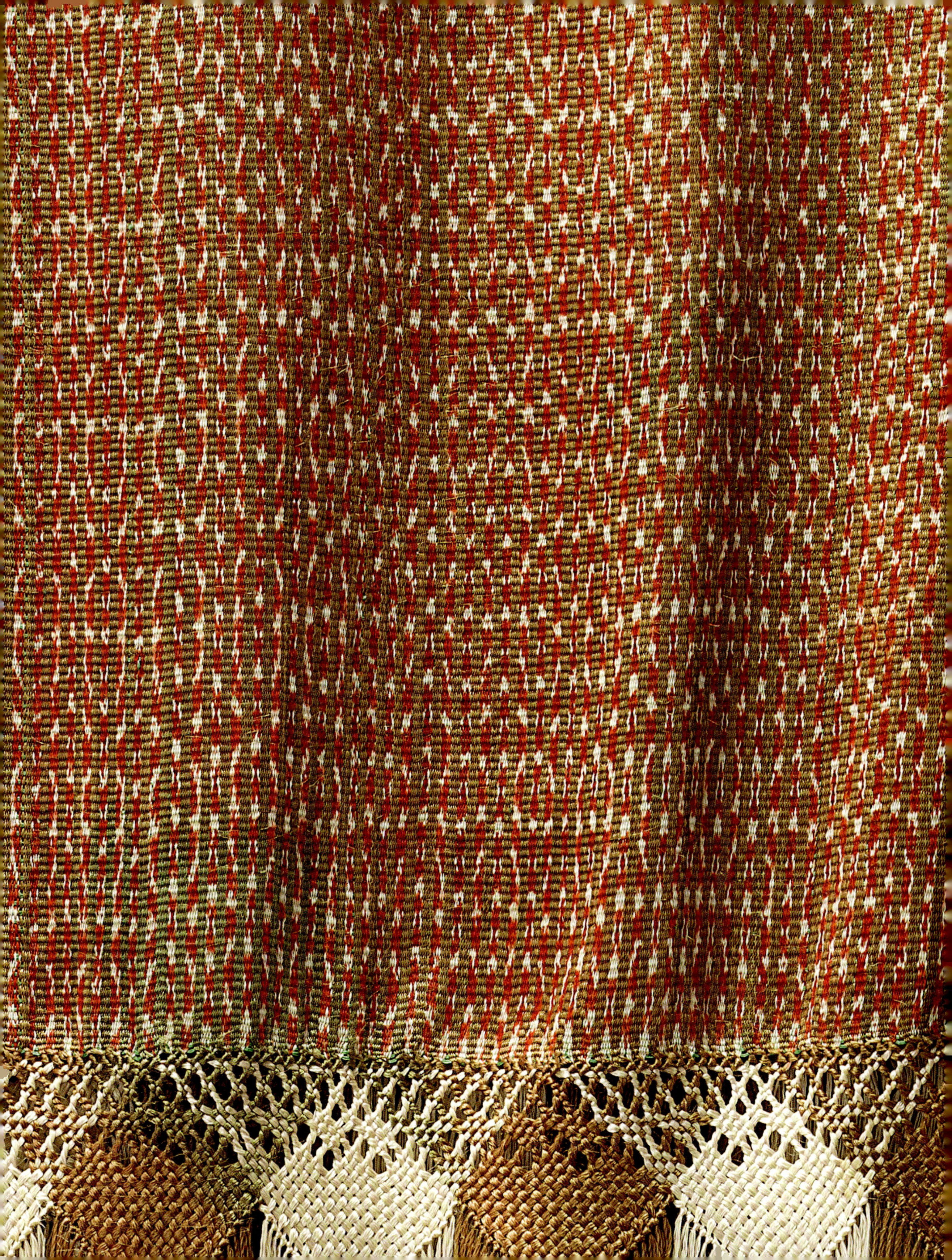

Appearances Can Be Deceiving – Frida Kahlo's Construction of Identity: Disability, Ethnicity and Dress

CIRCE HENESTROSA

What do I need feet for if I have wings to fly? 1953

Frida Kahlo's image was immortalized in her self-portraits and through the lens of many photographers, including Nickolas Muray, who took the iconic portraits of the artist we recognize today. Muray's archive contains one particular photograph – published in a 1939 edition of *Life* magazine – in which Kahlo and Rivera are pictured in their studio house in Mexico City, along with their friends Miguel and Rosa Covarrubias. Muray himself is crouched on the floor, and on the left, there are two other people, perhaps less well-known internationally: my great-aunts Alfa Ríos Henestrosa and Nereida Ríos [27].

Alfa Ríos was married to Andrés Henestrosa, one of the most prominent writers in Mexico at that time, and a close friend of Kahlo and Rivera.[1] Alfa came from the Isthmus of Tehuantepec, a region in the state of Oaxaca in the south-east of Mexico, composed predominantly of indigenous Zapotec peoples. It is a matriarchal society in which women dominate, and dress in Tehuana attire comprising floor-length skirts, richly embroidered blouses and long woven shawls, their hair dressed elaborately with ribbons and flowers. Growing up, I was surrounded by these colourful garments from Tehuana, and the sartorial traditions of this society were passed down to me by my aunt Cibeles, Alfa's daughter [28]. In our family it was said that Kahlo's first Tehuana dresses were given to her by Alfa, a fact that has since been confirmed by Kahlo scholars.[2] Having worn the Tehuana style of dress myself, I wanted to know why Kahlo had chosen this particular style as her signature look.

'To the average city Mexican, a Tehuana is as romantic and attractive a subject as a South Sea maiden to an adolescent American.'[3]

The traditions of the Isthmus of Tehuantepec have been well-documented for many centuries. Howard Campbell and Susanne Green's history of representations of Isthmus Zapotec women in particular provides an extended account of visitors' reactions to this region.[4] Their descriptions of the Tehuantepec women include stories of Zapotec women's market activity, and the cotton blouses and skirts they wore.[5] It was not until the painter and anthropologist Miguel Covarrubias published *Mexico South: The Isthmus of Tehuantepec* in 1946, including reproductions of his

27. NICKOLAS MURAY
FROM LEFT: ALFA RIOS HENESTROSA, ROSA COVARRUBIAS, NEREIDA RIOS, NICKOLAS MURAY, DIEGO RIVERA, MIGUEL COVARRUBIAS AND FRIDA KAHLO, SAN ANGEL, MEXICO CITY, 1938
Nickolas Muray Photo Archives

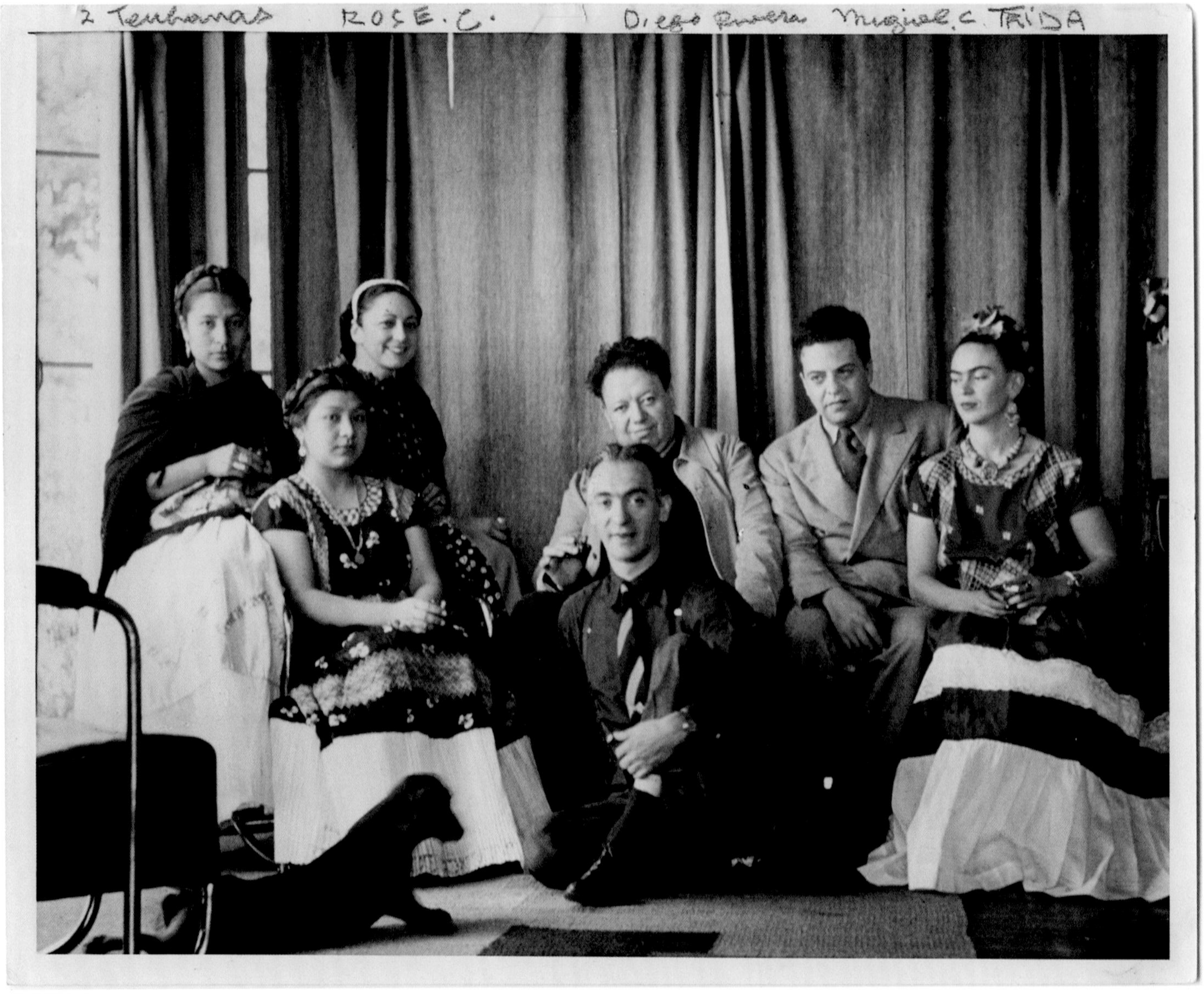

28. PHOTOGRAPHER UNKNOWN
FROM LEFT: TEODORO TOLEDO, NATALIA NADER, ALFA RIOS, ANDRÉS HENESTROSA AND THEIR DAUGHTER CIBELES HENESTROSA, AT THE WEDDING OF TEODORO AND NATALIA TOLEDO-NADER, C.1950
Private collection

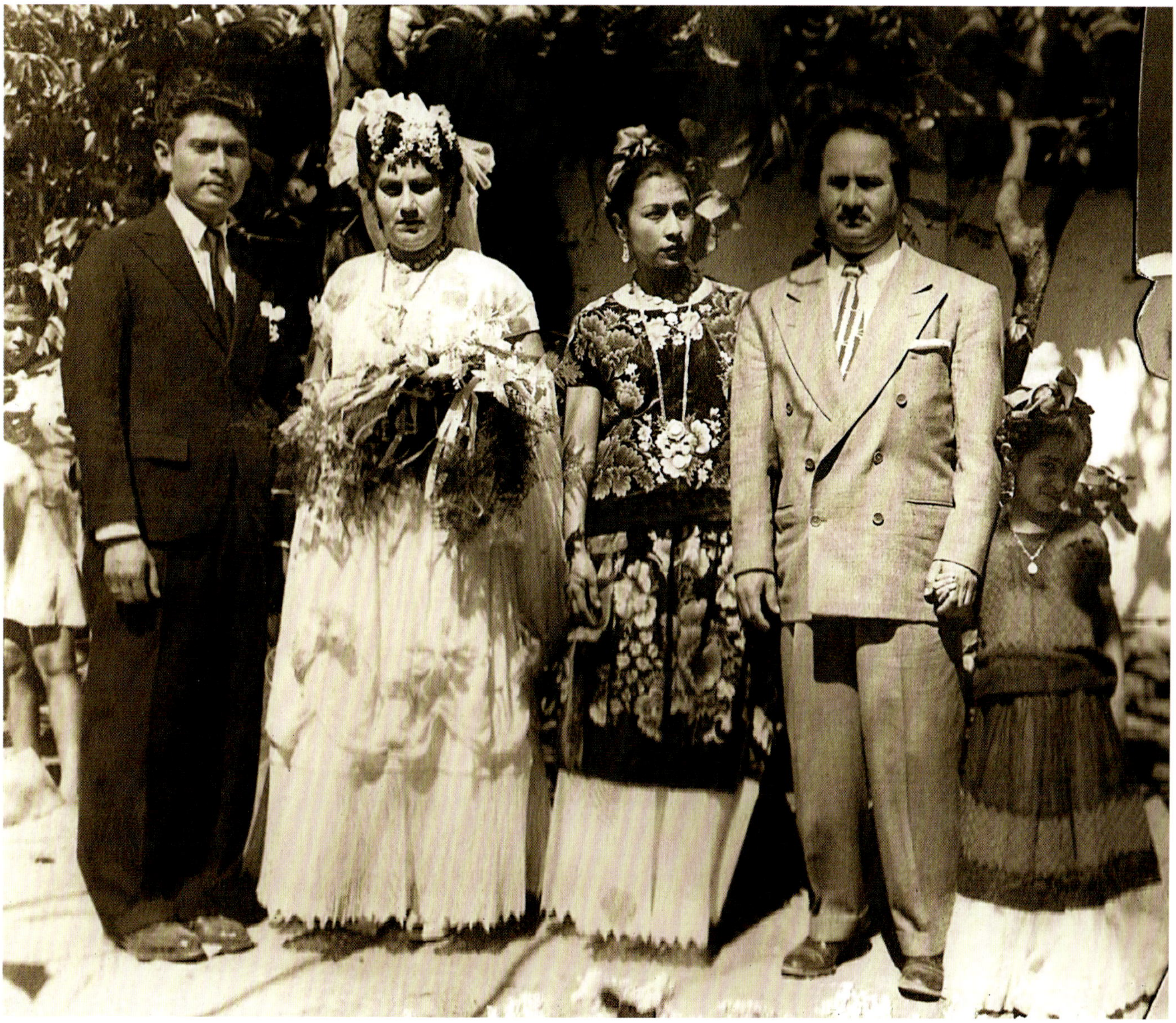

own studies of Zapotec people and the evolution of the Tehuana dress, that the region's traditions were truly recognized and made available to a broader audience [29].[6] Covarrubias's ethnography of Isthmus customs and history became a seminal text of Isthmus Zapotec studies, appreciated by both academic anthropologists and local intellectuals such as Andrés Henestrosa and Manuel Matus. His writings are one of the most important sources of information about Zapotec culture.

Covarrubias celebrated the indigenous, Zapotec culture that had survived in the region of Oaxaca. It was a society that appealed to the left-wing politics of the time. His commentary also struck home with the Zapotecs themselves, emphasizing the beauty of their women and reinforcing a fierce pride in their customs and identity. During the 1920s, artists, intellectuals and politicians found in the Tehuana the perfect symbol to represent a new, inspired, post-revolutionary Mexico – a Mexico that could embrace its native cultures and unite as a proud nation. Henestrosa's description of the Tehuana women said it all: they 'walked in verse and … their gait was pure poetry'.[7] Among the artists responsible for disseminating this romantic depiction of the Isthmus Zapotecs as symbols of the new Mexico were Covarrubias, Rivera and Jose Vasconcelos. Rivera travelled to Tehuantepec in 1926, gaining inspiration before creating the murals that cover the first-floor balcony of the *Secretaría de Educación Pública* in Mexico City, and which glorify the life of the local Tehuanas. Kahlo is portrayed as a Tehuana in these murals, and she also portrayed herself dressed in Zapotec attire in numerous canvasses of her own.[8]

Kahlo and Rivera shared a romanticized attachment to indigenous people, as did so many of the radical left at this time. The matriarchal society of the Tehuanas held a particular appeal for Kahlo, who was building her own image as an outsider: independent, but faithful to tradition, while at the same time embracing a modern, liberated lifestyle. Themes of female empowerment would be directly incorporated into her artwork through her self-portrayal in the style of the Isthmus women. According to Mexican art critic and historian Teresa del Conde, many educated, middle-class women wore regional costumes in the 1920s and 1930s.[9] Women such as Rosa Covarrubias [30], Alfa Henestrosa [28] and

29. MIGUEL COVARRUBIAS
HISTORICAL EVOLUTION OF REGIONAL COSTUME
IN ISTHMUS OF TEHUANTEPEC, C.1945
PAPER. 20.6 × 27.4 CM
Archivo Miguel Covarrubias,
Universidad de las Américas Puebla (UDLAP). 31122

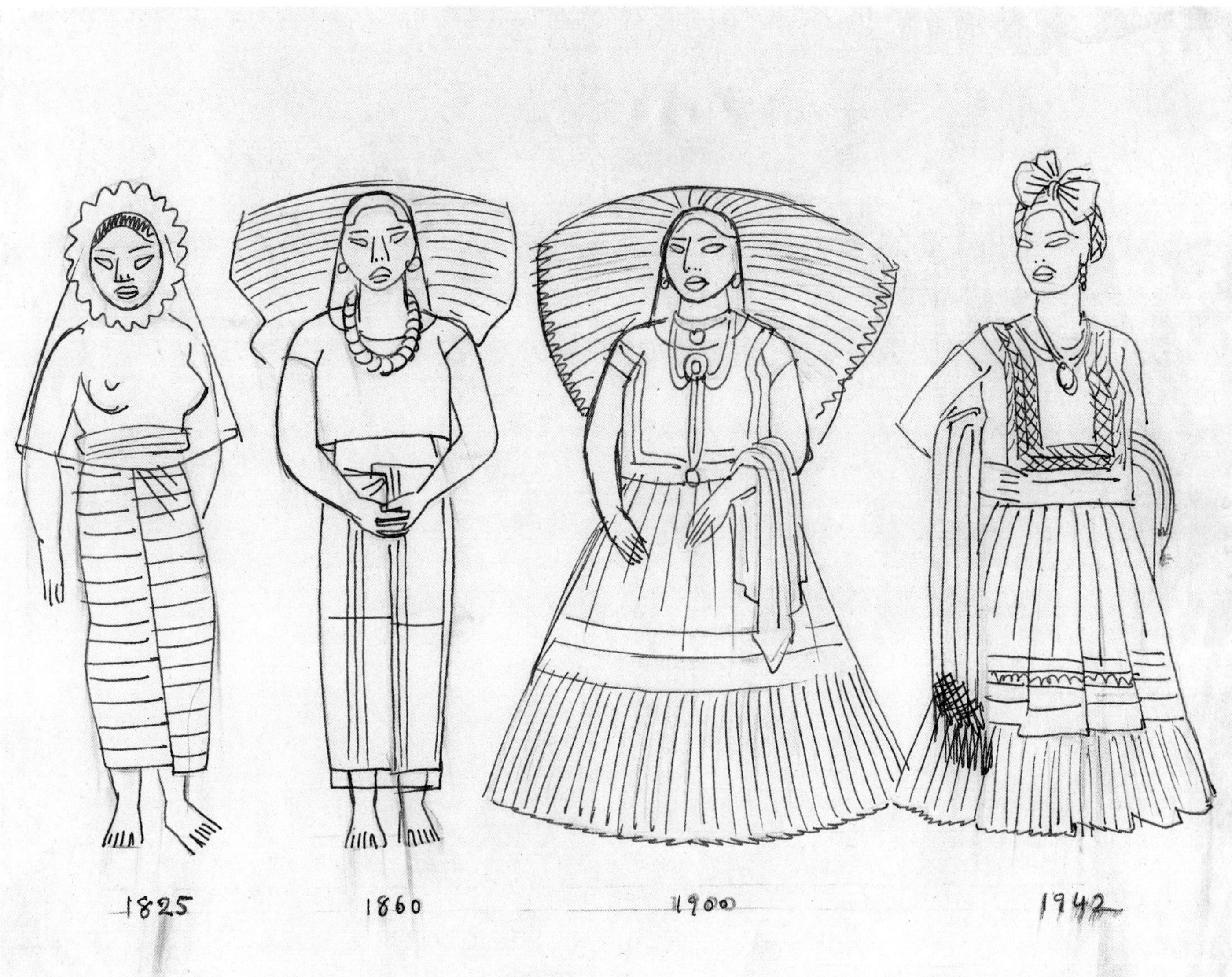

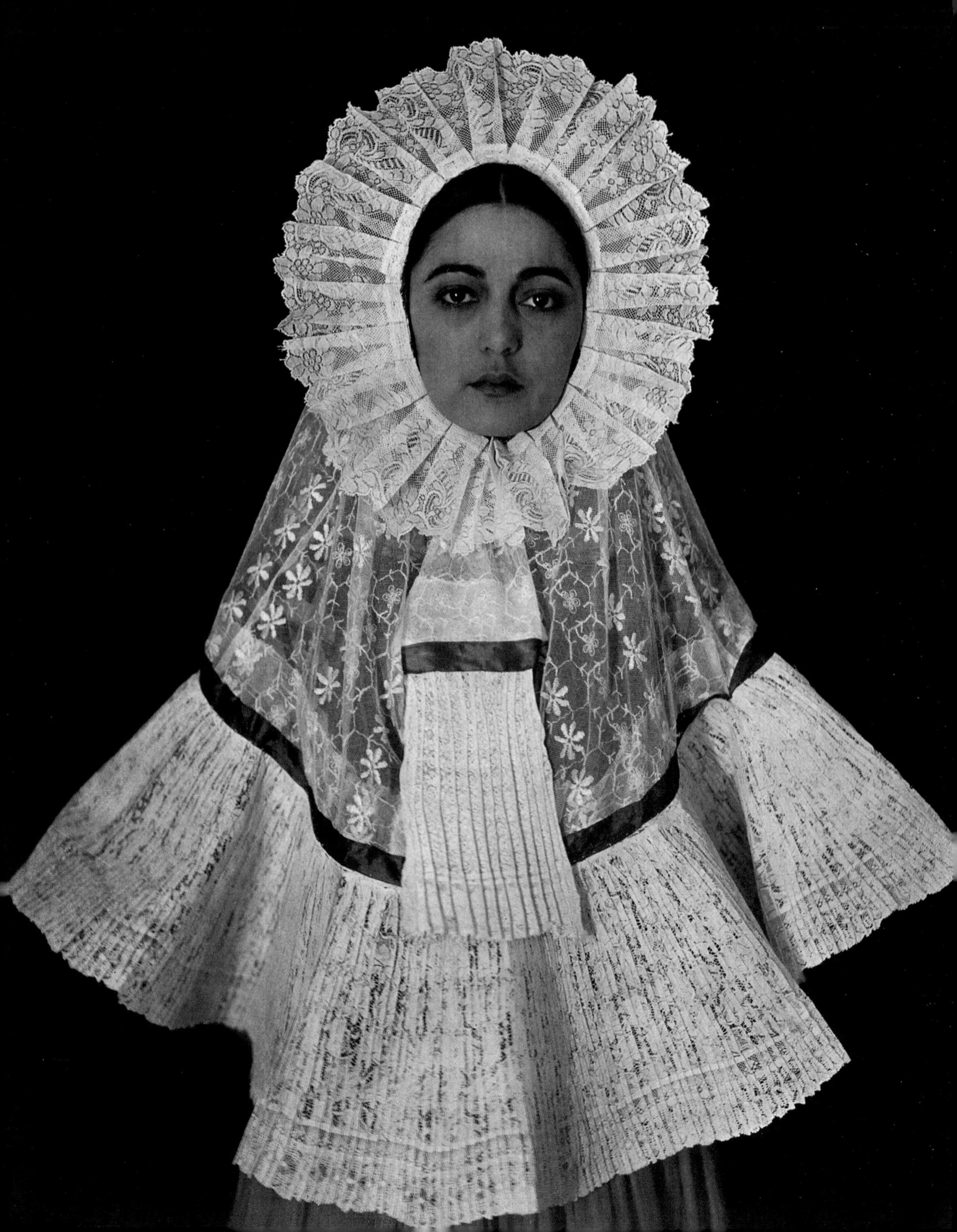

30. EDWARD WESTON
ROSA COVARRUBIAS DRESSED AS A TEHUANA, N.D.
GELATIN SILVER PRINT. 23.2 × 18.5 CM
Archivo Miguel Covarrubias. Universidad de las Américas Puebla (UDLAP) 32759

Dolores Olmedo embraced the look, but none used as many different versions of traditional dress, styled in the Tehuana tradition, with the same consistency and frequency, as Kahlo.

In late 2003, permission was granted to access the bathroom adjacent to Kahlo's bedroom at her former home, the Blue House, in Mexico City, in which her belongings had been stored since Rivera's death in 1957. When the door was unlocked, our eyes were opened again to the messages Kahlo's clothes conveyed, forging an immediate connection with Kahlo as a person. The clothes in Kahlo's wardrobe teach the modern eye something new about the artist herself – something of her essence that had been misplaced by time. Her vibrant collection was composed mostly of traditional Mexican pieces from Oaxaca and beyond. There were also garments from Guatemala and China, a collection of European and American blouses, as well as jewellery, accessories, orthopaedic devices, shoes and make-up. In addition there were 16 Tehuana blouses and 25 Tehuana skirts, some of them sewn and personalized by Kahlo herself.[10]

A photograph of Kahlo's maternal family was also found inside the bathroom, an image that has become another important source of inspiration for Kahlo scholars: it shows Kahlo's mother fully dressed in the Tehuana tradition [31], revealing Kahlo's relationship with this attire long before meeting Rivera. As Mexican anthropologist Marta Turok later observed: 'the myth that Diego encouraged her to assume this attire began to crumble with (this) discovery'.[11]

Kahlo was, and is, the very model of the bohemian artist: unique, rebellious and contradictory; a cult figure who has been appropriated by feminists, artists, fashion designers and popular culture. She continues to cause sensation with her enigmatic coquettish gaze and deep, dark brown eyes holding the viewer for a moment too long. At once commanding yet fragile, instantly recognizable with her trademark unibrow and bold Tehuana dress, she assembled all the appropriate elements of an icon – the ultimate modern day icon. Some of her closest friends, such as the painter Lucile Blanch, recalled that 'Frida had an aesthetic attitude about her dress'.[12] Herrera described how Kahlo would take special care in choosing each one of her garments, styling herself from head to toe with the most beautiful silks, lace, shawls and skirts. And during a visit to San Francisco

31. RICARDO AYLUARDO
FAMILY OF MATILDE CALDERÓN Y GONZALEZ, 1890
INSCRIBED: 'MOTHER (OAXACA) MATILDE CALDERÓN
7 YEARS OF AGE 1890. MATILDE CALDERÓN,
NOW KAHLO, WITH FOUR DAUGHTERS MATITA,
ADRI, FRIDA, AND CRISTI.'
GELATIN SILVER PRINT. 20.2 × 25.2 CM
Museo Frida Kahlo

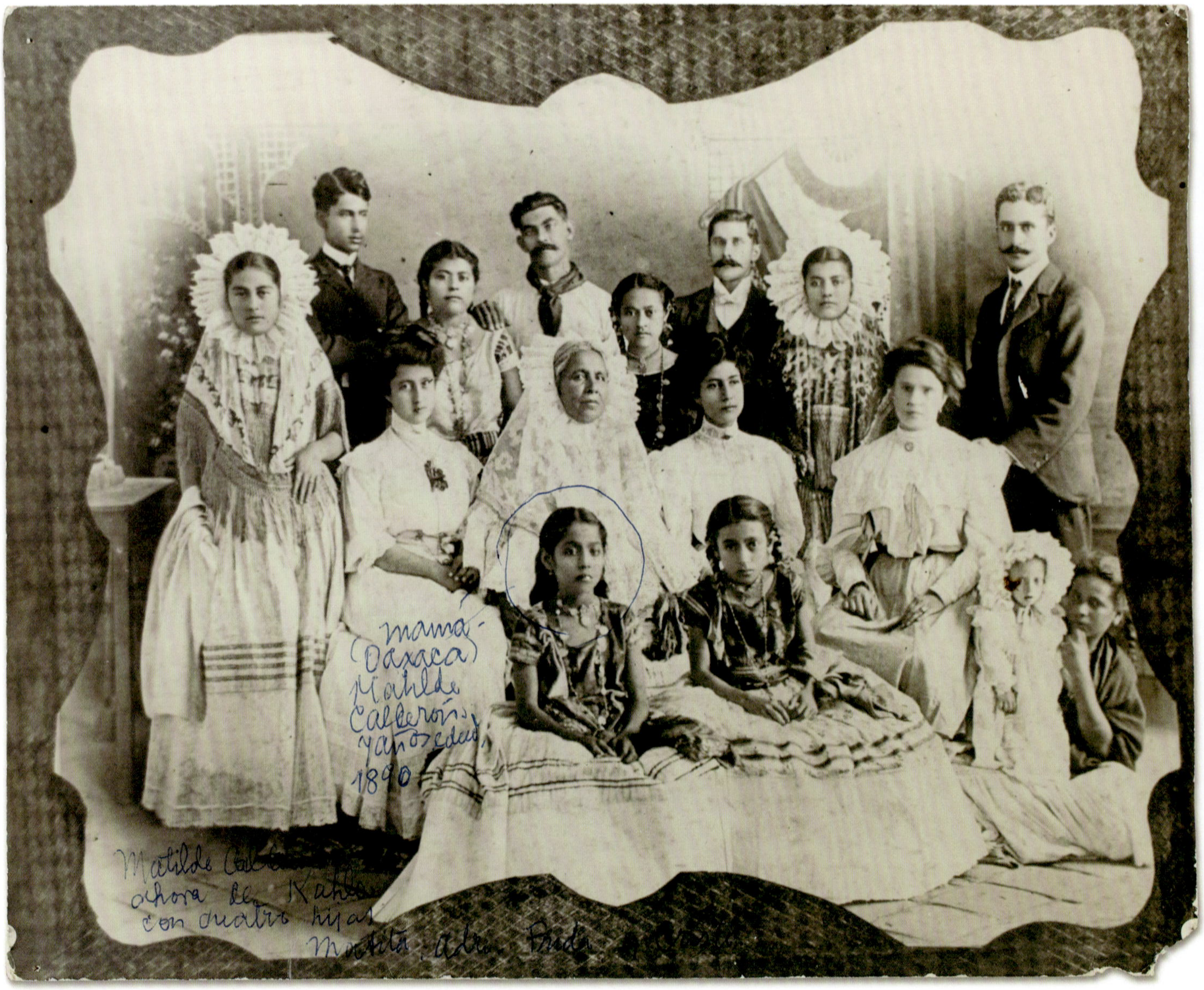

in 1930, children in the street would ask her 'where is the circus?' but she would just smile graciously and carry on walking.[13]

As a woman, an artist, an icon, Kahlo has achieved a rare, almost universal, acclaim. In a society often obsessed with tearing down the walls of the private self, Kahlo is the very embodiment of the ethos *du jour*. The choices she made reflected an intuitive ability to use a bold visual identity to situate herself in the art world at a time when women artists were fighting to win recognition for their work. In her case, recognition as an autonomous figure distinct from her famous husband. For someone whose entire œuvre was 'heart on sleeve', why would her wardrobe be any different? As Kahlo's biographer Hayden Herrera has pointed out:

> Kahlo is an alluring victim, for those drawn to notions of victimization and sadomasochism. On the other hand for those interested in psychological health, terminal illnesses and appalled by drug abuse, the gritty strength with which she endured her pain is salutary.... Although her paintings record specific moments in her life, all who view them feel Kahlo is speaking directly to them.[14]

However, with this universal acceptance something has been lost. The links to Kahlo's heritage and political beliefs have been superseded by her beatification. It is the aim of my research to recapture this lost message, which can be visually expressed through dress. As the art historian Oriana Baddeley has explained:

> Kahlo's popularity (means) her 'Mexican-ness' has become a stylistic gloss, decorative, colourful, pretty ... the colonised body which Kahlo clothed in revolutionary idealism has lost its function as a symbol of nationhood, becoming instead an icon of female suffering. What is obscured by this process is that it was through clothing, in both art and life that Kahlo attempted to redress the wrongs of history.[15]

It has been suggested by various scholars that Kahlo adopted the Tehuana dress to please her husband, who admired powerful Zapotec women.[16] But I would argue that her use of a hybrid dress was a calculated

32. CUSTOMISED SILK ANKLE BOOTS
Museo Frida Kahlo

33. FLORENCE ARQUIN
FRIDA KAHLO, 1941
GELATIN PRINT. 24.13 × 16.51 CM
Throckmorton Fine Art Inc., New York

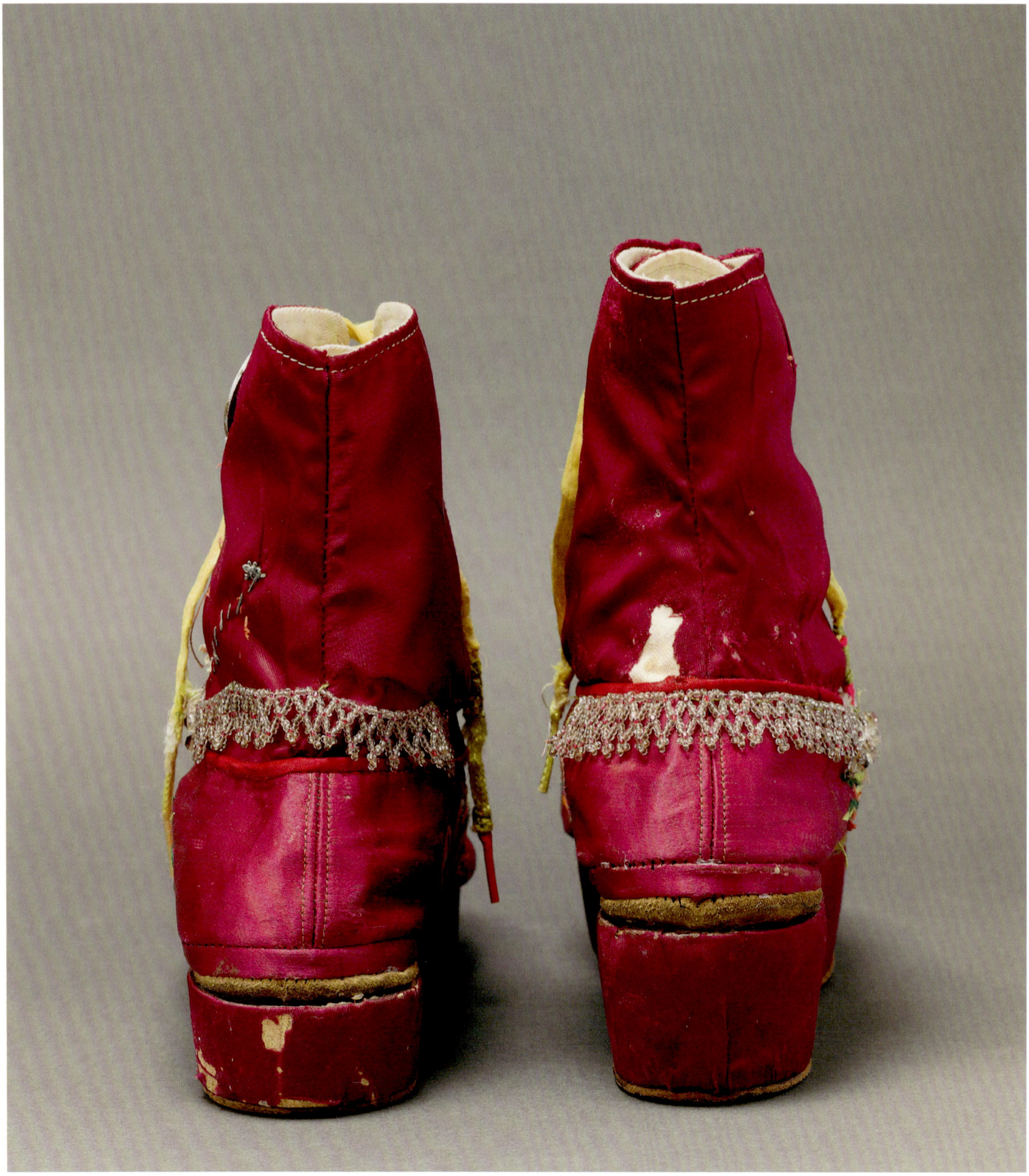

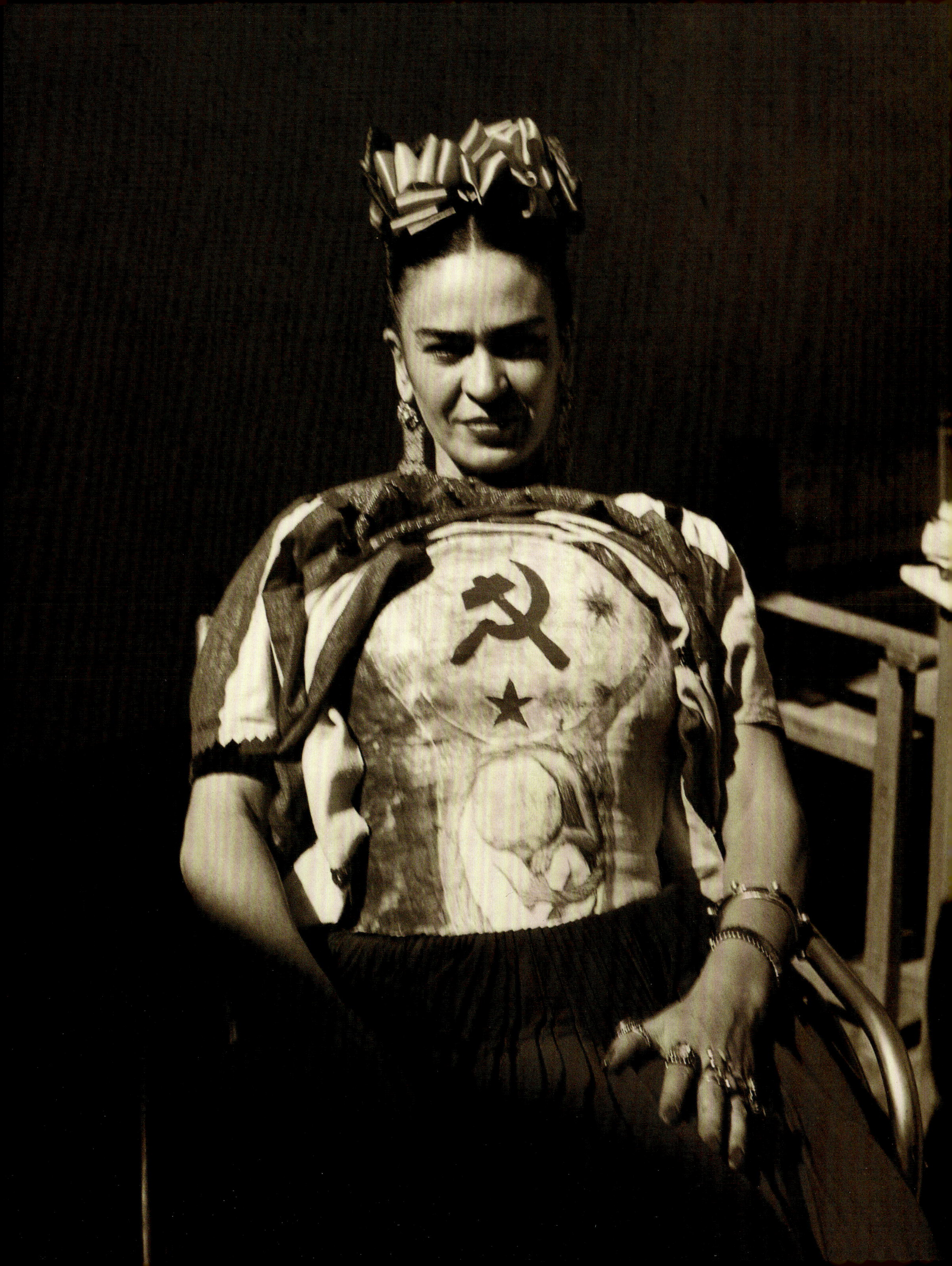

34. NICKOLAS MURAY
FRIDA KAHLO IN NEW YORK, 1939
Nickolas Muray Photo Archives

stylization. Kahlo was able to perceive the semiotic quality of clothing, and the ease with which it could be understood by others. Kahlo used traditional dress to strengthen her identity, while simultaneously reaffirming her political beliefs.[17]

The discovery of the photograph of Kahlo's maternal family encourages us to look anew at other defining moments in Kahlo's life, strengthening the argument that her choice to wear Mexican traditional dresses was not merely to please Rivera, or at the very least, not for that reason alone. Kahlo's choice of style and dress was rooted in an ongoing search for self-affirmation. The quest for apparel that would help her deal with the impact of ill-health was possibly a driving force that would eventually lead her back to her mother and to the familiarity of the stylistically rigid and traditional forms of the Tehuana. Her adoption of this dress was conscious and considered, both distracting and purposeful: a complex combination of her communist ideology, her *Mexican-ness*, constructed from her personal traditions and as a reaction to her disabilities.

Kahlo was aware of the power of clothes from a very young age. But she was equally aware of her fragmented body after contracting polio at the age of six and suffering a near-fatal accident aged 18. These incidents caused her lasting pain and formed the core subject of her art, but they also informed her personal style. As a result of the polio she was left with a wasted and shorter right leg, which is one of the reasons why she often wore long skirts. From a young age, she would wear three to four socks on her thinner calf and also wore shoes with a built-up heel to mask her asymmetry [71].[18]

Kahlo would carefully decorate her shoes with bows, pieces of silk embroidered with Chinese dragon motifs or add little bells. Her footwear has a distinctly contemporary and avant-garde feel; a pair of lilac 'Converse' style shoes demonstrates Kahlo's visionary aesthetic [32]. A series of three identical red boots decorated with green Chinese embroidery match her prosthetic leg – they are arguably the most enigmatic and modern objects in the collection.[19]

Evidence of the trauma Kahlo suffered is also evident in her orthopaedic devices. Kahlo's relationship with the corset was one of support and need – her body was dependent on medical attention – but

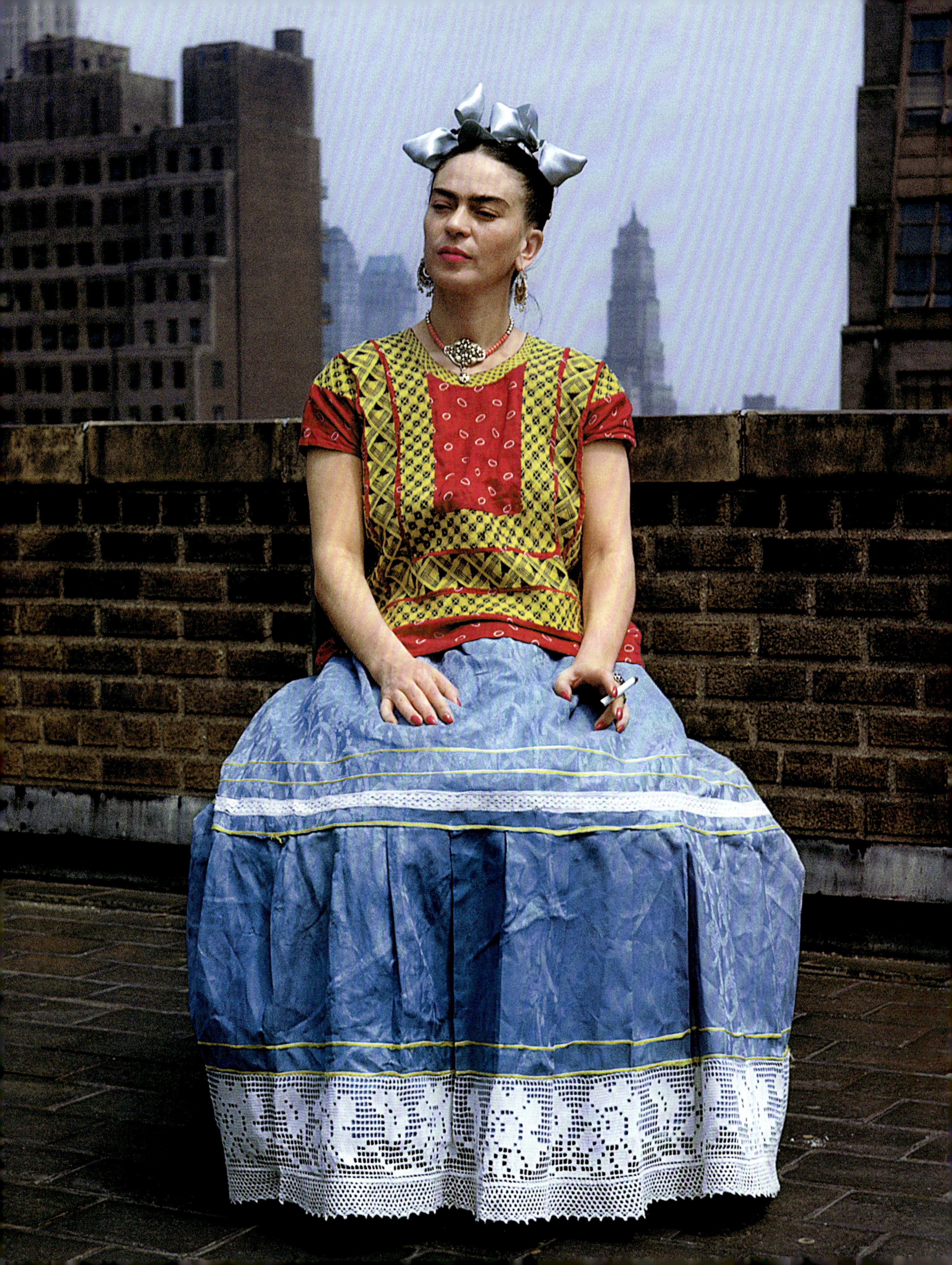

35. PHOTOGRAPHER UNKNOWN
JOHN J. KAN, DIEGO RIVERA (CUT OUT), FRIDA KAHLO (CUT OUT), DR LAYMAN AND MISS WOLF (DIEGO RIVERA'S FORMER ASSISTANT) AT THE CATHAY HOUSE RESTAURANT, UNITED STATES, C.1940
GELATIN SILVER PRINT. 20.4 × 25.5 CM
Museo Frida Kahlo

also one of rebellion. Far from allowing the corset to define her as an invalid, Kahlo decorated and adorned her corsets, making it appear as though she had explicitly chosen to wear them. She included them in the construction of her style as an essential wardrobe item, and they functioned as her second skin. Her self-fashioning was not purely visual; most of her clothes were made of lightweight fabrics such as cottons and silks, which she chose for comfort. The breathability of these fabrics allowed her to wear corsets comfortably beneath beautiful Mexican blouses [33].

The heavily adorned and fragmented composition of the traditional Tehuana dress enabled Kahlo to manipulate the geometry of her body's proportions. Comprising three key elements; below, a long skirt – the *enagua* – with a gathered waistband; above, a square-cut geometric blouse – the *huipil*; and, lastly, a hairstyle composed of braiding and flowers, Kahlo's stylistic interpretation of the Tehuana attire allowed her to draw attention to her head and torso, shifting the viewer's focus away from her lower body. The *huipil*, thanks to its geometric construction, helped Kahlo to look taller and, when she was seated, prevented the fabric from bunching up around her waist, thereby avoiding discomfort [34]. Kahlo always worked within this tripartite template, even when combining European pieces with Tehuana dress.

Kahlo's interest in manipulating her body's proportions and dissecting herself in geometrical forms is evident in several cut-out photographs found in the archive.[20] In these images, it is almost as if she intentionally wanted to crop herself from the viewer [35, 36 and 37]. These photographs show how she would edit and cut herself in a geometrical shape from the torso up – keeping just her head and heart – the elements she was most interested in exploring and displaying. As curator Judith Clark has pointed out: 'it is impossible to know which fragment was more important, the face or the square void'.[21]

Kahlo's response to her disability illuminates the complex relationship between fashion and dress, functionality and self-expression; she bares all and hides all through her personal styling. According to sociologist Joanne Entwistle: 'fashion and dress have a complex relationship to identity: on one hand the clothes we choose to wear can be expressive

36. PETER A. JULEY & SON
FRIDA KAHLO'S BODY, SAN FRANCISCO, CALIFORNIA, 1931
GELATIN SILVER PRINT. 13.5 × 16.1 CM
Museo Frida Kahlo

37. PETER A. JULEY & SON
FRIDA KAHLO'S HEAD, SAN FRANCISCO, CALIFORNIA, 1931
GELATIN SILVER PRINT. 6.3 × 5 CM
Museo Frida Kahlo

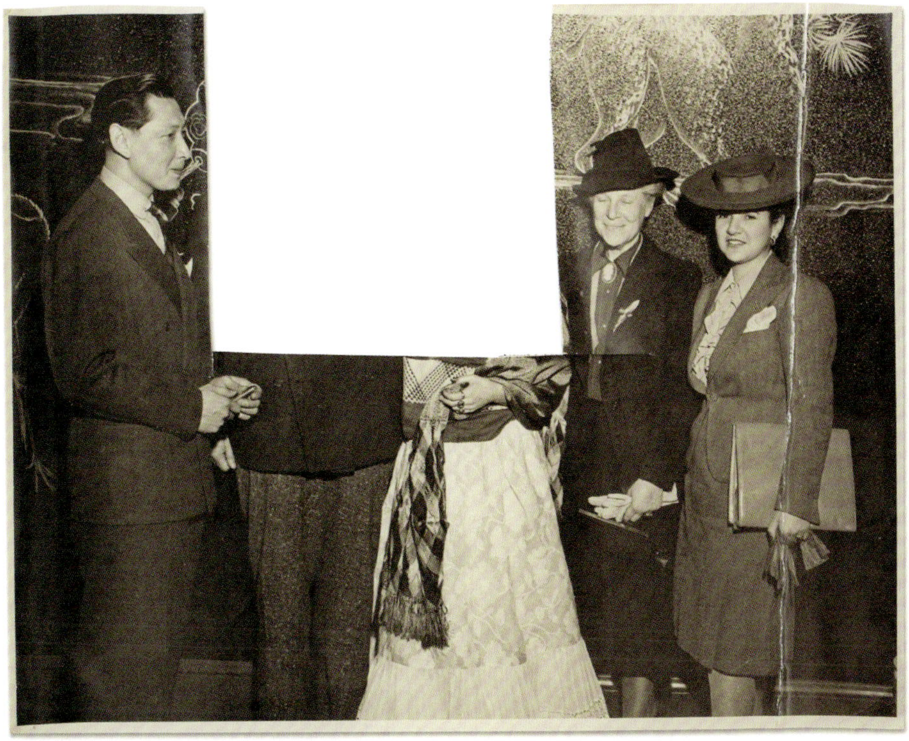

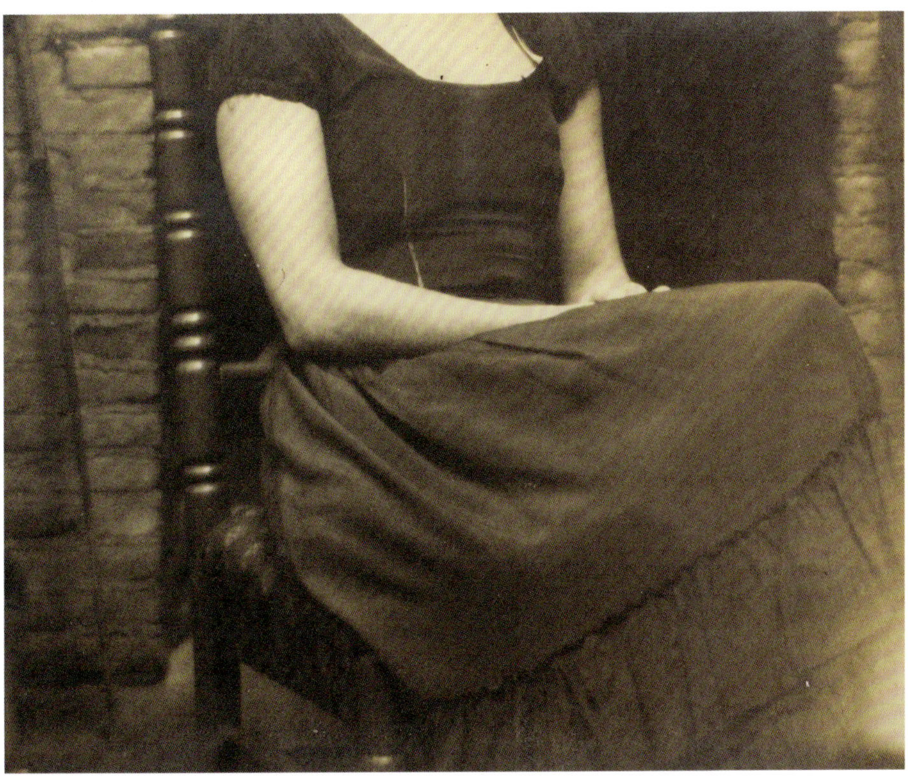

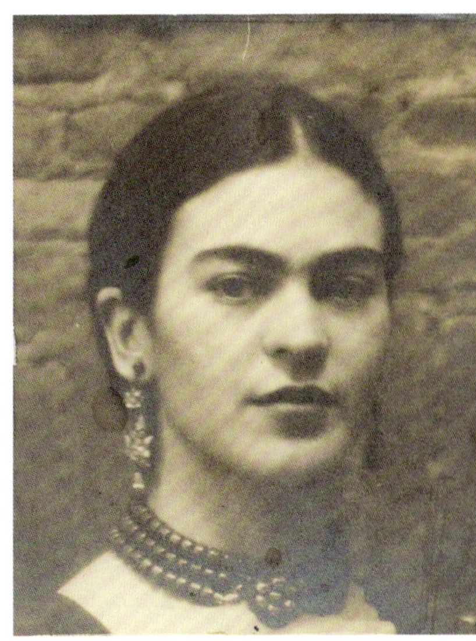

38. FRIDA KAHLO
APPEARANCES CAN BE DECEIVING, N.D.
CHARCOAL AND COLOURED PENCIL ON
PAPER. 29 × 20.8 CM
Museo Frida Kahlo

of identity, telling others something about our gender, class, status and so on; on the other, our clothes cannot always be "read", since they do not straightforwardly "speak" and can therefore be open to misinterpretation.'[22] This tension between clothes as revealing and clothes as concealing of identity has also been addressed by sociologists Richard Sennett and Joanne Finkelstein, who analyzed the ways in which identity is inherent in appearance and yet can also be hidden behind a disguise.[23] While Kahlo would style herself from head to toe with ethnic dress, allowing her disability to be covered, she was prepared to uncover her disability unflinchingly through her art. For example, in a drawing inscribed 'Appearances can be Deceiving', Kahlo depicts her fractured body hidden beneath a transparent skirt, blouse and *rebozo*, covering and uncovering perhaps her greatest creation: herself [38].

Placing disability at the forefront of my interpretation of Kahlo's personal style provokes questions about disability as part of human experience, its relationship to fashion, dress, femininity and identity.[24] It was through her self-portraits and the adoption of traditional Mexican dress that Kahlo was able to examine her life, her political views, her health struggles, her accident, her turbulent marriage and her inability to have children. When Kahlo's wardrobe was discovered, I felt I had met her personally for the first time, understanding her through her unique wardrobe, and viewing her through the lenses of disability, ethnicity, fashion and dress. It has been a long personal journey, from dancing as a child at my great-uncle's birthday celebration, a Tehuantepec *vela*, to my own Tehuana wedding at which I danced the traditional *zandunga*, with my skirt swaying and flowers in my hair. My research has been an attempt to rediscover this powerful and fascinating woman, to truly understand her through her unique wardrobe. Through her clothes, the spectre of Kahlo's essence is conveyed to us anew. We do not stare or observe – we meet, face-to-face.

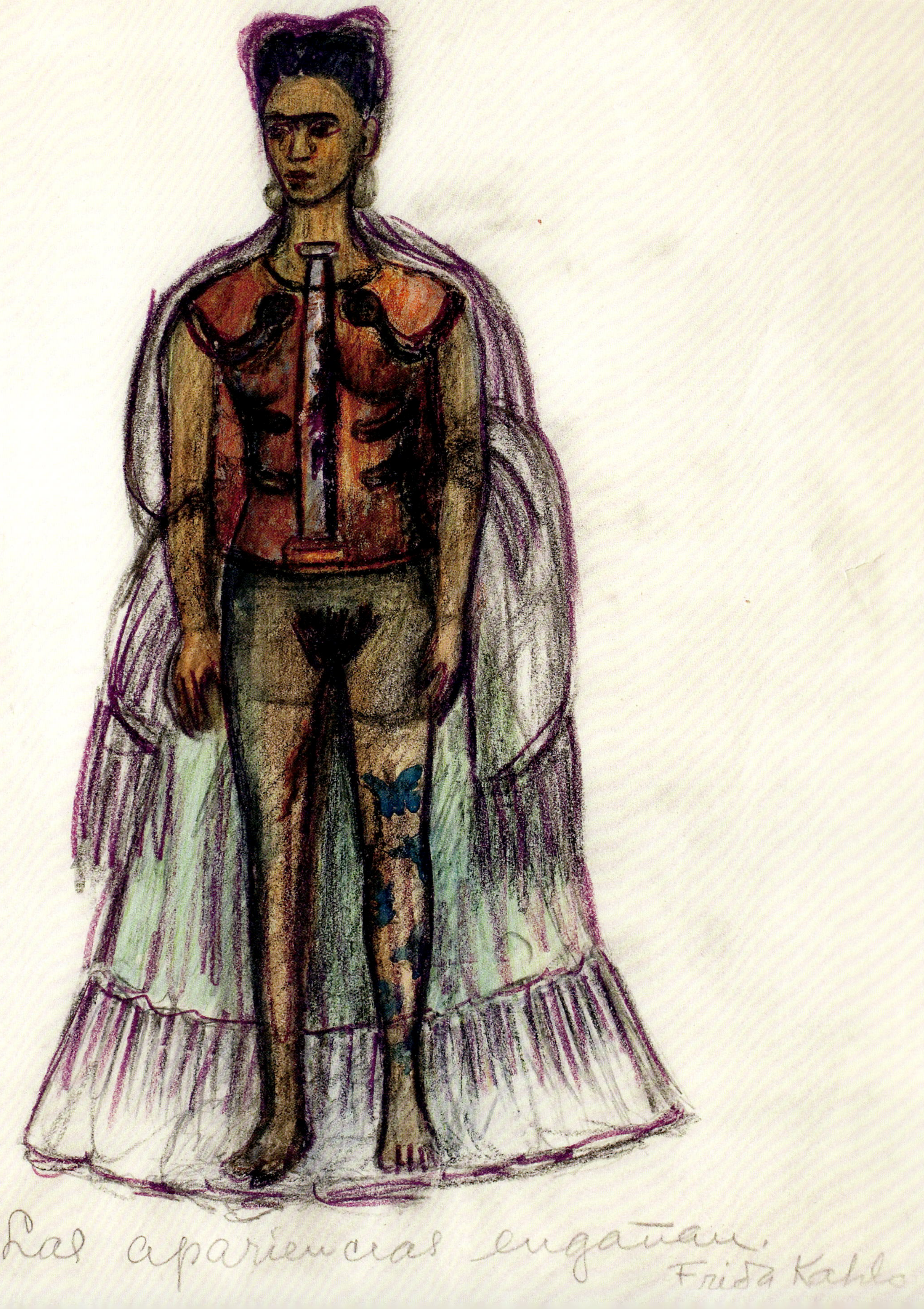
Las apariencias engañan.
Frida Kahlo

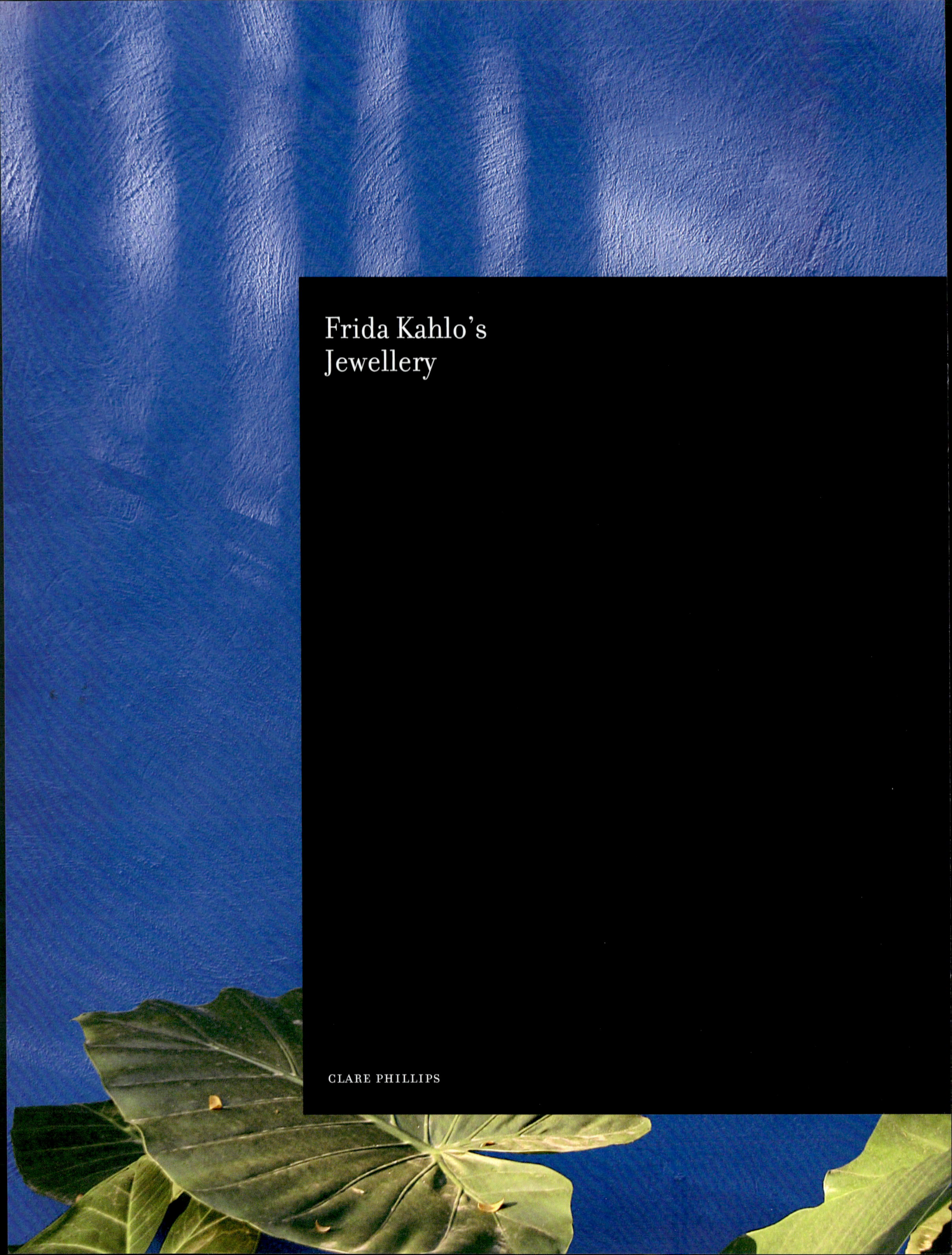

Frida Kahlo's Jewellery

CLARE PHILLIPS

As a shopping companion Frida Kahlo was described by the American muralist Lucienne Bloch as having 'an extraordinary eye for the genuine and the beautiful.'[1] This ability to recognize the exceptional, regardless of context or convention, informed the eclecticism of Kahlo's jewellery and the dramatic way in which she wore it. Jewellery mattered to Kahlo intensely, and the energy and passion she brought to her quest to obtain it are evident in Bloch's description of her ripping through New York dime stores 'like a tornado ... she'd find cheap costume jewelry and she'd make it look fantastic.'[2] Yet Kahlo was equally at ease with, and from the evidence of photographic portraits, drawn more profoundly to, the irregular stone beads that connected her with Mexico's pre-Columbian past, the delicate regional jewellery worn to accompany Mexican traditional dress, and the innovative Mexican silver jewellery being pioneered by contemporary designer-craftsmen. These three very different strands, all self-consciously Mexican, are the dominant themes within Kahlo's jewellery collection.

The exact source of the grey-green stone beads worn by Kahlo is not known, but they are most likely to have come from recently excavated Maya sites in southeastern Mexico. The Maya prized jade highly and during the Classic Period (*c.*250–900 AD) beads were often buried with the dead. In addition, simple bangles cut from the rims of large shells, similar to those preserved with Kahlo's possessions, have been found in slightly earlier Maya burials. Kahlo's acquisition of such archaeological treasures should be seen in parallel with Diego Rivera's much more extensive amassing of pre-Columbian art, and it would certainly have been facilitated by his contacts and frequent attendance at archaeological sites. The beads, whether water-worn pebbles or laboriously shaped using primitive tools, have an ancient beauty and would have appealed both aesthetically and intellectually to Kahlo who wore them in large quantities, in spite of their weight [75].

Of pre-Columbian gold, a single ornament in the shape of a bat or bird remains, attached as a pendant, to one of Kahlo's long gold chains. Whether there was once more is unclear. Photographer Gisèle Freund wrote of Kahlo's 'many gold Indian necklaces'[3] and the American art historian Parker Lesley recalled 'her Tehuana dress and all Diego's gold

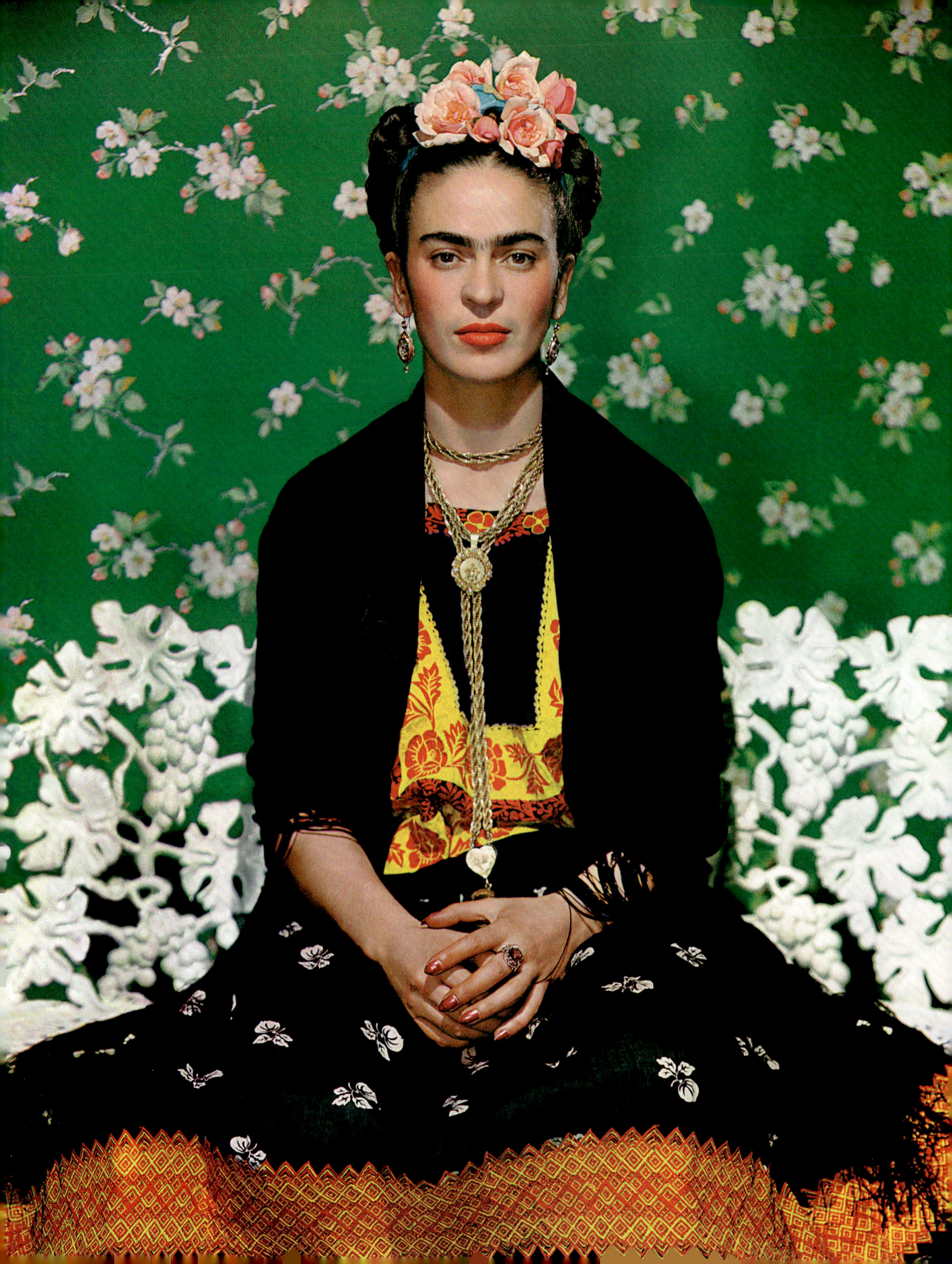

39. NICKOLAS MURAY
FRIDA KAHLO ON THE BENCH, 1939
Nickolas Muray Photo Archives

jewelry ... [she] clanked like a knight in armour.'[4] This auditory effect accords with another description of 'the jangling of [her] sumptuous jewellery drown[ing] out the sounds of the orchestra' at Mexico City's Palace of Fine Arts.[5] *Cascabeles*, or little gold bells, are a distinctive feature of pre-Columbian jewellery found in many parts of Mexico, and the jangling sound may have been created by the 'jingle bells' that Kahlo sewed onto her petticoats.[6] Another, equally invisible, aspect of Kahlo's jewellery was her gold teeth. The dental necessity of plain gold gave way on special occasions to specially commissioned gold incisors set with rose-cut diamonds.[7]

Kahlo's adoption of Tehuana dress was appropriately accessorized by long chains or *torzales* hung with diverse pendants, by her coral beads and filigree, and by elaborate earrings [39]; similar combinations were still being worn by significant numbers of Mexican women [40]. The three long chains that have survived are distinctive of the area around Oaxaca. In each the links are made of two circles of flattened gold wire (like a four-lobed sphere). These may be connected singly to form a light lacy chain, or through two loops concurrently to form a denser rope. The links of the denser rope may additionally be staggered to give a twisted effect which gives rise to the name *torzales*. The closeness to the neck could be varied by an ornamental slide, typically decorated with flowers of textured gold and fresh-water pearls [39]. From one of Kahlo's chains hangs a gold American 20 dollar coin dated 1903. This single coin evokes the necklaces of Tehuantepec famed for the gold coins hung along their length. There is no record of where Kahlo's traditional jewellery was acquired, but such pieces had been worn in the fairly recent past by her mother's family [31].

Mexican contemporary jewellery was enjoying a period of excitement and creativity in the first half of the twentieth century, with a growing number of skilled designers and craftsmen working in silver rather than the traditionally favoured gold. Geometric designs by Antonio Pineda, and densely ornamented and whimsical designs by Matilde Poulat (who had been a contemporary of Rivera's at the San Carlos Academy of Art) are amongst those worn by Kahlo [III.5 and III.6]. Her extensive collection of rings is mostly modern and some would have been locally

40. PHOTOGRAPHER UNKNOWN
WOMEN IN TEHUANTEPEC, OAXACA, MEXICO, 1937
POSTCARD. 9 × 14 CM
DeGolyer Library, Southern Methodist University
Ag2000.1370

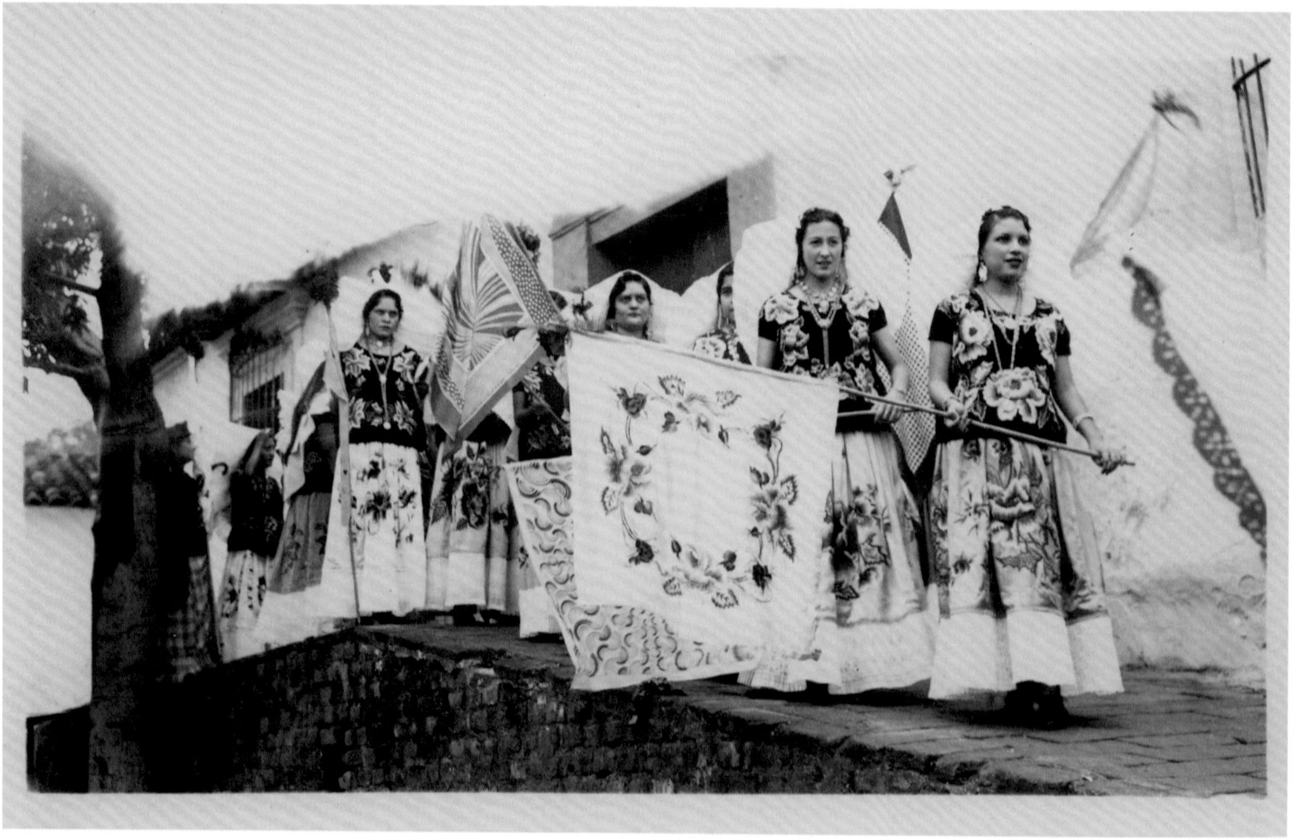

41. GISÈLE FREUND
FRIDA KAHLO'S HANDS AND BONITO, 1951
GELATIN SILVER PRINT. 20.2 × 25.4 CM
Museo Frida Kahlo

42. FLORENCE ARQUIN
FRIDA KAHLO, 24 JANUARY 1948
PHOTOGRAPHIC PRINT. 11 × 8 CM
Archives of American Art, Smithsonian Institution

43. DETAIL OF DARK NAVY WOOLLEN SLEEVED GARMENT, WITH CROSS-STITCHED 'TREE OF LIFE' DESIGN, SEE P.108

made. It is possible that Kahlo sometimes contributed to the design. Adelina Zendejas describes visiting her in August 1953 when she drew a peacock ring that she wanted and requested 'I have a few little stones here. Go out into the street and look for more.'[8] Zendejas duly gathered the stones and brought them to her. On occasion ancient and contemporary combine in one piece. Florence Arquin's photographs of the late 1940s show Kahlo wearing a (now lost) pendant mounted with a ceramic figure believed to have been excavated at Tlatilco on a silver necklace attributed to Héctor Aguilar [42].[9]

Kahlo's jewels were not a static or carefully documented collection but an ever-changing resource. They were tokens of friendship given and received: earrings of carved hands given by Picasso, one of which remains; the earrings she gave to Peggy Guggenheim who wrote 'I like them better than any I have'[10]; the amethyst necklace with its carved jade figure which she gave to Paulette Goddard[11]; and her rings which Hayden Herrera has described as 'a constantly changing exhibition … people gave them to Frida, and with impulsive generosity, she just as often gave them away'[12] [41]. Freund recalled that 'she would shower you with gifts large and small … a charm, a tiny brass ex-voto … as well as the heavy jewelry she was crazy about.'[13]

Relatively few pieces are known to survive. Much would have been dispersed at her death, indeed so desperate were people to have a memento of her that even as her body moved towards the crematorium fire, onlookers pulled at her rings.[14] An unquantified but substantial loss appears to have been a robbery at the time of her death, noted by Lola Álvarez Bravo who was among those who laid out her body: 'Diego told us to put all her jewels on her and Ruth [Diego's daughter] came back to tell me there was nothing left, everything had been stolen. We told Diego and he began to throw curses and bang his head against the wall.'[15] It is perhaps unsurprising that firm details surrounding this most distressing moment are scarce.

For all the uncertainties that linger, Kahlo's jewels were a crucial and carefully considered part of the face (and hands) she presented to the world, offering a compelling vision of strength and power which transcended her physical frailty. For Parker Lesley she epitomized

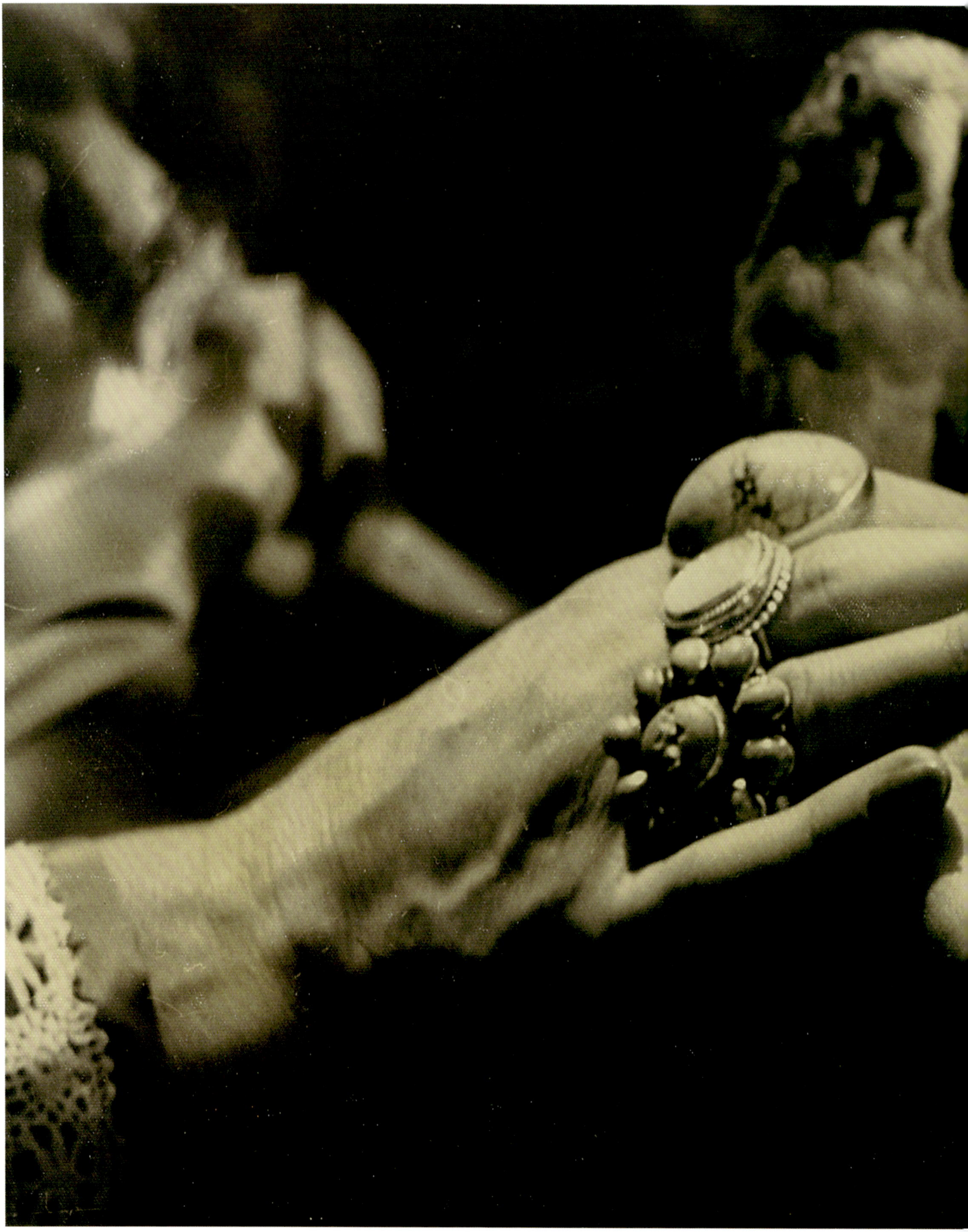

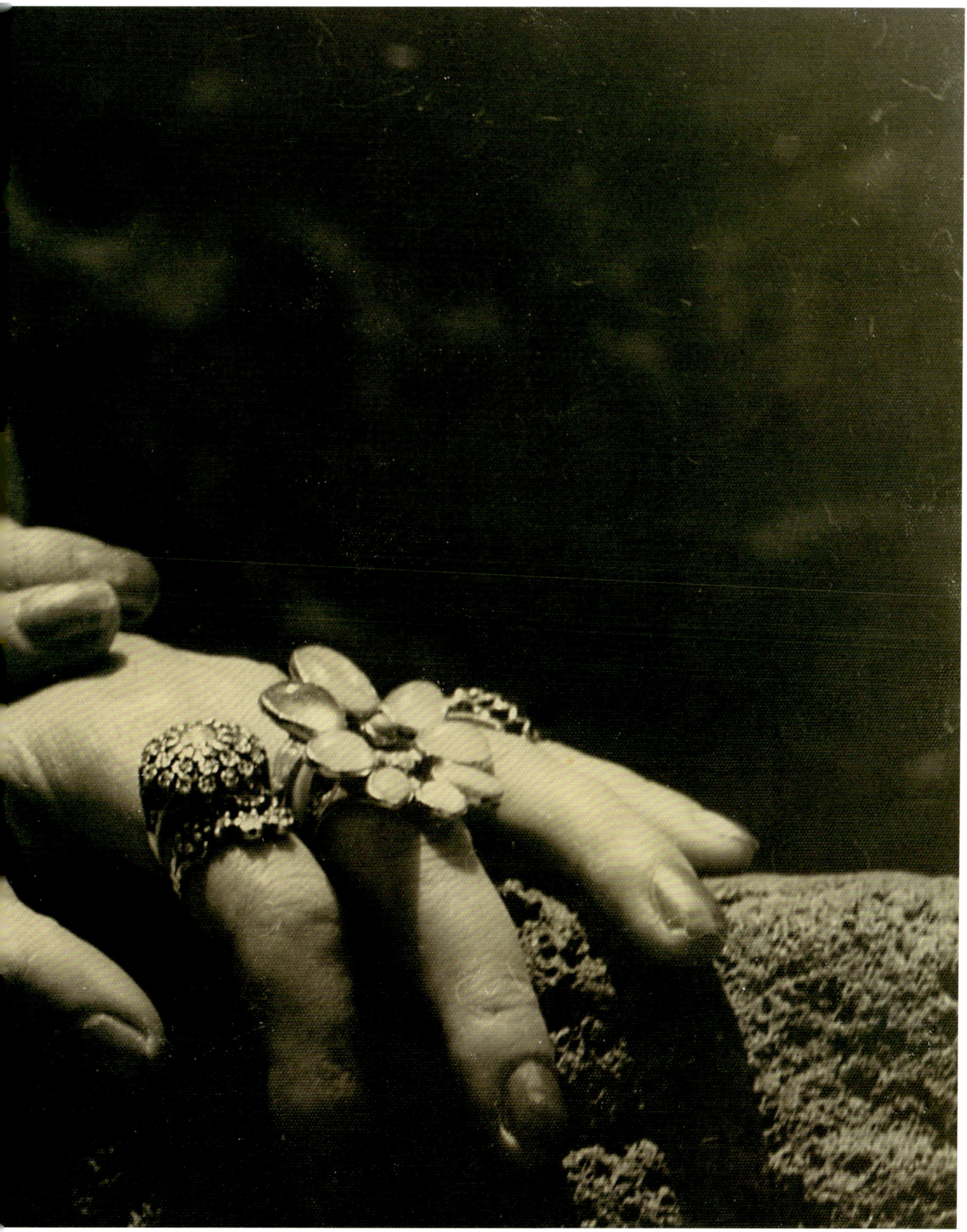

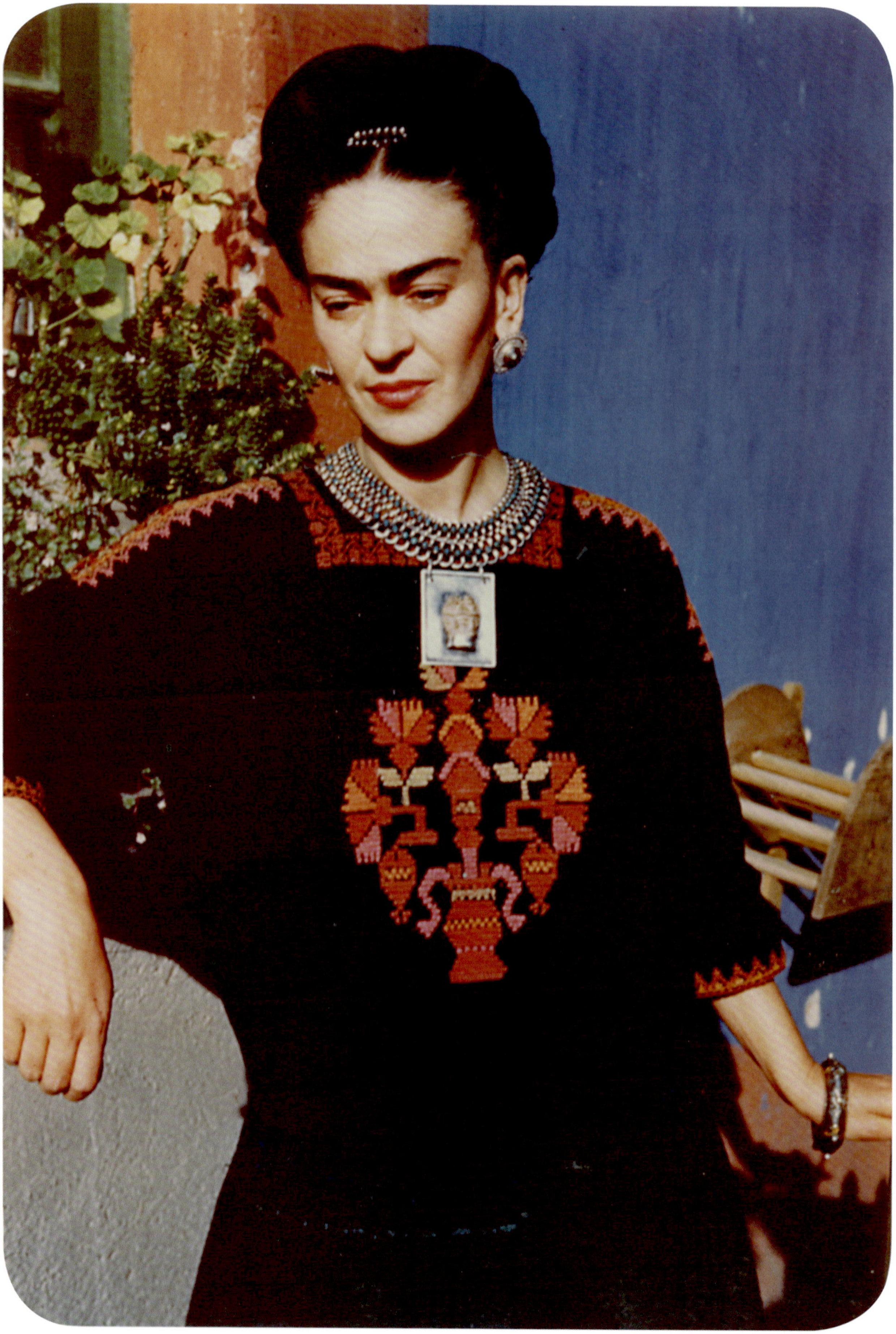

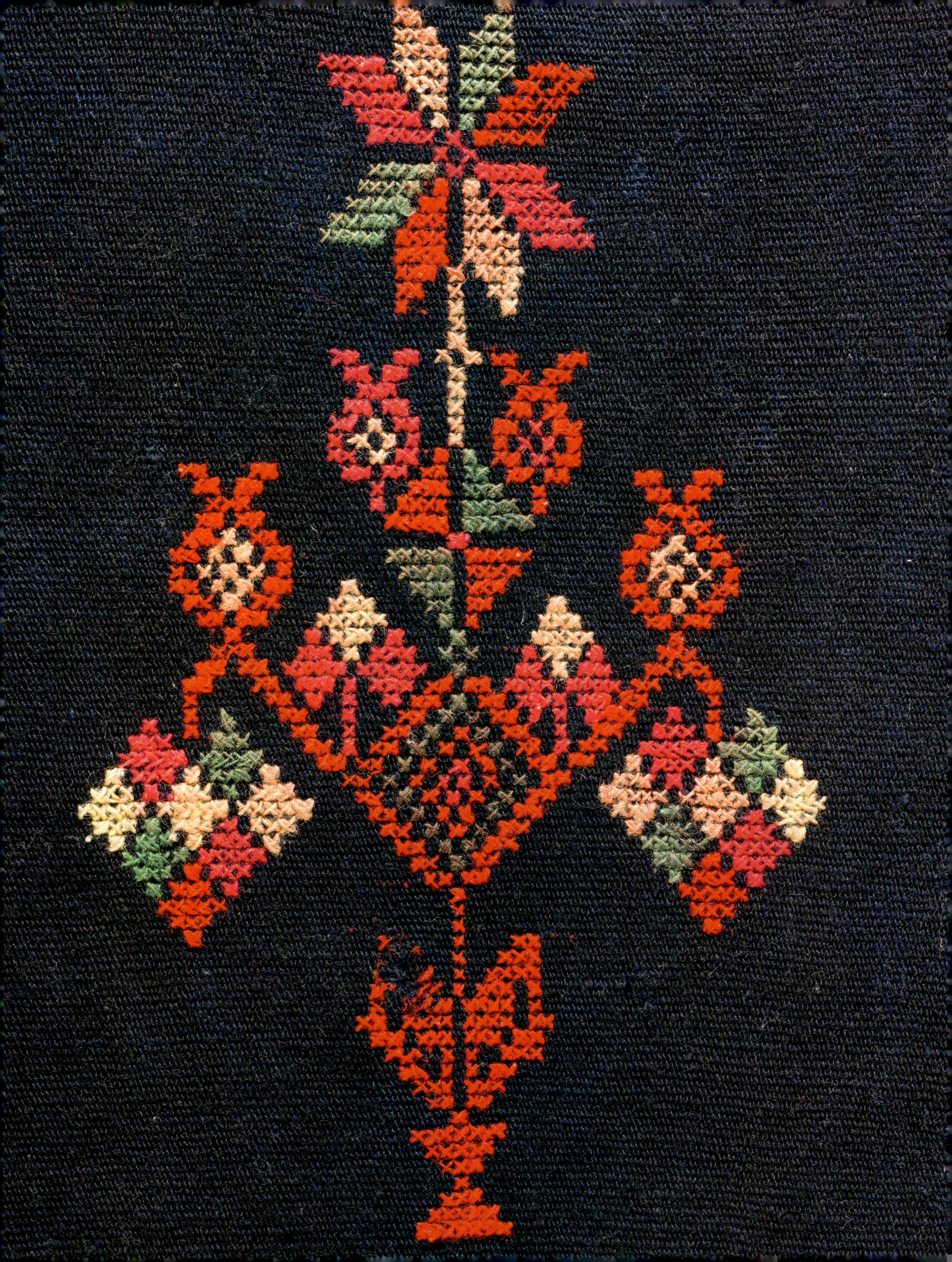

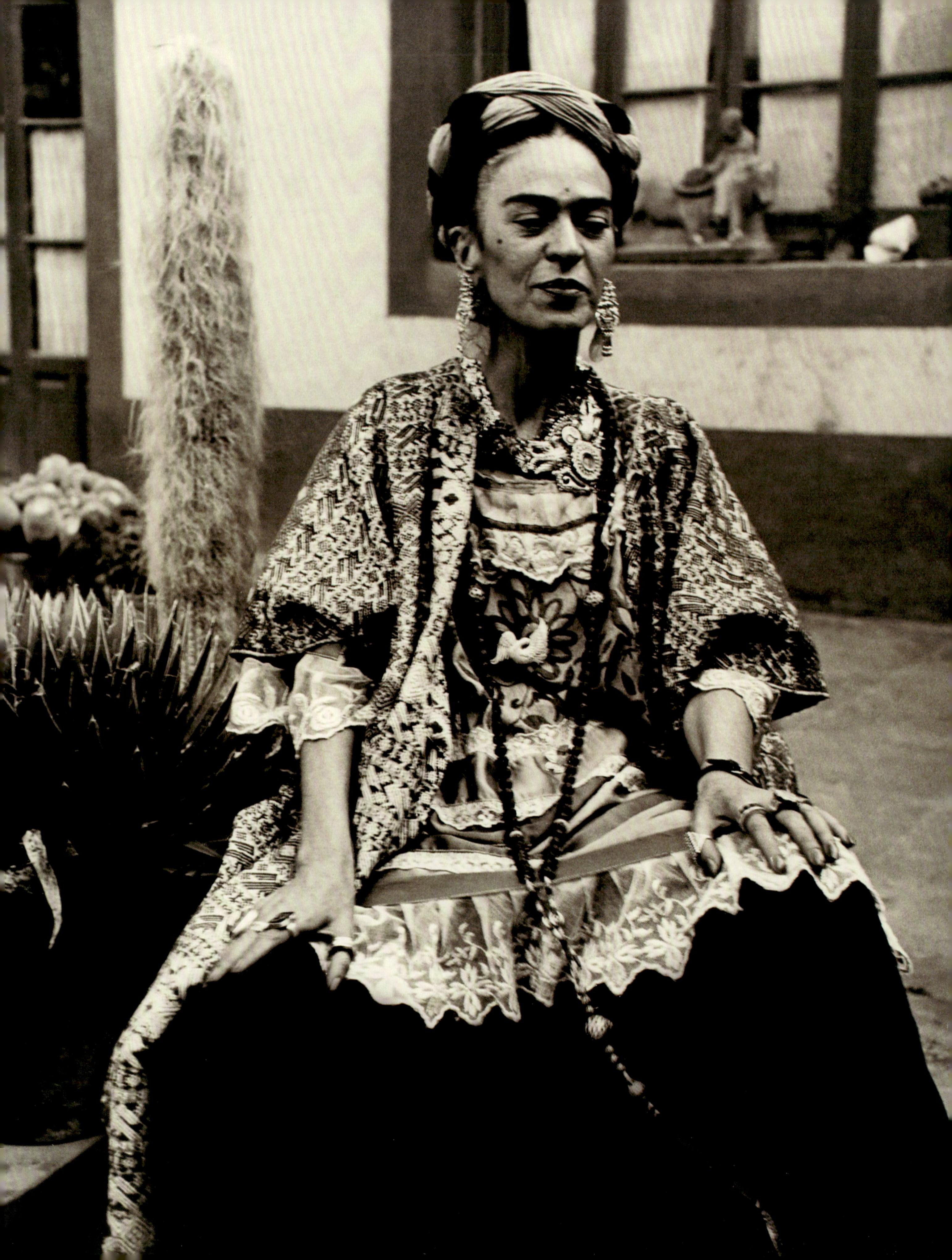

44. BERNICE KOLKO
FRIDA KAHLO, 1952
GELATIN SILVER PRINT. 25.2 × 20.3 CM
Museo Frida Kahlo

pp.96–7
DETAIL OF GUATEMALAN COTTON COAT, SEE P.113
Museo Frida Kahlo

'the Byzantine opulence of the Empress Theodora, a combination of barbarism and elegance.'[16] Likewise on their first meeting in the early 1950s, Freund encountered a 'thin and fragile young woman lying on a chaise lounge' but her description was of 'an Aztec princess ... every one of her fingers bear[ing] enormous rings with finely carved precious stones.'[17] It is a regal hauteur and a delight in extraordinary jewels that is captured again and again in both her self-portraits and in photographs [44].

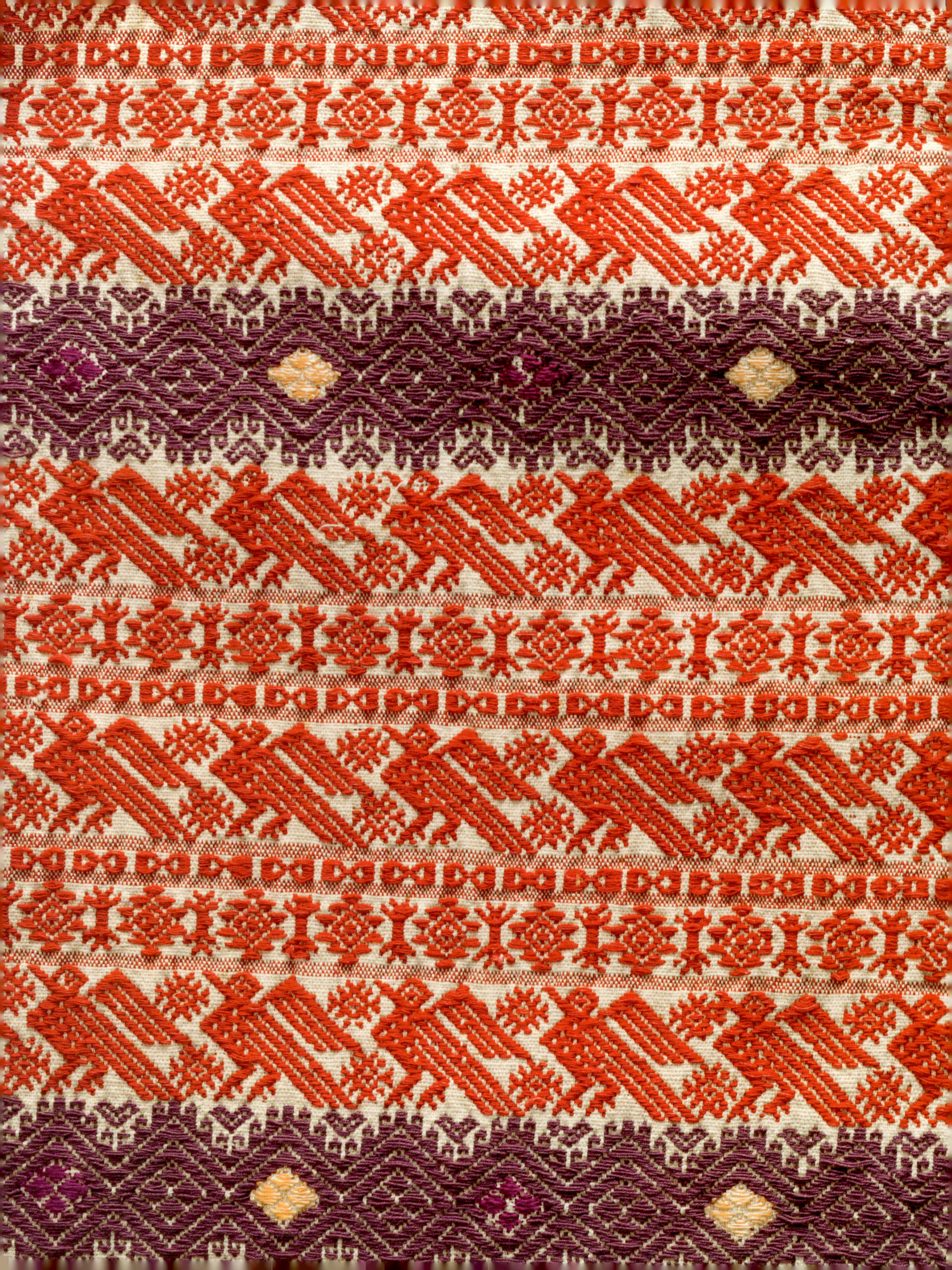

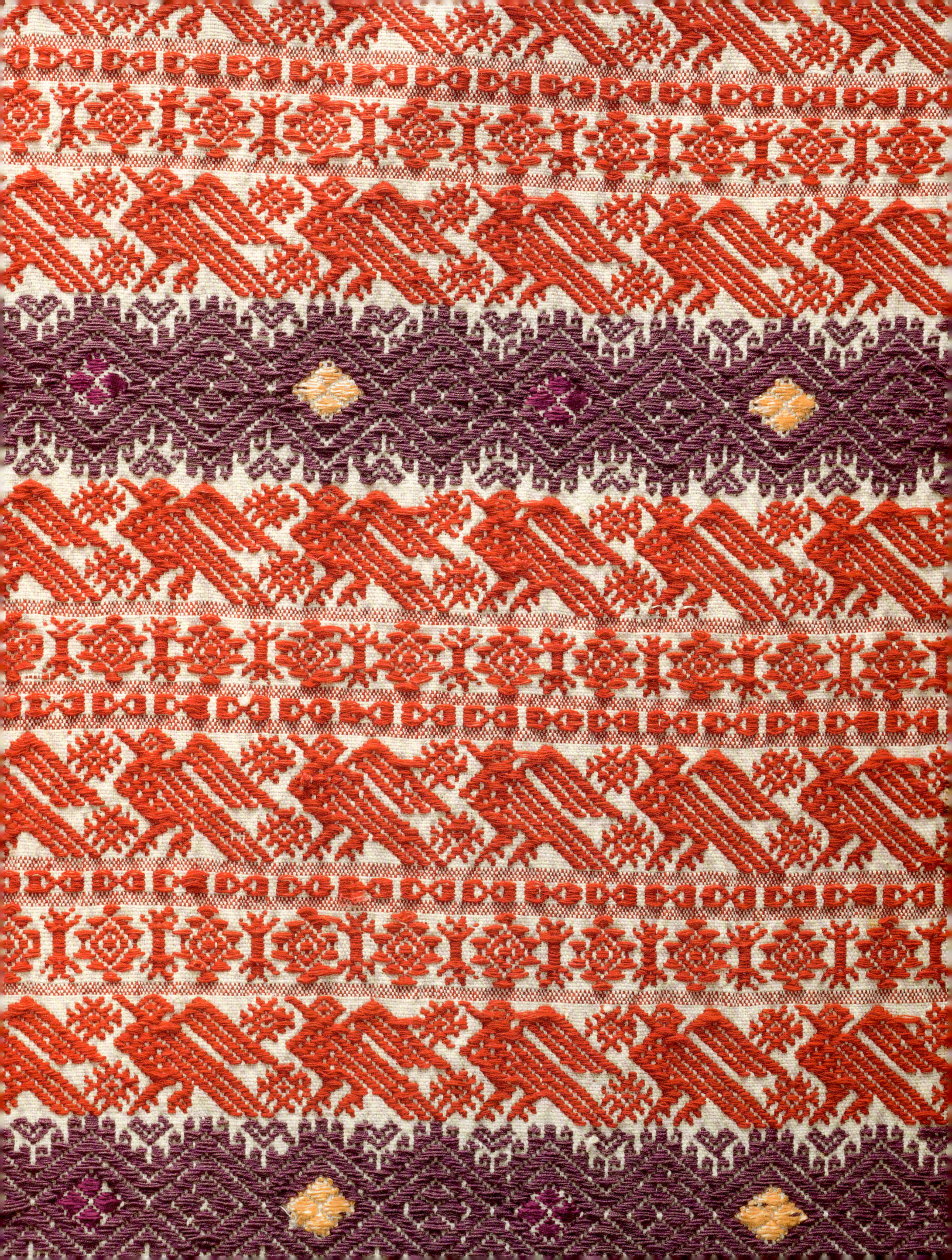

Frida Kahlo's Wardrobe

CHLOË SAYER

Frida Kahlo took great pleasure in combining indigenous garments from different regions of Mexico. Photographs show her wearing trousers with a beaded blouse from Puebla, a patterned Guatemalan coat over an embroidered *huipil* from Oaxaca, fringed *rebozos* (rectangular shawls) with colourful skirts from Tehuantepec or Juchitán. Her unique dress style continues to inspire designers the world over. Importantly, it also focuses attention on the technical prowess and enduring heritage of weavers and embroiderers across Mexico and Guatemala.

During the late 1920s, 1930s and 1940s — when post-revolutionary idealism and national fervour were at their height — regional diversity was widely celebrated. According to the Mexican census of 1930, 29 per cent of the population (over four million people) were indigenous. In the state of Oaxaca, the indigenous total was 69 per cent.[1] Distinctive styles of dress were intimately linked with cultural identity in Oaxaca and other ethnically diverse regions.

When Spanish *conquistadores* reached Mexico in 1519, they praised the achievements of local dyers and weavers who transformed white and naturally occurring brown cotton.[2] Now, as in the past, skilled weavers in indigenous communities continue to create cloth of great beauty and complexity using the native backstrap loom.[3] Traditional garments are not tailored in the European manner: instead they are assembled from squares or rectangles of cloth. Texture and patterning are crucially important. Brocading, often mistaken for embroidery, uses supplementary weft threads to embellish garments with flowers, birds, animals and geometric motifs.[4] Gauze-weaving is another ancient skill: threads, crossed by hand, form open-meshed cloth with the delicacy of lace.

After the Spanish conquest of 1521, settlers introduced new materials, techniques and clothing styles. Silk and wool were widely adopted; the European treadle loom allowed weavers to produce wide cloth-panels at speed. European needlework skills were taught in mission centres, while further inspiration was provided by textiles imported from China and the Philippines.[5] The twentieth century saw the spread of chemical dyes, synthetic and semi-synthetic fibres like rayon and acrylic, sewing machines (much used on the Isthmus of Tehuantepec to embroider clothing), factory-made ribbons, machine-lace and printed cloth.[6]

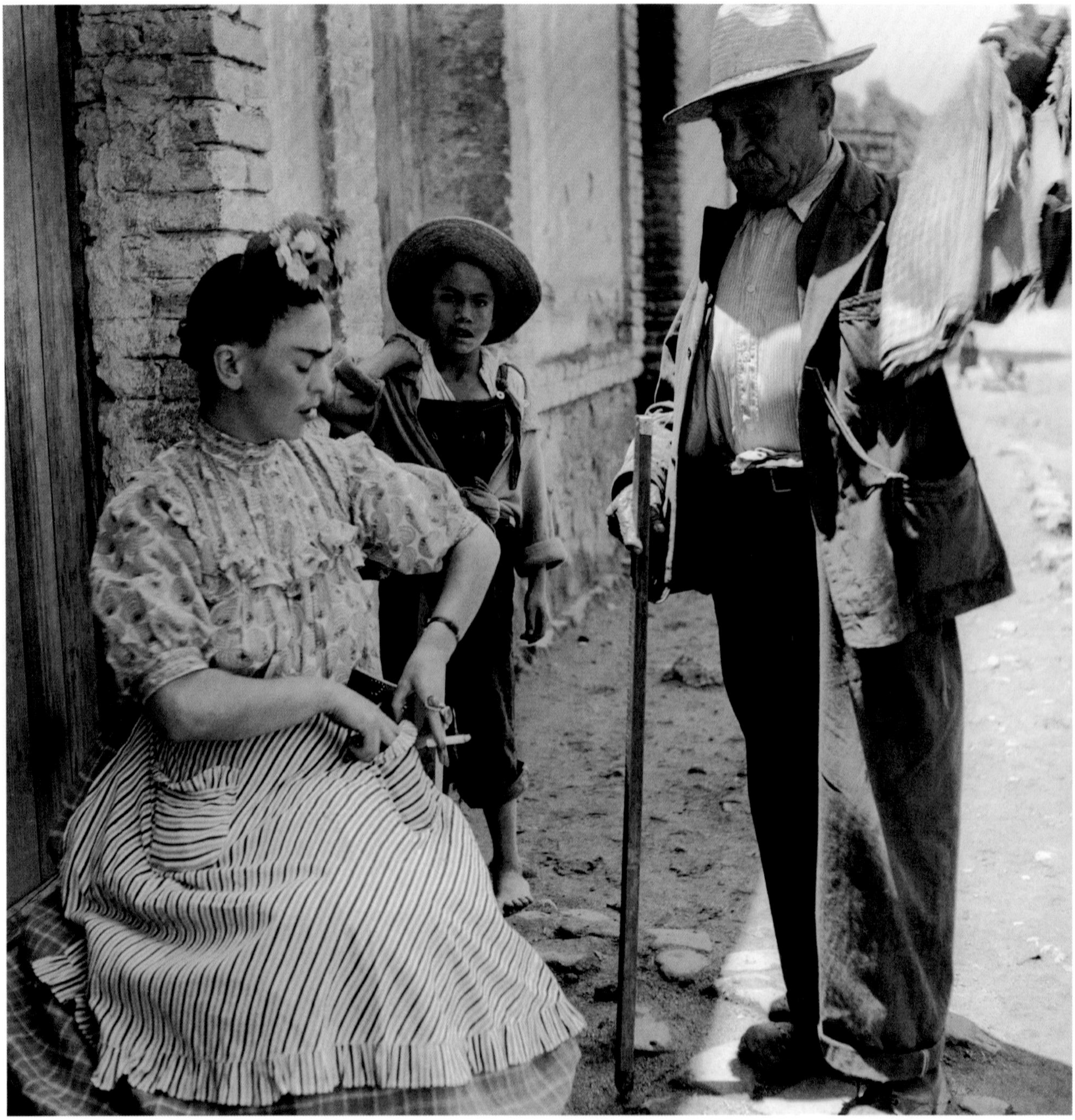

In most indigenous communities, textile skills centre on the creation of clothing. Many women still wear wrap-around skirts, held in place by a waist-sash. Also of pre-conquest origin are the *huipil* and the *quechquemitl*. The *huipil* resembles a sleeveless, rectangular tunic made from one, two or three panels. While some styles are ankle-length, others are tucked into the skirt or stop at the waist. The *quechquemitl* is best described as a closed shoulder-cape. European-inspired garments include skirts on waistbands, aprons, and square-cut blouses. The *rebozo* evolved during the colonial period to become a symbol of femininity and — after Independence — nationhood.

p.100

45. LEO MATIZ
FRIDA KAHLO BUYING CLOTH, 1946
Leo Matiz Foundation

p.102

46. COTTON HUIPIL WITH CHAIN STITCH EMBROIDERY; COTTON SKIRT WITH PRINTED FLORAL MOTIFS
Ensemble from the Isthmus of Tehuantepec, Oaxaca. The cotton huipil was probably made in Juchitán. The arrival of the Singer sewing machine at the start of the twentieth century generated a fashion on the Isthmus for geometric designs, densely worked in chain stitch. The skirt, locally termed a rabona, was made from printed cotton cloth with floral motifs. It displays a pleated flounce of the same material. Skirts of this style are still used on the Isthmus for everyday wear.

p.103

47. COTTON HUIPIL WITH MACHINE-EMBROIDERED CHAIN STITCH; PRINTED COTTON SKIRT WITH EMBROIDERY AND HOLÁN (RUFFLE)
Ensemble from the Isthmus of Tehuantepec, Oaxaca. The huipil was made from cotton, and the enagua from cotton cloth printed with floral designs. Because Tehuana women were fond of printed cloth from Manchester, England, it was widely sold throughout the region. Chain-stitched designs, on huipil and skirt, were done on the sewing machine with cotton threads of contrasting colours.

p.104

48. VELVET HUIPIL WITH MACHINE-EMBROIDERD CHAIN STITCH; COTTON SKIRT WITH PRINTED FLORAL MOFITS AND HOLÁN (RUFFLE)
Tehuantepec-style huipil of cotton velvet, lined with polka-dot printed cotton cloth. Criss-cross lines of stitching, worked in chain stitch on a sewing machine, pattern large areas. The central space was traditionally left unpatterned, so as to display the gold jewellery favoured by Tehuana women. Printed cotton cloth, probably imported, was used for the enagua, which retains its original lace-trimmed holán.

p.105

49. PRINTED COTTON BLOUSE; VELVET SKIRT WITH MACHINE-EMBROIDERY AND HOLÁN (RUFFLE)
Long-sleeved blouse of printed cotton cloth. Oversewn with rickrack braid, it features frills and a high neckline. Blouses of this type were widely worn in Mazahua communities in the state of Mexico. It is shown with a heavy velvet enagua from the Isthmus of Tehuantepec. It features a lace-trimmed holán. The handsome geometric designs were worked in chain stitch on a sewing machine.

p.106

50. COTTON BLOUSE WITH HAND-EMBROIDERY; SATIN SKIRT WORN WITH WOOL AND COTTON WAIST-SASH
Blouse of factory-made cotton cloth from the Nahua village of San Gabriel Chilac, Puebla. Hand-embroidered panels, delicately worked in synthetic silk thread, show birds and flowers. The voluminous satin skirt has a pleated flounce of the same material. This style of skirt, termed a rabona, was widely used on the Isthmus of Tehuantepec. The warp-patterned waist-sash of cotton and wool was woven on a backstrap loom in the P'urhépecha community of Santa Fe de la Laguna, Michoacán.

p.107

51. COTTON BLOUSE EMBROIDERED WITH GLASS BEADS; SATIN SKIRT WITH CHAIN STITCH AND FLORAL MOTIF EMBROIDERY; HOLÁN (RUFFLE) AND GUATEMALAN WAIST-SASH
An exceptionally fine ceremonial blouse from the Nahua village of San Gabriel Chilac, Puebla. Intricate designs, embroidered with imported glass beads on cotton cloth, include flowers, birds and 'Aztec' dancers. The Tehuana-style skirt, probably from Juchitán, displays geometric designs worked in chain stitch on a sewing machine. The floral motifs were embroidered by hand. The waist-sash is Guatemalan.

p.108

52. TOMICOTÓN: WOOLLEN SLEEVED GARMENT, WITH CROSS-STITCH EMBROIDERY; WOOLLEN SKIRT WITH SILK AND SATIN TRIM
A sleeved garment of handspun indigo-dyed wool. Known locally as a tomicotón, it was woven in two panels on a backstrap loom in the Nahua community of Hueyapan, Puebla. The larger panel is folded over, with a square-cut opening for the head. Sleeves are made from the second panel. Cross-stitched designs include a centrally positioned 'tree of life'. The heavy black skirt, termed a rollo, was woven on a backstrap loom; the maker has added lengths of green ribbon and a blue top-section of bought satin cloth. Skirts of this type were worn on ceremonial occasions by married women in the P'urhépecha community of Santa Fe de la Laguna, Michoacán.

p.109

53. COTTON HUIPIL HAND-EMBROIDERED IN BLACK THREAD; SEMI-SYNTHETIC FULL-LENGTH SKIRT
Cotton huipil, with hand-embroidered designs, from the Mazatec community of Huautla de Jiménez, Oaxaca. The maker has seamed together three widths of factory-made manta to simulate the three widths of cloth that would previously have been home-woven on a backstrap loom. Although peacocks are not native to Mexico, they became popular with Mexican embroiderers who saw them on pattern sheets. It seems likely that this huipil was made for sale rather than for local consumption. It is worn here over a long skirt of semi-synthetic material.

p.110

54. REBOZO WITH RAPACEJO (KNOTTED FRINGE); SILK SKIRT WITH CHINESE EMBROIDERED PANEL AND HOLÁN (RUFFLE)
Striped rebozo (rectangular shawl) from Guanajuato. The weaver has used artisela (a cellulose-based substitute for silk). Both ends are elegantly fringed. Professional knotters, known as empuntadoras, specialise in knotting warp threads in a range of designs. The silk skirt ties at the waist. It displays a panel of fine Chinese embroidery, and ends with a pleated flounce.

p.111

55. REBOZO AND COTTON HUIPIL; SILK SKIRT WITH WOVEN VELVET FLORAL MOTIFS
Fringed magenta rebozo, woven from artisela (synthetic silk) in Santa María del Río, San Luis Potosí. Floral designs pattern the silk skirt. The all-white huipil of handspun cotton demonstrates the immense skill of Kekchí-Maya backstrap weavers in the Cobán region of Guatemala. Three cloth-panels, brocaded with supplementary weft threads, show rows of maize-like plants and human figures with animals. Warp threads, crossed by hand, form areas of open-meshed cloth.

p.112

56. COTTON MAZATEC HUIPIL HAND-EMBROIDERED AND APPLIQUÉD; PLAIN FLOOR-LENGTH SKIRT
Huipil from the Mazatec community of Huautla de Jiménez, Oaxaca. Panels of cotton cloth display floral designs, hand-embroidered in cross-stitch. Satin ribbons, seamed together, form vivid bands of colour; the yellow frill suggests sleeves. Machine-lace and rickrack braid provide additional decoration. The huipil is shown here with a plain floor-length black skirt.

p.113

57. GUATEMALAN COTTON COAT WORN WITH MAZATEC HUIPIL AND PLAIN FLOOR-LENGTH SKIRT
Cotton coat, patterned with weft-brocaded repeat designs, worn over a Mazatec huipil and a black skirt. The intricately figured cloth of the coat was woven in two panels on a Guatemalan draw loom in San Marcos, Totonicapán or Quetzaltenango. The coat opens at the front: yellow and purple silk threads have been used to elegantly reinforce the edges of the cloth with buttonhole stitch.

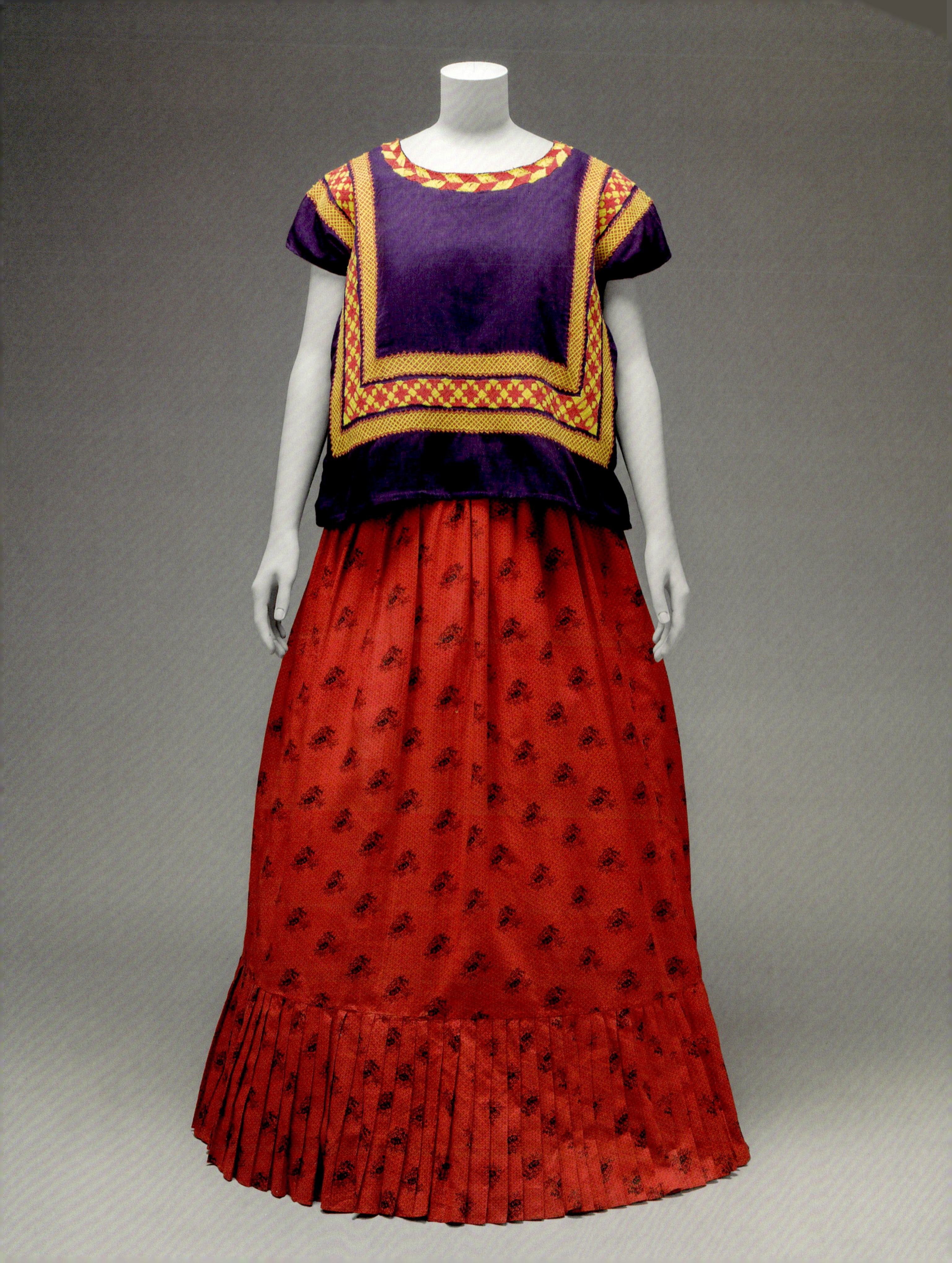

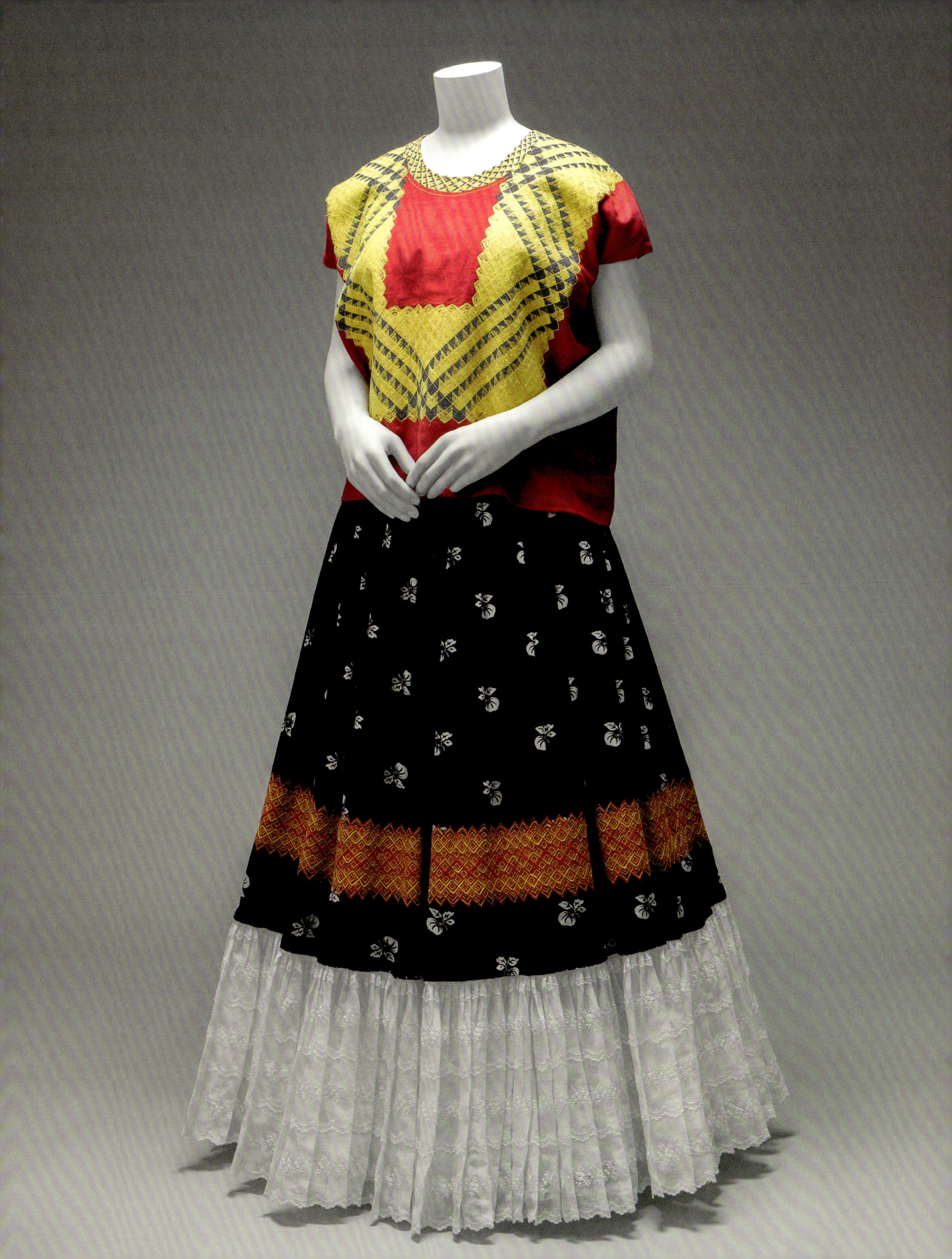

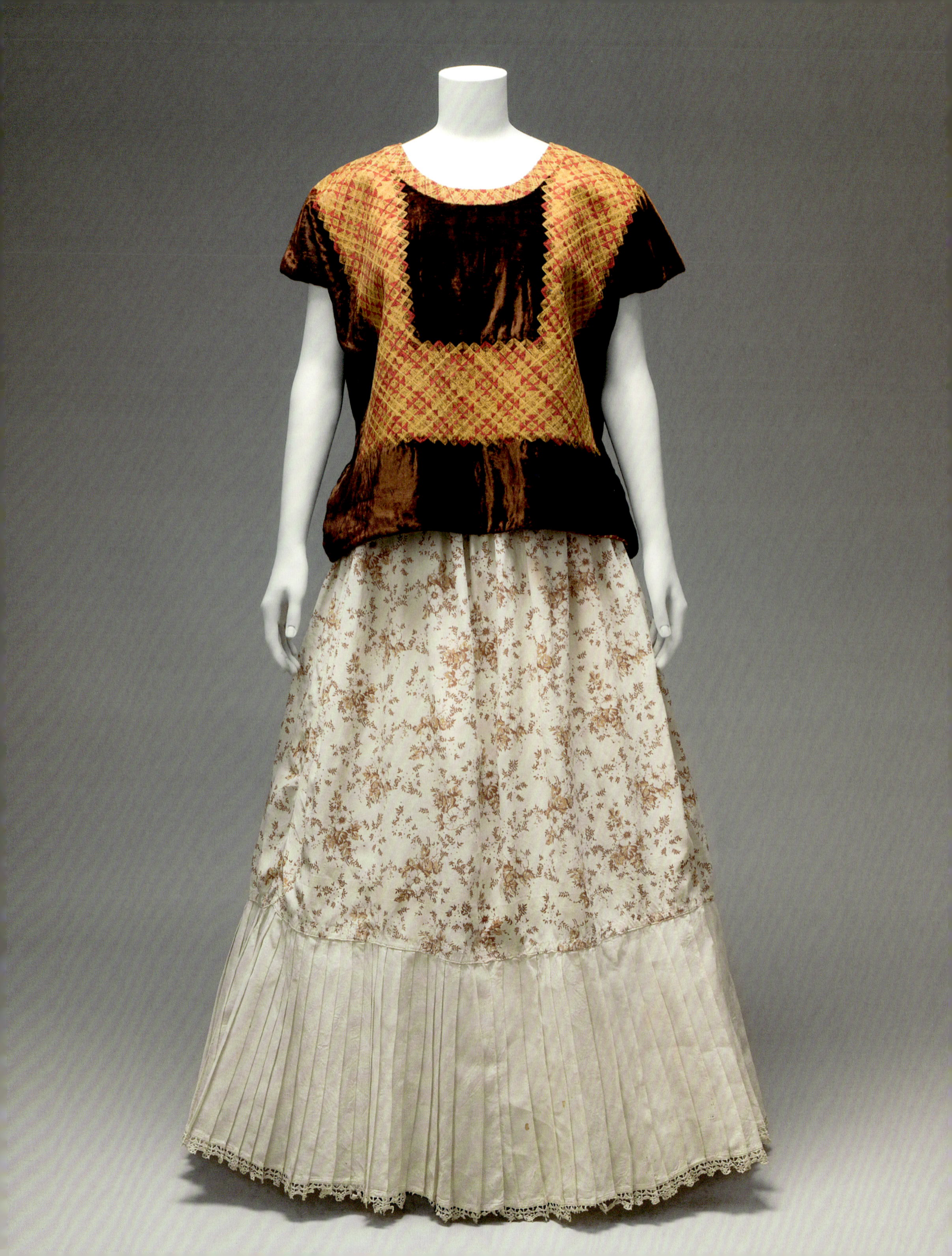

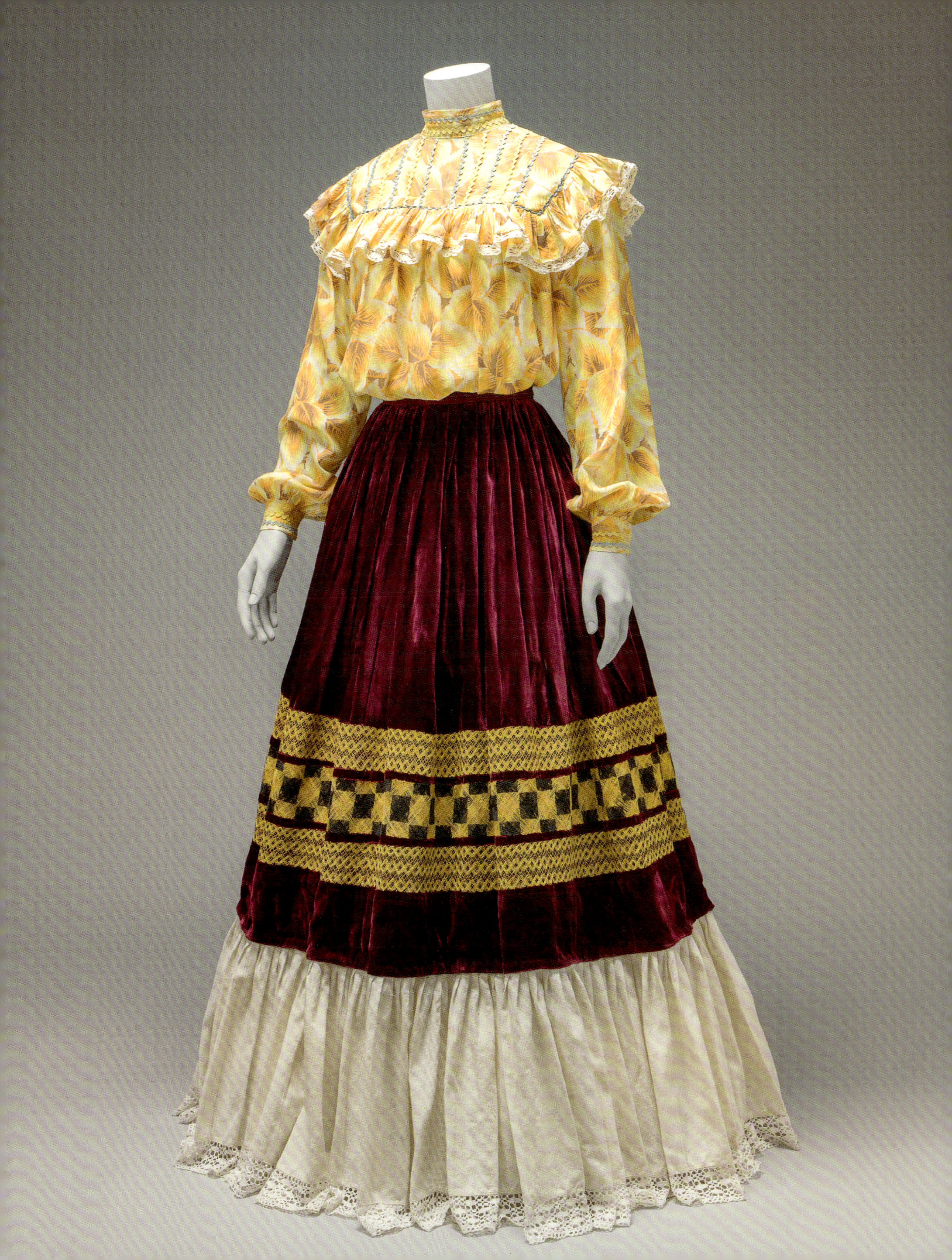

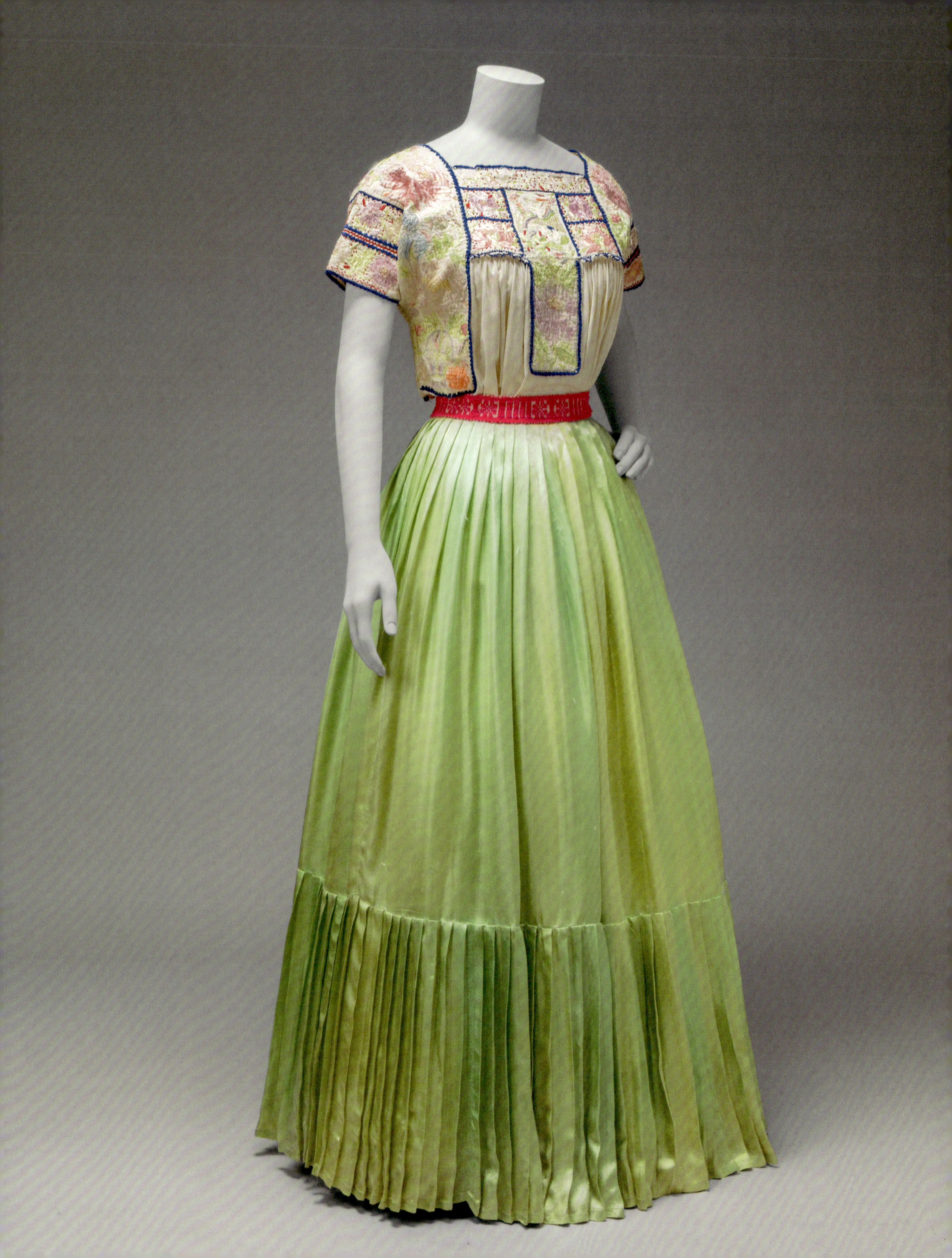

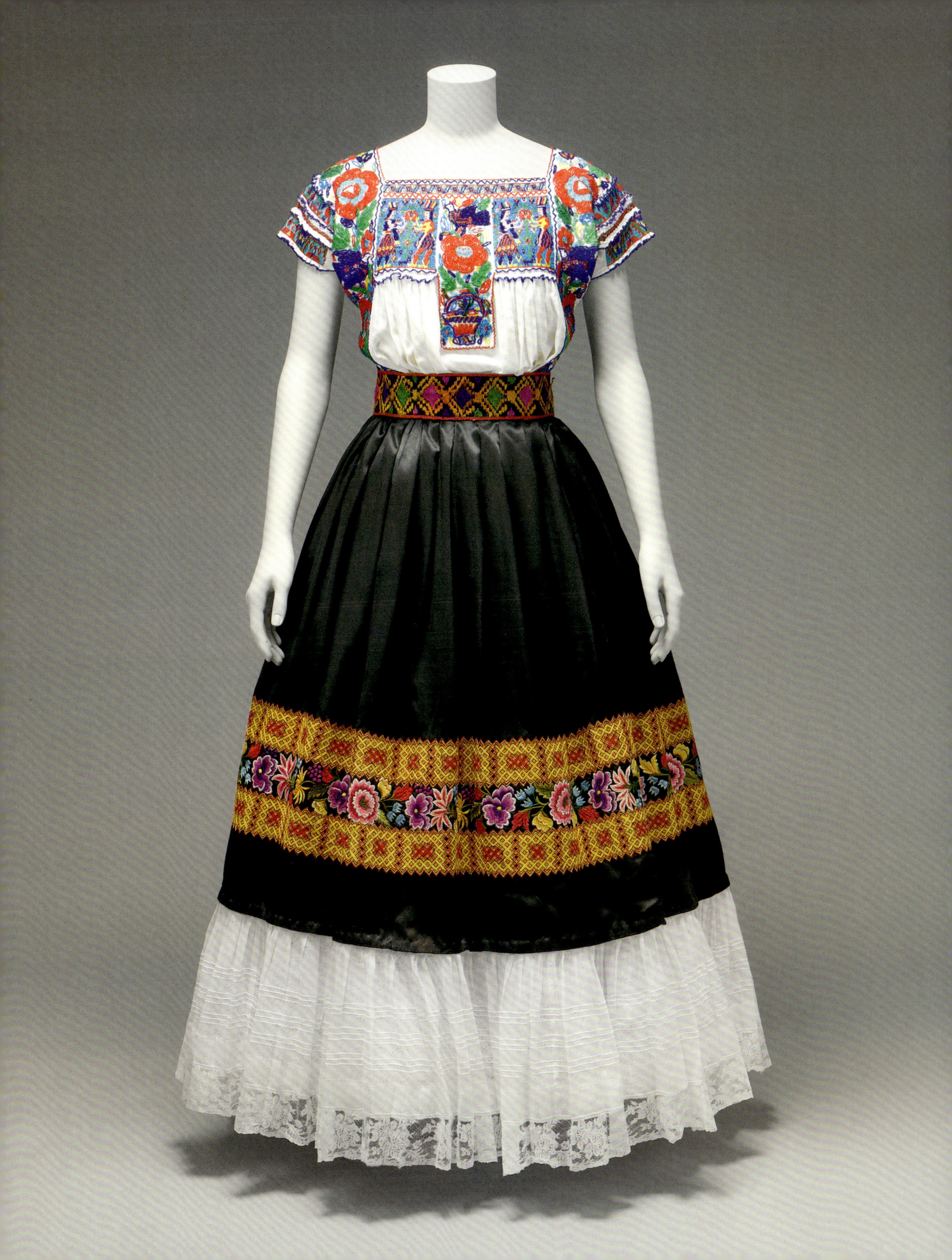

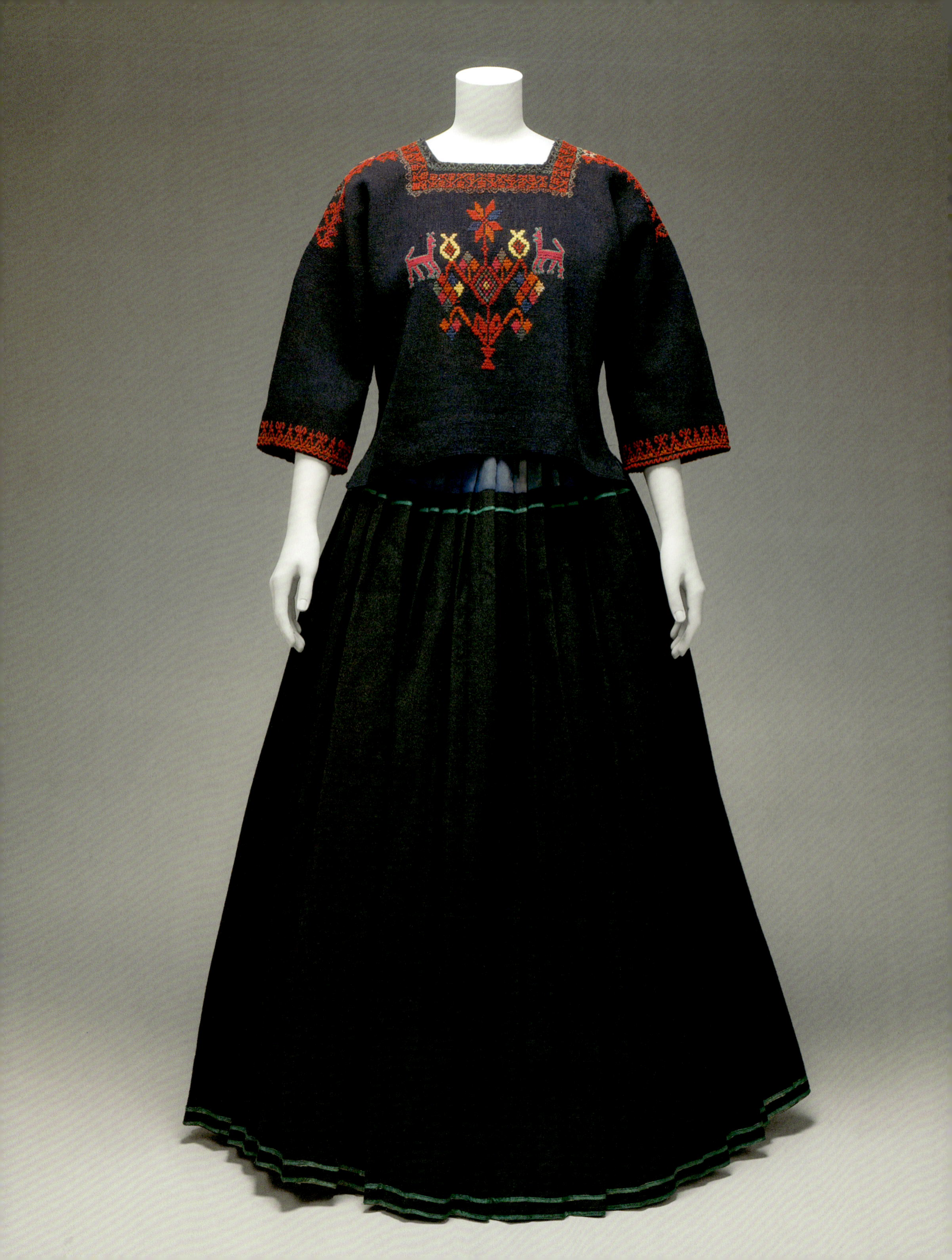

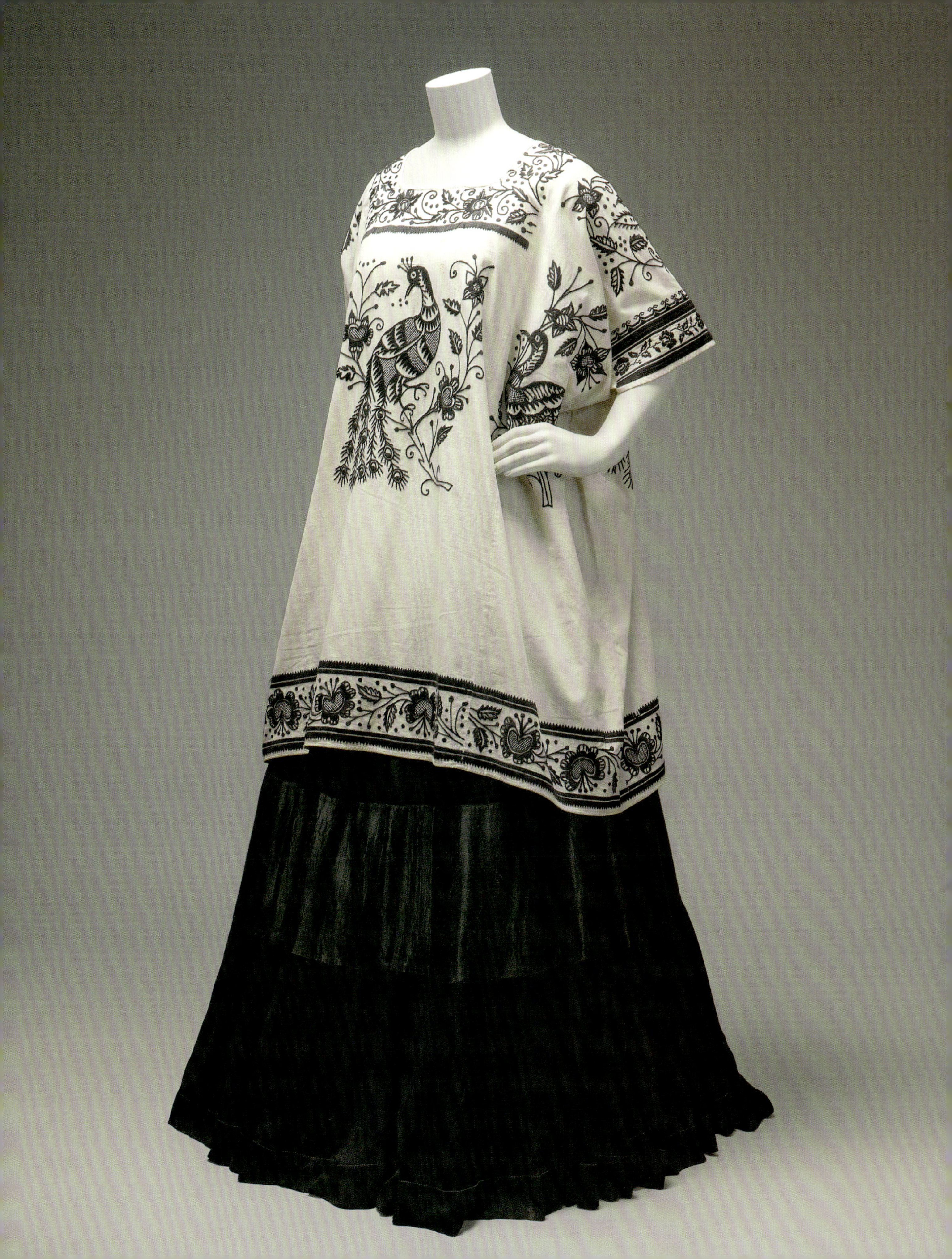

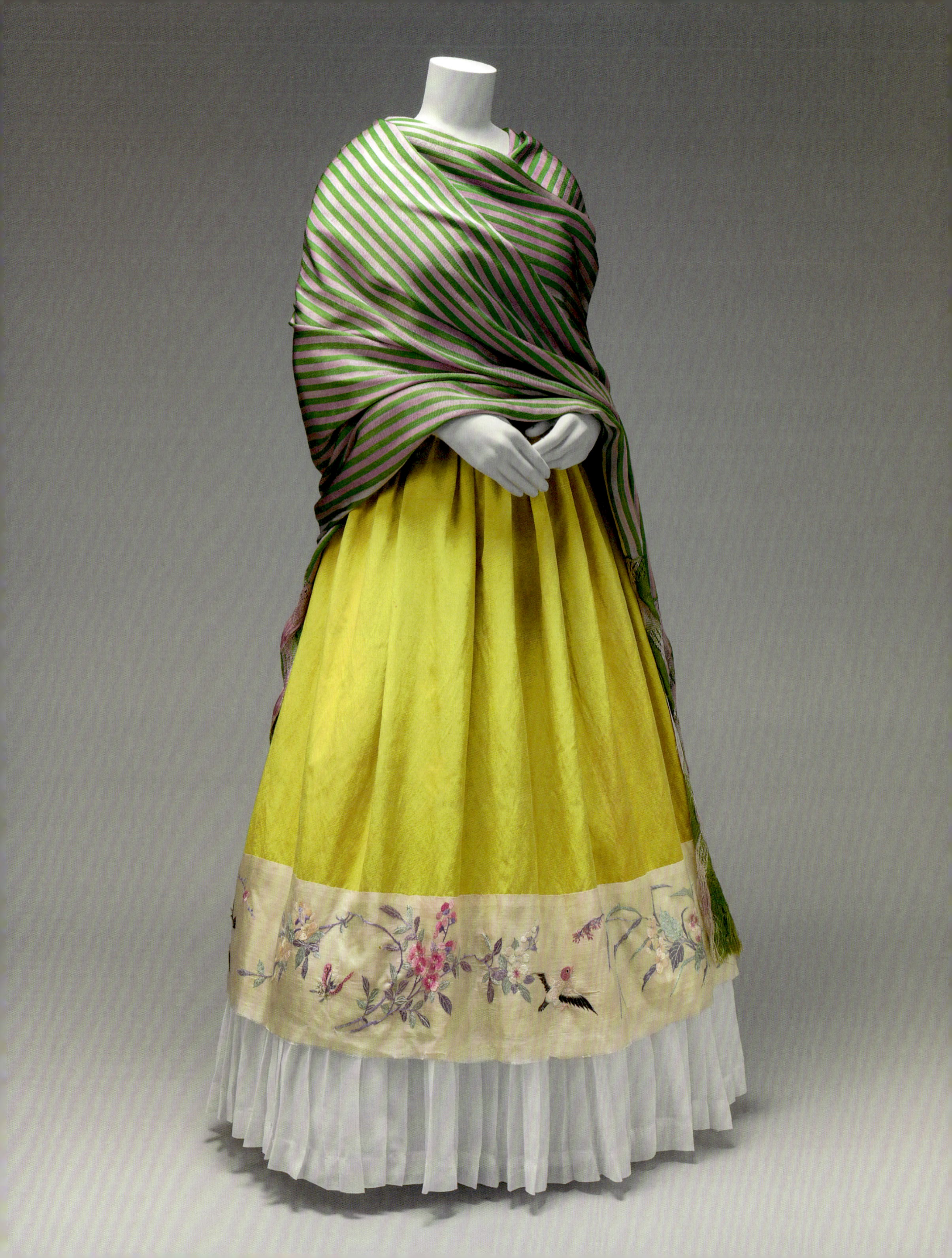

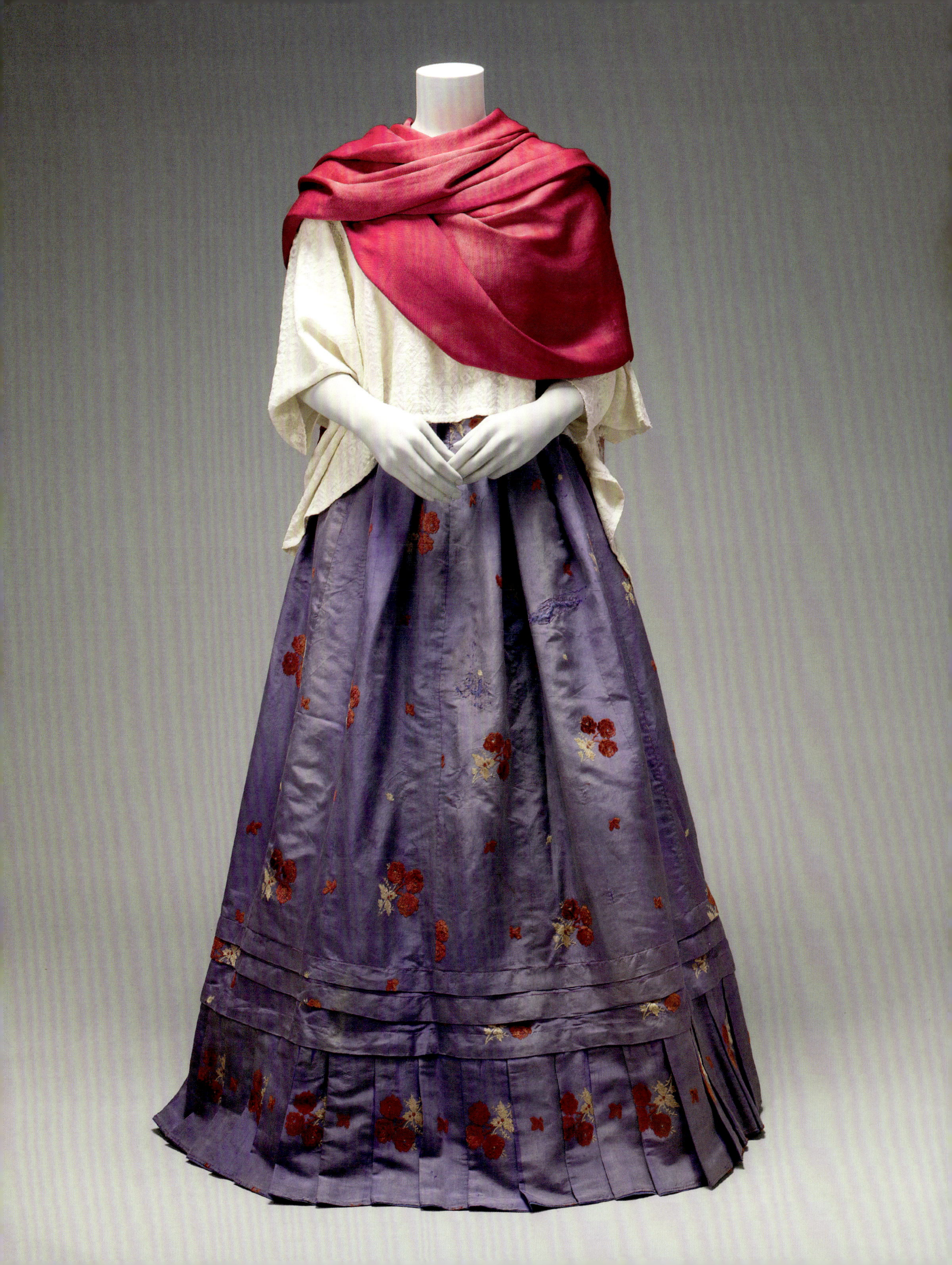

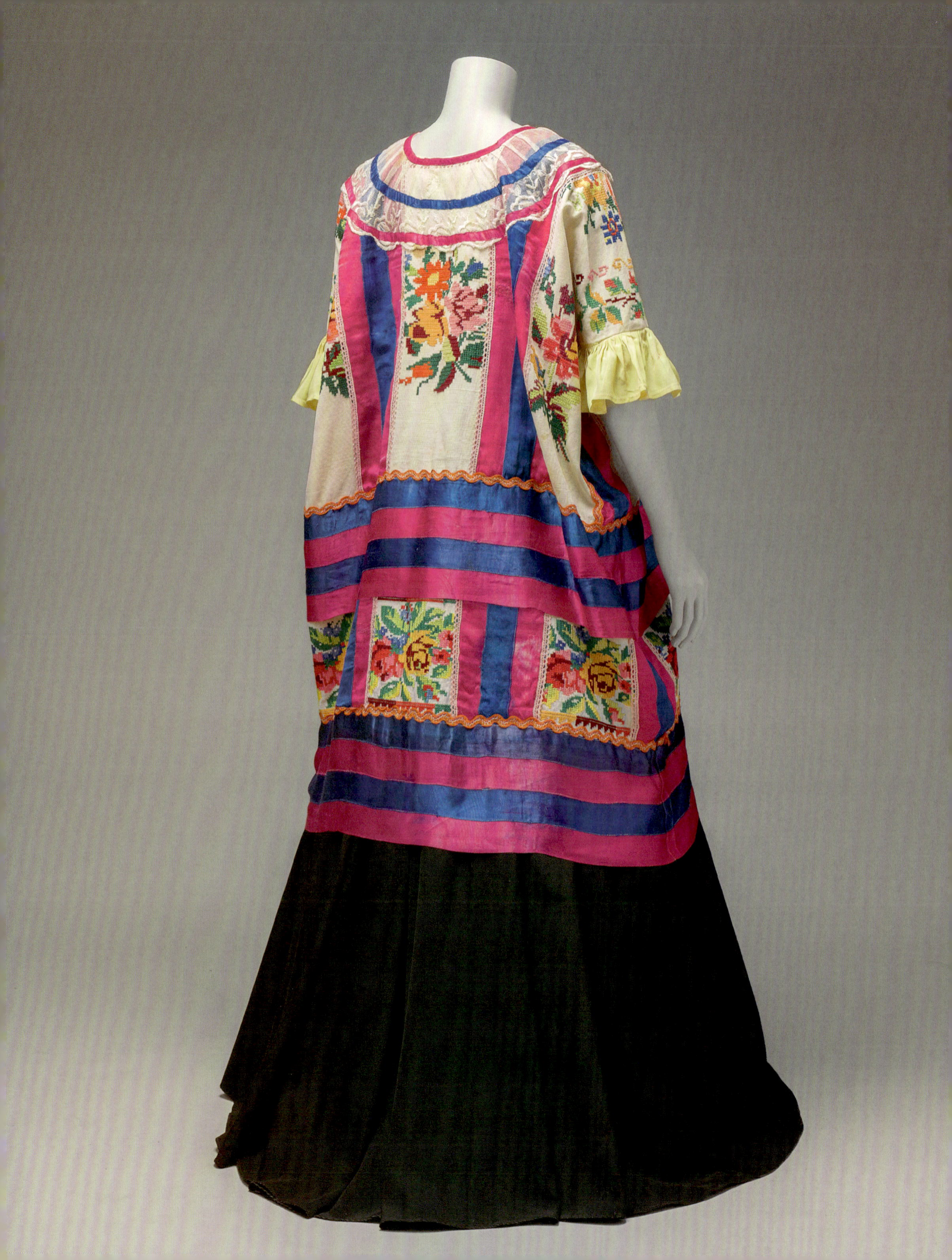

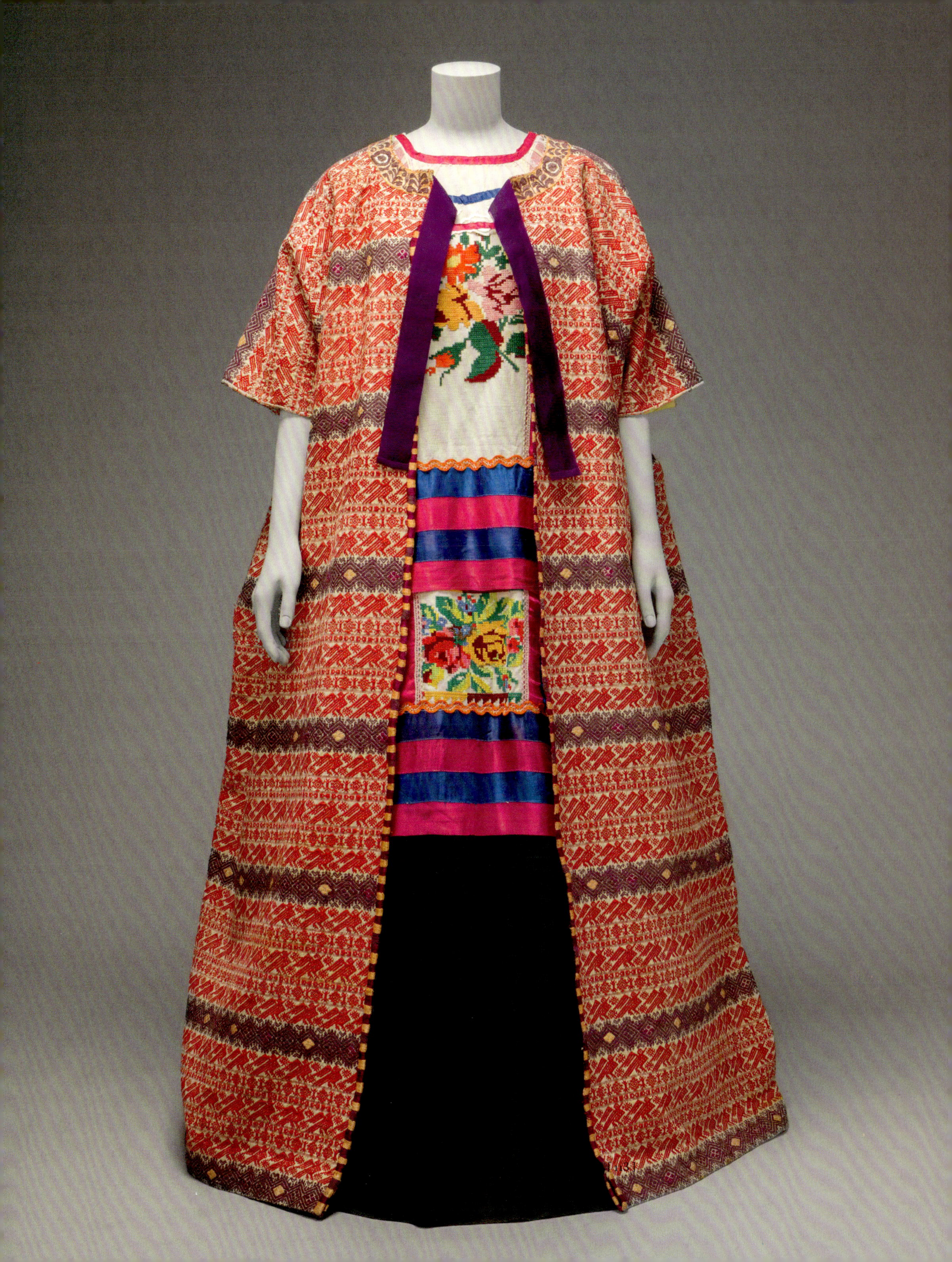

Frida Kahlo:
Making Her Self Up

CLAIRE WILCOX

> Her light-tan face was not pretty, perhaps, by established norms, but she possessed – and even radiated – a strange and alluring beauty.... She was always made-up and well dressed, even when she did not expect visitors.... She knew how to transform herself into a sensational beauty, irresistible and unique.[1]

Frida Kahlo paid great attention to her face. Of her small œuvre of paintings, about a third are self-portraits. From the late 1930s and throughout the 1940s, she created a series of likenesses that redefined female self-portraiture. In each, her tinted lips are tightly closed (Kahlo never revealed her teeth), and her upper lip distinctly moustached. Rouged cheekbones and dark, conjoined eyebrows frame her side-glancing eyes. In some, her features are set against, or arise from, verdant foliage; in others the background, with its shallow depth of field, has an ominous emptiness. In *Self-Portrait with Monkeys* (1943) [58] the unruly pets that roamed the Blue House crowd against the artist, their dark fur and cold eyes spirit-mirroring her own. In most, she is alone, adorned with pre-Columbian era beads and shells, while ribbons, thorns and strands of hair encircle her neck.

The head and shoulder format of these self-portraits allowed few sartorial details, although in *Self-Portrait with Red and Gold Dress* (1941) [59], painted in the year of her father's death, the just-visible embroidery picks up the hue of her lips and cheeks, ameliorating the sober palette of the upper half of the painting. Above her dark braided hair, Kahlo memorialized her name in large black script, followed by 'Mexico' and the date in Roman numerals. Disquieting and beautiful, the repetition of Kahlo's face in each painting suggests multiple versions of herself.

Of all her features, it was Kahlo's eyebrows that became her unique signifier. The doodles and dreamscapes of her diary are populated with figures whose brow marks act as a shorthand for self. Her brows also acted as a stage for her preoccupations: in *Thinking About Death* (1943), they bear aloft a skull and crossbones, in others, a third eye, while in *Self-Portrait as a Tehuana* (1943) [88], they form a sorrowful reproach to her husband Diego Rivera, while permitting his miniature to nestle within the cleft of her brows.[2] Rivera compared them to bird wings, recalling 'her

58. FRIDA KAHLO
SELF-PORTRAIT WITH MONKEYS, 1943
OIL ON CANVAS. 81.5 × 63 CM
The Jacques and Natasha Gelman Collection of 20th Century Mexican Art and the Vergel Foundation

hair was long; dark and thick eyebrows met above her nose. They seemed like the wings of a blackbird, their black arches framing two extraordinary brown eyes.'[3] Kahlo adopted Rivera's metaphor, incorporating it into the pencil drawing *Self-Portrait Dedicated to Marte R. Gómez* (1946) [60]. Here, she delicately transmuted the hairs of her brow into the feathers of a hummingbird with outstretched wings. Earlier, in *Self-Portrait with Thorn Necklace and Hummingbird* (1941) she had inverted this Mexican talisman of good luck by hanging a dead bird around her neck; images of wings, flight and flightlessness pervaded the lexicon of her art.[4]

Like many of Kahlo's works the drawing reflects an interior duality, with one side of her hair hanging loose like a curtain, blending into the frayed edges of the ribboned inscription, and the other neatly plaited. Despite the fact that Kahlo was nearly always photographed wearing earrings, such adornments do not often have a place in her observations of self. Exceptionally, the drawing features one of the pair of hand-shaped earrings given to her by Picasso, entwined with the fragile root of a flowering plant, rendered in the style of a botanical illustration.[5] The manipulation and adornment of Kahlo's hair, an essential part of her Tehuana *toilette*, operates like a spring-gauge of her psychological wellbeing; in *Self-Portrait with a Necklace* (1933) her hair is demure, topped with a neat cord bow while in *Self-Portrait with Braid* (1941) [61] her tresses have been reaffixed like a seething coronet, an act of redemption following the scissored violence of *Self-Portrait with Cropped Hair* (1940) [81].[6]

Snapshots of Kahlo with the Mexican artist and dancer Rosa Covarrubias and Italian–American photographer Tina Modotti show that she and many of her artistic circle retained their natural brows, rather than conform to Hollywood ideals of beauty by reducing them to a narrow arc, as fashionable women such as Kahlo and Rivera's patron Natasha Gelman did.[7] However, as well as emphasizing their allegorical properties in her self-portraits, Kahlo also enhanced her brows using cosmetics: a Revlon eyebrow pencil in 'Ebony' was discovered in 2004 amongst her hidden possessions, while Olga Campos's description of Kahlo's cosmetic rituals shows that she went further, using Talika, a French product that encouraged the growth of eyebrows and eyelashes.

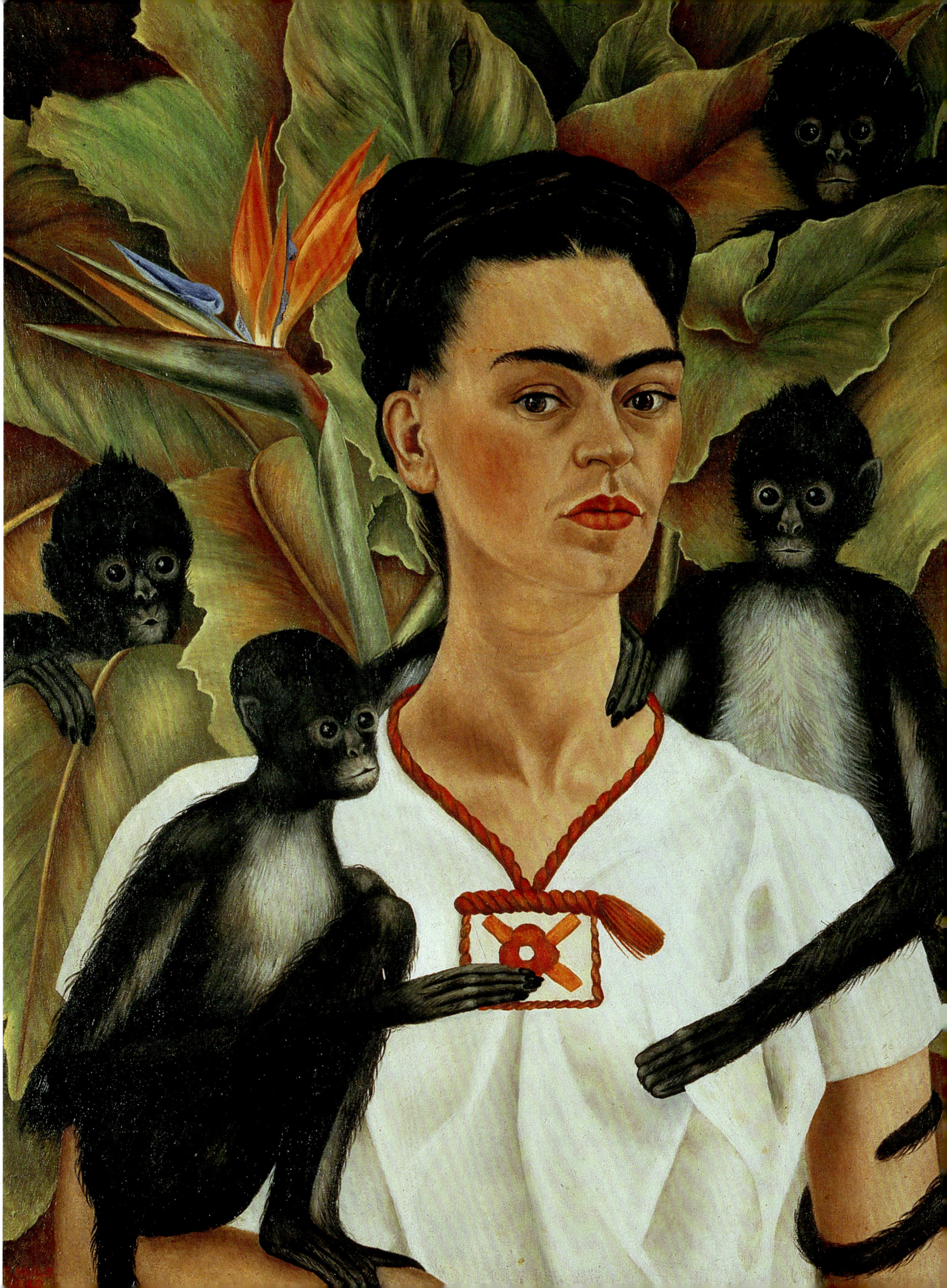

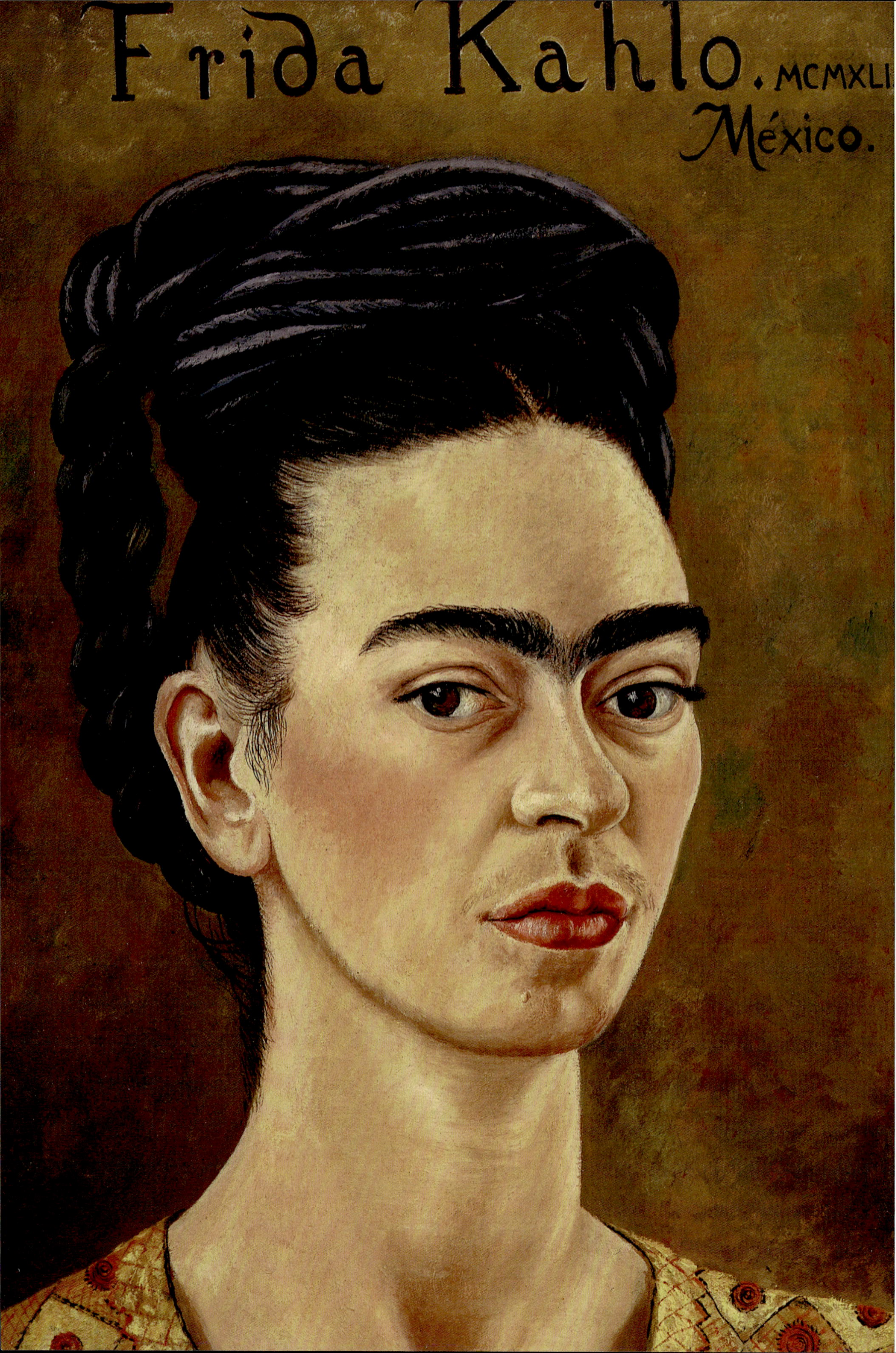
Frida Kahlo. MCMXLI
México.

59. FRIDA KAHLO
SELF-PORTRAIT WITH RED AND GOLD DRESS, 1941
OIL ON CANVAS. 39 × 27.5 CM
The Jacques and Natasha Gelman Collection of 20th Century Mexican Art and the Vergel Foundation

60. FRIDA KAHLO
SELF-PORTRAIT DEDICATED TO MARTE R. GÓMEZ, 1946
PENCIL ON PAPER. 38.5 × 32.5 CM
Private collection

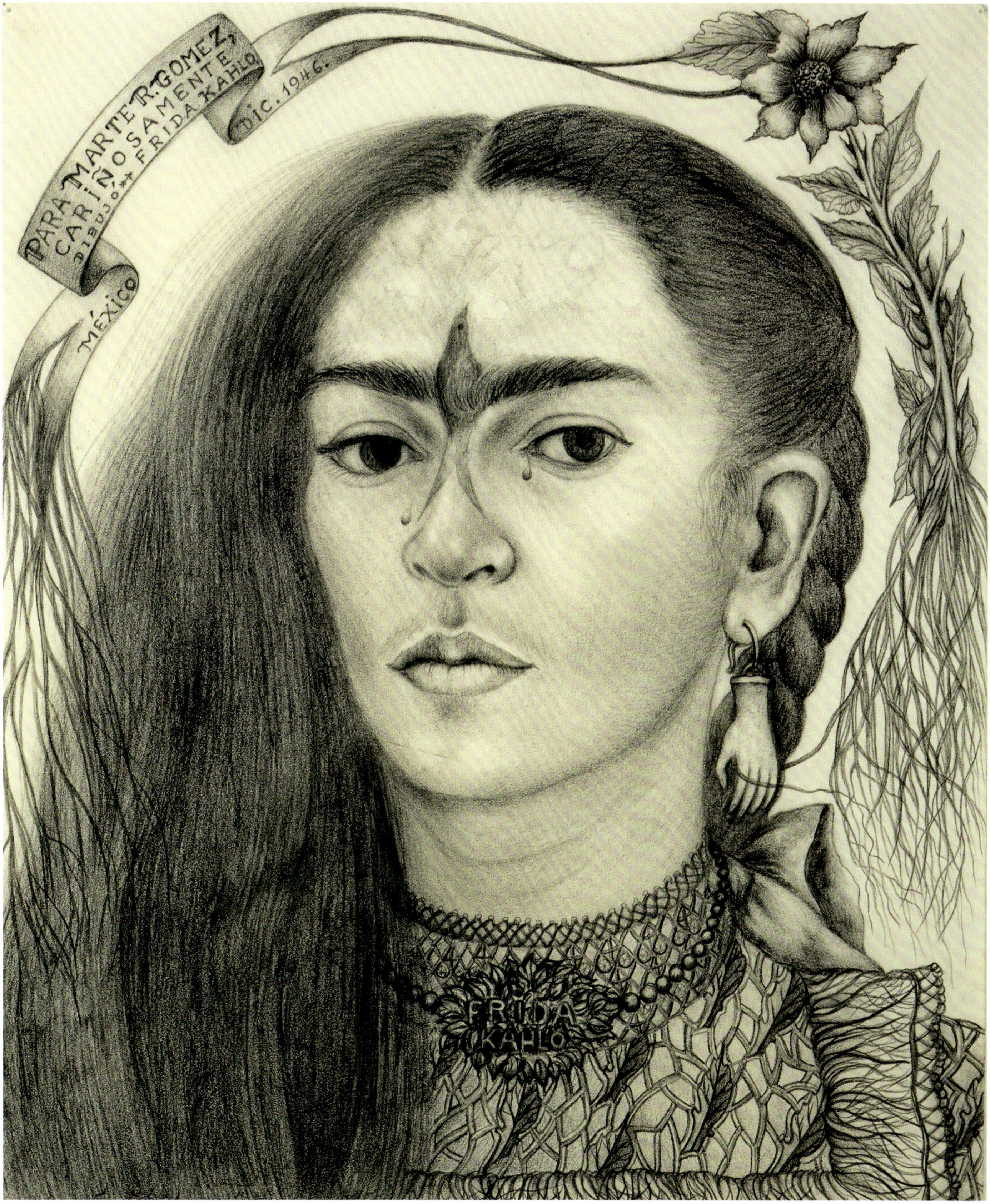

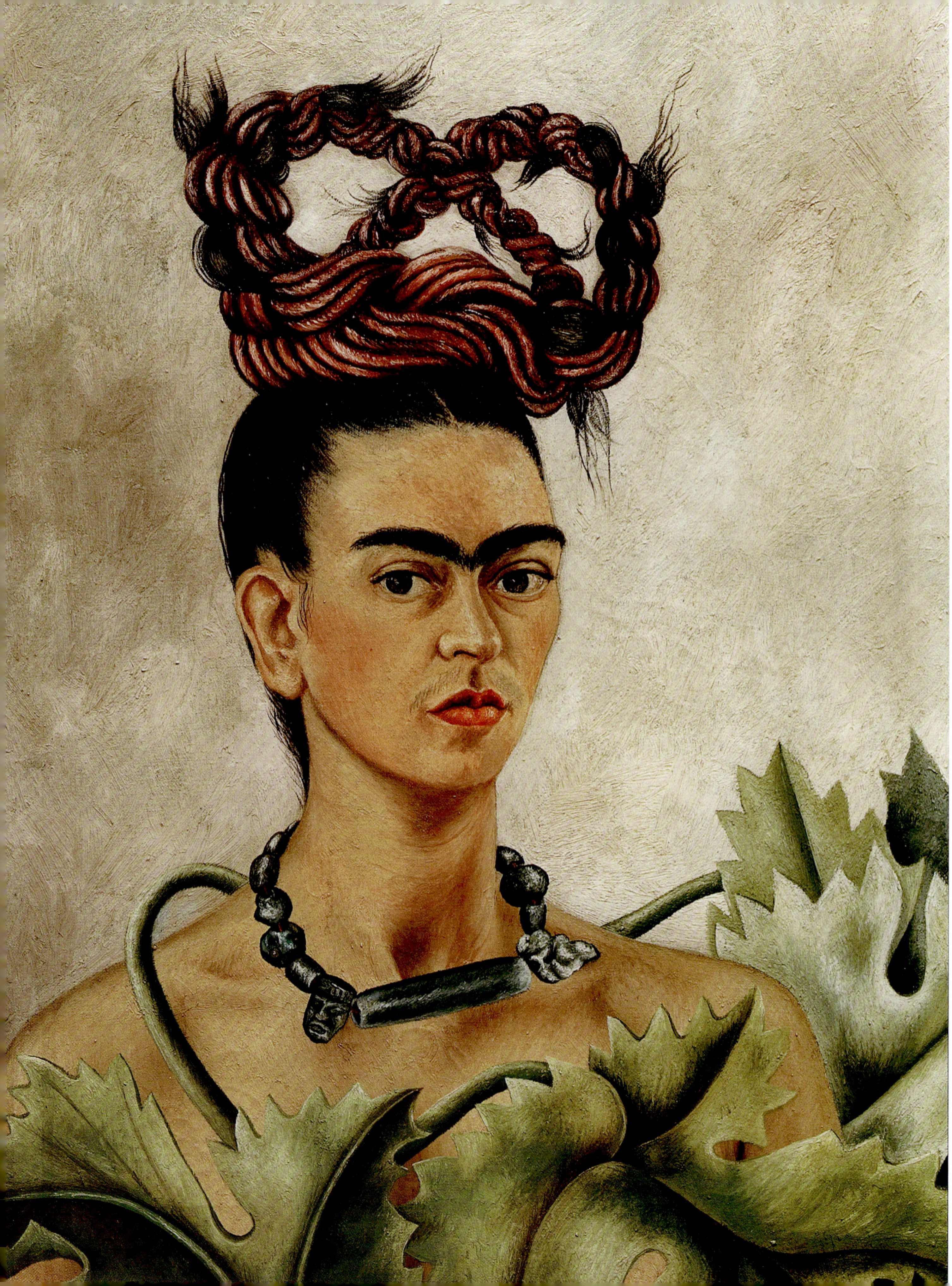

61. FRIDA KAHLO
SELF-PORTRAIT WITH BRAID, 1941
OIL ON HARDBOARD. 51 × 38.5 CM
The Jacques and Natasha Gelman Collection of 20th Century Mexican Art and the Vergel Foundation

However, even bolder than not plucking in-between her brows to individuate them, was Kahlo's refusal to depilate her moustache.[8] Her androgynous attributes were a composite part of her personality and complex sexuality. 'Of my face', she said, 'I like the eyebrows and the eyes. Aside from that, I like nothing ... I have the moustache and in general the face of the opposite sex.'[9] Kahlo's fascination with the face, and her German–Hungarian and Spanish–Indian heritage that informed her *mestizo* identity, is articulated in *My Grandparents, My Parents and I (Family Tree)* (1936) [62]. She described her mother, Matilde Calderón, as having 'beautiful eyes, a very fine mouth, and dark skin – she was like a Oaxaca bellflower.'[10] Here, she depicts Matilde's eyebrows as they appear in family photographs, but enhances the shadow on her upper lip, as if to identify it with her own, and to echo Guillermo Kahlo's resplendent moustache. Earlier, in *Self-Portrait with a Necklace* (1933), Kahlo's fine brush work had imbued her own facial hair with a delicate, unapologetic beauty.

In the 1940s, American cosmetics brands such as Coty, Max Factor, Helena Rubenstein and Elizabeth Arden began to expand their markets in Latin America. Kahlo's eyebrow pencil was not imported, like some of her other surviving products such as emery boards and nail varnishes, but manufactured in Mexico City, where Revlon had opened a manufacturing base in 1948.[11] Western ideals still pervaded, with the American actress Claudette Colbert penning a 'Taking Care of Your Beauty' column for the Mexican broadsheet *El Universal* in the 1940s. However, the flowering of the Mexican film industry at the same time – which made the Gelmans' fortune, and the success of Mexican film stars such as Maria Félix and Dolores del Rio, who were friends of the Riveras – also helped to redefine notions of beauty. While the beauty department in large stores such as *El Palacio de Hierro* sold American and French cosmetics and perfumes, new products developed for multiracial skin tones were also becoming increasingly available.[12] Campos describes Kahlo as using 'blush and rice powder by Coty' but her surviving skin products only include Revlon blusher and a powder compact.[13] A jar of Pond's dry skin cream, made in Mexico, has also been preserved. Pond's based its advertising campaigns not on race or colour, but on its appeal to universal beauty, being 'preferred by beautiful women in all parts of the world.'[14]

62. FRIDA KAHLO
MY GRANDPARENTS, MY PARENTS AND I
(FAMILY TREE), 1936
OIL AND TEMPURA ON ZINC. 30.7 × 34.5 CM
Museum of Modern Art, New York. 102.1976

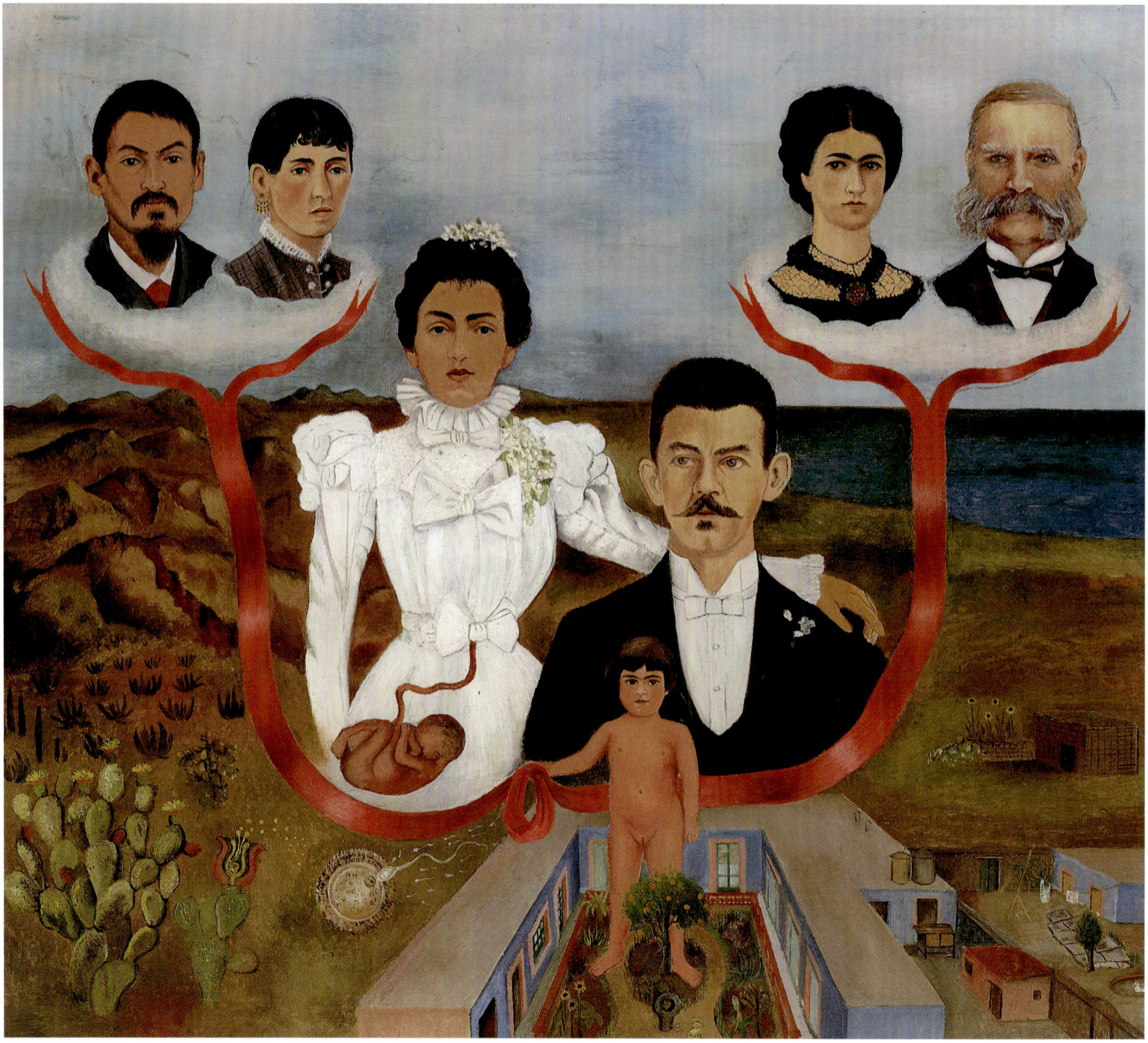

In 1930, during her visit to San Francisco with Rivera following their marriage (her first time away from home), Kahlo attracted the attention of photographers Edward Weston and Imogen Cunningham, who portrayed her at a moment of transition between ingénue and cultural sophisticate. Weston recalled Kahlo's impact – 'people stop in their tracks to look in wonder' – while Cunningham captured the 23-year-old, wrapped in her *rebozo*, with hands unadorned and face bare, almost upstaged by her heavy silver earrings and jadeite necklace [p.2]. However, from 1937 Kahlo became the subject of a far more knowing series of images, as she began a ten-year affair with Nickolas Muray – a pioneer of duotone colour photography and a regular contributor to fashion magazines such as *Vogue*. Muray's images, and his film footage shot in 1939, 'colour in' the monochrome of Weston and Cunningham's portraits, forming an illuminating record of Kahlo's Tehuana dress.[15] Its festivity is matched by her bright nail varnish, rings and newly 'made-up' face, using lipstick, rouge and face powder perhaps bought in San Francisco [65].[16]

Kahlo expressed affection with lipstick kisses on the letters, photographs and missives she sent to Rivera and other friends and lovers [64]. In 1939 she wrote to Muray: 'I am sending you here millions of kisses for your beautiful neck to make it feel better.' Kahlo signed off with a crimson kiss, writing 'To you, my loveliest Nick, all my heart, blood and all my being. I adore you. Frida.'[17] Lipstick gave Kahlo pleasure: in a further letter she describes a birthday present from her mother – 'a lovely new lipstick, in pale blue and gold on the outside.'[18] Kahlo's effects, uncovered in 2004, include Revlon's 'Raven Red' nail varnish, a smeared, well-used Revlon lipstick called 'Everything's Rosy' and an almost empty bottle of matching nail varnish.[19] The cosmetic industry's language of optimism in describing red, in all its shades, suggested that beauty and well-being were inextricably linked [63]. Kahlo too was preoccupied with the symbolic properties of colour, but for her the meanings were more profound. In her diary, she wrote of magenta 'blood? Well who knows?' and red frequently punctuates her paintings from the embroidery on her blouse in *Me and My Doll* (1937) [2], to the red of the ribbons, flowers, drops of blood and the veins that

63. REVLON'S 'EVERYTHING'S ROSY', C.1954
Private collection

64. PHOTOGRAPHER UNKNOWN
SUBJECTS UNKNOWN, N.D.
ON VERSO: FRIDA KAHLO'S STAMPED LIPS
SILVER GELATIN PRINT. 9.1 × 5.8 CM
Museo Frida Kahlo

65. NICKOLAS MURAY
FRIDA KAHLO WITH MAGENTA REBOZO, 1939
Nickolas Muray Photo Archives

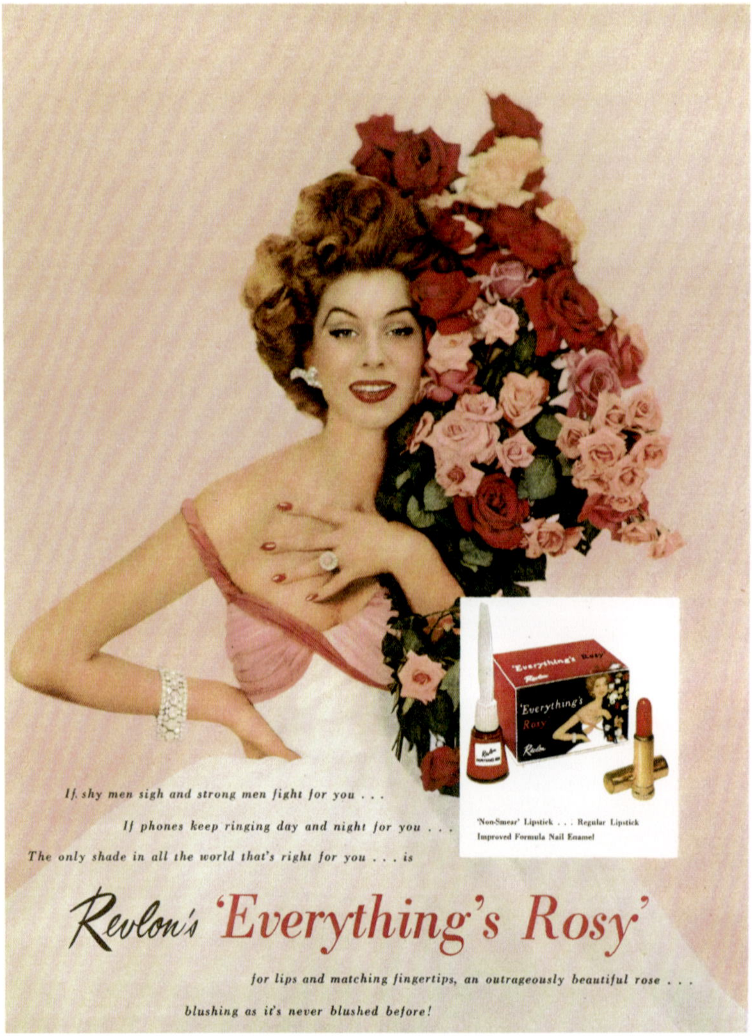

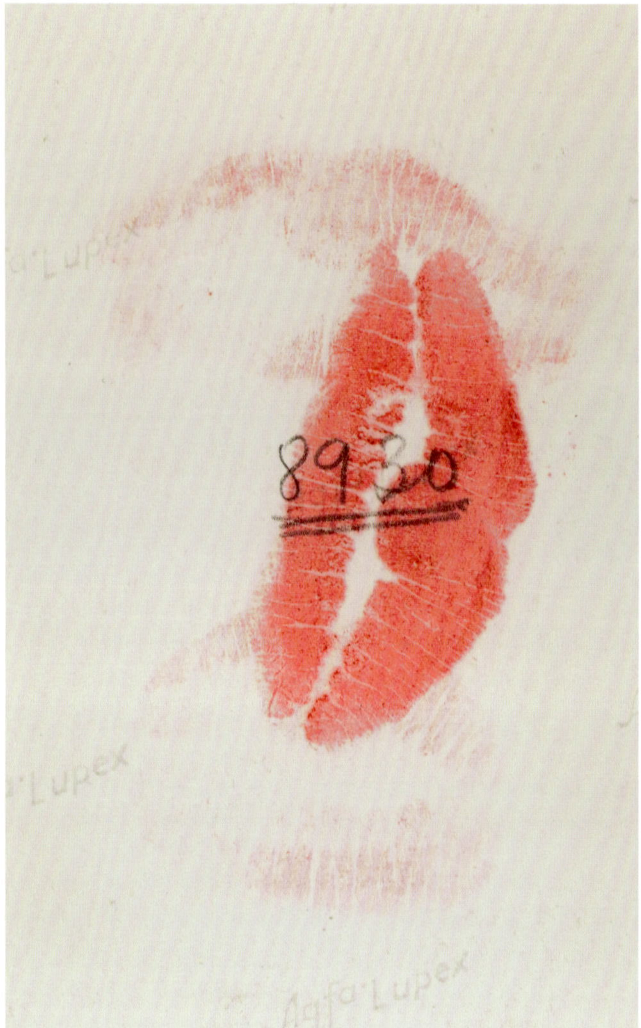

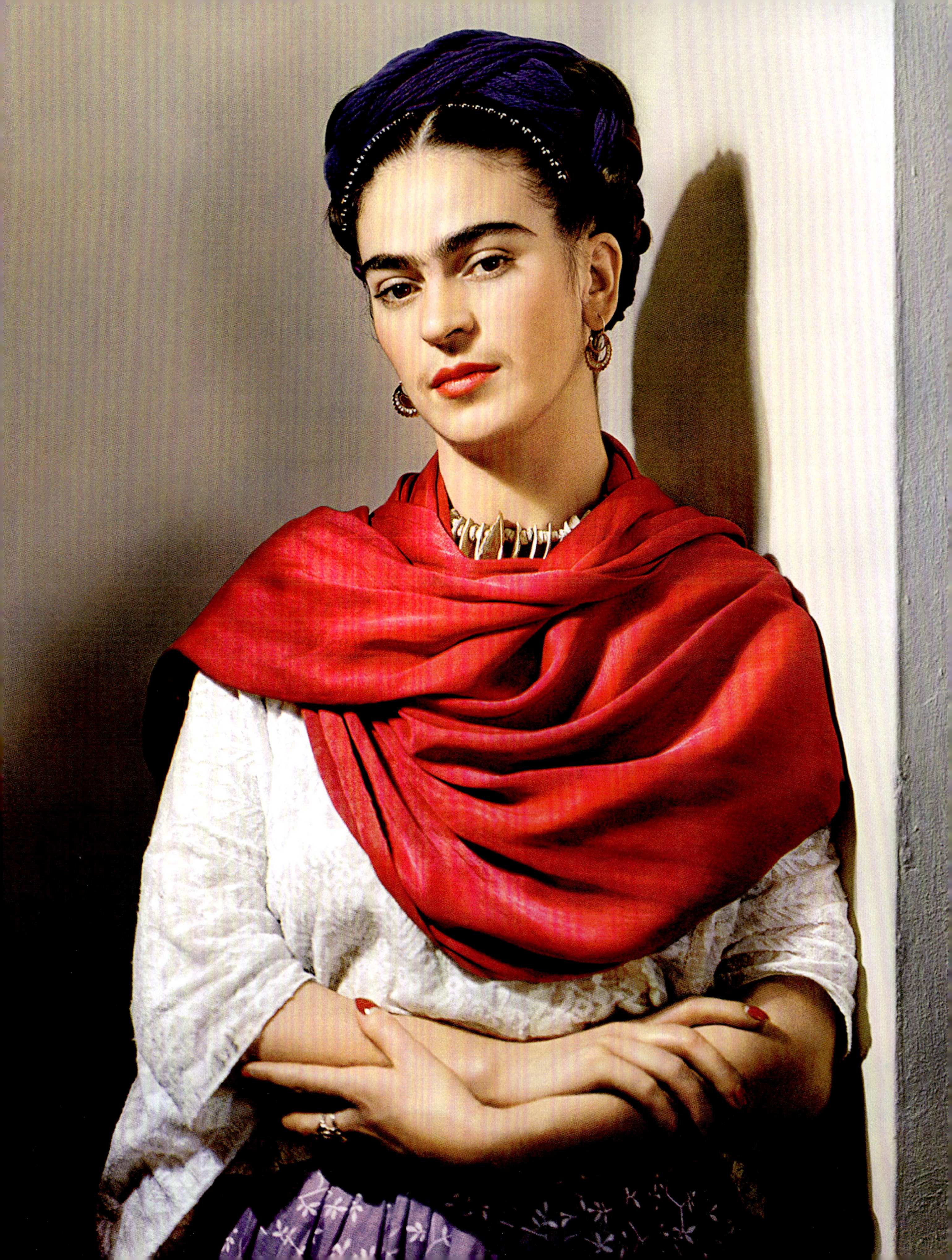

66. LOLA ÁLVAREZ BRAVO
FRIDA KAHLO ON HER BED, C.1945
GELATIN SILVER PRINT. 23.9 × 17.1 CM
Center for Creative Photography, University of Arizona, Tuson. 95.29.1

pp.128–9
DETAIL OF CHINESE EMBROIDERED PANEL FROM SILK SKIRT, SEE P.110
Museo Frida Kahlo

permeate others. While the warmth of Kahlo's lips and cheeks in her self-portraits suggest a feverish grip on life, their pallor in others such as *The Broken Column* (1944) [78] suggests a barely beating pulse.

The photographer Lola Álvarez Bravo recalled: 'Although she always had a precise way of dressing and making herself up and combing her hair, she always looked very natural. I never saw Frida too made up or looking ridiculous.'[20] It would be surprising if Kahlo was not as dexterous at applying make-up as she was paint, nor applied the same care.[21] Like the self-portrait, however, the application of make-up is impossible without mirrors. Cosmetic pioneers such as Helena Rubenstein – who sent powder compacts to Kahlo following a trip to Mexico in 1941 – recognized the importance of creating lipsticks, blushers and powders with an integrated mirror. Applying make-up on the go, and regarding the self in public, had become socially acceptable.

Álvarez Bravo wrote that Kahlo lived a life 'surrounded by mirrors' as her series of photographs taken in 1944–5 attest.[22] Here we see Kahlo reflected in the mirror inset into the canopy of her bed that allowed her to paint; in the wardrobe door in front of which she dressed; in the mahogany looking glass kept by her dressing table; in the insets in the walls in the courtyard of the Blue House; and Narcissus-like, in the canals of Xochimilco [66]. Towards the end of her life, Kahlo could no longer maintain the beautifying rituals so vital to her identity and sense of self-worth, and those around her had to become her mirrors: 'Each time Frida went into the operating room, Cristina carefully combed her sister's hair and powdered her face.'[23] In *Leaves of Grass*, which was beside Kahlo's bed when she died, Walt Whitman wrote of 'the pure extravagant yearning questioning artist's face…'.[24] His verse suggests the complexity of self, as read through the visage. In Kahlo's case, the aesthetics of her self-portrayal in both her personal styling and her self-portraits seem to be directed at expressing a set of identities for which beauty products were just one tool. In one of the many contradictions that made Kahlo unique, her assertion of *Mexicanidad* through regional dress, with its traditions rooted in the past, was offset by her thoroughly modern enthusiasm for adorning her face. Taken together they created a harmonious and radiant whole, for Kahlo, memorably, made her self up.

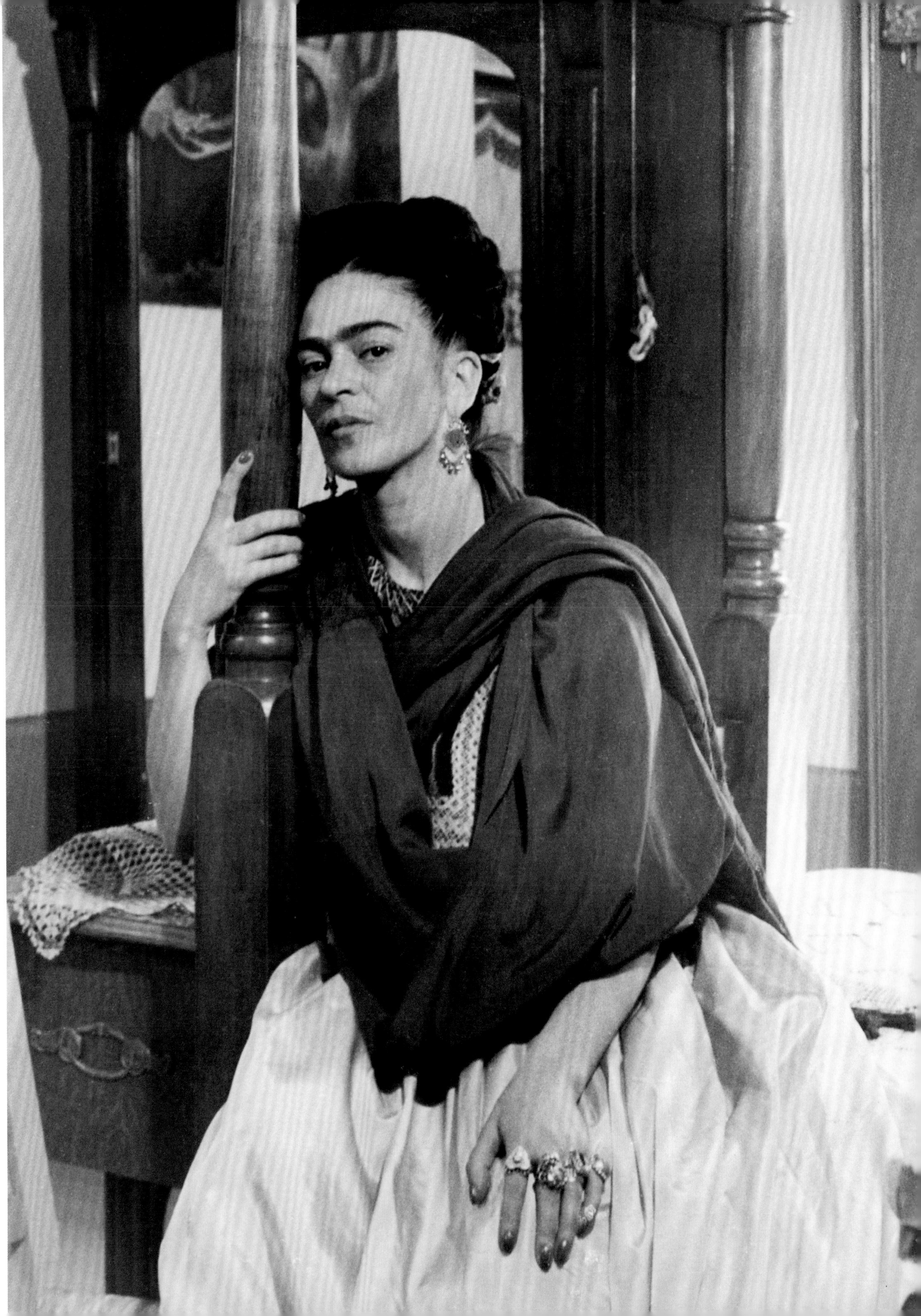

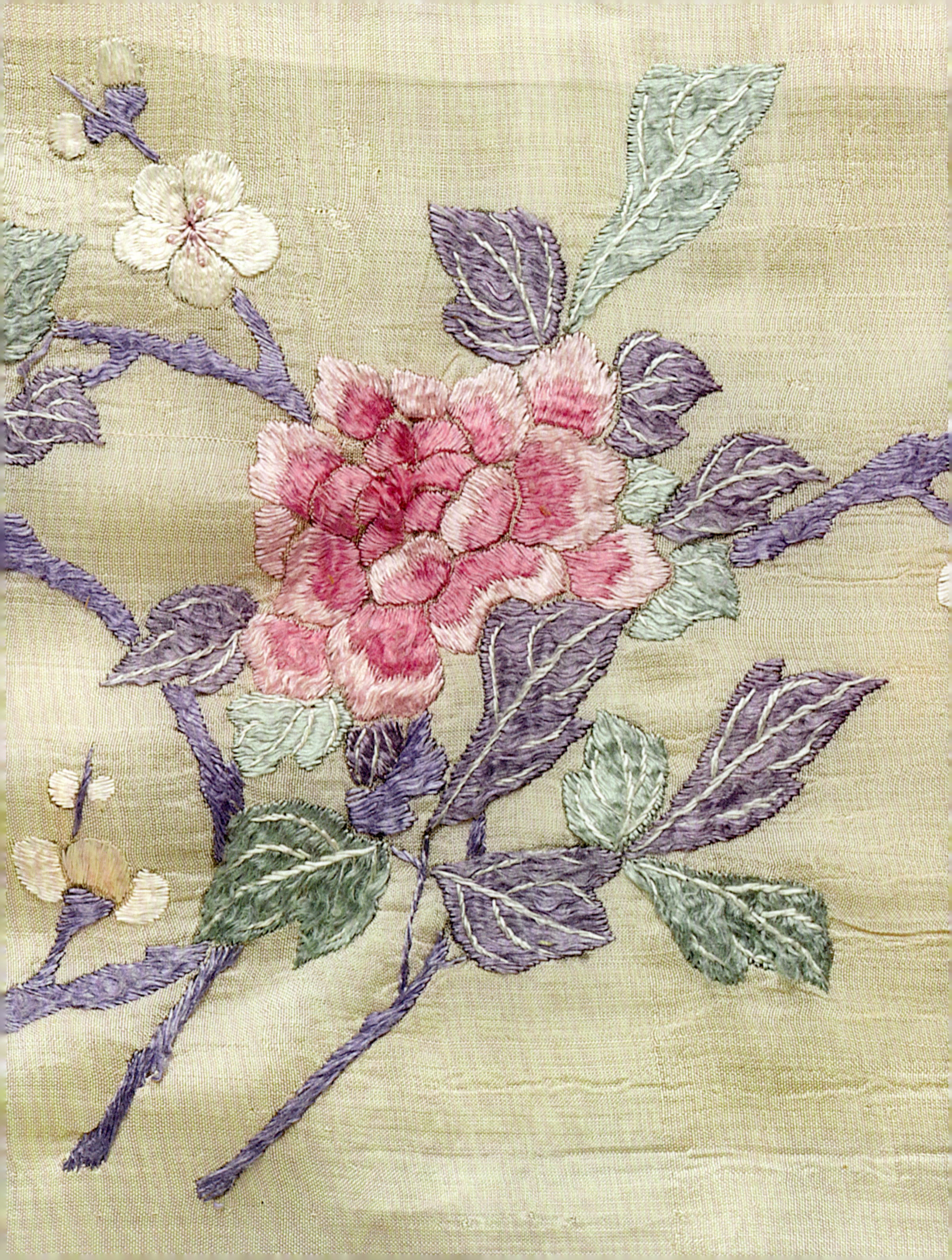

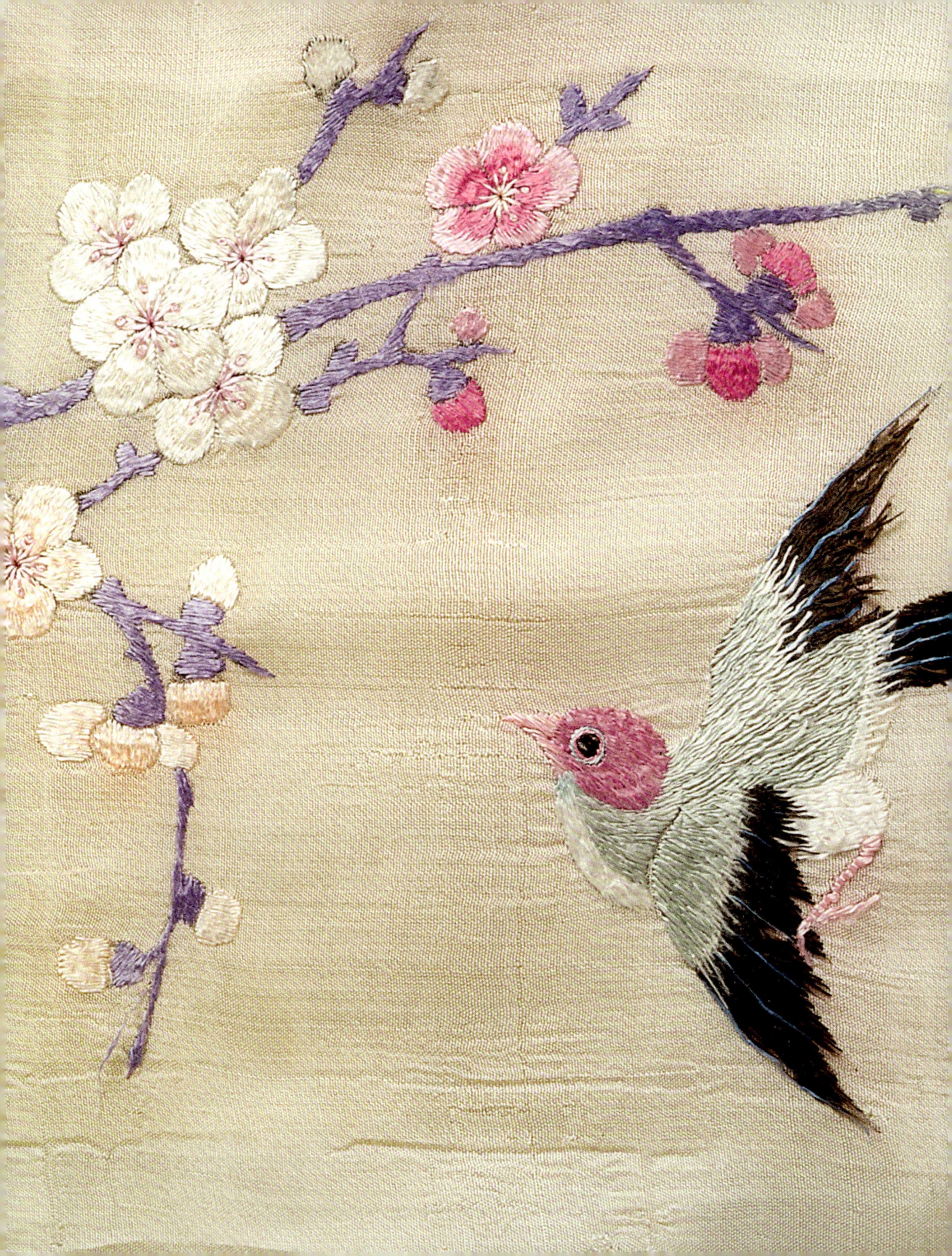

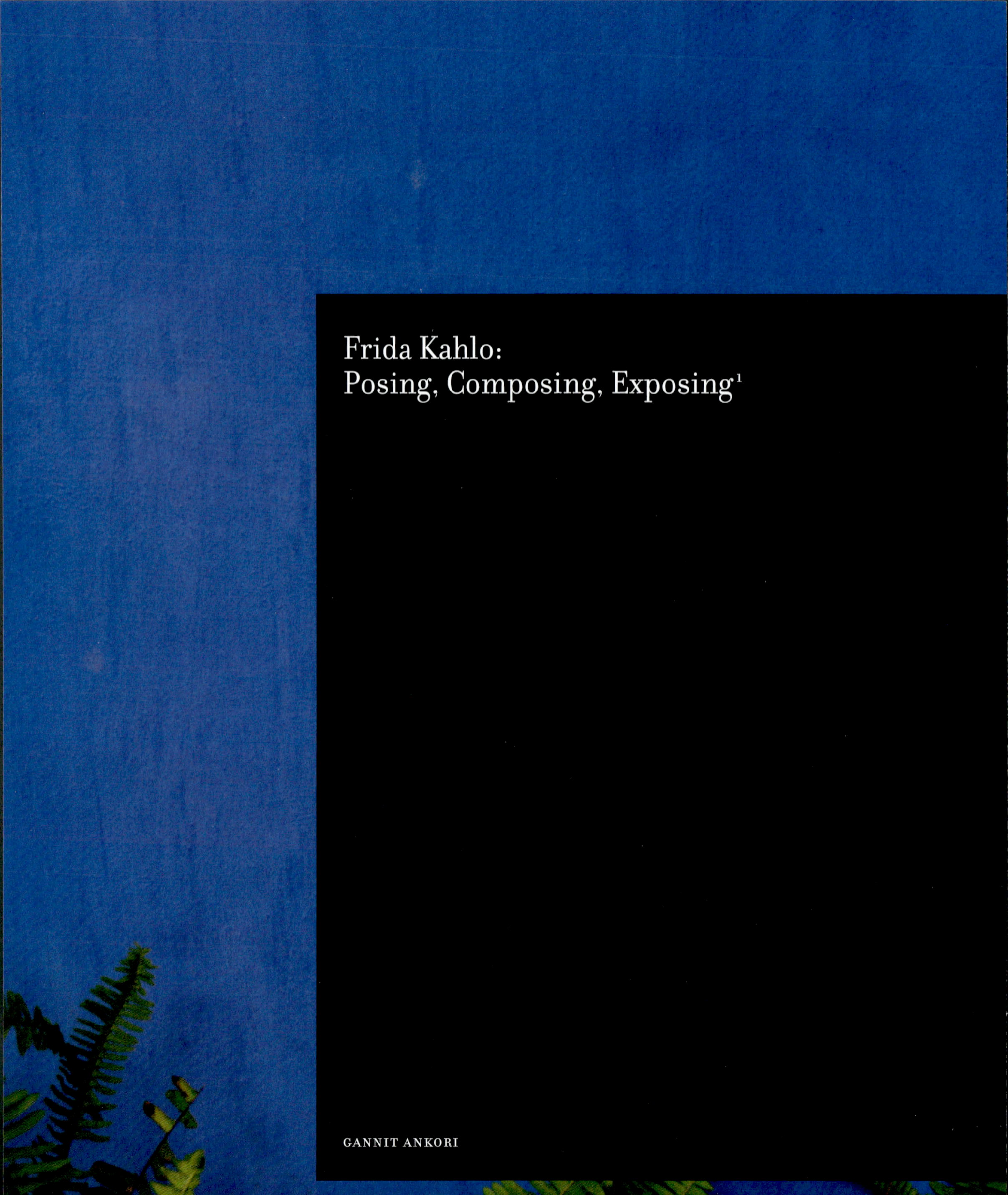

Frida Kahlo: Posing, Composing, Exposing[1]

GANNIT ANKORI

A few days before they were married in Coyoacán's town hall in August 1929, Frida Kahlo and Diego Rivera visited the studio of Victor Reyes where they posed stiffly for their wedding portrait in front of a backdrop of clumsily painted arches and vegetation [67]. Kahlo later told a reporter that she had borrowed the clothes and the *rebozo* she was wearing from a maid.[2] The series of pictures that Reyes ultimately produced emulates indigenous, turn-of-the-century wedding photographs.[3]

Just three and a half months earlier, an anonymous photographer captured candid shots of Kahlo and Rivera in their everyday clothes.[4] Marching briskly at a May Day demonstration, Kahlo looks like a totally different person [68]. Her narrow skirt, button-down shirt and tie and austere hairdo, present her as an androgynous-looking communist comrade. Rivera's biographer and close friend, Bertram Wolfe, described Kahlo's demeanour at that time as that of 'an adolescent boy'.[5]

Looking at photographs from this period, it becomes clear that 22-year-old Kahlo was an expert in having her picture taken. It is also apparent that she was still experimenting with a variety of sartorial styles and undergoing a process of self-construction with the aid of diverse costumes and accessories.

Significantly, long before she ever met Rivera, Kahlo learned how to strike a pose. Moreover, even as a teenager, she was precociously cognizant of the power of clothes to convey meaning, and, more specifically, to simultaneously perform and camouflage aspects of her developing identity. Also noteworthy is the fact that Kahlo's intense engagement with photography and fashion predated her becoming a painter by several years.

Since early childhood, Kahlo frequently posed for her doting father, Wilhelm (Guillermo) Kahlo, a professional photographer from whom she learned how to work both sides of the camera.[6] A German immigrant, Herr Kahlo, as his daughter called him in jest, was an architectural photographer, who professed to be a misanthrope and to despise portraiture. Yet, he clearly enjoyed taking pictures of Frida, who was, by all accounts, his favourite daughter.[7] In one of Guillermo Kahlo's photographs, four-year-old Frida appears leaning against the back of an armchair, glancing down happily at a doll that she cradles in her arms.[8]

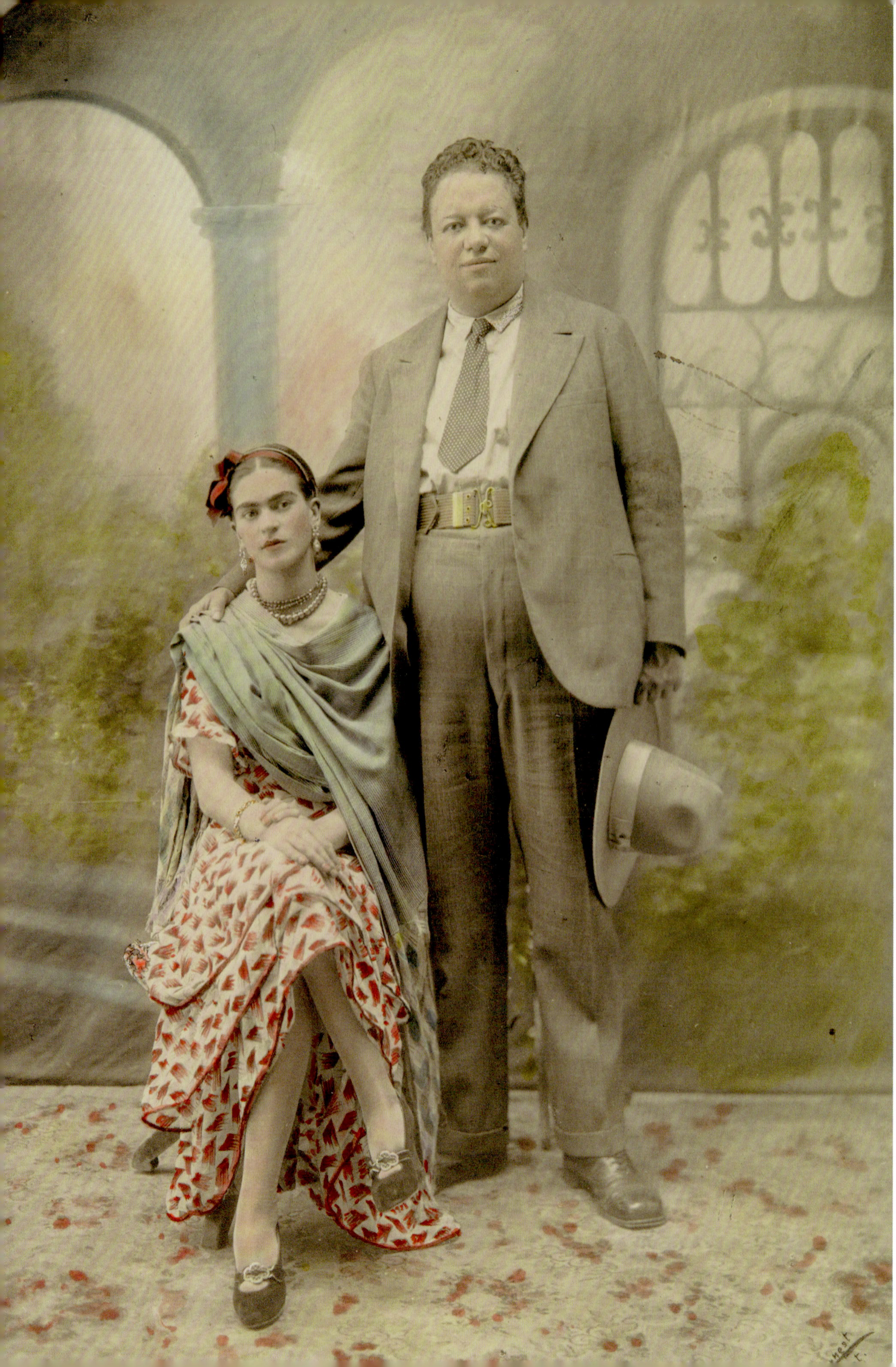

67. VICTOR REYES
WEDDING PORTRAIT OF FRIDA KAHLO AND DIEGO RIVERA, 19 AUGUST 1929. ON VERSO: 'FRIEDA KAHLO' AND 'DIEGO RIVERA'
GELATIN SILVER PRINT WITH HAND-APPLIED TRANSPARENT WATERCOLOUR. 18 × 12.6 CM
Museum of Fine Arts, Boston. 2016.112

68. PHOTOGRAPHER UNKNOWN
FRIDA KAHLO AND DIEGO RIVERA IN MAY DAY PROTEST, MEXICO CITY, 1 MAY 1929

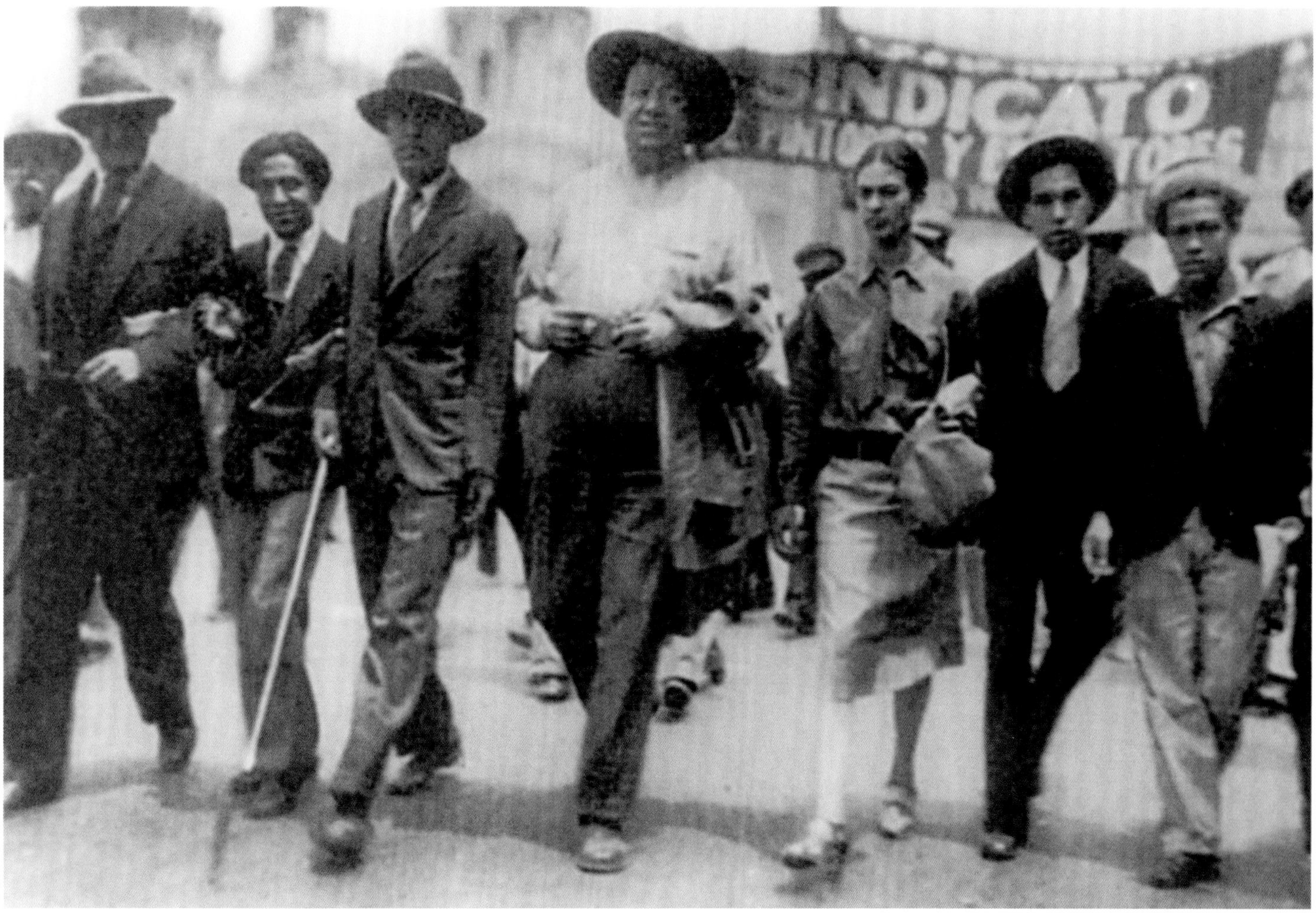

In the pendant photograph, she holds onto the chair with both hands, smiling sweetly at the photographer, her beloved father [I.*3*]. By 1919, just a few years later, a pensive 12-year-old Frida with a huge ribbon in her hair, replaced the smiling toddler [I.5]. She looks subdued – somewhat sad, with a piercing gaze that would later become a trademark of her iconic look. Kahlo later noted that suffering from polio at the age of six completely transformed her from a vivacious child to an introverted and lonely little girl. Henceforth, in the numerous photographs of Kahlo that have come to light, she almost never smiles.[9]

In a delicate (probably unfinished) pencil drawing dated 1931, Kahlo traced the contours of her face, based on photographs taken at different stages of her life (including the two images discussed earlier) [69]. This triple self-portrait reveals the direct influence of photographs on Kahlo's self-portraiture and highlights her creative process.[10] It also underscores Kahlo's ongoing self-reflective exploration and visualization of her process of growing up. The following year, Kahlo's mode of painting changed dramatically.[11] However, she continued to examine her process of maturation with added force in a series of nine paintings that comprise her 'Childhood Series', launched with the startling and taboo-breaking painting *My Birth* (1932).[12]

Memory (1937) is part of Kahlo's 'Childhood Series' [70]. Like the aforementioned drawing, it visualizes the artist's coming of age and includes three distinct self-portrayals. However, in addition to this, *Memory* also presents Kahlo's choice of garb as inextricably linked with her transformation from little girl to adult woman. The painting displays an adult 'Frida' as its central protagonist. She stands precariously between land and sea. Her hair appears cropped and permed, and her face is blotted with tears. She is wearing a mottled leather bolero over a white skirt and blouse. This atypical hairstyle and outfit may also be observed in a few photographs of the artist from 1934–5 [71].[13] This strange-looking 'Frida' is flanked by two empty, one-armed costumes that dangle from the sky on red strings and coathangers. On the left side of the composition is a little girl's dark blue skirt and white shirt, referencing the German School uniform that Kahlo wore as a child.[14] On the right side of the painting, an adult woman's Tehuana costume hovers. Ignoring the outstretched hand of the

69. FRIDA KAHLO
UNTITLED DRAWING, 1931
Private collection

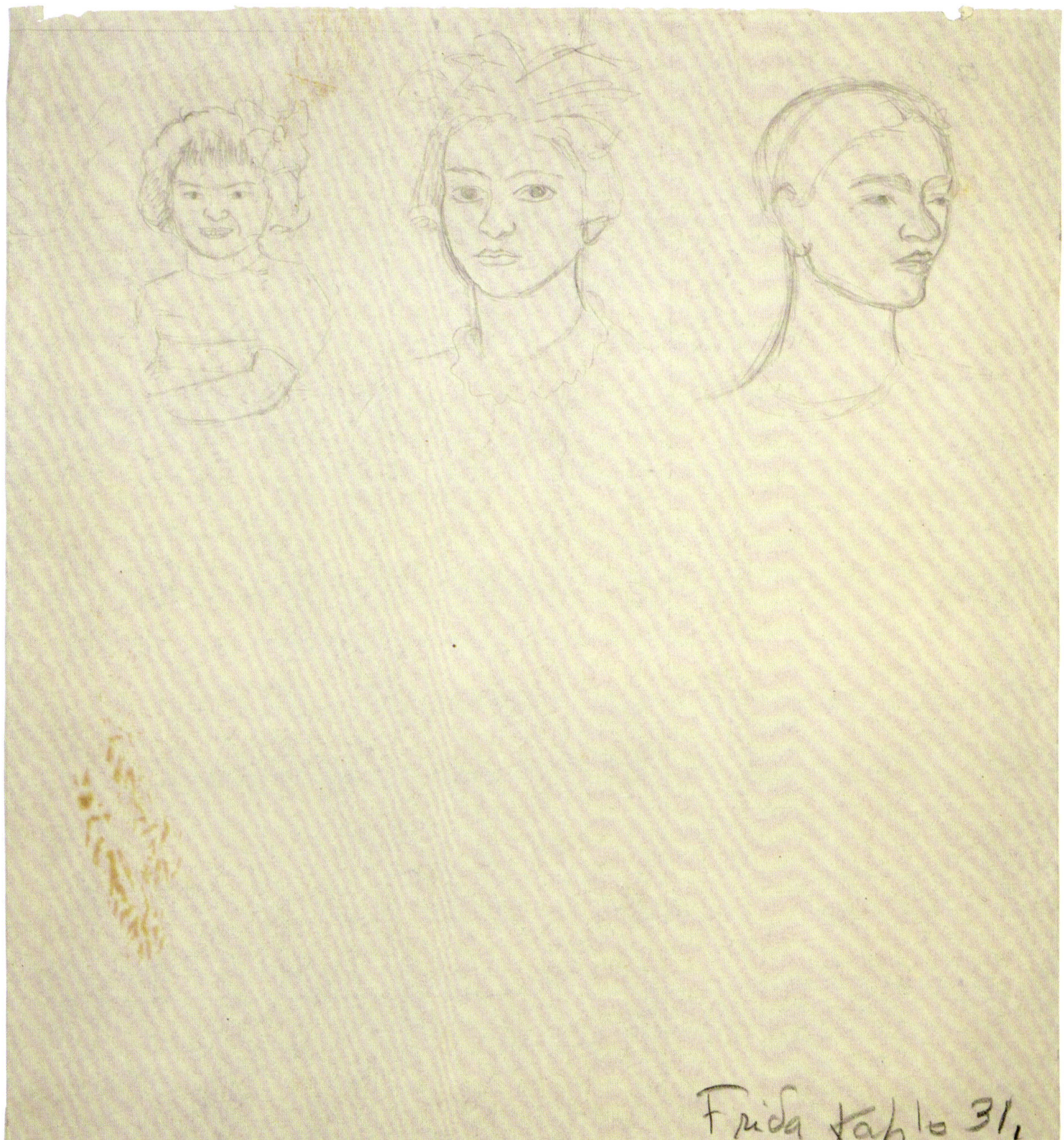

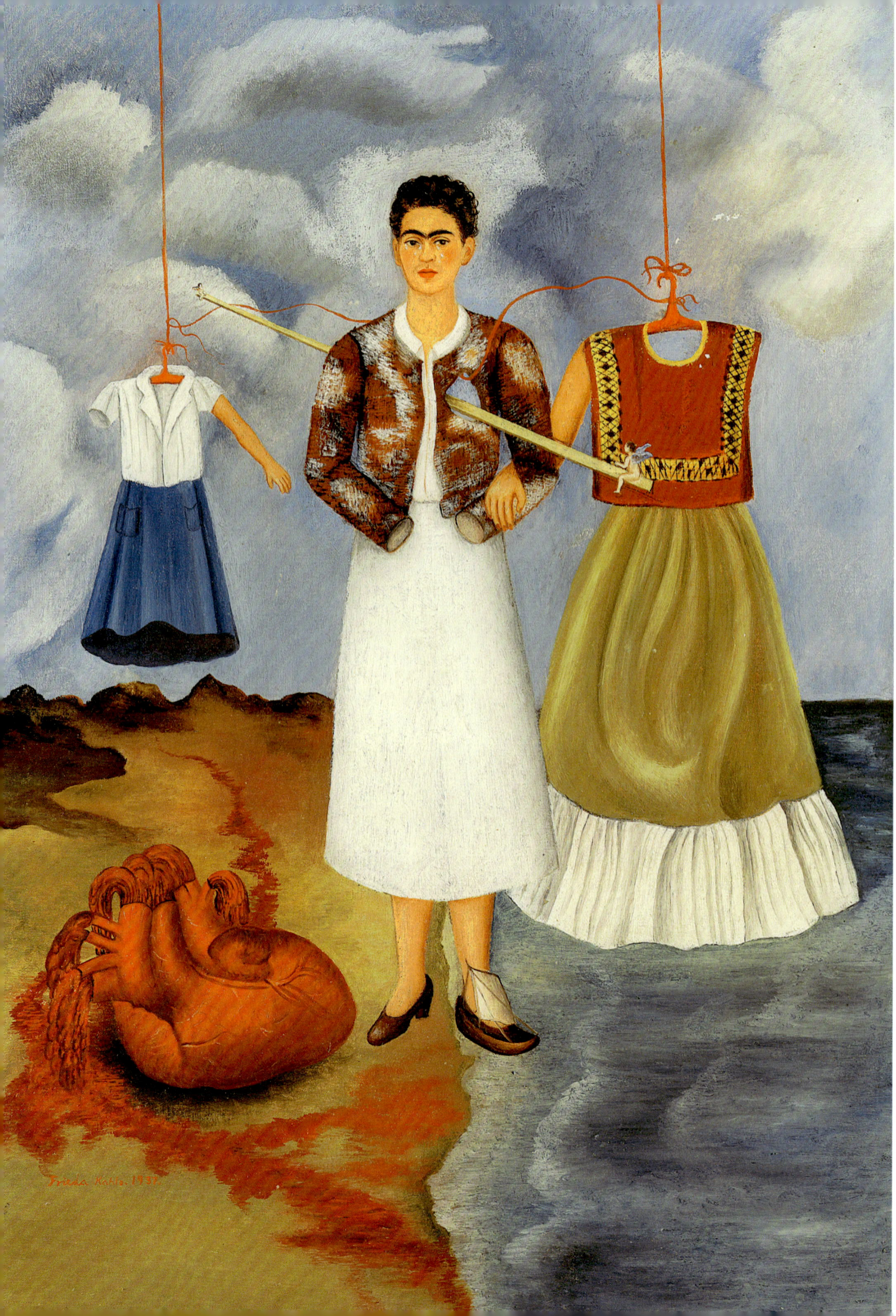

70. FRIDA KAHLO
MEMORY OR THE HEART, 1937
OIL ON METAL. 40 × 28 CM
Private collection

71. LEO MATIZ
DIEGO RIVERA, MIGUEL COVARRUBIAS, FRIDA AND CRISTINA KAHLO, C.1934
Leo Matiz Foundation

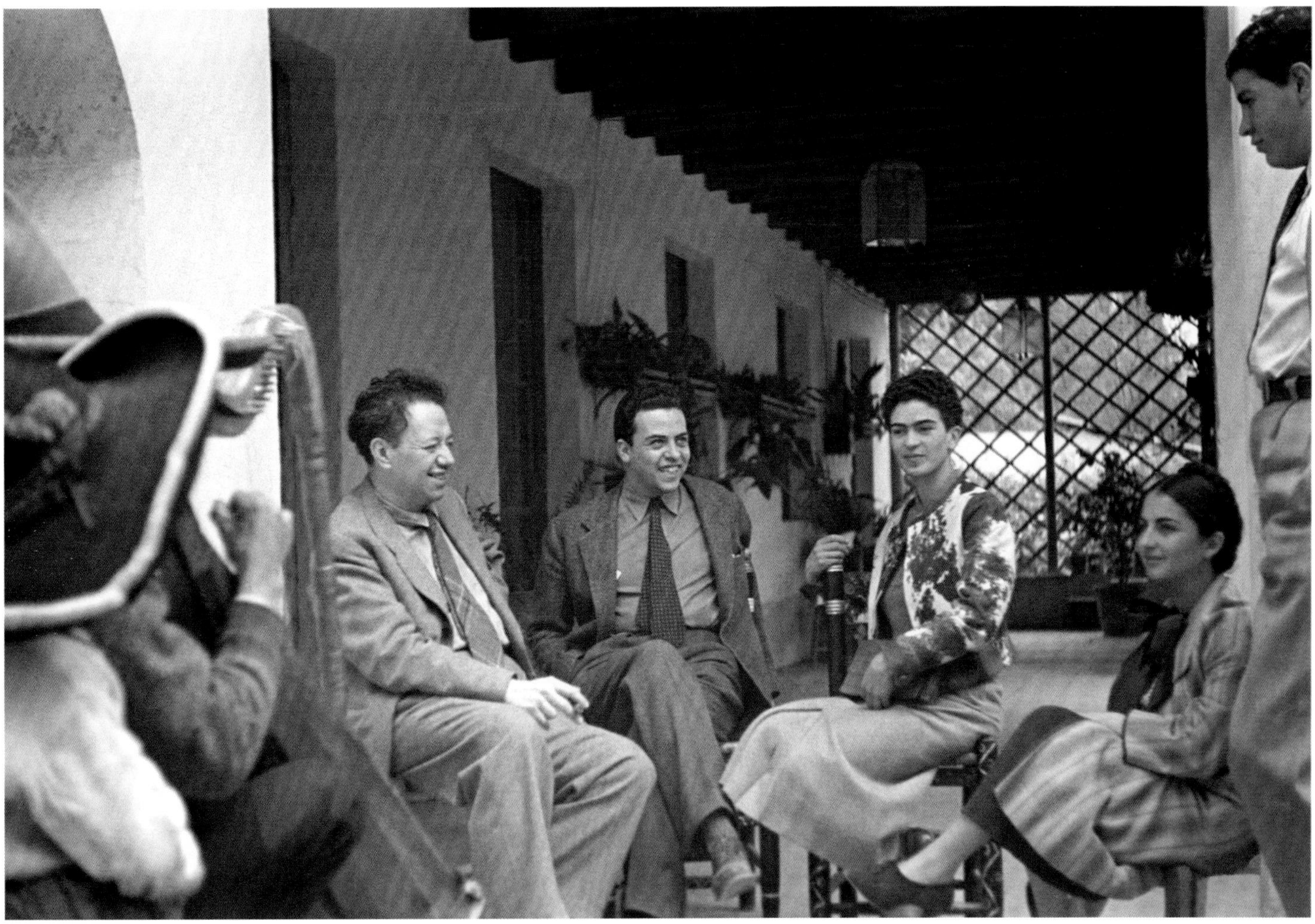

little school girl, the central 'Frida' chooses instead to link arms with the Tehuana costume, symbolizing Kahlo's choice to pursue the identity of the paradigmatic Mexican woman, *La Mexicana*. However, this choice is shown to be a wounding experience, as is indicated by Kahlo's profuse tears and the huge bleeding heart that dominates the painting. The line that charts the coastline – separating land and sea – ascends vertically along Kahlo's skirt and blouse, seemingly 'cutting' her body in half, suggesting a painful internal conflict. The figure's lack of hands renders her helpless in the face of this predicament. Kahlo's ship-shaped bandaged foot and the gaping hole in her torso – which is penetrated by a rod – allude to the two physical traumas that bracketed Kahlo's childhood: contracting polio at age six and the tragic accident she suffered when she was 18 years old.[15]

Memory demonstrates how Kahlo emphatically associated growing up with dressing up, and how both elements are part and parcel of her deliberate process of self-construction. The painting also clearly exemplifies the close affinities between the artist's photographs, her sartorial choices and her self-portraiture. However, a critical examination of these three distinct activities reveals that they are not synonymous and that, ultimately, they do not always perform the same functions within Kahlo's world. Indeed, whereas all of three involve 'posing' and 'composing' – Kahlo's paintings alone engage in the self-conscious act of 'exposing'.

Circe Henestrosa's curatorial thesis demonstrates that Kahlo's wardrobe was designed by the artist as a way to assert her ethnic identity, but also in order to hide her disability.[16] Almost every photograph of Kahlo (with the exception of a few private images by Nickolas Muray from the 1940s)[17] functions in much the same way: carefully displaying Kahlo as a flamboyant Mexican woman, while diverting attention away from her wounded body. In sharp contrast, Kahlo's art – as it developed from 1932 onwards – served a very different purpose and performed a more multifaceted task. Whereas it did involve Kahlo 'posing' and 'composing' – in addition it became a sophisticated form of 'exposing' the physical and psychological pain and the complexities of her identity, which her elaborate garments, eye-catching accessories and beautiful photographs masked so expertly.[18]

Two drawings illustrate this process: *Self-Portrait Drawing* (*c*.1937) [72] clearly depicts the artist 'posing' and 'composing', while *Exposing the Scar* (1938) [73] presents her 'exposing' her disabled body as well. Salomon Grimberg described the first drawing, which may have been a preparatory sketch for an unknown painting, as follows: 'Frida Kahlo, seated at work, wearing an embroidered dress from San Juan Chilateca, Oaxaca.... Paradoxically, she is self-conscious of every detail of her looks in order to appear natural. She wants to be perceived precisely as she wishes to be remembered.' Kahlo depicts herself with five arms with which she 'composes' herself as she 'poses' and 'composes' a self-portrait. Grimberg provides more details: 'Kahlo uses each of five hands to fix herself: one hand arranges her hair, two steady the face, one holds the sketchbook, one falls to the side. With her left hand [the mirror image of her right hand] she draws.'[19] *Exposing the Scar* and a very similar (now lost) painting from the same year, *Remembrance of an Open Wound*, both portray a seated Kahlo, wearing a Tehuana costume. However, rather than using her long flowing skirt to hide her limbs, she lifts her costume dramatically and 'exposes' her bandaged, bleeding foot and the long scar that runs along the inside of her thigh.[20] In this drawing, Kahlo also renders herself headless and her clothes transparent, exposing the red heart beating in her chest. As she often does, Kahlo merges the real and symbolic into palpable images of her body.

The propensity to dress up in order to cover up her disability harks back to Kahlo's formative years. Her childhood friend, Adelina Zendejas, remembered that following her being afflicted by polio, Kahlo's right leg grew thin and she developed a slight limp. Teased by classmates, nicknamed 'Frida peg-leg' and ashamed of her maimed limb, she began to wear layered socks in order to hide her 'deformed paw'.[21] After her near-fatal accident, Kahlo also chose to wear clothes that covered her withered limb and diverted attention away from the lower part of her body that had been ravaged by the crash.[22]

On 7 February 1926, just four and a half months after her accident, Guillermo Kahlo staged a photo session, taking several group photographs as well as individual portraits of members of his family. In one photograph, 19-year-old Frida sits elegantly with two books in her

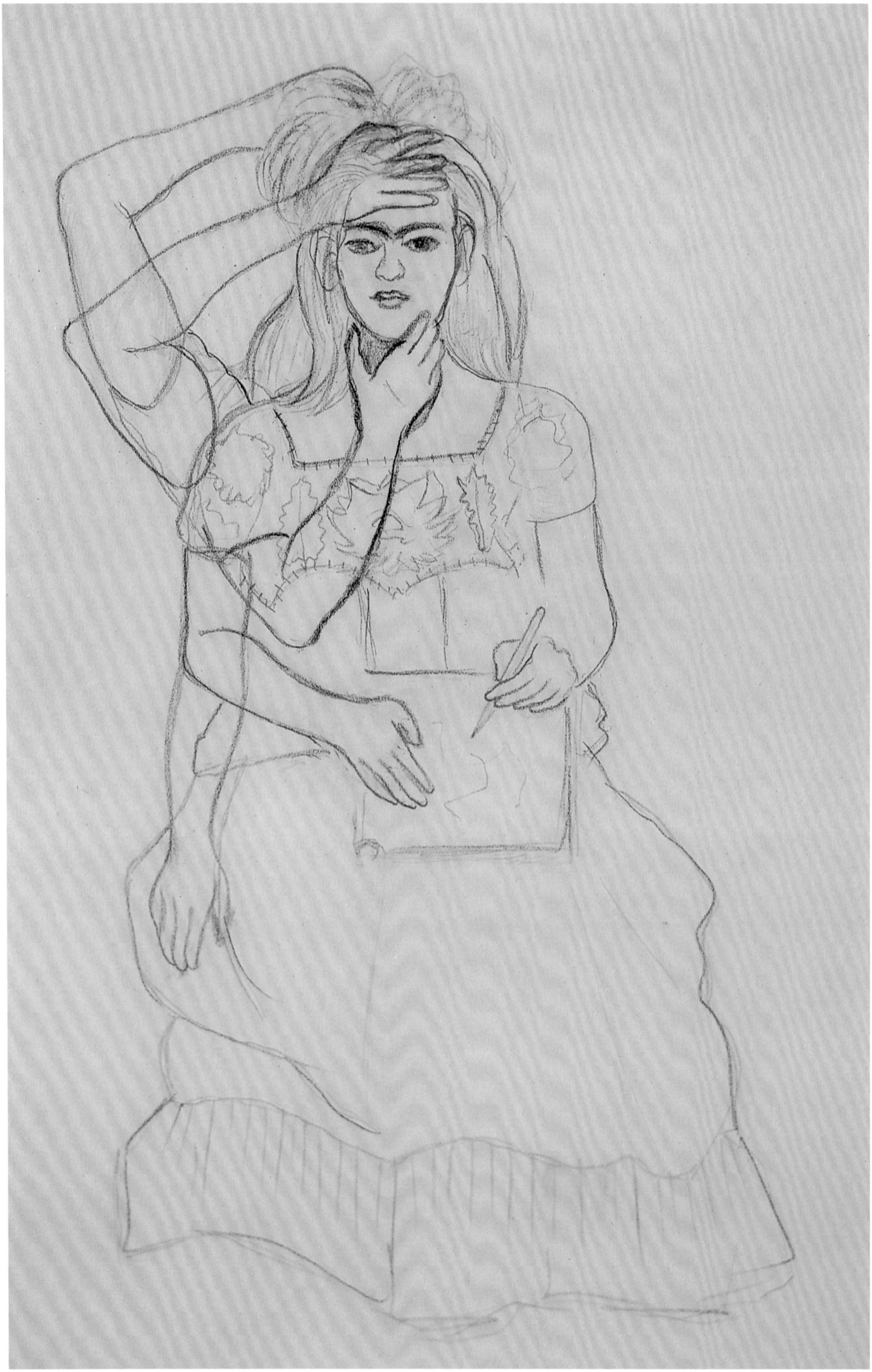

72. FRIDA KAHLO
SELF-PORTRAIT DRAWING, C.1937
PENCIL AND COLOURED PENCIL
ON PAPER. 29.7 × 21 CM
Private collection

73. FRIDA KAHLO
EXPOSING THE SCAR, 1938
Private collection

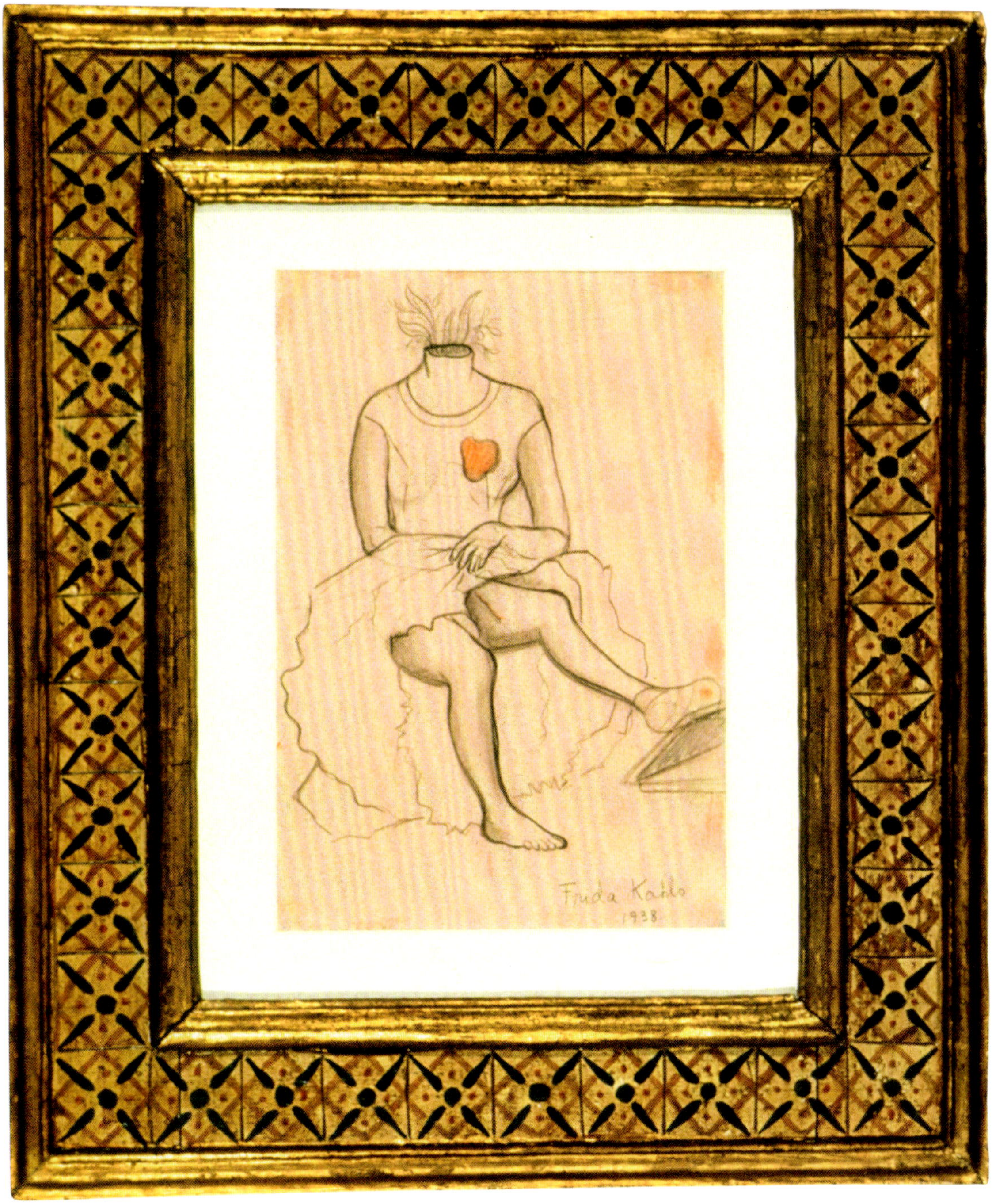

74. PHOTOGRAPHER UNKNOWN
MATILDE CALDERÓN Y GONZÁLEZ POSING AS A SOLDADERA, N.D.
Museo Frida Kahlo

lap [II.3].[23] She places her left leg in front of her right one, rendering her disability imperceptible. Her glossy black hair is parted at the centre and pulled back tightly. Two ornate flowerpots, the grid form created by closed double doors in the background and the geometrically patterned carpet make for a balanced and pleasing composition. The same day and in the same location, Guillermo shifted the orientation of the carpet, changed the positioning of other props, and took a series of group photographs of members of his extended family [II.4]. In several seemingly conventional pictures, Frida's mother, Matilde Calderón, sits in matronly fashion; Frida's sister, Cristina strikes a ladylike, coquettish pose; and the male relatives look dignified in their jackets and ties. Flaunting her unconventional spirit within this traditional-looking gathering, Frida distinguishes herself by donning a man's three-piece-suit. In additional photographs that comprise this series, she leans against a stylish walking stick like a dapper dandy, or wears a close-fitting cap that accentuates her masculine appearance.[24] All the photographs hide Frida's disability with elegant sophistication, project her flare for flamboyant and unconventional clothes and reveal her mesmerizing and exceptionally photogenic presence.

The close and loving relationship between Frida Kahlo and her first photographer – her father – has been studied in depth, based on visual and verbal testimonies by the artist herself.[25] However, a virtually overlooked fact, only uncovered when hitherto unknown family photographs were published by the Museo Frida Kahlo in 2010, is that in their youth, both of Kahlo's parents also posed for photographs in a variety of costumes. This may have inspired Kahlo later on. Guillermo Kahlo was an exceptional self-portraitist, who presented himself in various guises, and also posed in the nude. As a young woman, Kahlo's mother playfully posed wearing outlandish hats, but also dressed up as a *soldadera* [74][26] and in a traditional Tehuana costume, as her daughter would decades later [31].[27]

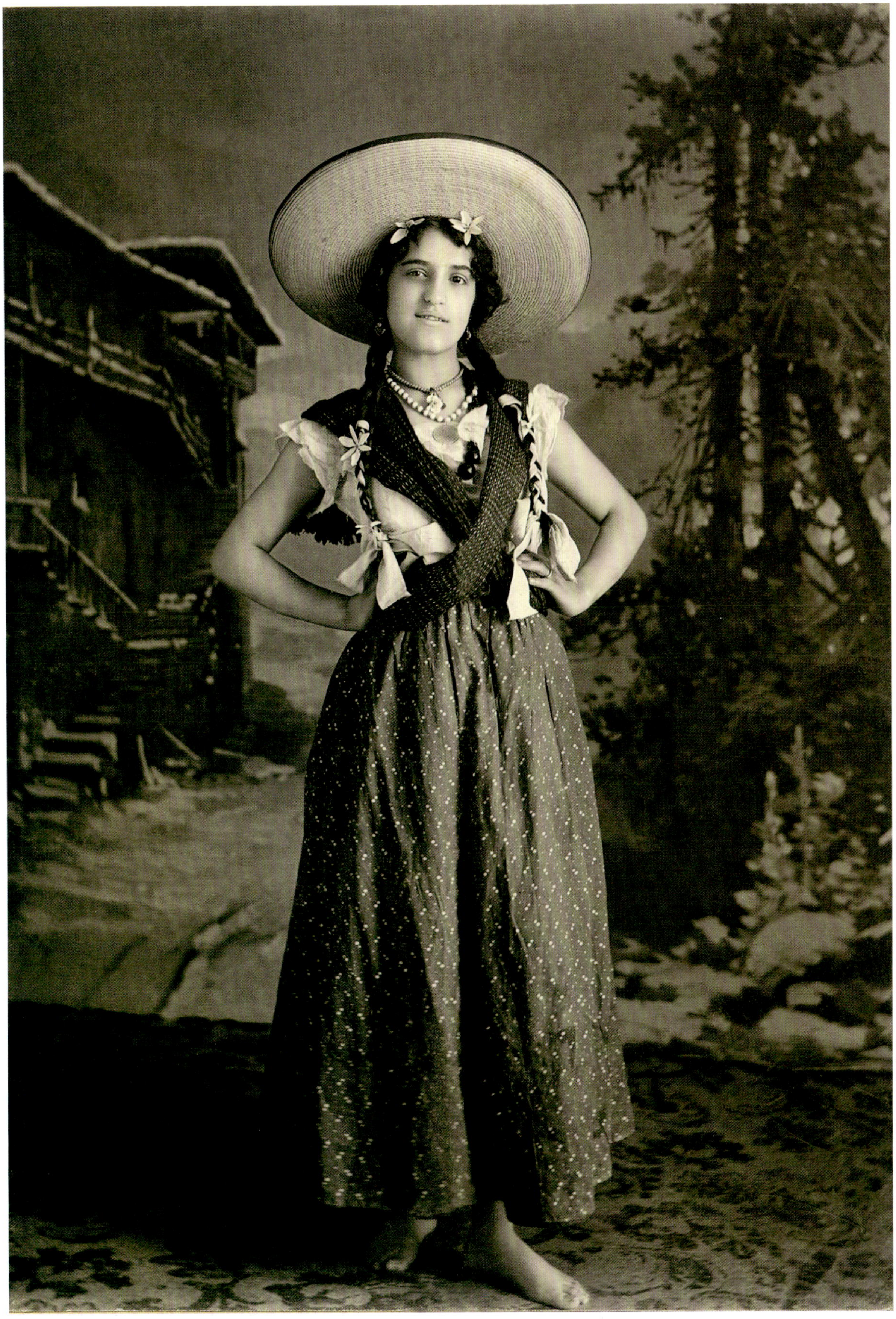

STYLING LA MEXICANA: ACCESSORIES, DRESSES AND TRESSES

As a disabled child, Kahlo was forced into a position of 'otherness'.[28] One of her coping mechanisms was to embrace her distinctiveness, embellish it and eventually construct unique and unconventional identities. She transformed being 'different' into being 'special'. This pattern continued with added force into adulthood. New material has recently come to light, which allows us to trace the chronology of Kahlo's sartorial development. The transformation seems to have begun in 1929, but accelerated after Kahlo and Rivera arrived in the United States in 1930, where her carefully choreographed indigenous Mexican costumes and jewellery were completely outside the norm.

Indeed, in post-revolutionary Mexico, and certainly within the social, political and cultural milieux in which Kahlo had been immersed since her teenage years at the National Preparatory School, the espousal of all things Mexican was a prevalent ideological position.[29] More specifically, indigenous costumes, especially from the Isthmus of Tehuantepec, were championed and often photographed, filmed, collected and worn in Mexico and even within the Kahlo-Calderón household. Outside Mexico, in sharp contrast, they were perceived as extraordinary, flamboyant, 'exotic' and extremely unusual.

Kahlo began to develop her native Mexican look gradually, with the aid of two accessories. Both items – her *rebozo* (Mexican shawl) and an Aztec necklace – first appear in photographs of Kahlo from 1929 and link her to Rivera. While posing for her 1929 wedding portrait, Kahlo dons a *rebozo* for the first time [67]. Grimberg has observed that from that day forth, the *rebozo* is the garment that Kahlo would wear most often:

> It may not be a coincidence if one considers that in some parts of Mexico a man gives a *rebozo* to the woman he wishes to marry instead of a ring, which is likely in Kahlo and Rivera's case for she never wore a wedding band. Thereafter, photographs of her wearing the garment are seen with growing frequency. Kahlo becomes as inseparable from her *rebozos* as children from their security blankets.[30]

The second item, a gift from Rivera, is an Aztec necklace of round jade beads punctuated by a flat central stone, inscribed with the Nahuatl glyph 'Nahui Olin'. The necklace adorns Kahlo's neck in photographs and paintings from 1929 and 1931 [II.5 and p.2].[31] By wearing a pre-Columbian necklace, Kahlo asserts her identification with indigenous Mexican culture. The specific Nahuatl glyph is a coded reference to one of Rivera's former lovers, and positions Kahlo as Rivera's woman.[32] Kahlo's espousal of the Aztec 'Nahui Olin' necklace is one of many examples of the artist's overt embrace of *Mexicanidad* and coded expression of more personal messages. Hence, for example, the coral bead necklace from the Museo Frida Kahlo [III.3] is a clear celebration of indigenous belonging. However, the silver legs threaded between the beads, recall popular *Milagros*, and allude to Kahlo's maimed limb. The more contemporary Matilde Poulat necklace [III.7] includes the yin-yang symbol that also pervaded Kahlo's drawings and diary entries and influenced her worldview and compositions (for example, *The Love Embrace*) during the last decade of her life.

In November 1930, Kahlo and Rivera travelled to San Francisco, where Rivera was commissioned to paint a mural at the San Francisco Stock Exchange.[33] It was there that Kahlo proceeded to assemble her repertoire of accessories, dresses and tresses. This was Kahlo's first trip outside of Mexico and she relished every moment. Her extensive correspondence from this time reveals her excitement and childlike joy at discovering a brand new world: 'San Francisco is very beautiful. Our way here was also very beautiful. For the first time I got to see the Ocean, and I loved it! The city is in a beautiful location, from everywhere you can see the sea. The bay is beautiful and ships arrive from China and from everywhere in the Orient...'.

Kahlo wrote at length about Chinatown and other ethnic enclaves in the city, which she happily explored. Residing on Montgomery Street, just a few short blocks from San Francisco's bustling Chinatown, Kahlo cultivated her budding predilection for exuberant fabrics, handmade embroideries and ethnic crafts: 'Imagine', she wrote to her '*Papacito lindo*' ('dearest daddy') with enthusiasm: 'there are 10,000 Chinese here, in their shops they sell beautiful things, clothing and handmade fabrics

75. EDWARD WESTON
FRIDA KAHLO AND DIEGO RIVERA, SAN FRANCISCO, 1930
GELATIN SILVER PRINT. 24.3 × 19 CM
Center for Creative Photography, University of Arizona, Tuscon 81.276.1

of very fine silk, when I return I'll tell you all about it in detail.'[34] By the time she did return to Mexico (in May 1931), she had acquired multiple Chinese items, which she would later integrate into her wardrobe.[35]

In addition to discovering this new and beautiful world, Kahlo discovered who she wanted to become and how to use her clothing to compose this spectacular persona. 'The *gringas* really like me a lot and pay close attention to all the dresses and *rebozos* that I brought with me, their jaws drop at the sight of my jade necklaces,' she wrote to her '*Mamacita linda*' ('dearest mummy') on 21 November 1930, soon after her arrival.[36] Increasingly aware of the sway and impact of her exotic-looking appearance and bold sense of style, Kahlo thrived in the limelight. 'All the painters want me to pose for them', she wrote home with unbridled delight.[37]

Kahlo's self-styled persona became a sensation. A newspaper article about Rivera's revolutionary art, included references to his exotic spouse: 'Frida, Diego's beautiful young wife, is part of the picture. She wears the native costume, a tight-bodied, full-skirted muslin dress, the classic *rebozo* draped about her shoulders and a massive string of Aztec beads about her slender brown throat.'[38] The writer John M. Weatherwax composed a play and a short story about Kahlo entitled *The Queen of Montgomery Street* (c.1930). Referring to Kahlo as an enchanting regal presence, Weatherwax wrote:

> Everyone has been looking at her. She is bewitching in her long, high-waisted grass-green dress. Over her shoulder is a bronze open-work shawl. About her neck is a heavy jade-green *chalchihuitl* necklace. Her black hair is parted in the middle and drawn into a little knot at the back of her neck. Her cheeks and lips have just the right amount of rouge.[39]

Much to her delight, many of the best photographers in the world took pictures of this newly minted, self-styled Kahlo. Edward Weston recalled:

> I photographed Diego again, his new wife – Frieda – too: she is … petite, a little doll alongside Diego, but a doll in size only, for she is strong and quite beautiful, shows very little of her father's German

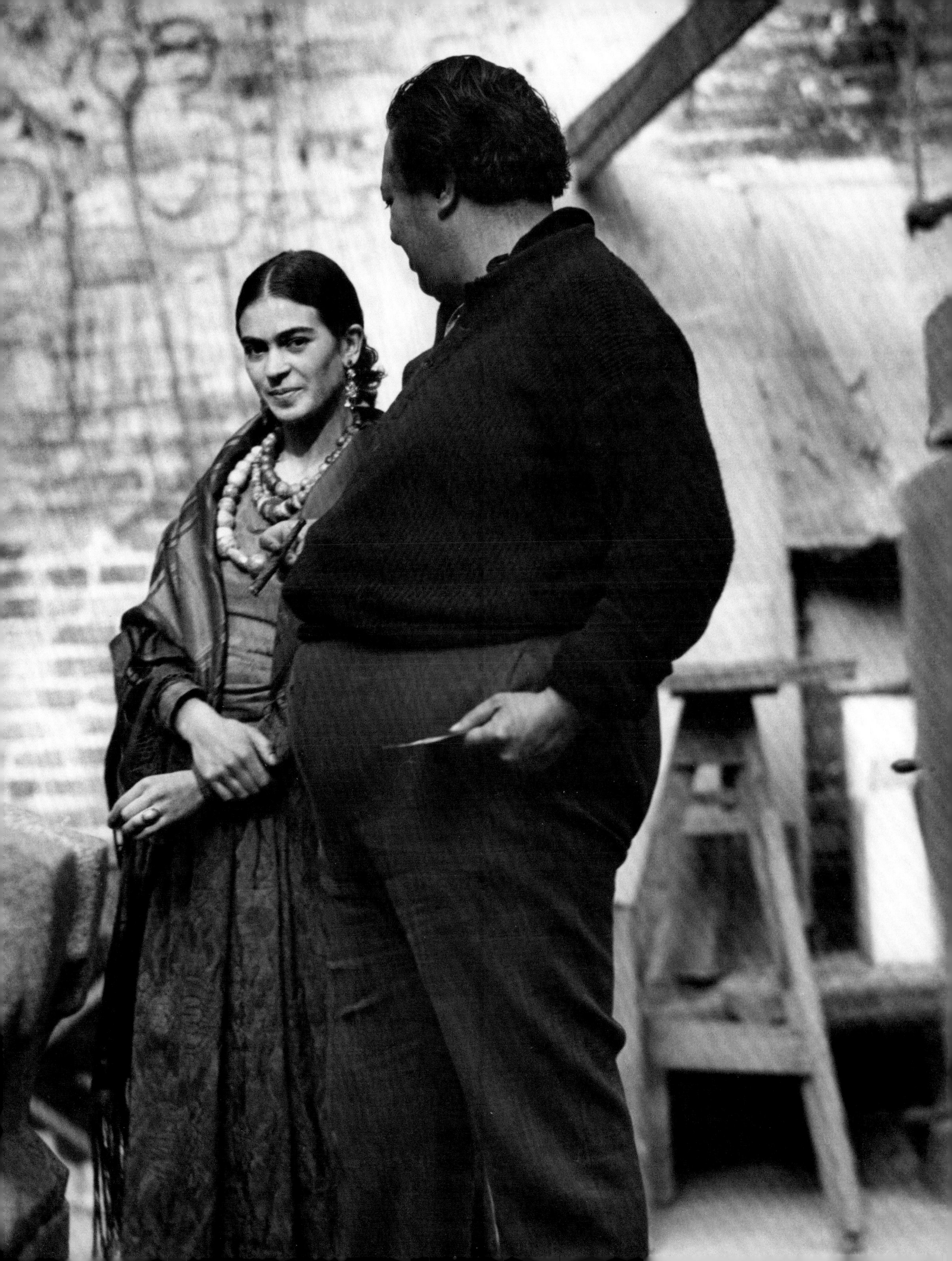

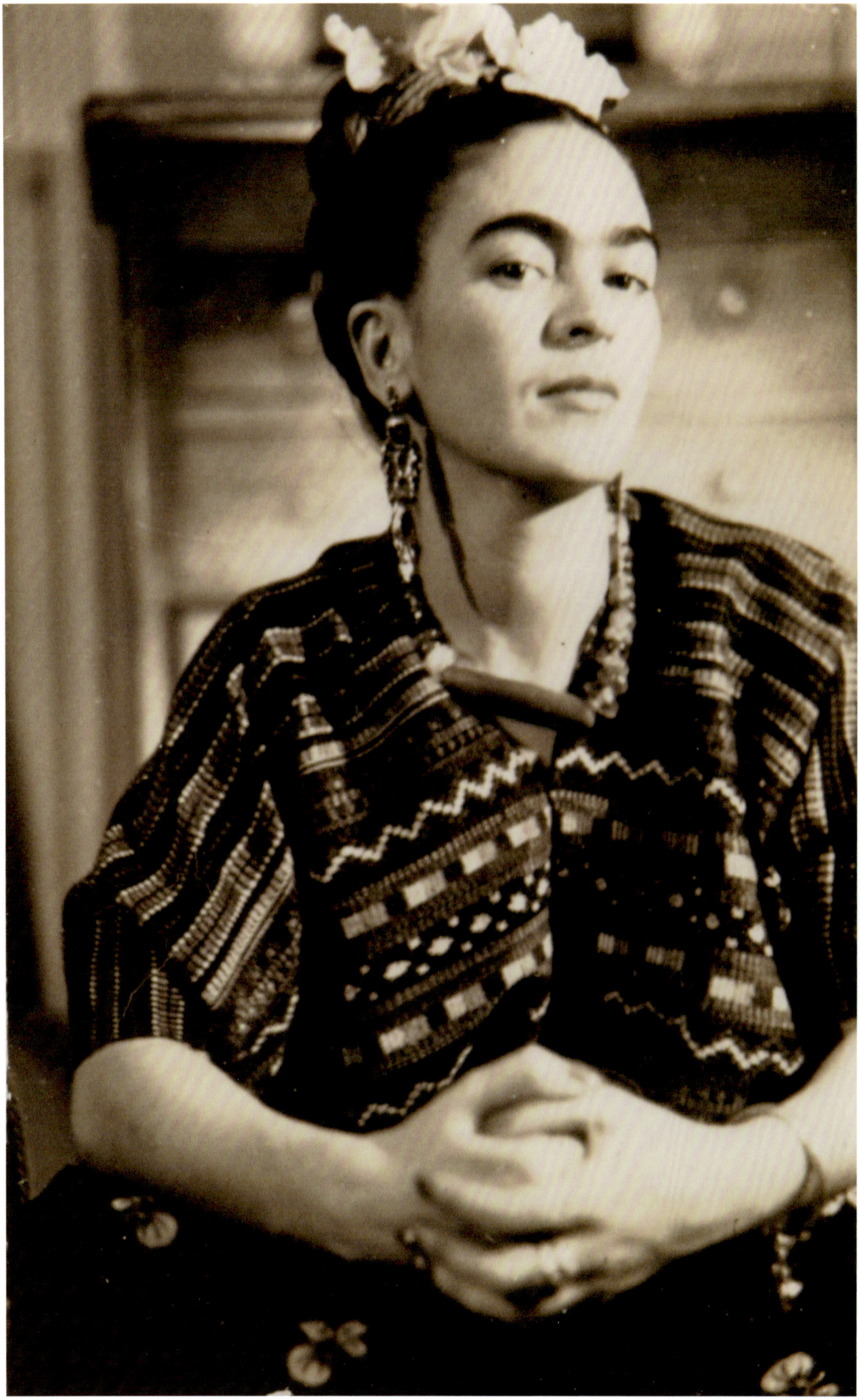

76. JULIEN LEVY
FRIDA KAHLO, C.1938
GELATIN SILVER PRINT. 3.4 × 2.2 CM
Philadelphia Museum of Art
125th Anniversary Acquisition. The Lynne and Harold Honickman Gift of the Julien Levy Collection, 2001.
2001-62-609

77. JULIEN LEVY
FRIDA KAHLO, C.1938
STRIPS OF CONTACT PRINTS. 3.7 × 2.5 CM
Philadelphia Museum of Art
125th Anniversary Acquisition. The Lynne and Harold Honickman Gift of the Julien Levy Collection, 2001.
2001-62-620 (negs. 15 and 16); 2001-62-621 (negs. 17 and 18); 2001-62-619 (negs. 21 and 22); 2001-62-617 (negs. 23 and 24)

> blood. Dressed in native costume even to huaraches, she causes much excitement on the streets of San Francisco. People stop in their tracks to look in wonder [75].[40]

Following her San Francisco sojourn, Kahlo identified with her image as *La Mexicana* to such an extent that in three paintings from the 1930s, an empty Tehuana costume appears as the artist's alter-ego. Elsewhere I have analyzed the multi-layered iconographies of *My Dress Hangs There* (1933) [96], *Memory* (1937) [71] and *What the Water Gave Me* (1938).[41]

In addition to the sumptuous indigenous costumes and the eclectic assortment of accessories and jewellery she accumulated, Kahlo also developed elaborate coiffures that framed her distinct facial features. By 1938, when she had her first and only solo exhibition in New York (at the Julien Levy Gallery), Kahlo's hairdo was already an integral part of her iconic look. Levy himself professed to have been totally infatuated with Kahlo, who flirted with him while also 'carrying on' with other suitors [76]. In addition to this, he was fascinated by what he termed 'Frida's litany of arranging her hair' and convinced her to let him photograph her in the process of braiding and fixing her hair. This series of private photographs show a topless Kahlo unbraiding her hair with expertise and flair [77].[42]

The 1 November 1938 issue of US *Vogue* magazine published an article entitled 'The Rise of Another Rivera' in conjunction with the Julien Levy exhibition. Penned by Bertram Wolfe (Rivera's biographer and by now a close friend of both Kahlo and Rivera), it was one of the earliest texts that addressed Kahlo's paintings, and the first to link her self-fashioning with her art:

> From the bright, fuzzy, woolen strings that she plaits into her black hair and the color she puts into her cheeks and lips, to her heavy antique Mexican necklaces and her gaily colored Tehuana blouses and skirts, Madame Rivera seems herself a product of her art, and, like her work, one that is instinctively and calculatingly well composed.[43]

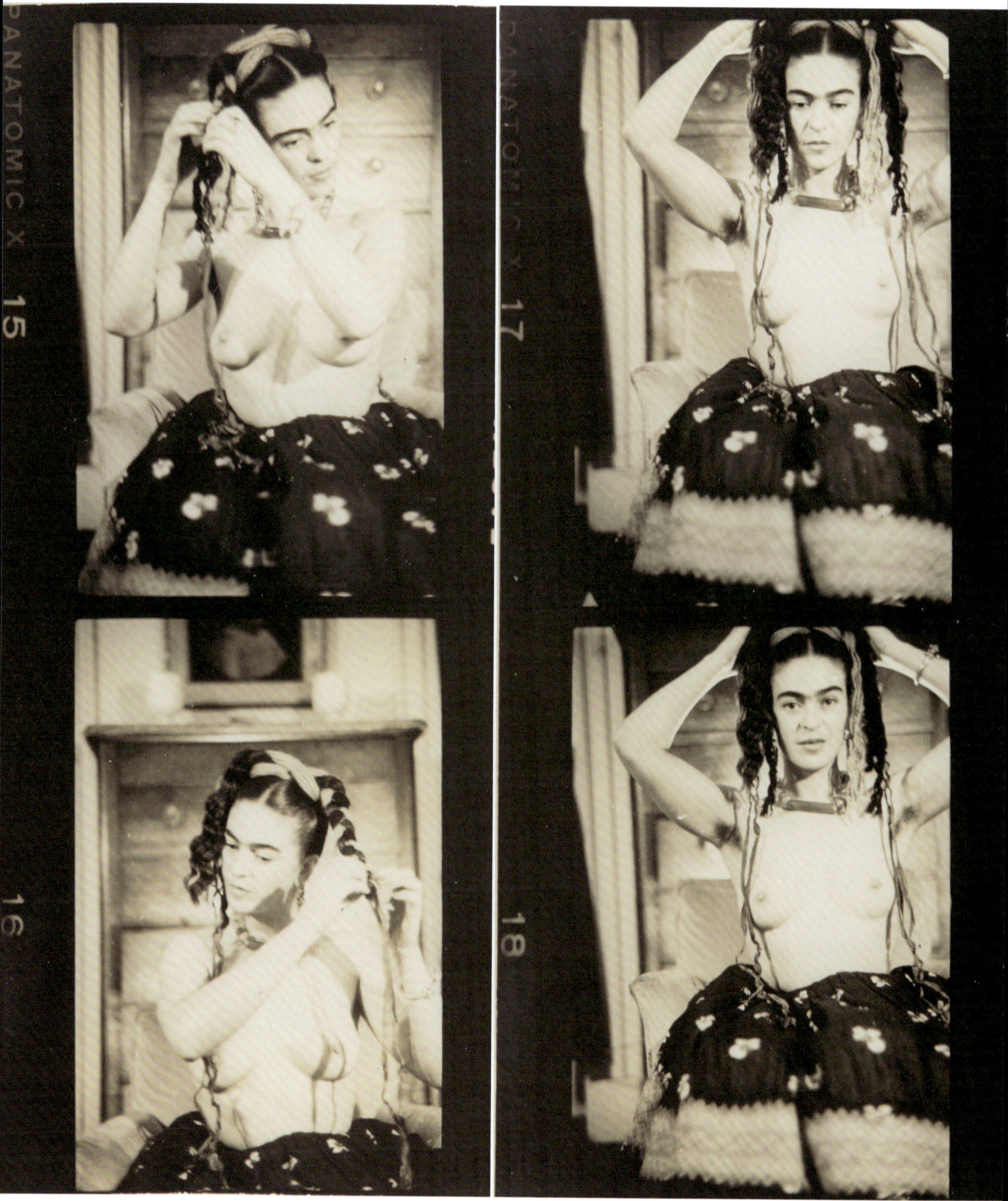
PANATOMIC X 15
16
PANATOMIC X 17
18

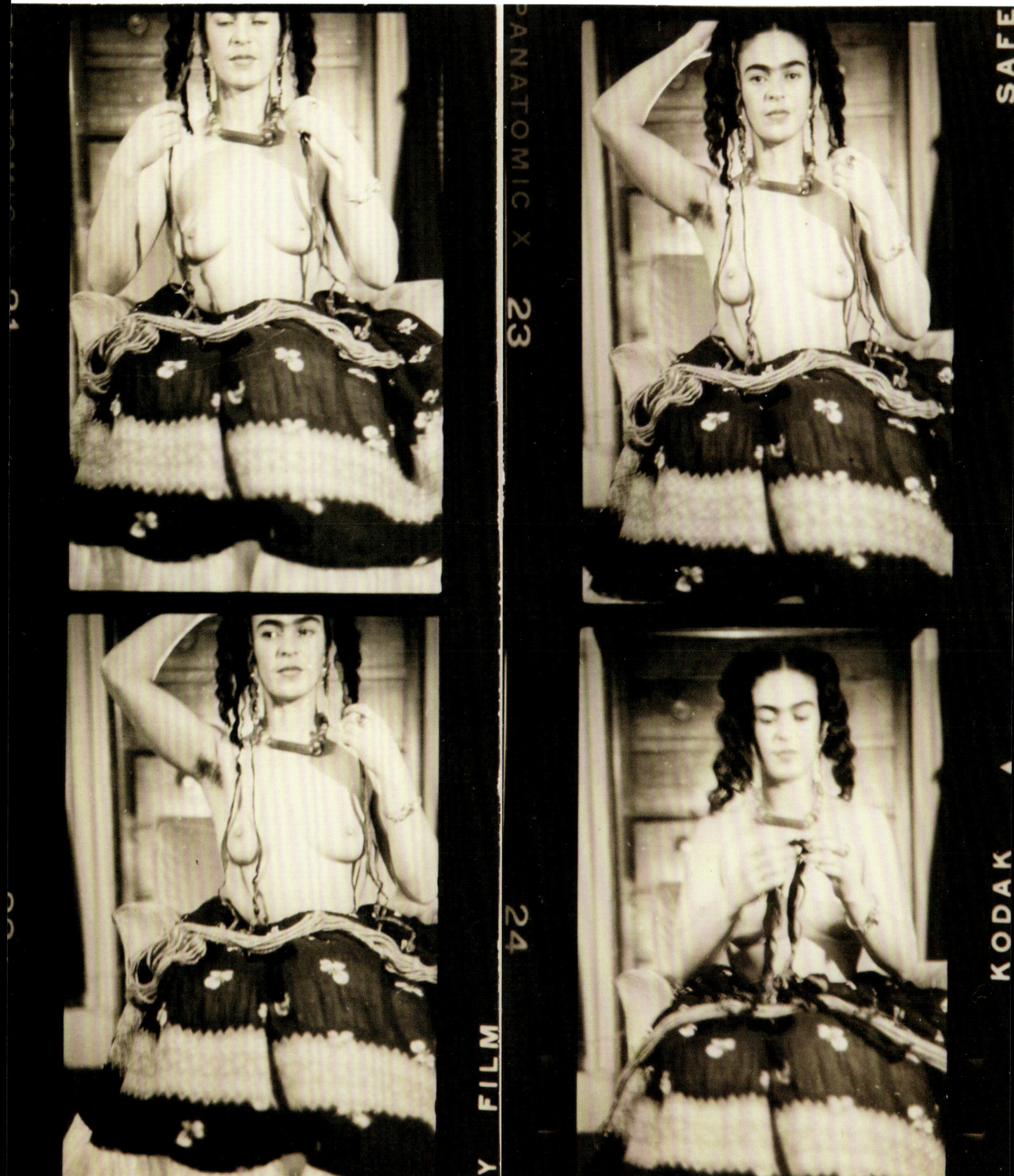
PANATOMIC X
23
24
SAFE
KODAK
FILM

78. FRIDA KAHLO
THE BROKEN COLUMN, 1944
OIL ON CANVAS. 40 × 30.5 CM
Museo Dolores Olmedo Patiño, Mexico City

THE GREAT CONCEALER

The 'well composed' Madame Rivera – described by Wolfe and immortalized in numerous stunning photographs – appeared impeccable and spectacular. Countless people who had encountered Kahlo since the 1930s, stressed her regal, extraordinary and seamless self-presentation. But Kahlo's drawings and paintings reveal that the seemingly perfect appearance was, in fact, a façade. In a newly discovered drawing, Kahlo depicts her costume as camouflage. Rendering her clothes transparent, she allows us to peer through the layers and observe the medical corset and the mismatched legs underneath her colourful costume. The drawing also penetrates her body to expose the broken column hidden behind the mask of *La Mexicana* [38]. Driving this point home, Kahlo scribed a caption just above her signature, verbalizing what the image asserts: that 'Appearances can be Deceiving'. Other paintings by Kahlo, among them *The Broken Column*, likewise strip away the façade to expose Kahlo's broken body, medical apparatus and internal wounds [78]. *Tree of Hope*, painted after Kahlo's spinal fusion operation in 1946, is a double self-portrait [80]. On the right, a fully dressed, bejewelled, coiffed and adorned Kahlo sits in a wooden chair holding a medical corset and a flag in her hands. She seems to be wearing a second corset underneath her clothes. Behind her, another portrait of Kahlo, covered by a white sheet, appears lying upon a gurney, her back partially exposed, her hair dishevelled, her face completely hidden from view. This horizontal figure is based on a photograph by Nickolas Muray [79]. Two bloody incisions on Kahlo's back reference the surgical procedure she underwent in New York.[44] Kahlo's divided and broken sense of self, visualized in this painting as two distinct 'Fridas', is echoed in other elements of the composition, including the binary sun and moon; night and day; and the fissured stony landscape.

Addressing Kahlo's inner conflicts and tenuous sense of identity, her lifelong friend, Alejandro Gómez Arias, reflected: 'Who was Frida Kahlo? It is not possible to find an exact answer. So contradictory and multiple was the personality of this woman, that it may be said that many Fridas existed. Perhaps none of them was the one she wanted to be.'[45]

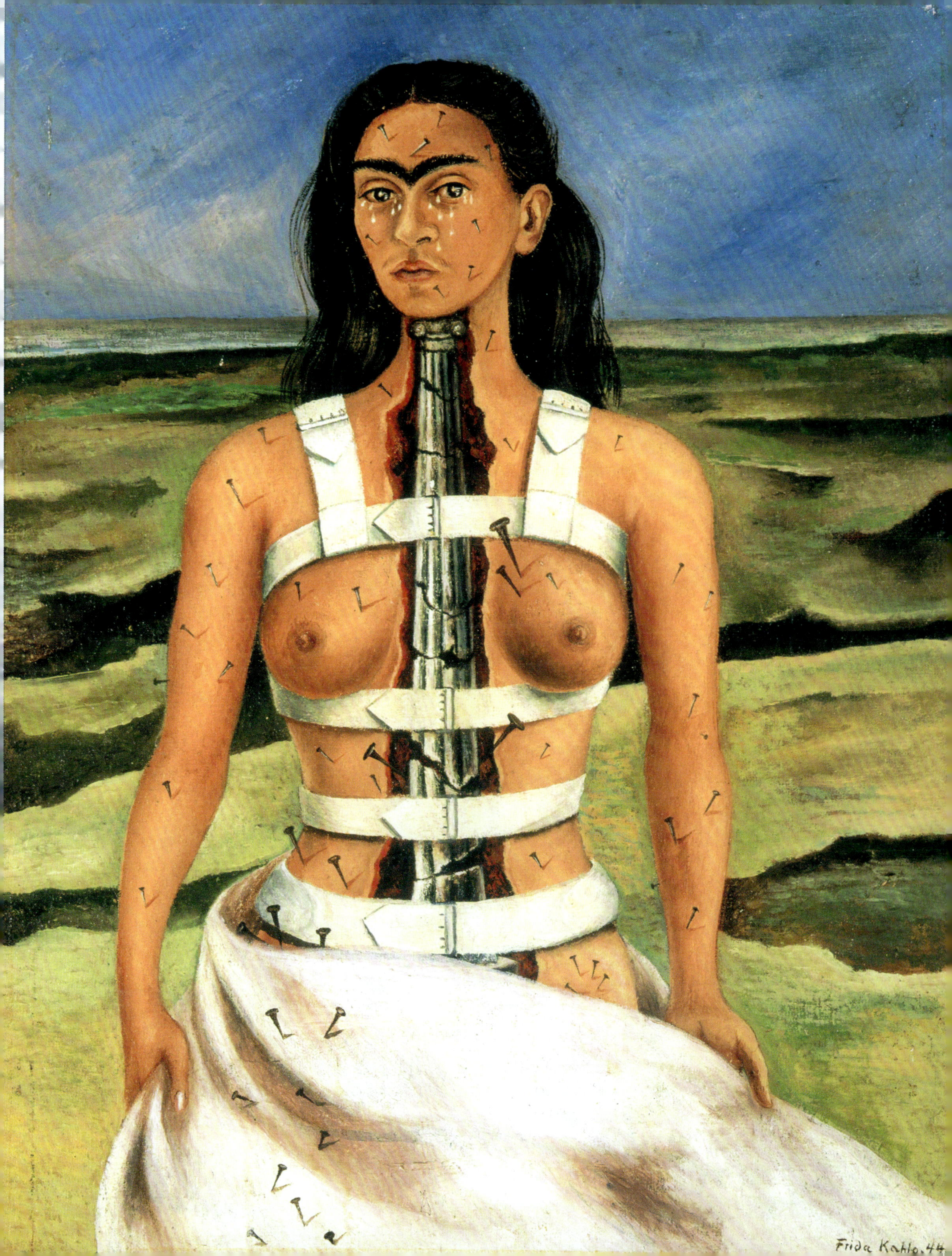
Frida Kahlo. 44

79. NICKOLAS MURAY
FRIDA KAHLO IN NEW YORK, 1946
Nickolas Muray Photo Archives

80. FRIDA KAHLO
TREE OF HOPE, KEEP FIRM, 1946
OIL ON HARDBOARD. 55.9 × 40.6 CM
Private collection

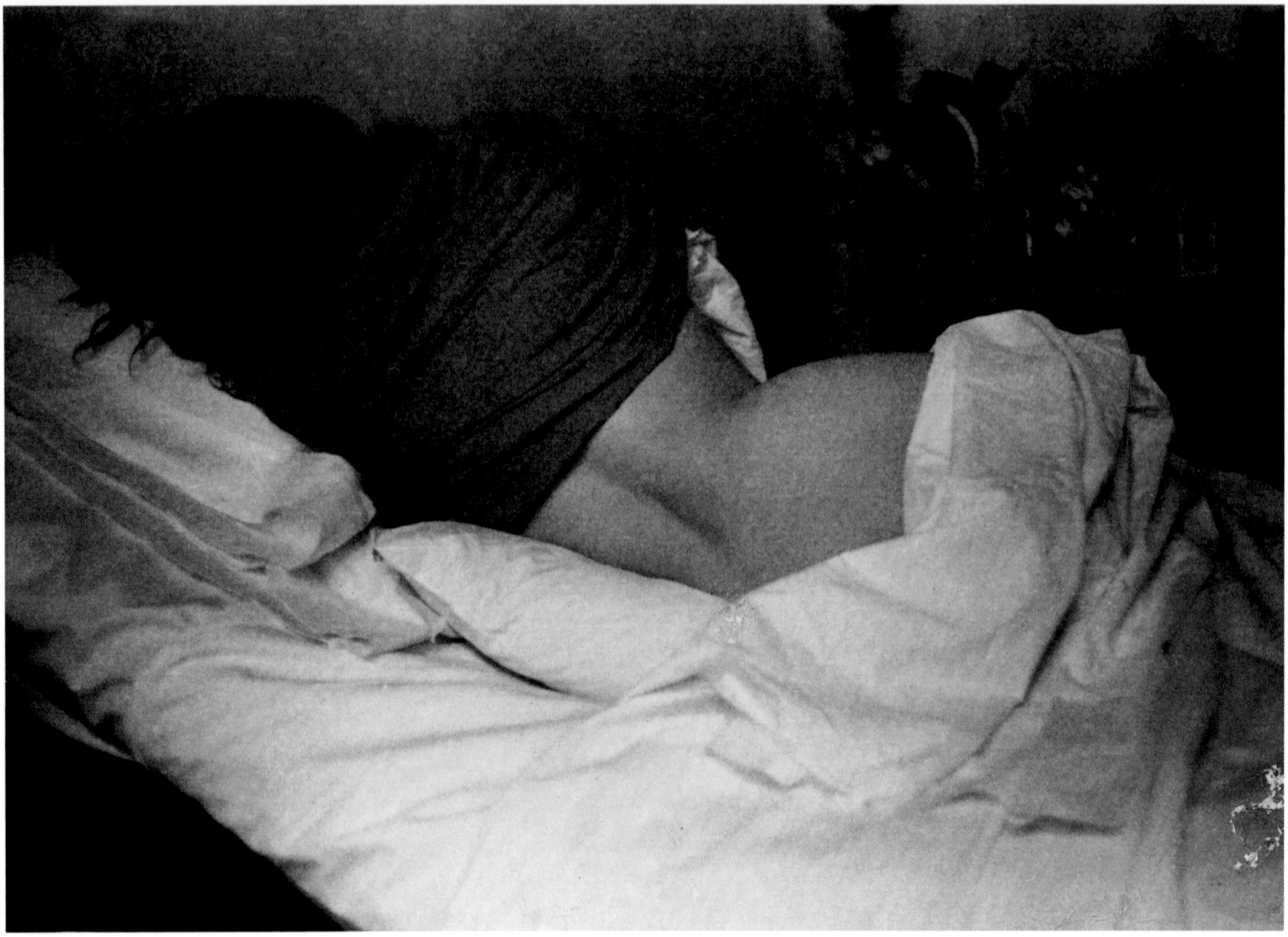

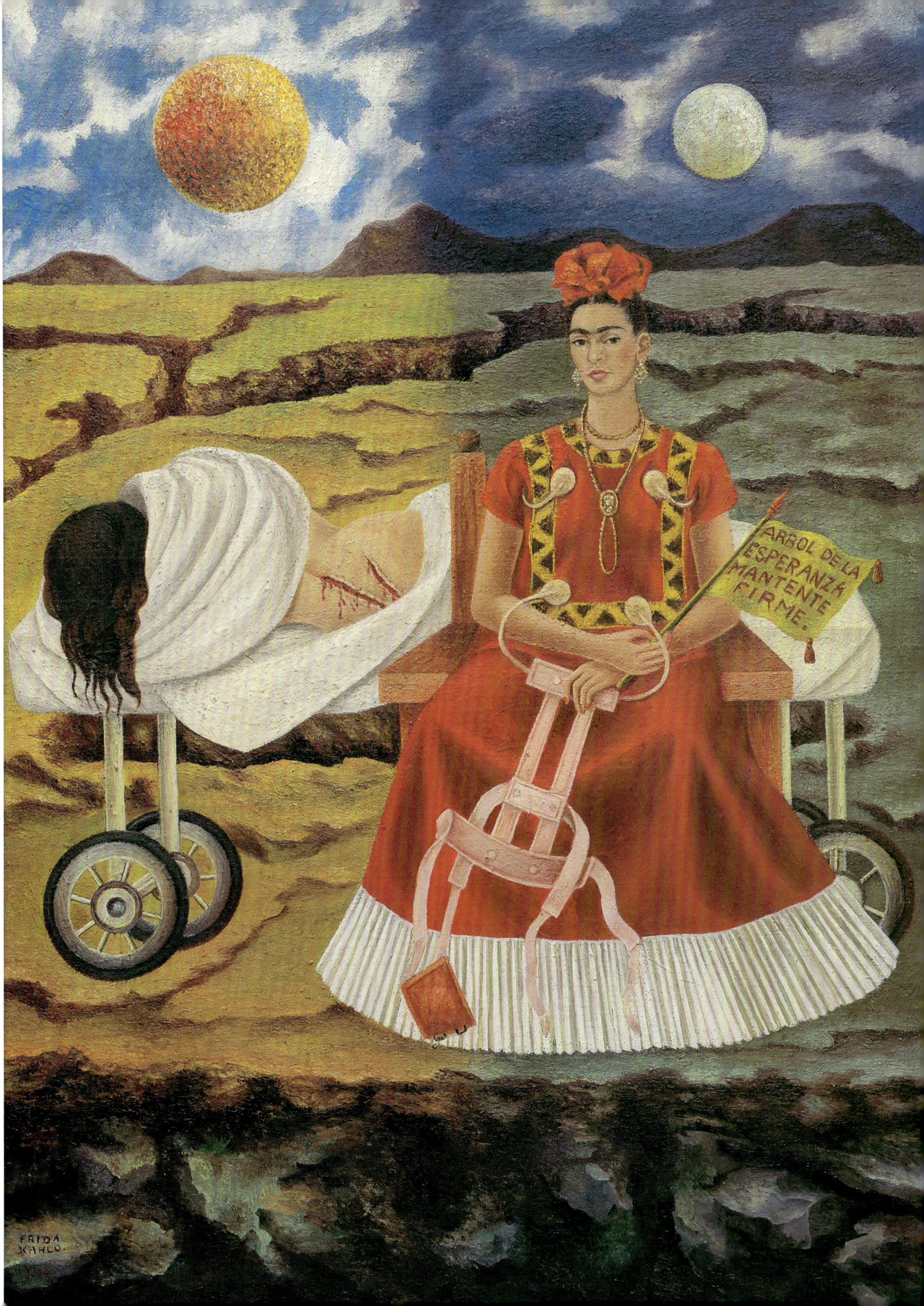

ARBOL DE LA
ESPERANZA
MANTENTE
FIRME.
FRIDA
KAHLO.

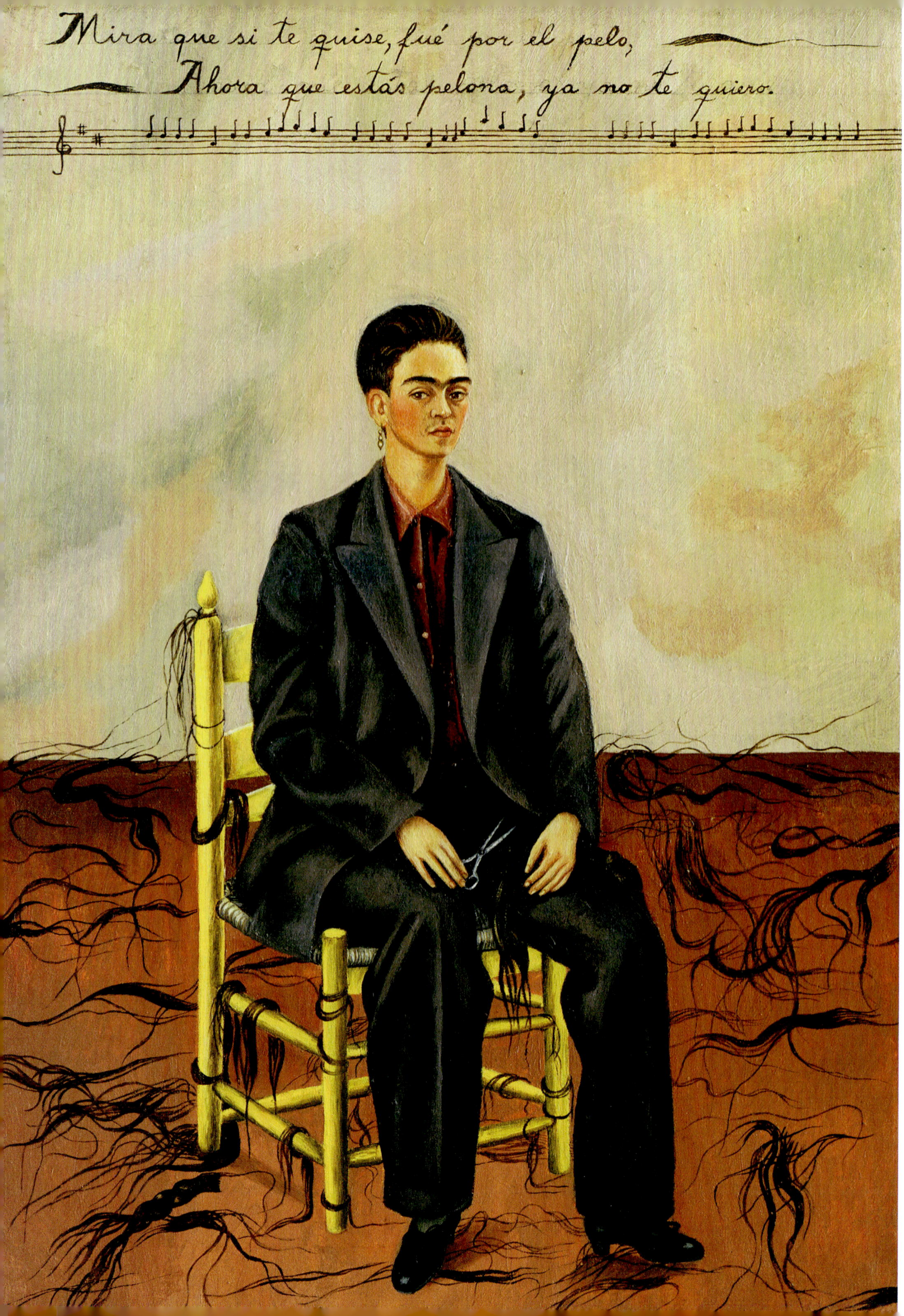
Mira que si te quise, fué por el pelo,
Ahora que estás pelona, ya no te quiero.

81. FRIDA KAHLO
SELF-PORTRAIT WITH CROPPED HAIR, 1940
OIL ON CANVAS. 40 × 28 CM
Museum of Modern Art, New York. 3.1943

The inner schisms that plagued Kahlo went well beyond the gap between her elaborate Tehuana façade and her broken and ailing body. Kahlo's paintings expose many additional fissures and contradictions that riddled her complex identities. For example, her 'feminine' coiffure of beribboned braids decked with colourful yarn and flowers sharply contrasts with her accentuated unibrow and emphatically painted moustache. Kahlo's 1940 *Self-Portrait with Cropped Hair* presents an explicit – and thoroughly studied – example of Kahlo performing her gender non-conforming identity [81]. In other paintings, for example, *Las Dos Fridas*, she explores her mixed cultural heritage and her failed attempt to fit into conventional gender roles, like 'wife' and 'mother' [82]. In other paintings, she espouses the clothes and attributes of a 'Crowned Nun', a Christ figure, *La Llorona* and *La Malinche*.[46]

Kahlo's multiple identities also manifested themselves in the nomenclature she adopted. She took on names that alluded to her German, Mexican, Nahuatl and Hindu affiliations, marking her multiple modes of being in the world. Yet perhaps the most telling name of all, used by her and Rivera, relates to her masking and camouflaging propensities. It was Kahlo who aptly named herself 'The Great Concealer'.[47]

82. FRIDA KAHLO
THE TWO FRIDAS, 1939
OIL ON CANVAS. 173.5 × 173 CM
Museo de Arte Moderno, Conaculta-INBA, Mexico

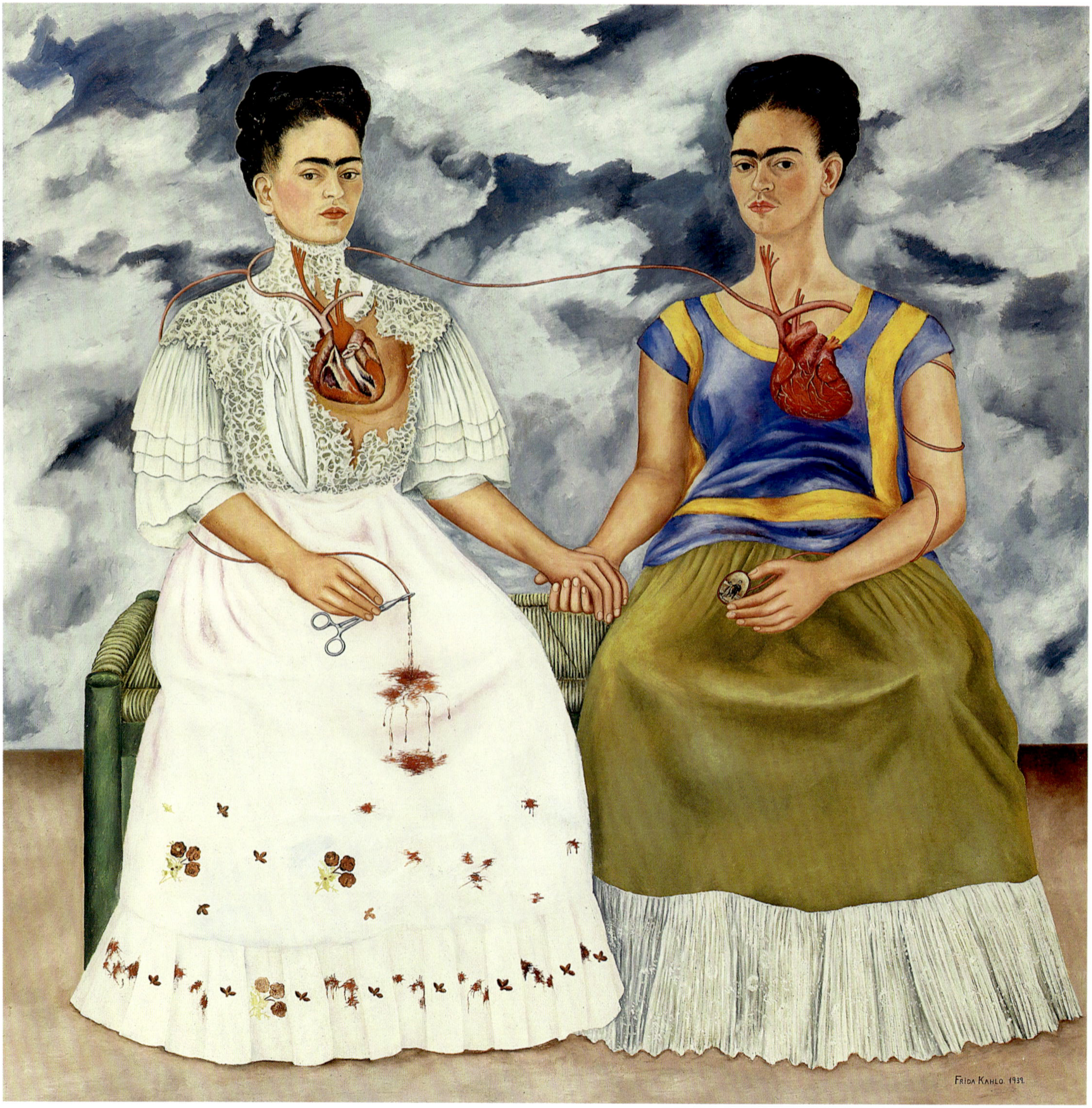

pp.160–1
REBOZO; DETAIL OF RAPACEJO (KNOTTED FRINGE), SEE P.110
Museo Frida Kahlo

CODA: DECOMPOSING

During a tearful interview in the 1960s, Judith Ferretto, Kahlo's devoted nurse and caretaker, recounted the last year of the artist's life. Kahlo's deteriorating medical condition transformed the vivacious Kahlo into a homebound and often bedridden woman. She could hardly paint, but when she did, Ferretto would place her in her wheelchair and secure her by tying her *rebozo* to the back of the chair in order to help her sit up straight. At this point, it was the nurse who bathed, dressed and adorned Kahlo and pleated her hair 'like a child's'. The headboard of Kahlo's bed became a repository for photographs, reminding the artist of her glory days and keeping pictures of her loved ones close. The end was inevitable after the amputation of Kahlo's right leg. Ferretto recalled arriving at the Blue House and finding a desperate and unkempt Kahlo in crisis, completely dishevelled, with her hair in disarray and her clothes dirty. Ferretto bathed her, dressed her up and fixed her hair, allowing Kahlo to regain a semblance of her previous self. At that moment, Ferretto said, she knew that Kahlo would never recover: Kahlo's dresses and tresses were such an integral part of her identity that for her to abandon these aspects of her being was a harbinger of her death.[48]

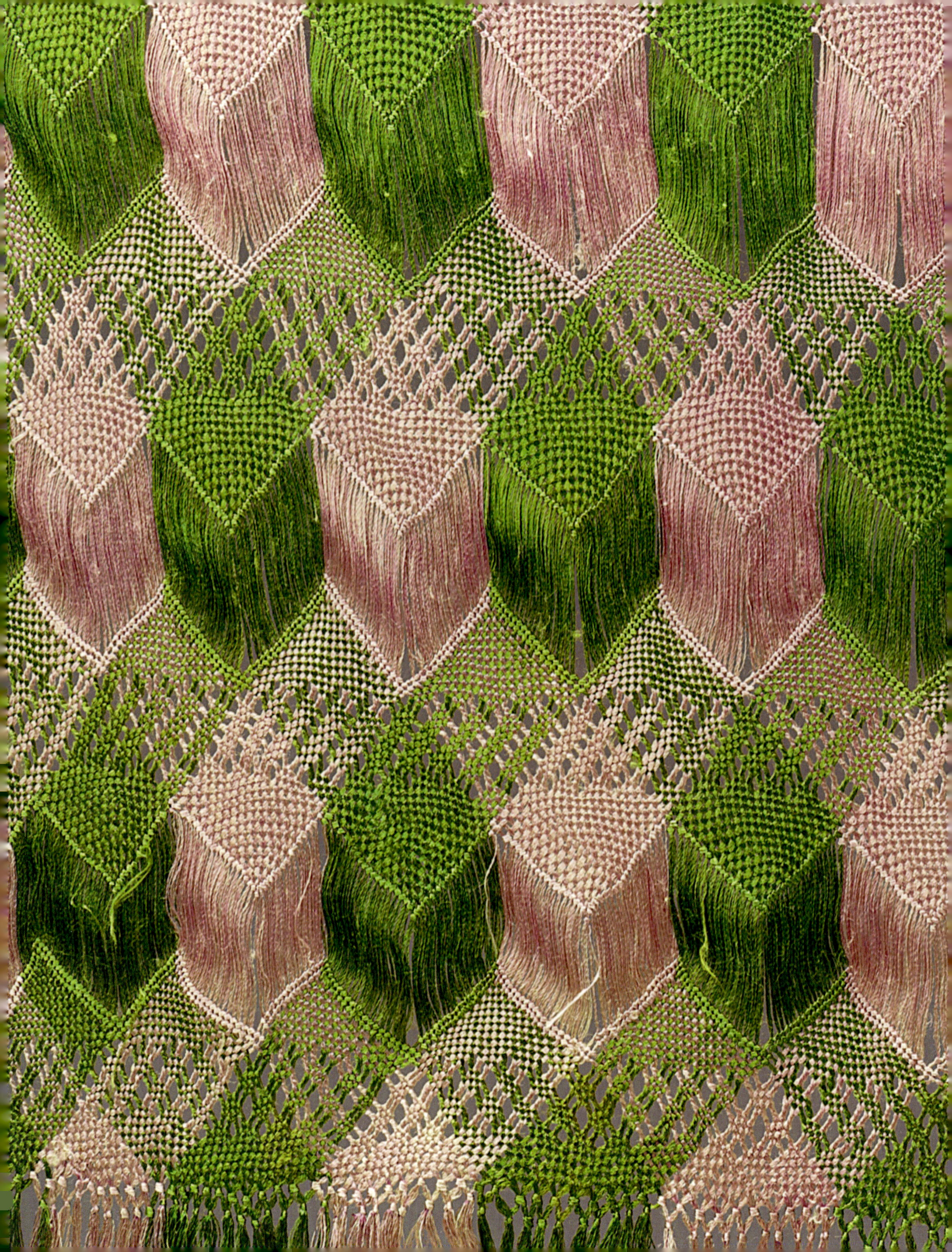

pp.160–1
REBOZO; DETAIL OF RAPACEJO (KNOTTED FRINGE), SEE P.110
Museo Frida Kahlo

CODA: DECOMPOSING

During a tearful interview in the 1960s, Judith Ferretto, Kahlo's devoted nurse and caretaker, recounted the last year of the artist's life. Kahlo's deteriorating medical condition transformed the vivacious Kahlo into a homebound and often bedridden woman. She could hardly paint, but when she did, Ferretto would place her in her wheelchair and secure her by tying her *rebozo* to the back of the chair in order to help her sit up straight. At this point, it was the nurse who bathed, dressed and adorned Kahlo and pleated her hair 'like a child's'. The headboard of Kahlo's bed became a repository for photographs, reminding the artist of her glory days and keeping pictures of her loved ones close. The end was inevitable after the amputation of Kahlo's right leg. Ferretto recalled arriving at the Blue House and finding a desperate and unkempt Kahlo in crisis, completely dishevelled, with her hair in disarray and her clothes dirty. Ferretto bathed her, dressed her up and fixed her hair, allowing Kahlo to regain a semblance of her previous self. At that moment, Ferretto said, she knew that Kahlo would never recover: Kahlo's dresses and tresses were such an integral part of her identity that for her to abandon these aspects of her being was a harbinger of her death.[48]

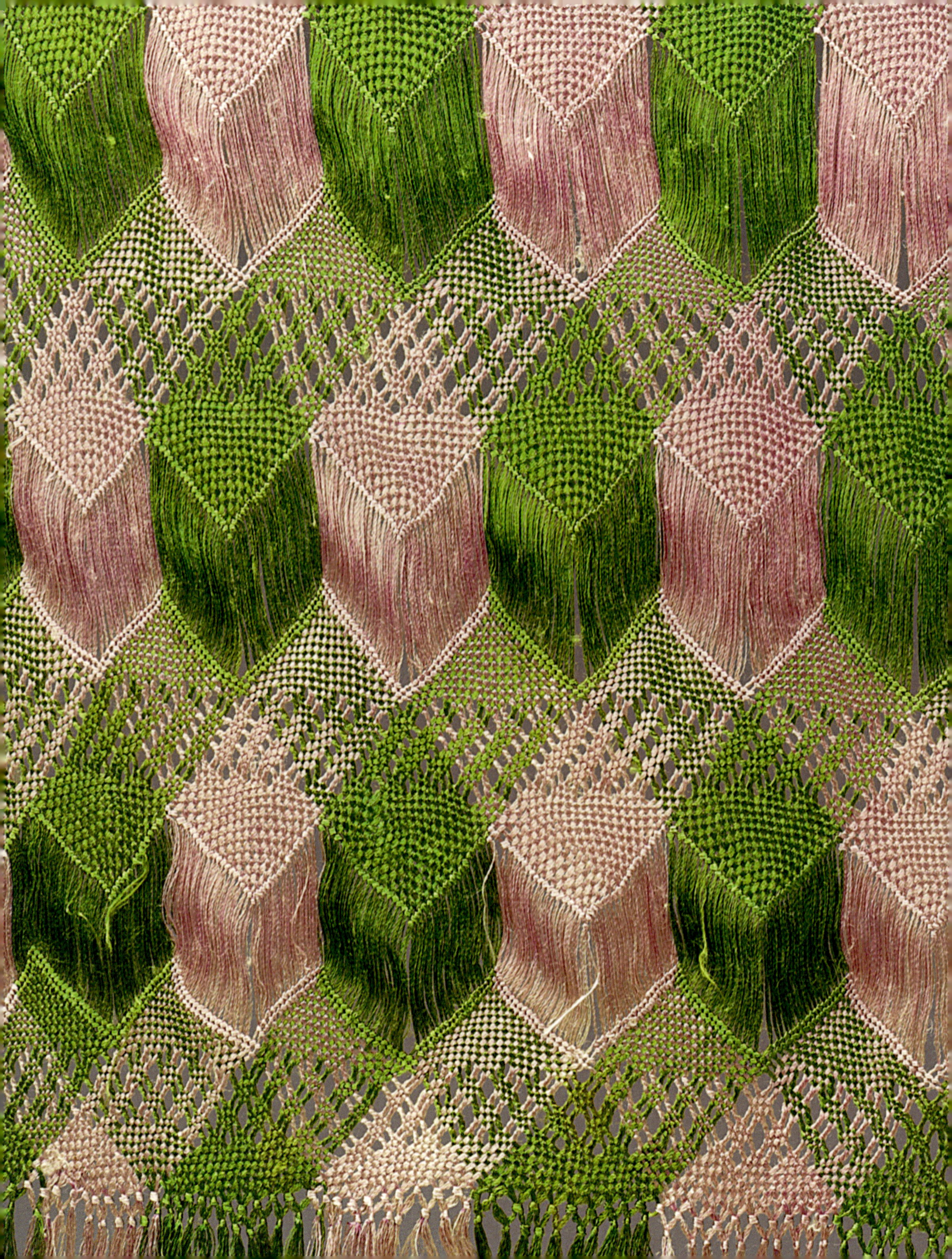

GUILLERMO KAHLO
SELF-PORTRAIT, C.1907
GELATIN SILVER PRINT. 16.3 × 8.5 CM
Museo Frida Kahlo

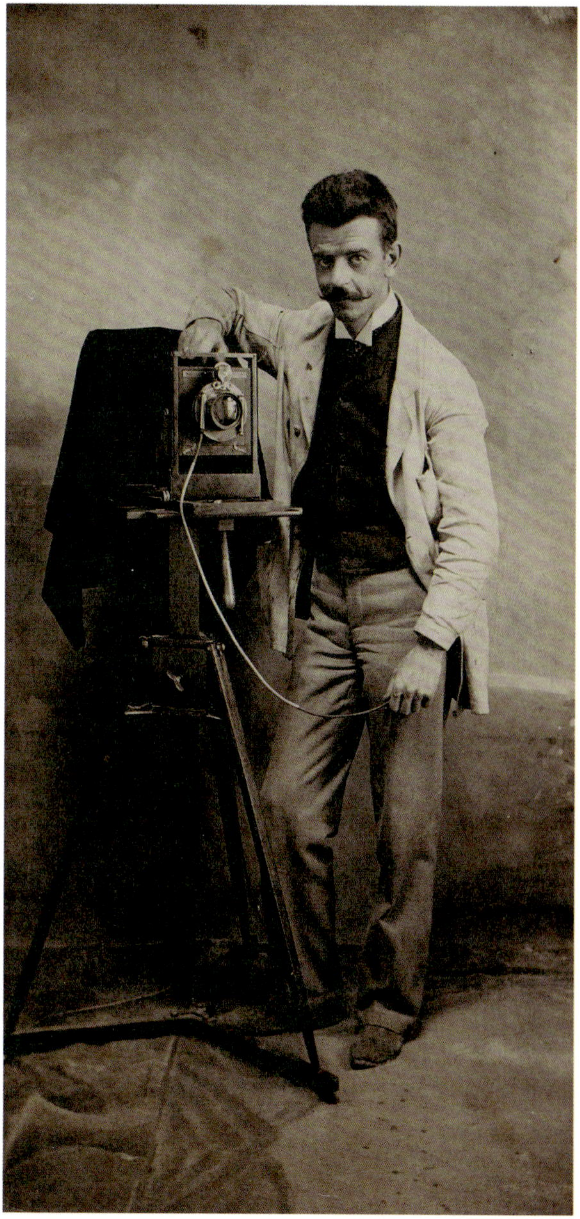

I.7

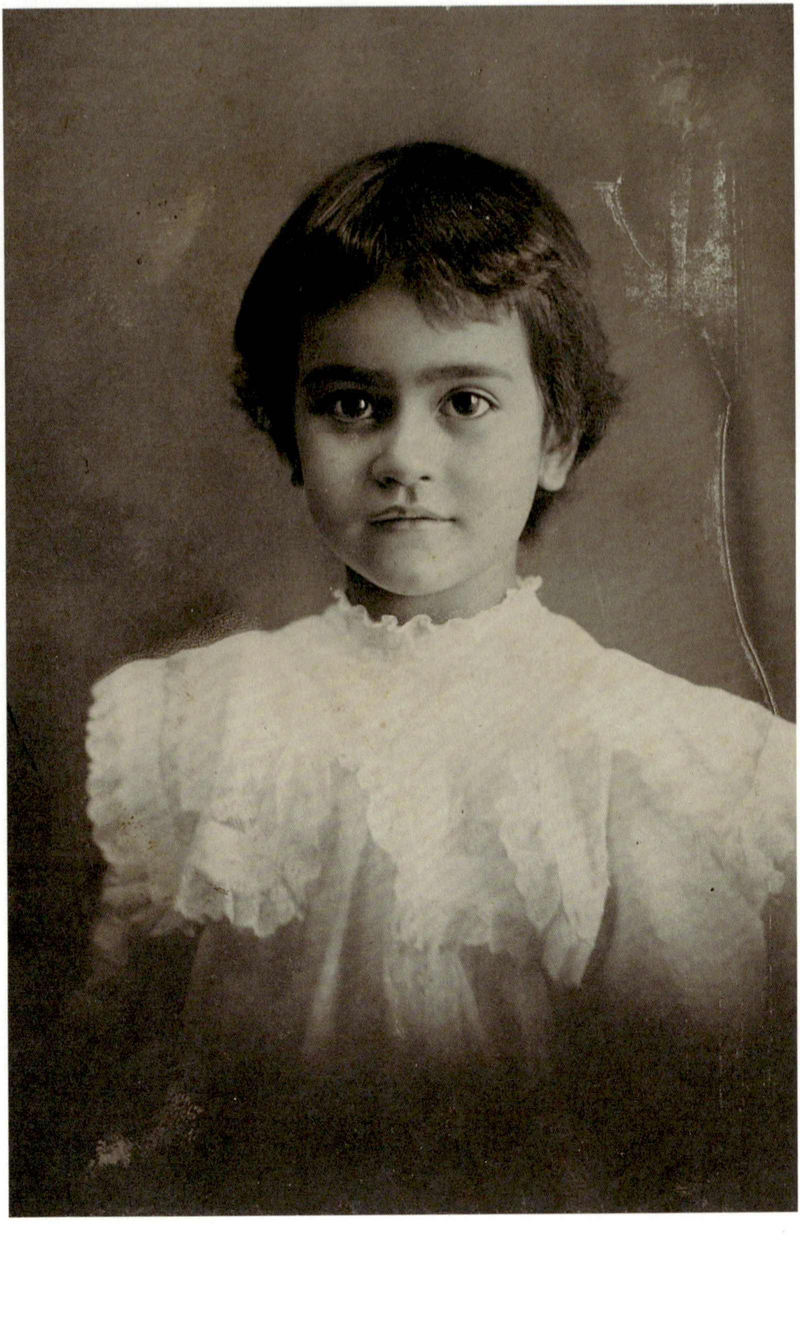

I.2

GUILLERMO KAHLO
SELF-PORTRAIT, C.1907
GELATIN SILVER PRINT. 16.3 × 8.5 CM
Museo Frida Kahlo

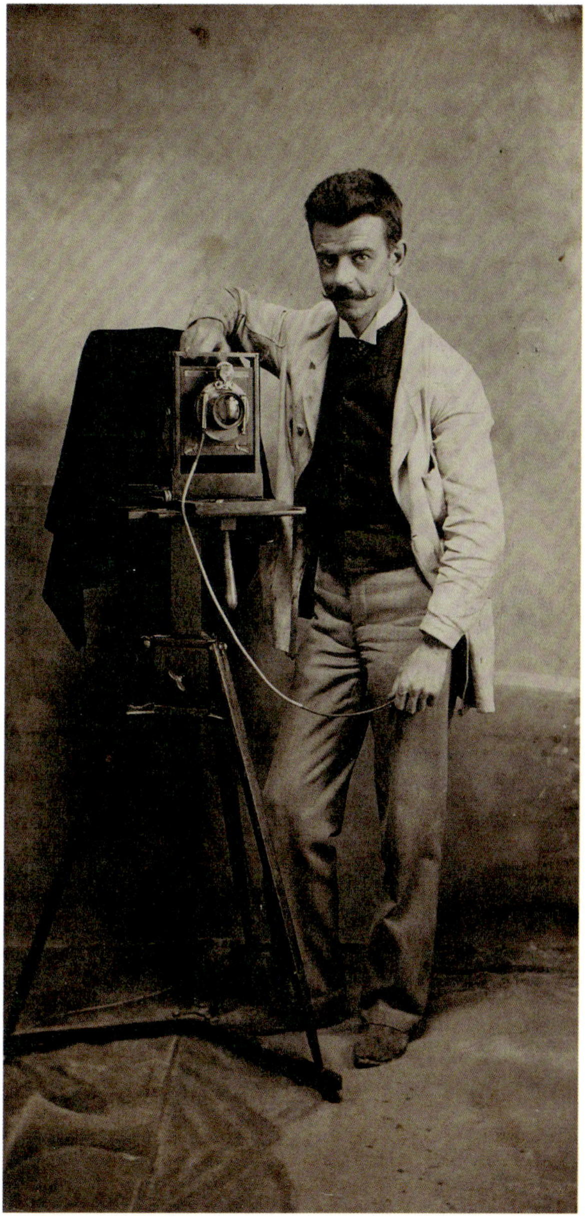

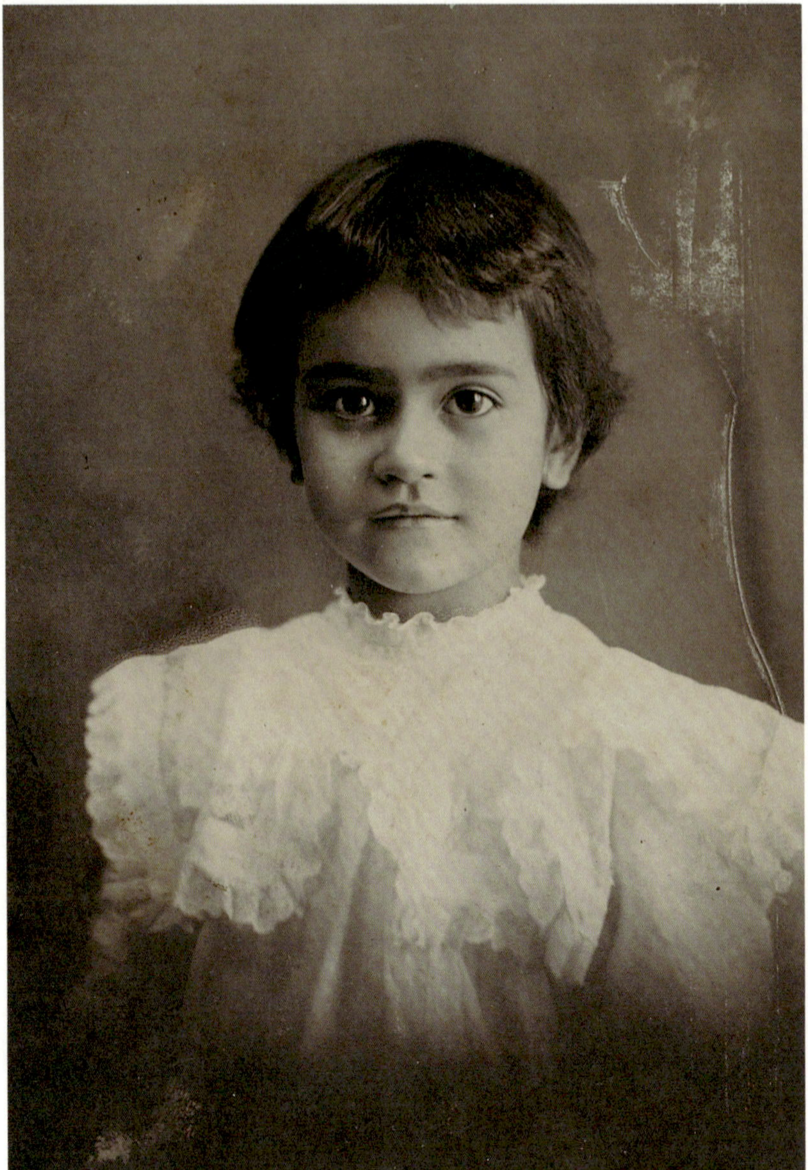

I.2

GUILLERMO KAHLO
FRIDA KAHLO, C.1909
ON VERSO: 'FRIDA AT 2 YEARS'
GELATIN SILVER PRINT. 14.3 × 10 CM
Museo Frida Kahlo

GUILLERMO KAHLO
FRIDA KAHLO, 1911
ON VERSO: 'AGED FOUR 1913'
GELATIN SILVER PRINT. 17.1 × 12 CM
Museo Frida Kahlo

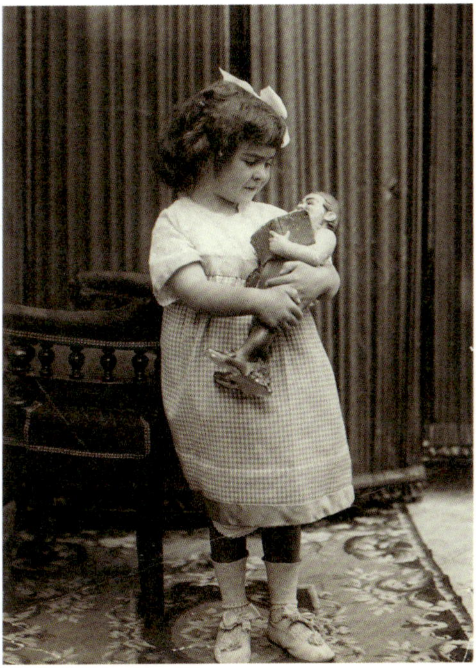

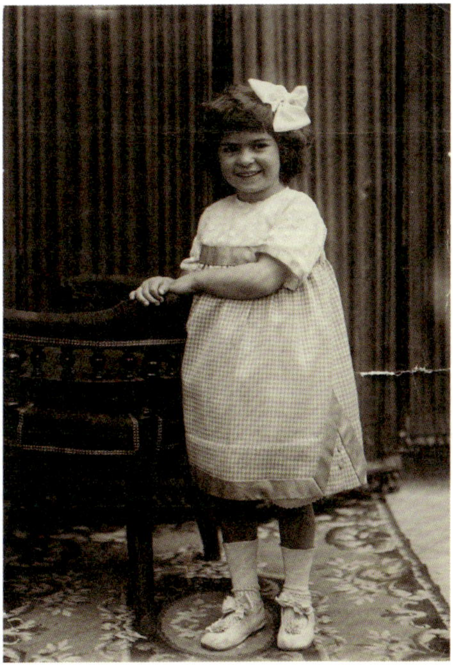

GUILLERMO KAHLO
FRIDA KAHLO, 15 JUNE 1919
ON VERSO: 'AGED 9'
GELATIN SILVER PRINT. 24.4 × 19 CM
Museo Frida Kahlo

In later life, Kahlo changed the year of her birth from 1907 to 1910, perhaps to align herself with the Mexican Revolution. Hence, the dates or ages she inscribed on the reverse of her childhood photographs are often erroneous.

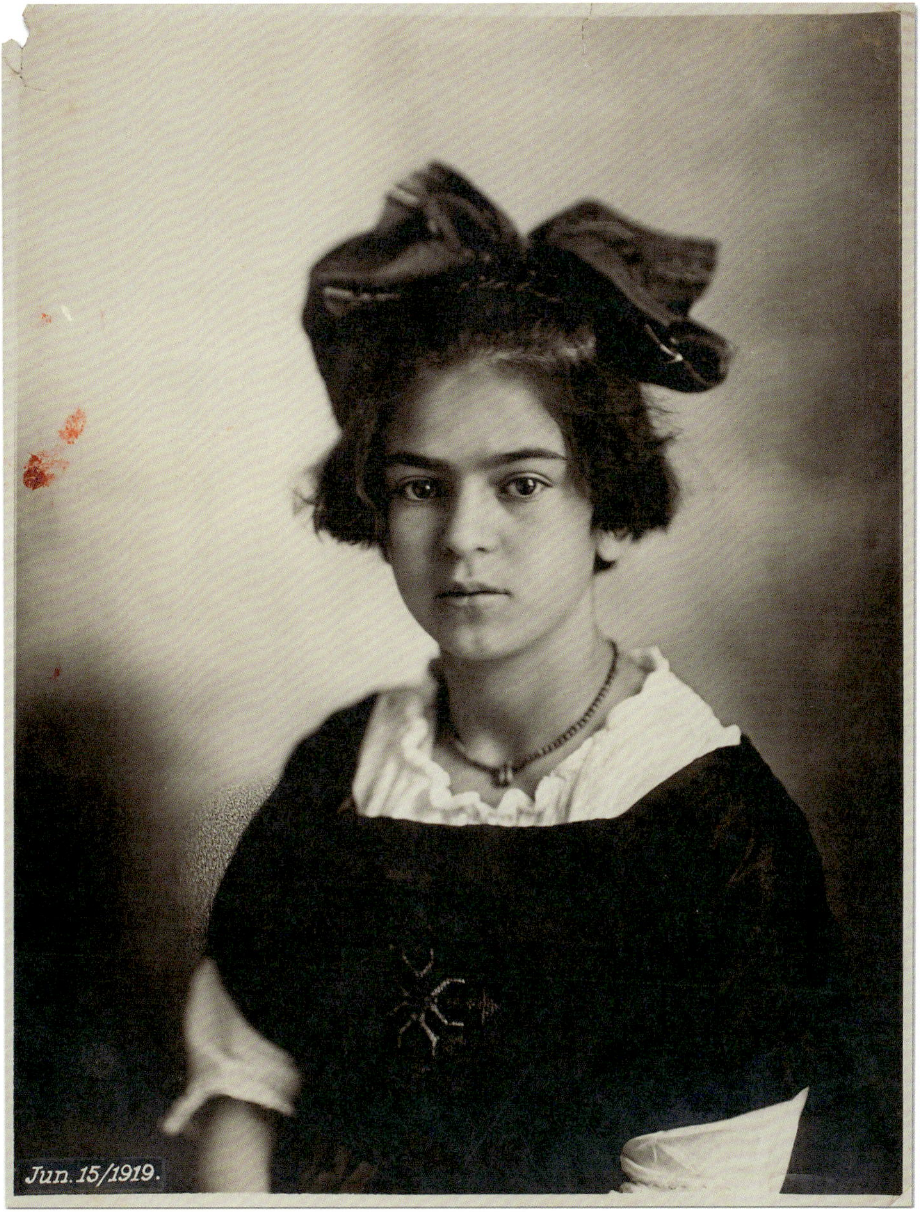

1.5

GUILLERMO KAHLO
FRIDA KAHLO, 1917
ON VERSO: 'FRIDUCHITA IN 1920 WHEN SHE
RECEIVED HER FIRST COMMUNION, AT THE AGE OF 10'
GELATIN SILVER PRINT. 19.9 × 15.7 CM
Museo Frida Kahlo

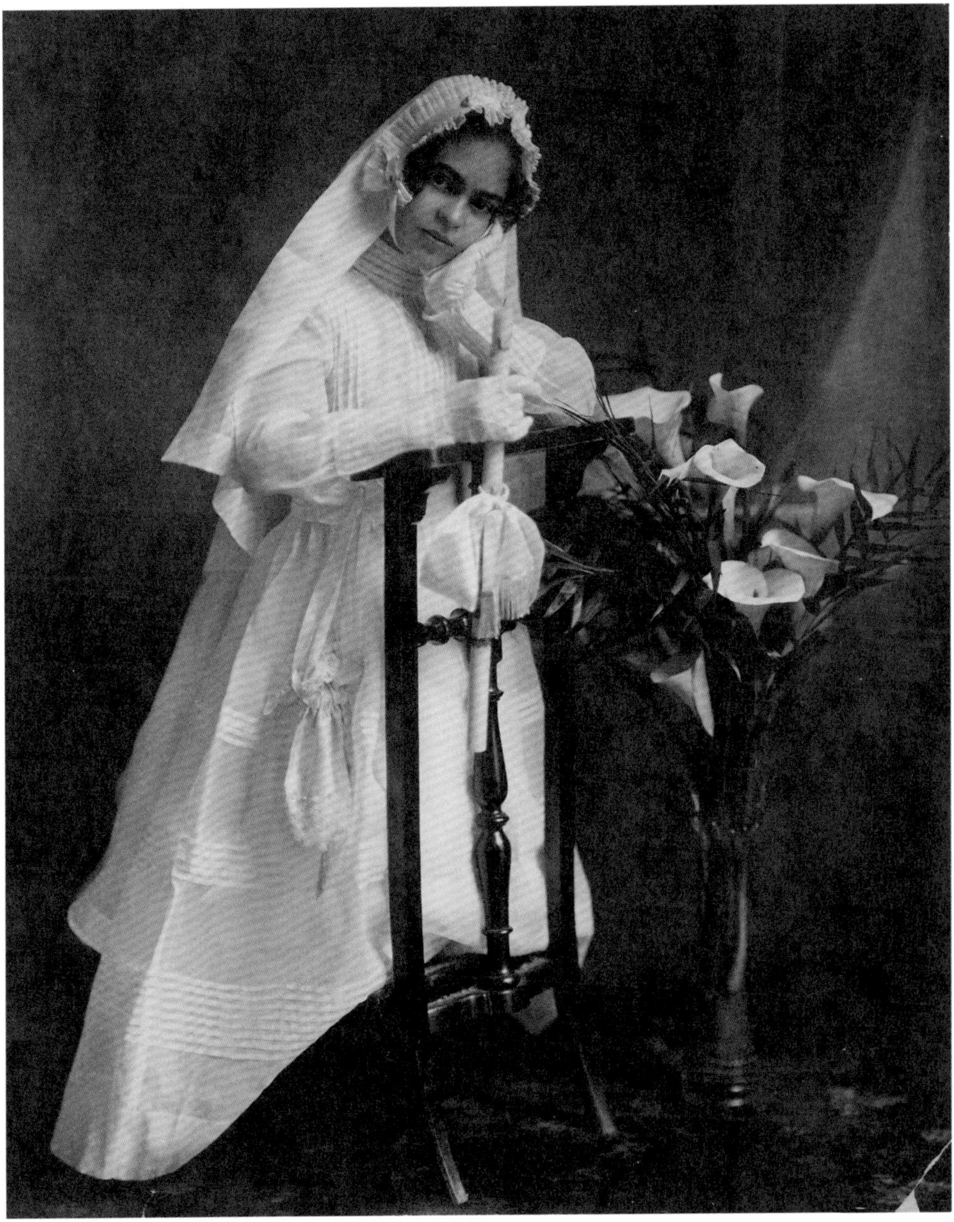

I.7

'FRIEDA. 14 AÑOS'
ON VERSO: 'FRIDA KAHLO. AGED 14, 1923.
NATIONAL PREPARATORY SCHOOL. MEXICO'
SILHOUETTE. 12.6 × 8 CM
Museo Frida Kahlo

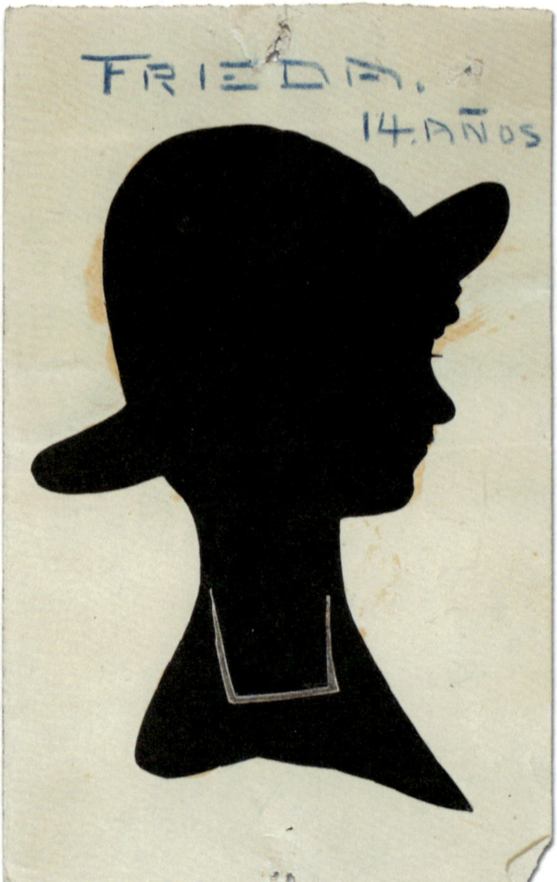

PLASTER CORSET.
MEDICAL BANDAGES, PLASTER, COTTON FABRIC,
HEMP YARN, COTTON STRAPS AND FRICTION BUCKLES
Museo Frida Kahlo

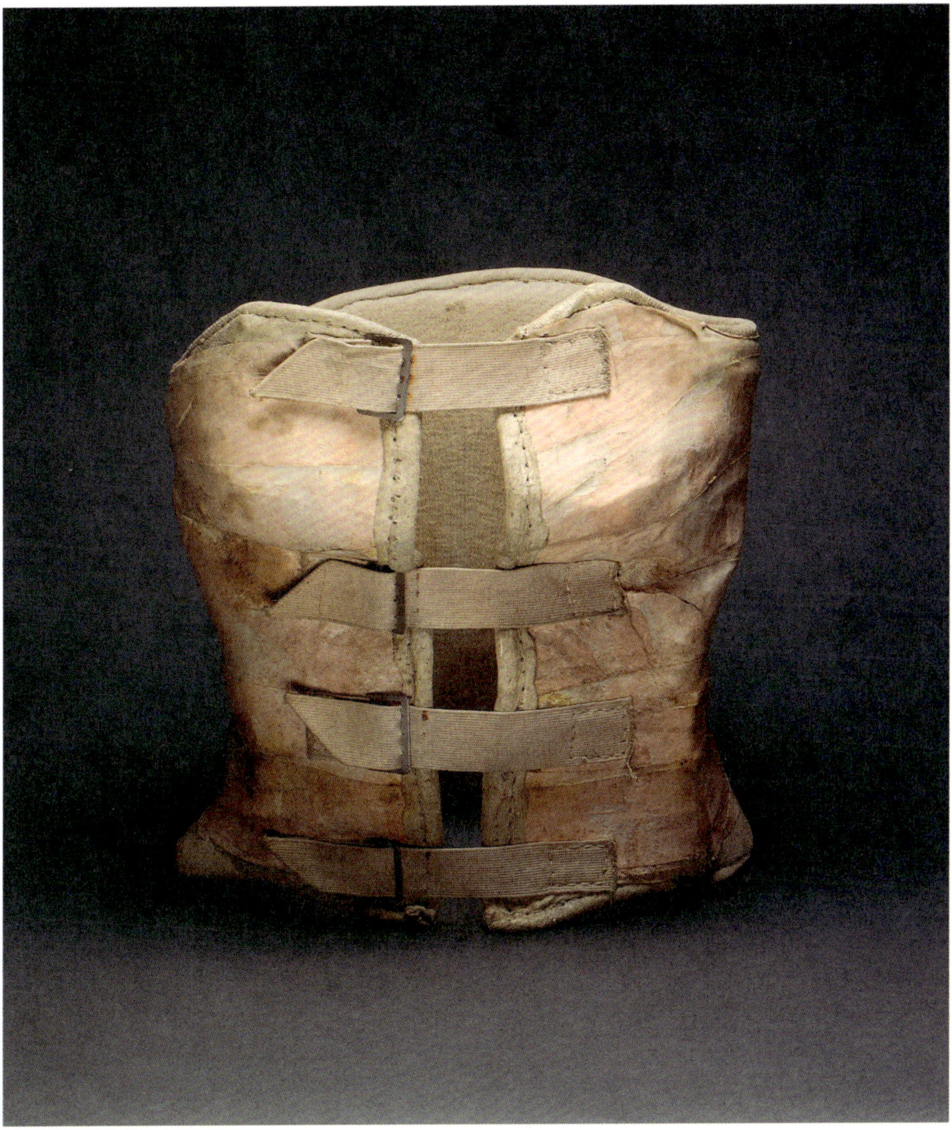

LEATHER CORSET WITH METAL FRAME.
LEATHER, COTTON STRAPS, FELT AND METAL BUCKLES
Museo Frida Kahlo

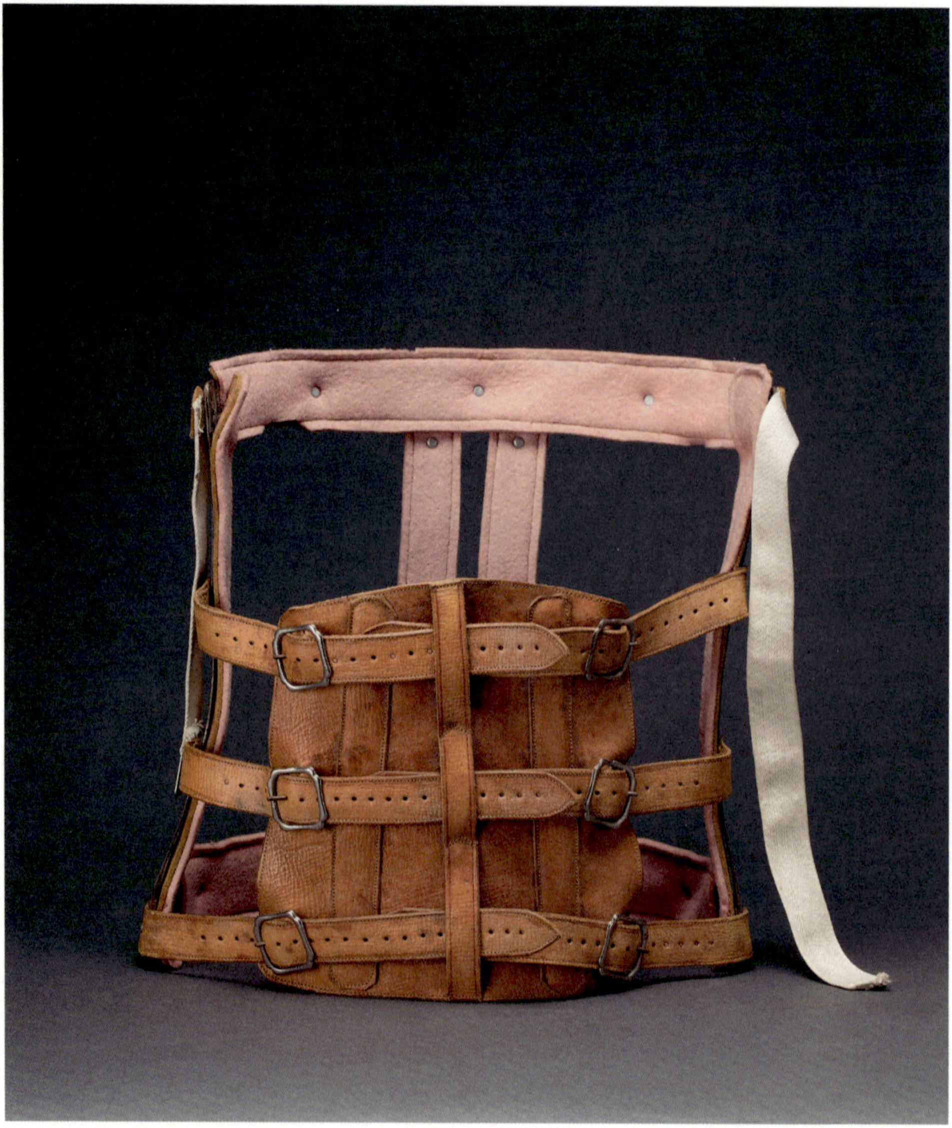

LEATHER CORSET WITH INTERNAL METAL FRAME.
LEATHER STRAPS, METAL BUCKLES AND LACING TO FASTEN
Museo Frida Kahlo

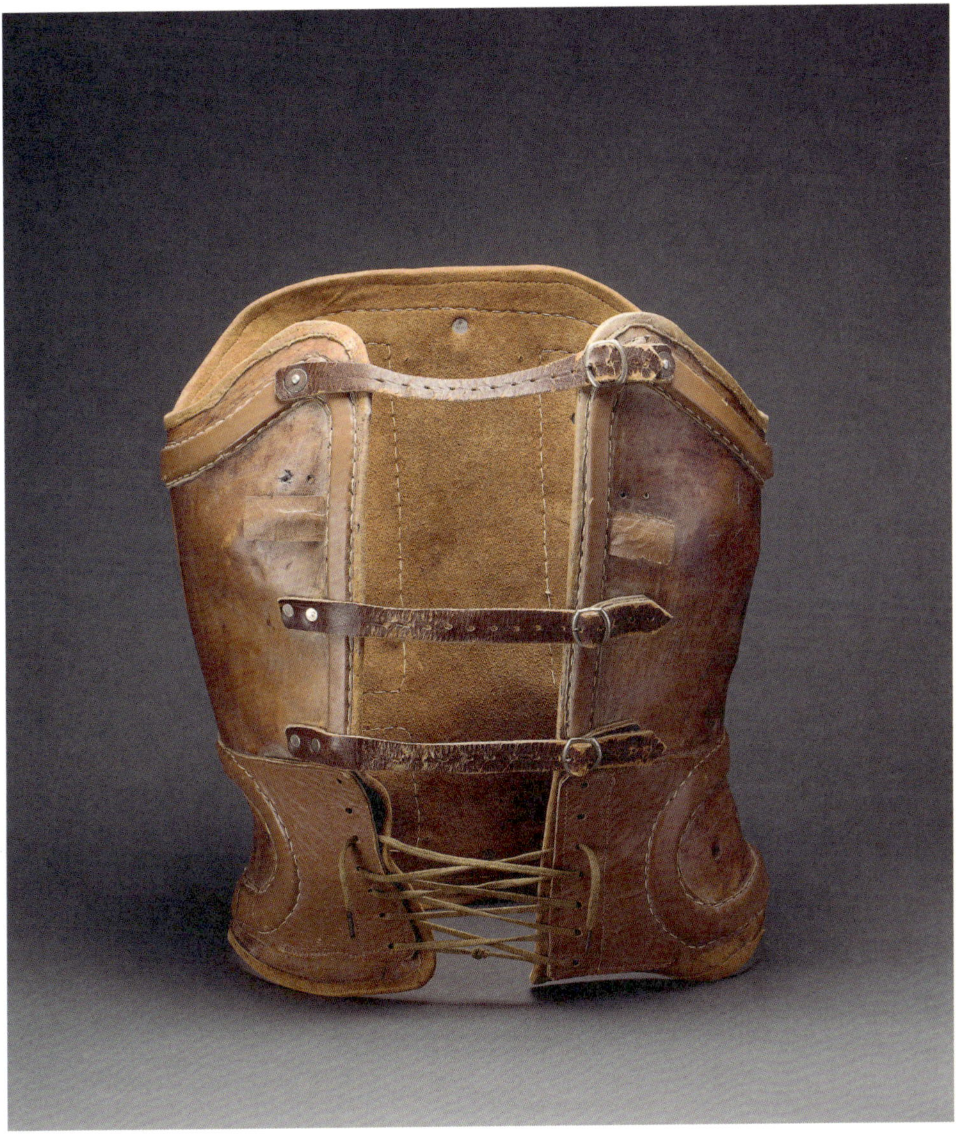

BACK BRACE.
METAL, LEATHER, COTTON TAPES, BRUSHED COTTON AND METAL BUCKLES
Museo Frida Kahlo

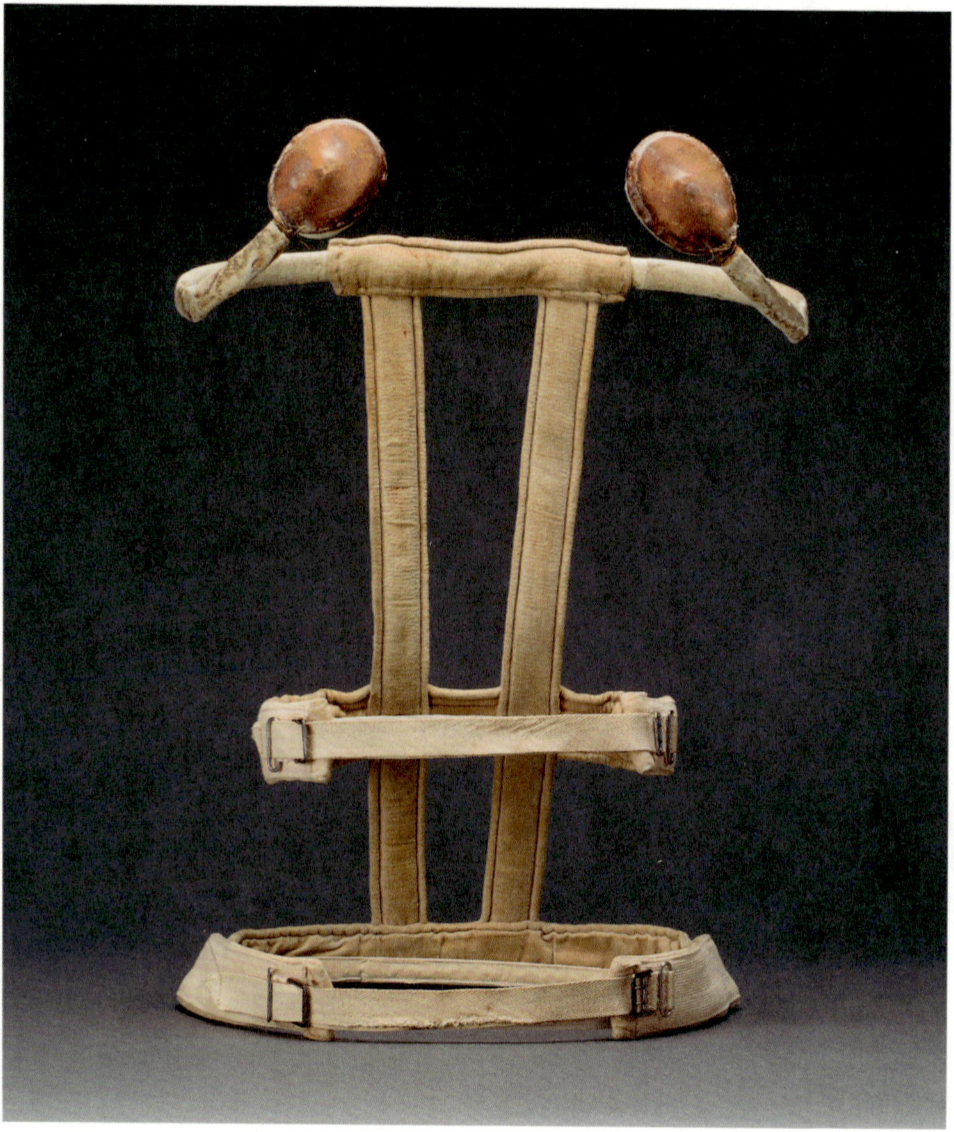

PLASTER CORSET.
PAINTED AND DECORATED BY FRIDA KAHLO
Museo Frida Kahlo

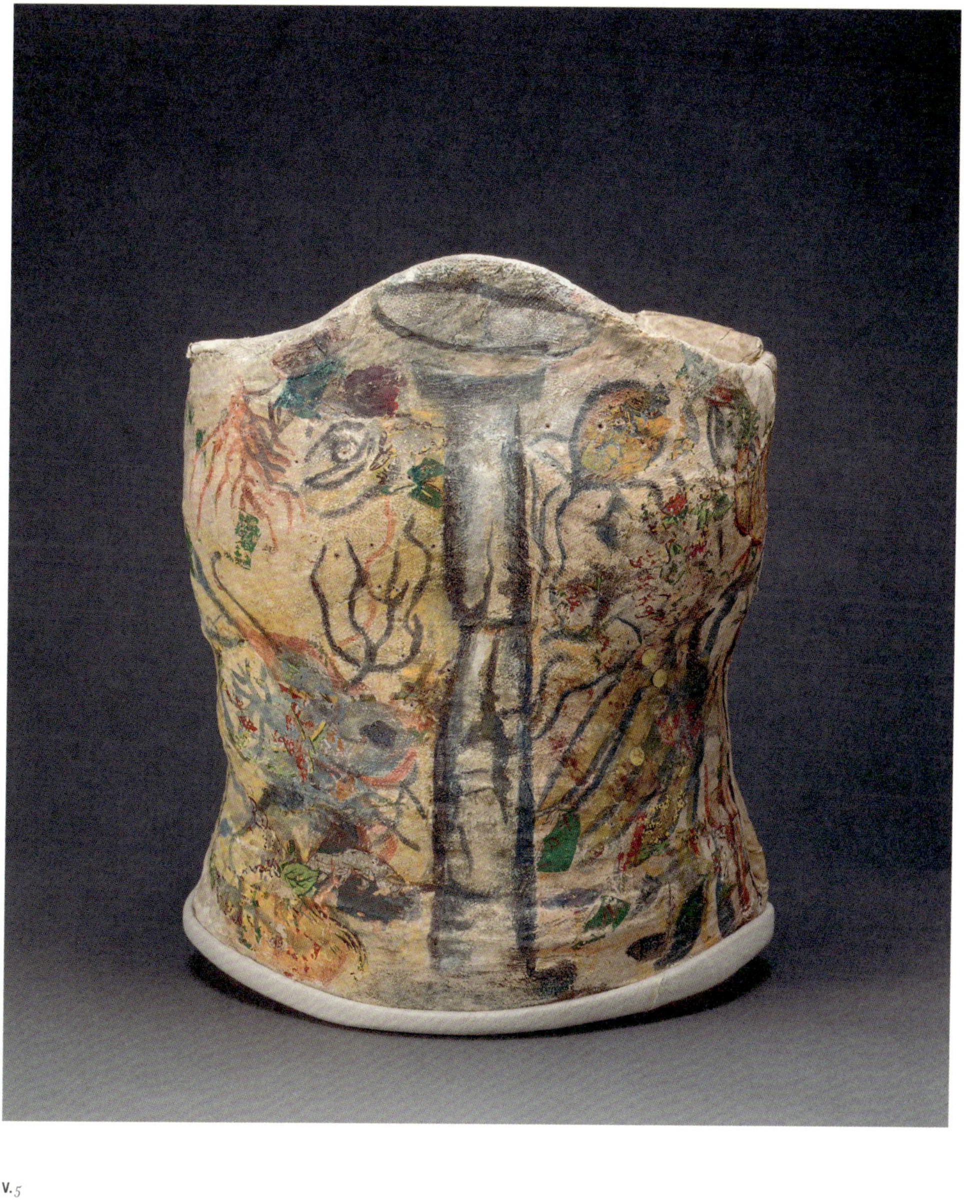

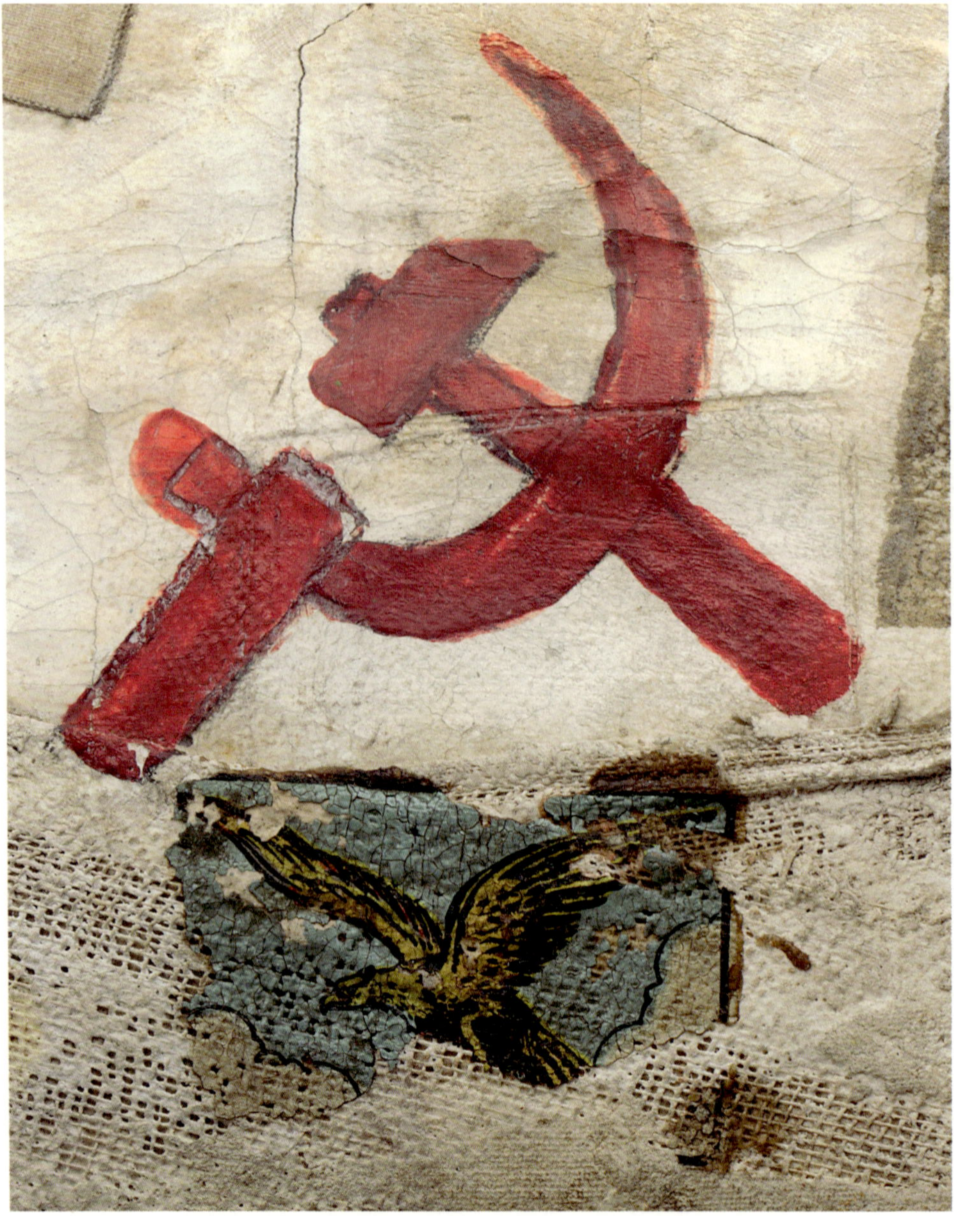

V. 6

PLASTER CORSET.
PAINTED AND DECORATED BY FRIDA KAHLO
Museo Frida Kahlo

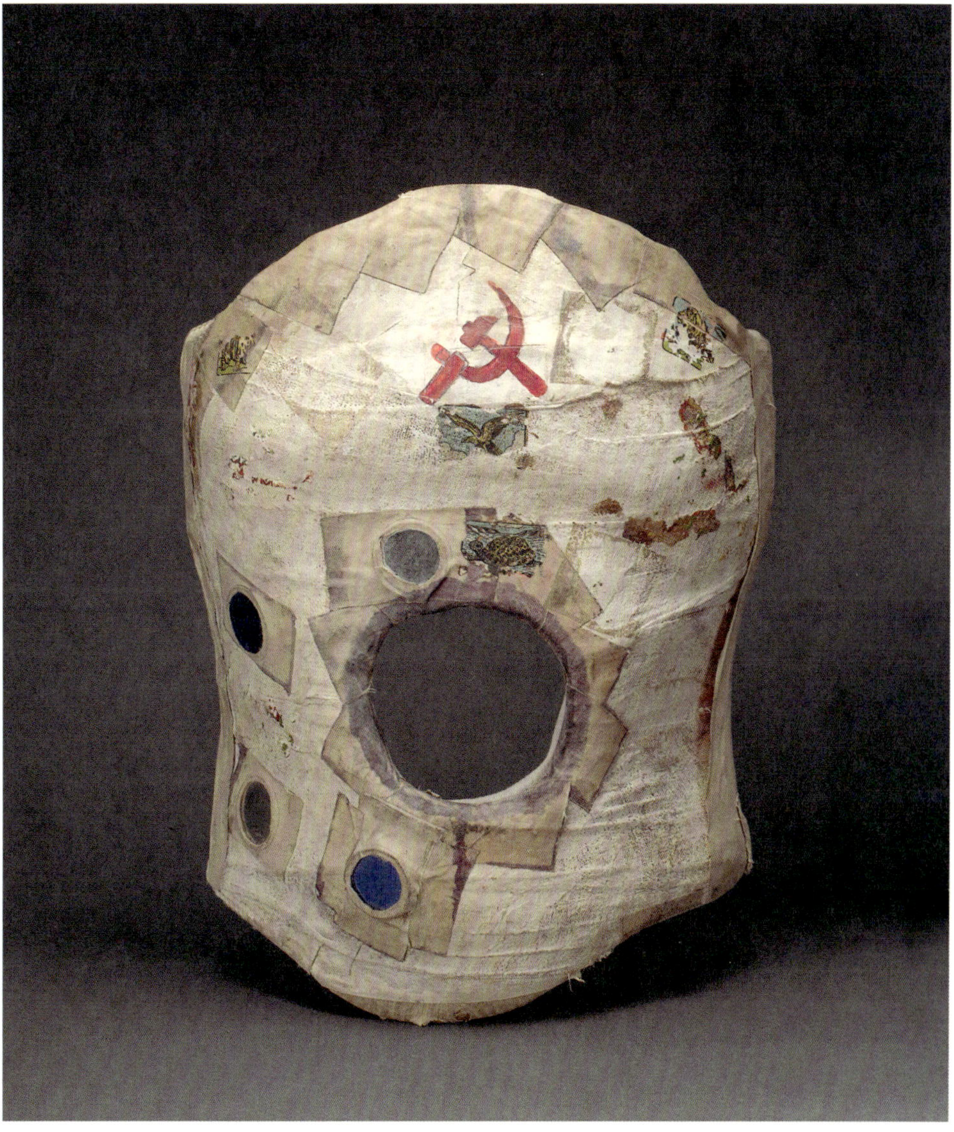

PROSTHETIC LEG WITH LEATHER BOOT.
APPLIQUÉD SILK WITH EMBROIDERED CHINESE MOTIFS
Museo Frida Kahlo

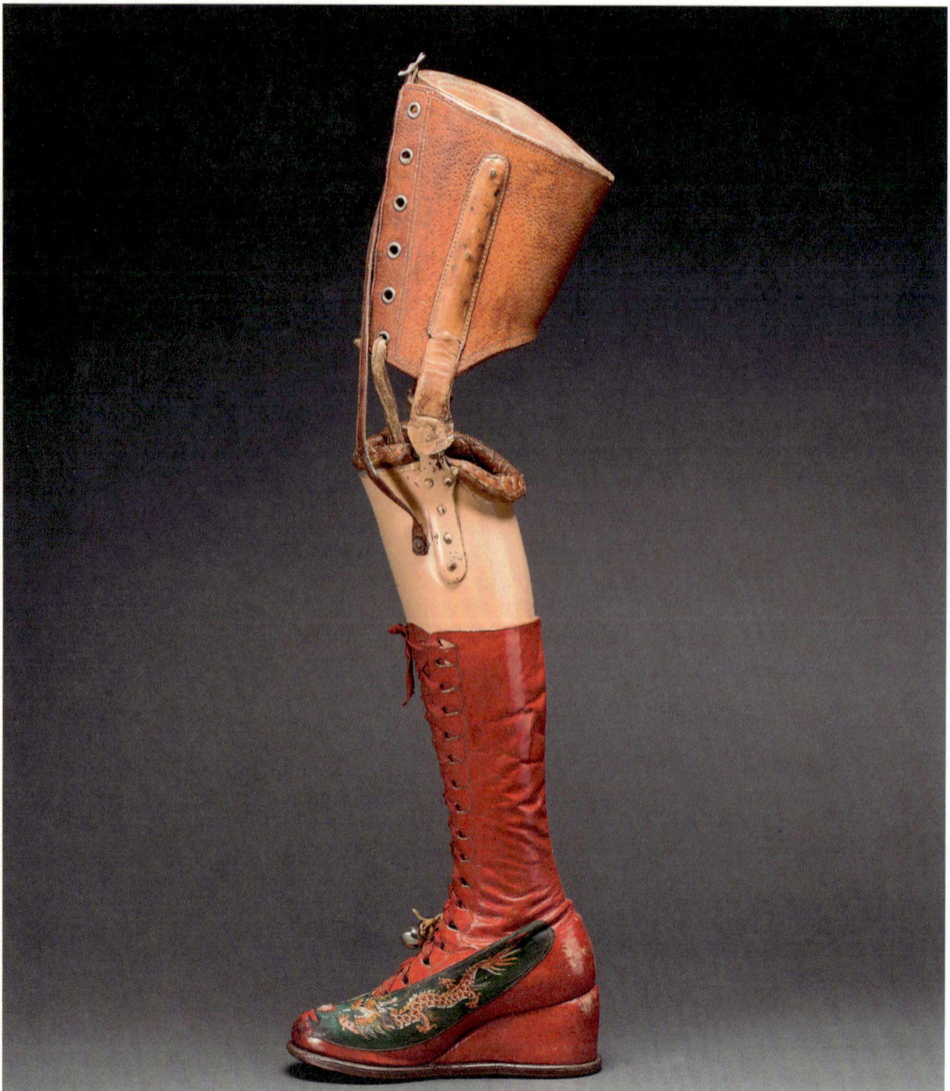

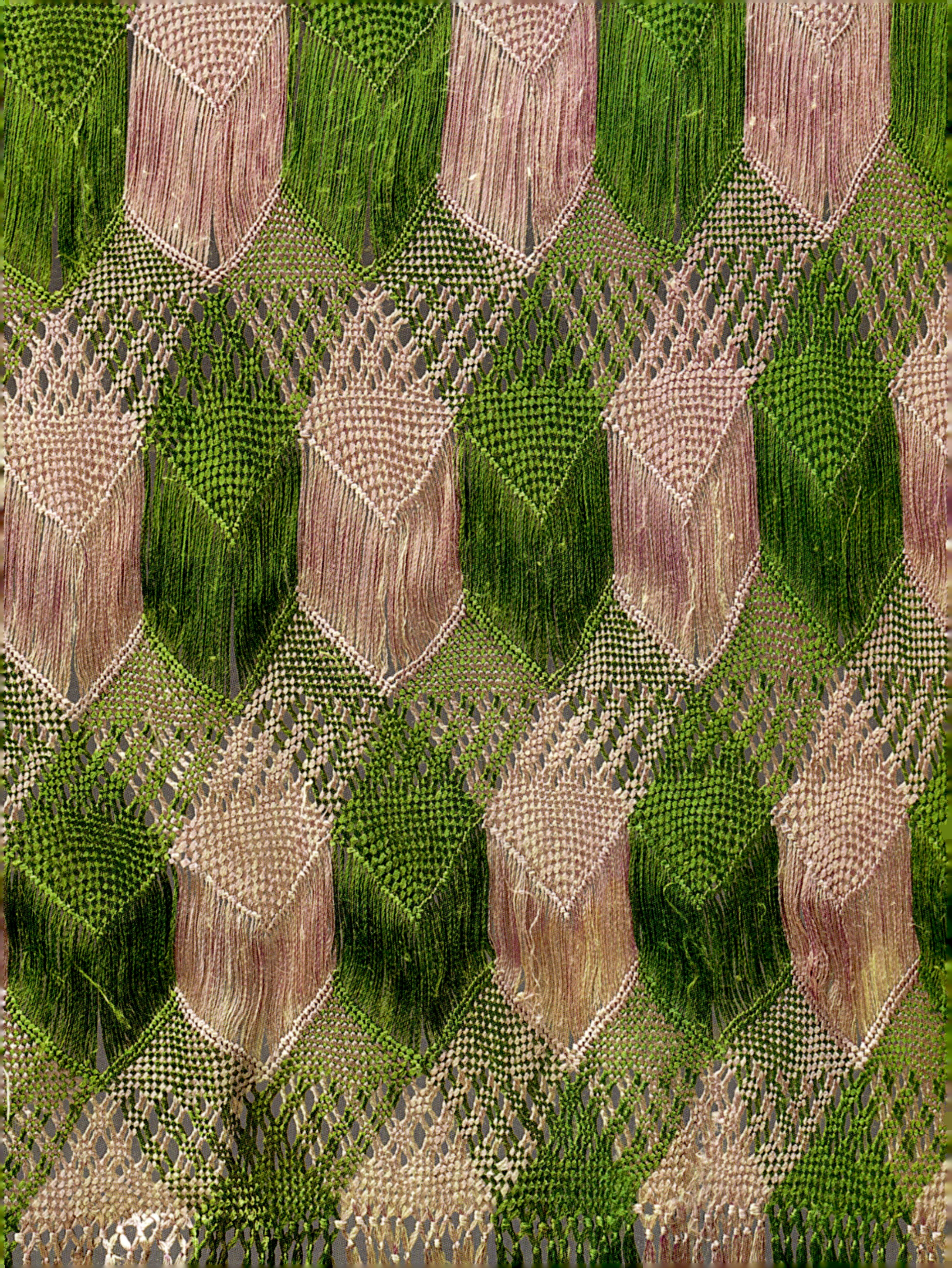

The *Resplandor*: Cultural and Spiritual Significance in Two Self-Portraits

KIRSTIN KENNEDY

Throughout her life, Frida Kahlo's choice of elaborate hair styles and headdresses to crown her head and frame her face deliberately reflected her political and personal identity. The student group '*los Cachuchas*', to which she belonged whilst studying at the *Escuela Nacional Preparatoria* in the 1920s, took its name from the floppy cloth caps worn by members.[1] After her marriage to Diego Rivera in 1929 until her death in 1954, she consistently adopted the traditional dress of the Zapotec women of Tehuantepec, on the Pacific coast of the province of Oaxaca.[2] Photographs and self-portraits show her wearing an *enagua* (a long skirt), an embroidered *huipil* (a loose-fitting tunic) and a *rebozo* (a long scarf or shawl), her hair gathered on top of her head and interwoven with ribbons, cords or flowers (embellishments which harked back to pre-Columbian traditions).[3] On one level, this reflected the sense of pride in Mexican history and culture which politicians, artists and intellectuals increasingly felt in post-revolutionary Mexico, and which in the 1920s and 1930s was particularly inspired by the region of Tehuantepec.[4] On another, recent research suggests that Kahlo's own family heritage motivated her sartorial choices.[5] Although she never visited the region of Oaxaca, Kahlo's mother Matilde was born there, and a photograph of Matilde as a child with her family shows them wearing traditional Tehuana dress [31].[6] Some family members also wear the 'small *huipil*' or *resplandor* (in Spanish, literally, 'radiance'), a lace *huipil* worn as a headdress in which the woman's head is framed by the lace collar and the redundant sleeves hang below the chin and over the neck. The origins of this garment, which emerged as a defining characteristic of Tehuana dress in the nineteenth century, are obscure.[7] In 1930s and 1940s Mexico this female aesthetic would have been familiar across the country: ten *peso* notes of the period featured the smiling head of a woman framed by a *resplandor* [83].[8]

Despite her interest in Mexican culture, and in Tehuana dress in particular, photographs of Kahlo wearing the *resplandor* are infrequent, which suggests that for her the garment was freighted with a particular significance. She owned two examples, and an undated photograph of around 1940 shows her wearing one of them standing before her diverse collection of Mexican art [84].[9] Figures of Adam and Eve stand

83. TEN-PESO BANKNOTE
ISSUED BY BANK OF MEXICO,
3 SEPTEMBER 1947

84. BERNARD SILBERSTEIN
FRIDA KAHLO IN TEHUANA COSTUME, C.1940
GELATIN SILVER PRINT. 24.6 × 19.5 CM
Cincinnati Art Museum, Ohio. 1986.574

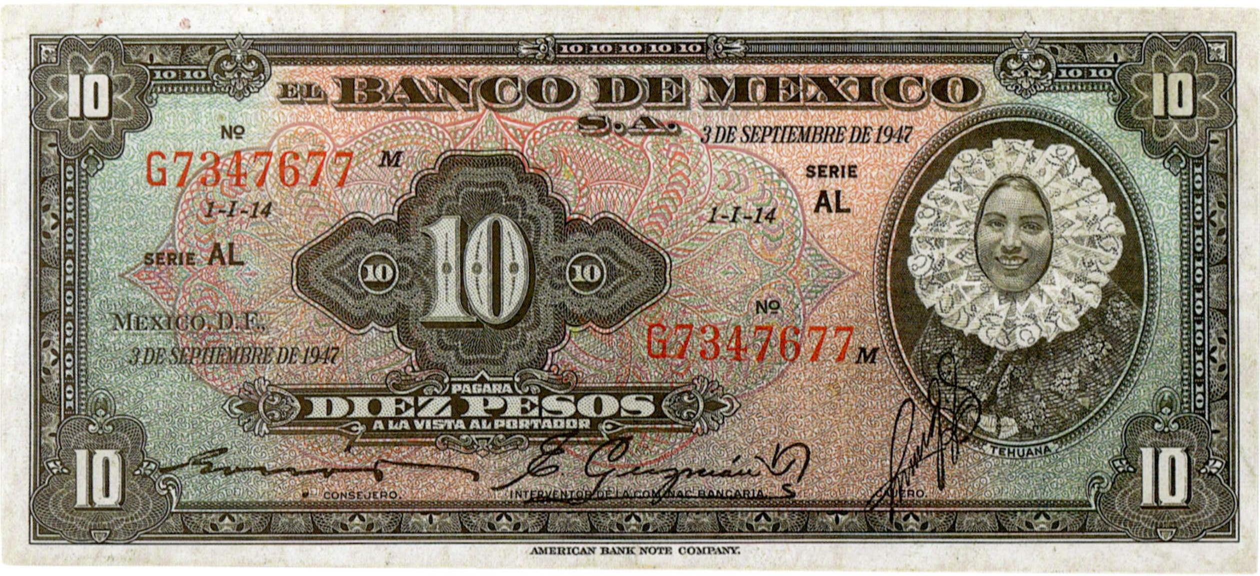

above oxen, horses and a miniature skull. It would seem from these juxtapositions that Kahlo wore the *resplandor* deliberately in this image to link herself with Mexico's Spanish, Catholic past as well as its pre-Columbian heritage.

Kahlo seldom painted herself in a *resplandor* in her self-portraits, but in the 1940s she did so twice. The paintings discussed here have been analyzed in terms of Kahlo's emotional relationship with Rivera, which is understandable, given that he appears in the earlier of the two self-portraits.[10] However, the inclusion of the *resplandor*, a garment of particular significance for Kahlo, suggests her desire to convey a different message about the various cultural strands of her heritage, and the relationship between the earth, sex, life and death. Like the photograph of Kahlo standing in her *resplandor* before objects spanning very different aspects of Mexico's cultural heritage, these two paintings of Kahlo's face framed by an aureole of lace invite deliberately contrasting interpretations based on different artistic and religious traditions. In both portraits, Kahlo depicts herself wearing the *resplandor* in a style appropriate to church-going.[11] Kahlo had rejected her mother's devout

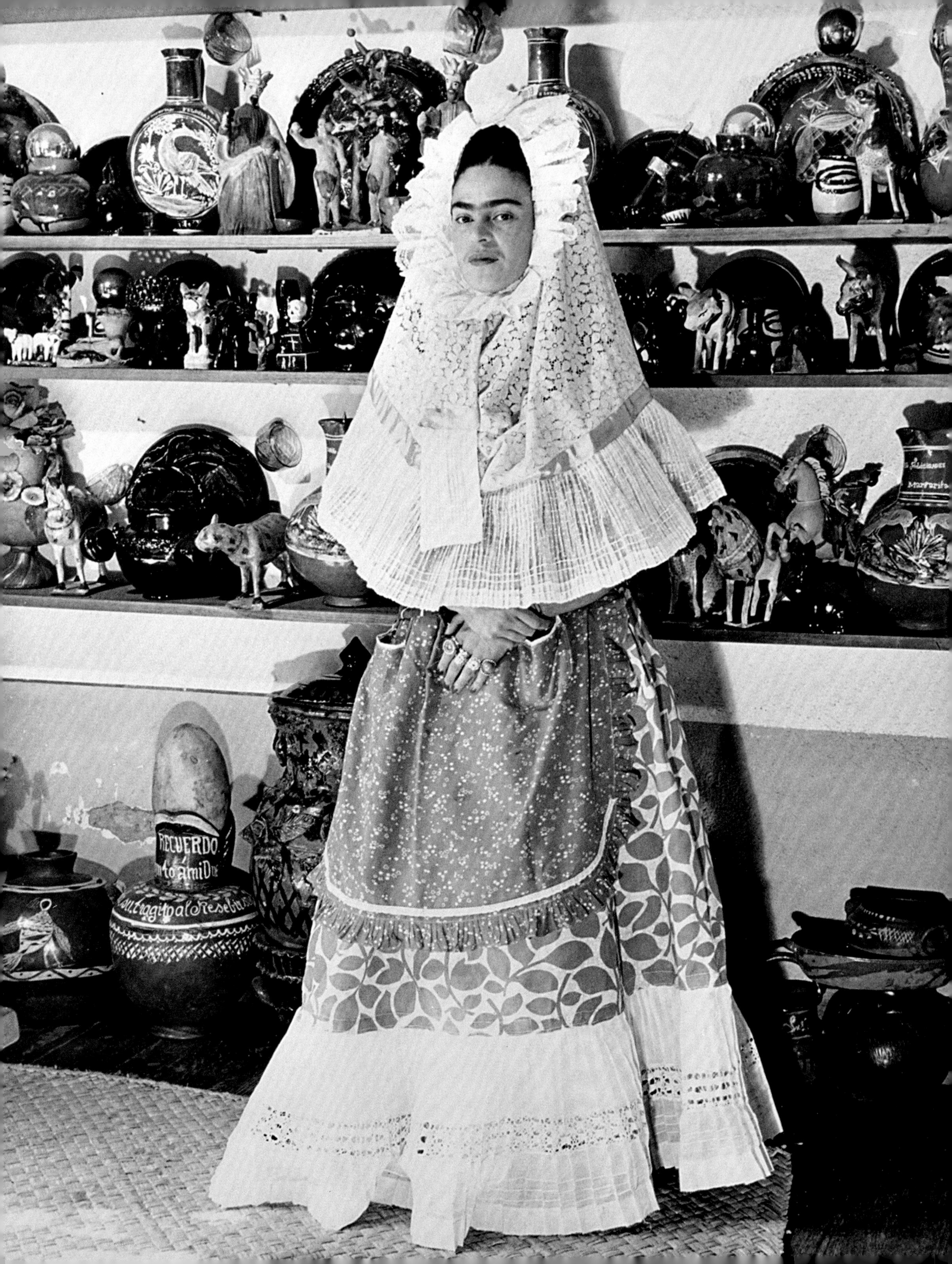
RECUERDO

85. NICOLÁS ENRÍQUEZ
THE VIRGIN OF GUADELUPE WITH THE FOUR APPARITIONS, 1773
OIL ON COPPER. 56.5 × 41.9 CM
Metropolitan Museum of Art, New York. 2014.173

Catholicism, but the image of her head encircled in ray-like lace pleats, her upper body hidden beneath rich fabric, recalls depictions of the Virgin Mary, particularly the Virgin of Guadalupe, whose cloaked image surrounded by rays of light had miraculously appeared on a cloak worn by the Mexican Indian Juan Diego in the sixteenth century [85].[12] The sun-like quality of the pleats also introduces echoes of Aztec mythology, in which the sun was worshipped as a symbol of eternal rebirth. The small, pearl-like tears that run down Kahlo's impassive face in her *Self-Portrait* of 1948 would seem to continue the pre-Columbian theme [86]. In Nahua mythology, water and the sun were at the heart of all creation.[13] Alternativly, Kahlo's tears recall the weeping features of Mary in depictions of her Seven Sorrows (prompted by events in Christ's childhood and by His Passion). Unlike Mary, however, Kahlo's gaze is not modestly downcast, and her tears in this portrait equally suggest her identification with the weeping woman of Tehuantepec folklore *La Llorona* who, unwed and abandoned by her lover, murdered her own children.[14]

The tension inherent in Kahlo's allusion to herself simultaneously as Mary and *La Llorona*, framed by the rays of a Christian or an Aztec sun, continues in the role played by the natural world in the imagery of these self-portraits. The white flower designs on the white lace headdresses are accurate depictions of the *resplandores* owned by Kahlo, but they also carry Christian connotations of moral purity. This symbolism is reinforced by the floral headdress she wears in *Self-Portrait as a Tehuana* (1943) [88], which supplements the *resplandor* and recalls the elaborate crowns studded with artificial flowers worn by Mexican nuns at the moment of their profession, and on their death beds. Eighteenth- and nineteenth-century portraits of these 'crowned nuns' show them wearing and holding carnations, roses and lilies – scented flowers symbolic of the Virgin Mary and indicative of the nuns' own vocation as brides of Christ [89].[15] The focus on the adornment of the head suggests the importance of the mind in the quest for salvation. A 1725 biography of the saintly sister Barbara Josepha de San Francisco, of the Convent of the Holy Trinity in Puebla, Mexico, cited her symbolic interpretation of her veil and wimple. These, she said, 'made me understand how I should maintain purity in my five senses, and what

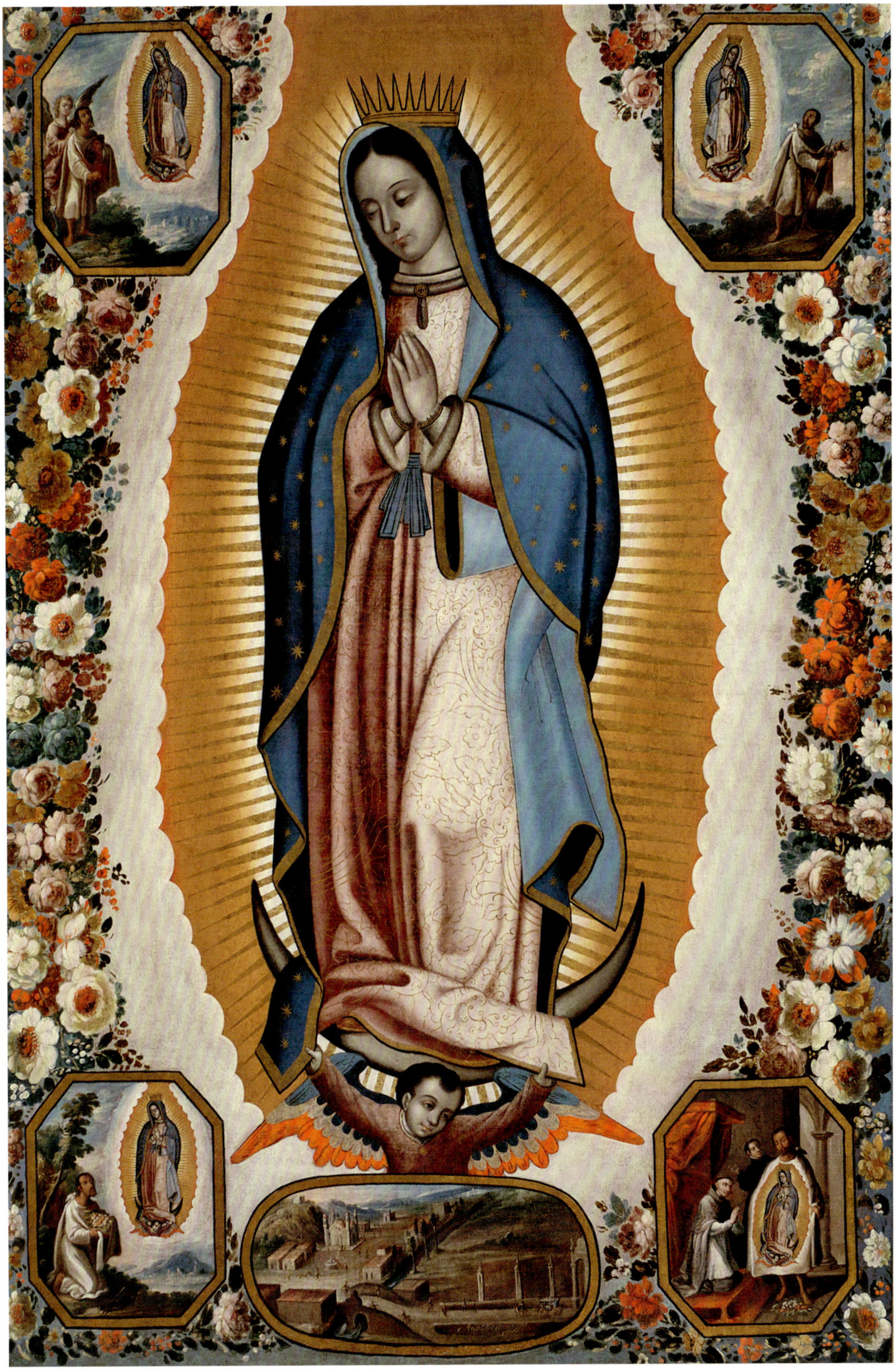

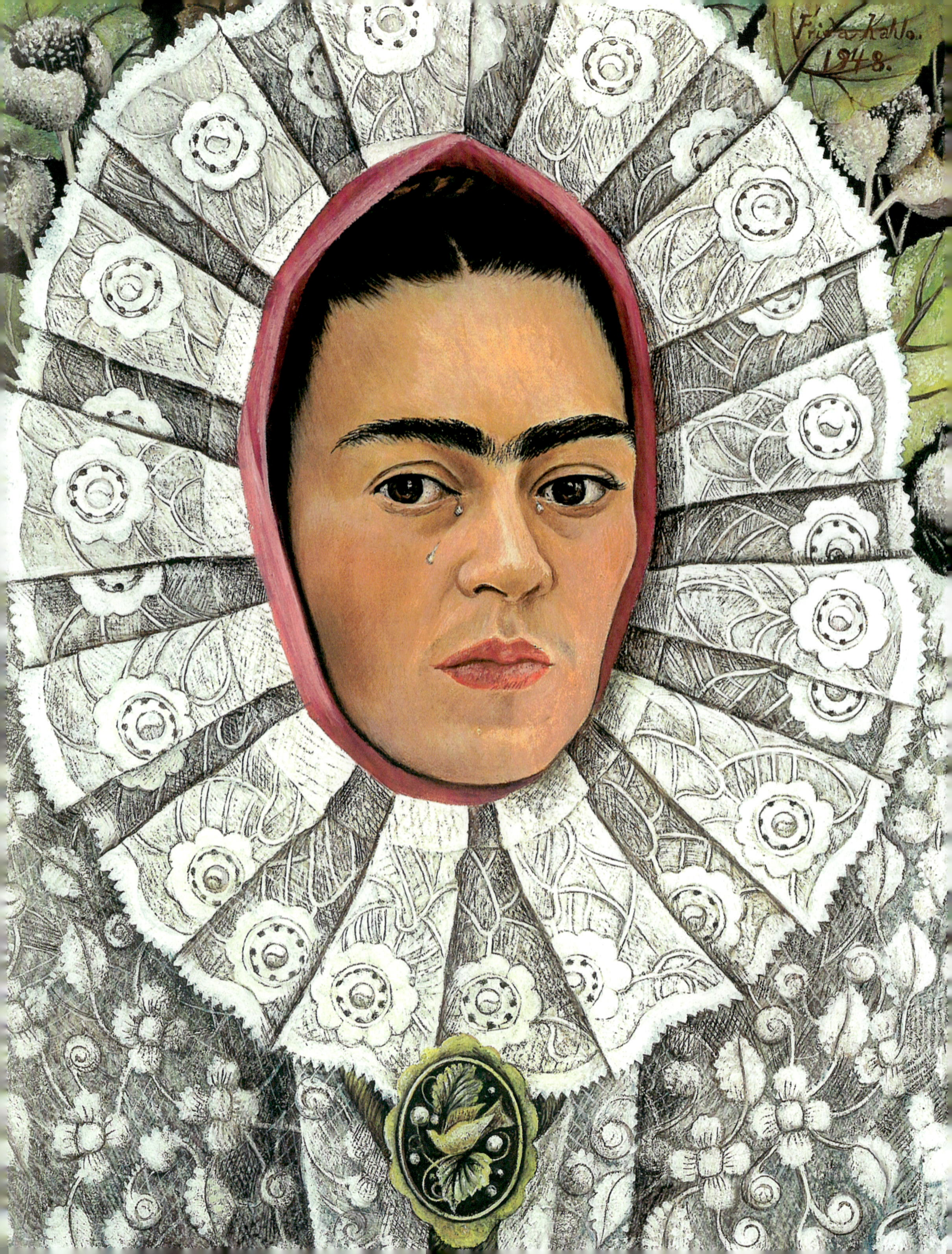
Frida Kahlo.
1948.

86. FRIDA KAHLO
SELF-PORTRAIT, 1948
OIL ON HARDBOARD. 50 × 40 CM
Private collection

I should do in each of these to martyr them, so that I might earn the palm and crown that had been put on me.'[16]

Again, however, Kahlo maps her own view of the universe onto these allusions to Catholic iconography. In *Self-Portrait as a Tehuana* [88], the focus of her thoughts is not salvation but her husband, whose portrait sits above her brow. The flowers in her headdress are not the roses and carnations of devotional imagery but purple bougainvillea, which flourished in the garden of the Blue House, and what could be the white-petalled 'Mexican violet' and arnica, both healing plants in traditional medicine.[17] The Nahua culture represented the life-force of the sun with a four-petalled flower; the leaves of the flowers in Kahlo's painting send forth a network of dark roots which mingle with white threads that emanate from the *resplandor*, threads which lend the headdress a living force of its own. The imagery appears to reflect Kahlo's understanding of the cosmos as an elaborate web of conducting threads (flowers and leaves in her hair sprout vein-like roots in her 1938 self-portrait, *Remembrance of an Open Wound*).[18] It also suggests how she viewed her sexual relationship with Rivera in the context of the natural world. Writing metaphorically about her relationship with him in her diary at an unspecified moment in the 1940s, Kahlo stated that 'I penetrate the sex of the whole earth, her heat chars me and my entire body is rubbed by the freshness of the tender leaves'. In the self-portrait of 1948, the lace flowers of the *resplandor* dominate the painting, marginalizing the leaves and flower-heads of living plants depicted in the background. 'There are always new things. Always linked to living ancient ones,' wrote Kahlo in her diary on 9 November 1951, three years before her death.[19] In these two self-portraits, Kahlo has taken a characteristic element of Mexican traditional dress, the *resplandor*, and turned it into a vital symbol of her artistic heritage, sexual desire and spirituality.

87. PHOTOGRAPHER UNKNOWN
FRIDA KAHLO WITH 'SELF-PORTRAIT AS A TEHUANA', C.1943
PHOTOGRAPHIC PRINT. 18 × 13 CM
Florence Arquin Papers, Archives of American Art, Smithsonian Institution

88. FRIDA KAHLO
SELF-PORTRAIT AS A TEHUANA, 1943
OIL ON HARDBOARD. 76 × 61 CM
The Jacques and Natasha Gelman Collection of 20th Century Mexican Art and the Vergel Foundation

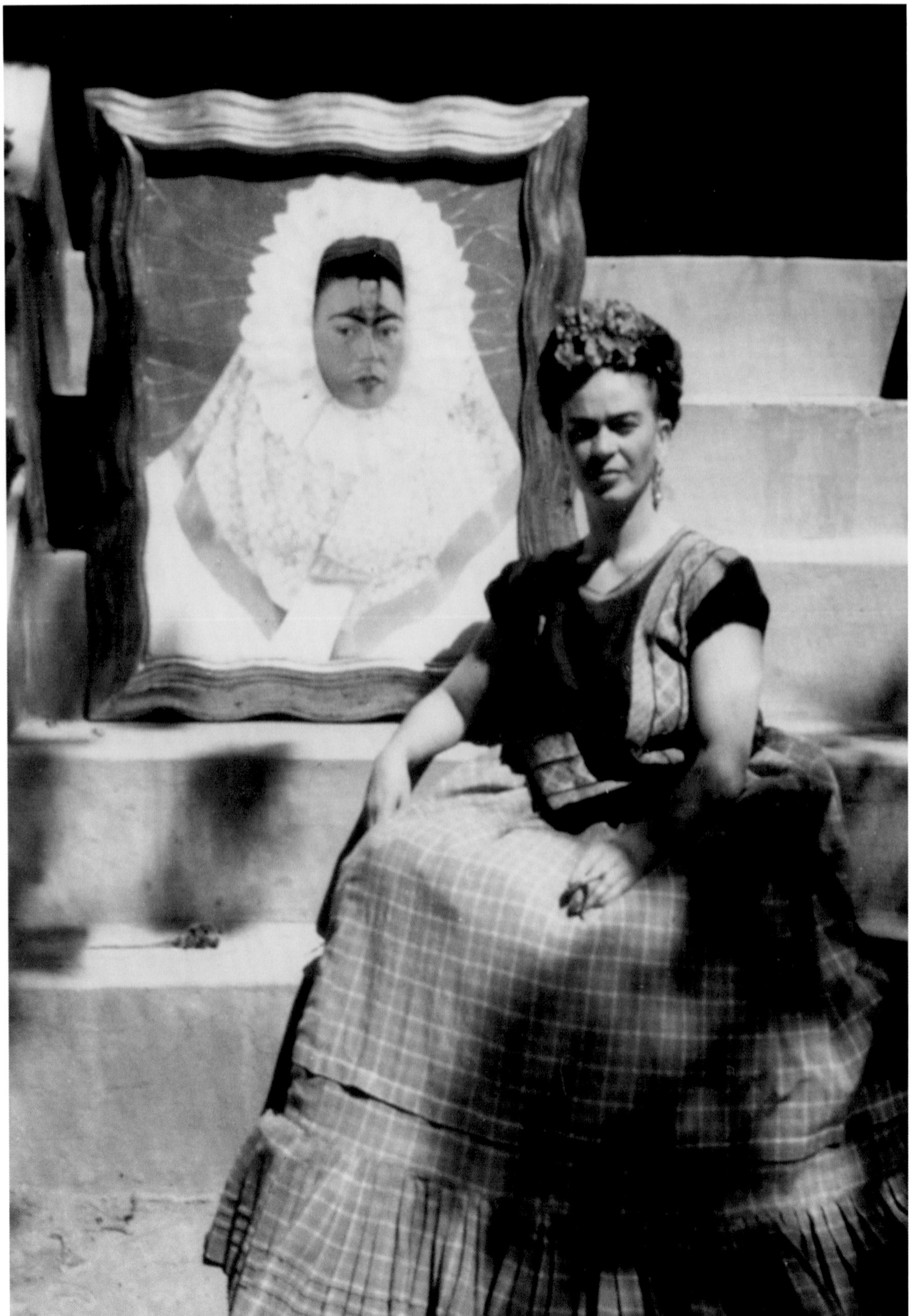

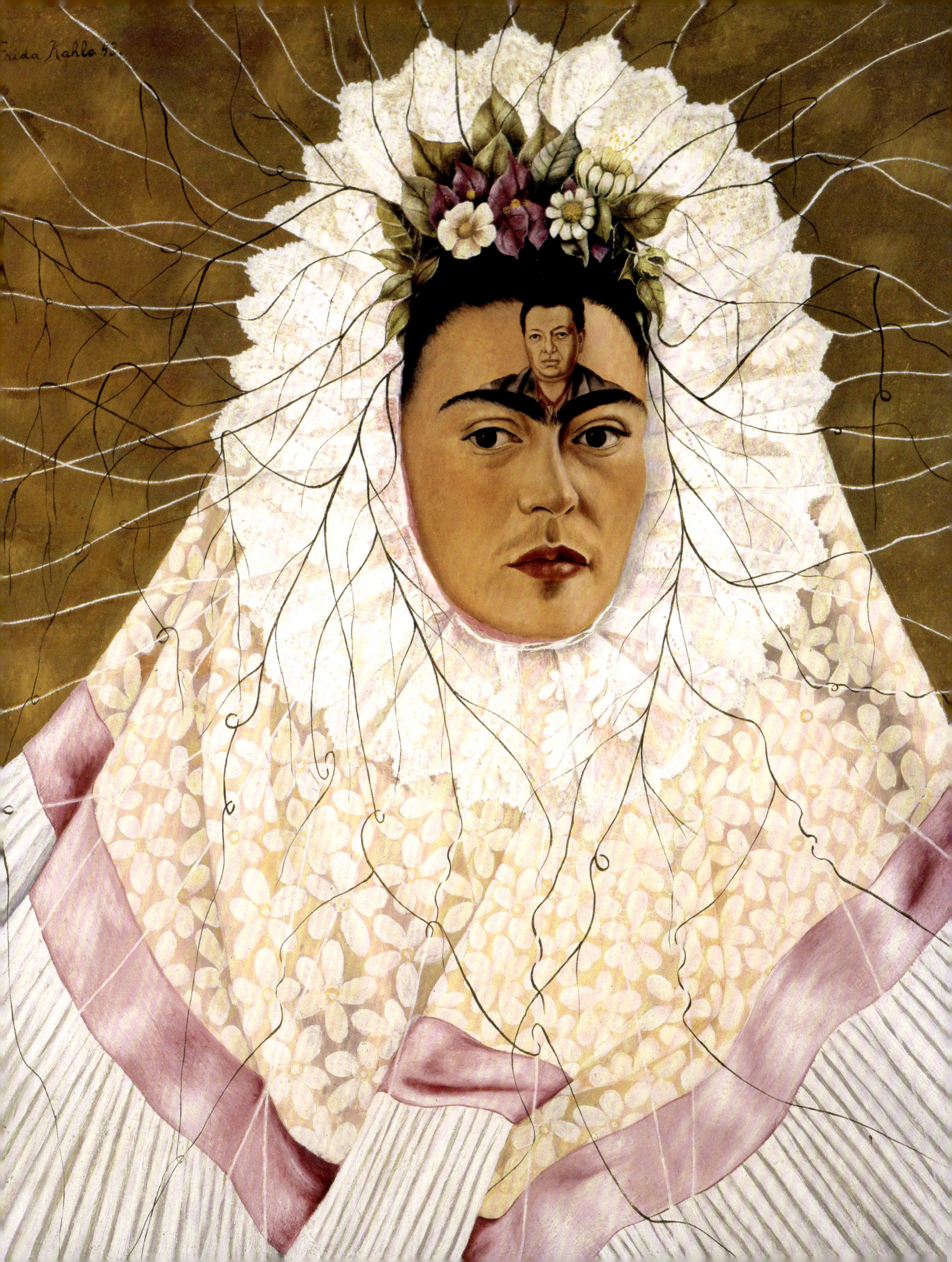
Frida Kahlo 43.

89. BIZNIETA DE HERNÁN CORTÉS
SOR JUANA INÉS DE LA CRUZ, C.1650
40.6 × 30.3 CM
Museo de America-Coleccion, Madrid

90. DETAIL OF RESPLANDOR
Museo Frida Kahlo

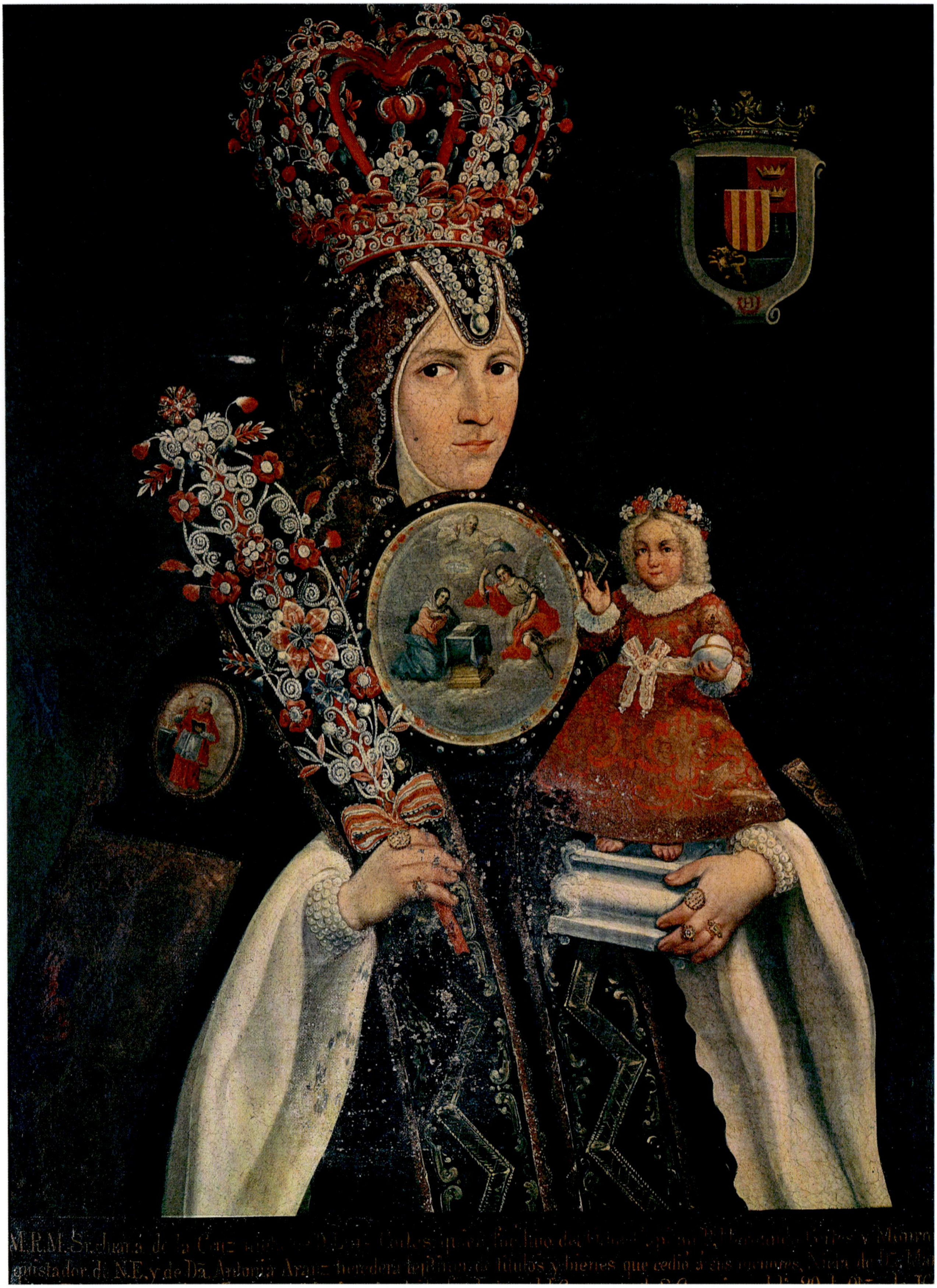

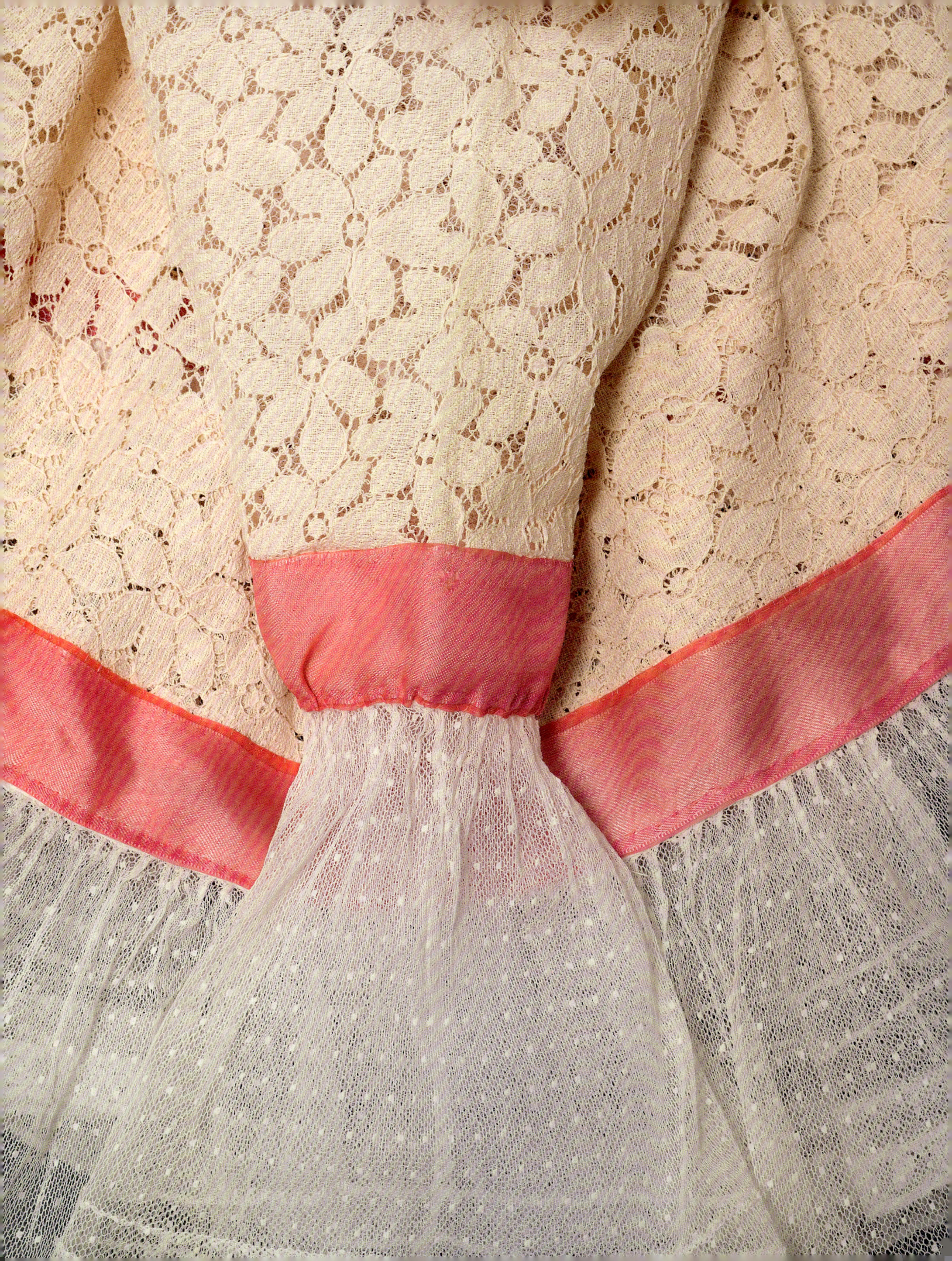

Frida Redressed

ORIANA BADDELEY

In January 1931, a small column, human-interest story and picture was published in the *San Francisco News* under the heading 'Artist's Mate has own Success' [91].[1] Diego Rivera and his team of assistants were busy painting a mural in the San Francisco Stock Exchange tower and the press were suitably intrigued by the visit of a world-famous artist to their city.[2] Having covered the work of the muralist himself in earlier articles, their attention turned to his companion. The article goes on to inform us that the 'little dark eyed, black haired woman' who greets the reporter is none other than 'Mrs Diego Rivera' and that she is 'revealed as portrait artist in own right'. We are also told in a slightly surprised tone that she paints in 'her own way', uninfluenced by the work of her famous husband. The accompanying awkwardly posed photograph shows the 'cordial' Mrs Rivera, a typical artist at her easel, paintbrush in hand, supposedly putting the final touches to the portrait of her friend, Jean Wight. It reads as an unthreatening story of sanitized bohemia reaching out from another time and place.

Seventy-five years later, few people would recognize Mrs Rivera but millions across the world think they know her alter-ego *Frida*. From cupcakes to tattoos, the signature eyebrows, the coils of hair, the decorative ornaments and ribbons all serve to identify the symbolic components of this mythical Frida. It may be an inspirational Frida, a creative Frida, a suffering Frida or a subversive Frida, but above all it is always an easily recognizable Frida.

Films, plays and children's books, have all drawn on Hayden Herrera's 1983 bestselling biography of the artist to flesh out the visual cipher of Frida with details of her life and character, making her someone we not only recognize but also think we know. Like a character from a favourite soap opera we anticipate her likes and dislikes, while audiences recognise her place in the complex twenty-first century pantheon of allegorical women.

Characteristics of her appearance, and the identity she carefully constructed throughout her life, have become so easily parodied that they are the stuff of popular mimicry, from Beyoncé's Halloween costume[3] to a myriad of Frida lookalike competitions [92].[4] In donning the costume of Frida, such admirers are not only 'dressing up', they are aspiring to the very particular values that her image now represents and, through

91. 'ARTIST'S MATE HAS OWN SUCCESS. MRS. DIEGO RIVERA REVEALED AS PORTRAIT ARTIST IN OWN RIGHT', SAN FRANCISCO NEWS, JANUARY 1931
Collection of the author

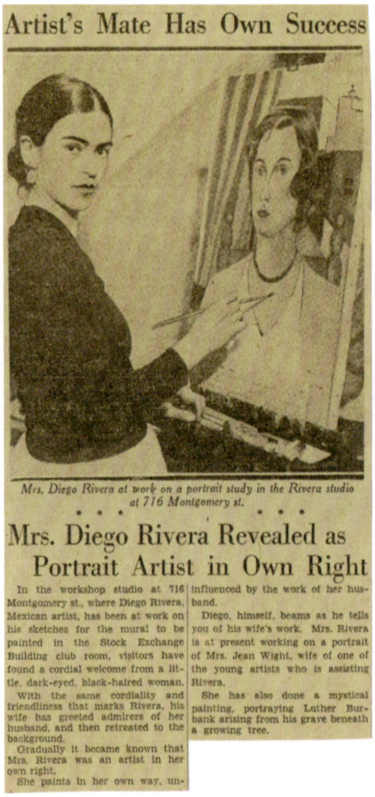

Artist's Mate Has Own Success

Mrs. Diego Rivera at work on a portrait study in the Rivera studio at 716 Montgomery st.

Mrs. Diego Rivera Revealed as Portrait Artist in Own Right

In the workshop studio at 716 Montgomery st., where Diego Rivera, Mexican artist, has been at work on his sketches for the mural to be painted in the Stock Exchange Building club room, visitors have found a cordial welcome from a little, dark-eyed, black-haired woman.

With the same cordiality and friendliness that marks Rivera, his wife has greeted admirers of her husband, and then retreated to the background.

Gradually it became known that Mrs. Rivera was an artist in her own right.

She paints in her own way, uninfluenced by the work of her husband.

Diego, himself, beams as he tells you of his wife's work. Mrs. Rivera is at present working on a portrait of Mrs. Jean Wight, wife of one of the young artists who is assisting Rivera.

She has also done a mystical painting, portraying Luther Burbank arising from his grave beneath a growing tree.

imitation, manifesting their own identifications with such values. Many of the qualities assigned to Frida in the popular imagination relate to very contemporary debates around identity and the body; to gender; to race; and perhaps above all to an assertive positioning in relation to these issues.

The elements of this visual characterization are parts of the iconography of Frida's identity – components of a symbolic embodiment of alterity, survival and empowerment. The combination of her natural, if unconventional, beauty and the self-aestheticization of what she called her 'broken' body[5] produced a form of 'Frida' costume that rests on a borderline between fashion and masquerade.[6] It is clear, however, that as an artist Kahlo was acutely aware of the iconographic significance of dress within the traditions of portraiture and she was always very precise in the ways in which she referenced clothing. She used costume in both her art and her self-presentation to empower or constrain, but never as simple ornament, it was always laden with symbolic meaning.[7]

And then there are the clothes themselves, frequently dramatic and evocative, functioning as both disguise and protective armour [95]. The precision and deliberateness of her choice of clothing on one level lends itself to parody and is easily absorbed into the fashion stylists' repertoire. From Jean-Paul Gaultier's famous appropriation of Kahlo's surgical corset in his 1998 spring/summer collection [93] to more recent explorations of Frida's style potential in *Vogue Italia* in 2014, there is no mistaking the inspirational image behind the re-workings [94]. In these and the many other popular evocations of Frida-mania, the particularities of dress are often subsumed by the accepted parodies of *Frida*. Eyebrows, hairstyle and decorative ornament all serve to connote the connection. The pointed symbolism in the artist's own choice of clothing is often subsumed by audiences into a generic homage to her Mexican heritage, even though it is usually far more specific in its meaning.

This is nowhere more evident than in her predilection for the Tehuana costume. For Kahlo, to wear Tehuana clothing was more than an assertion of her interest in Mexico's native heritage: it was also an adoption of gendered myths of identity popular in the post-revolutionary rhetoric of the Mexican avant-garde. The costume is particular to the women of

92. BEN HIDER
FRIDA KAHLO LOOKALIKE COMPETITION,
NEW YORK BOTANICAL GARDENS, 2015

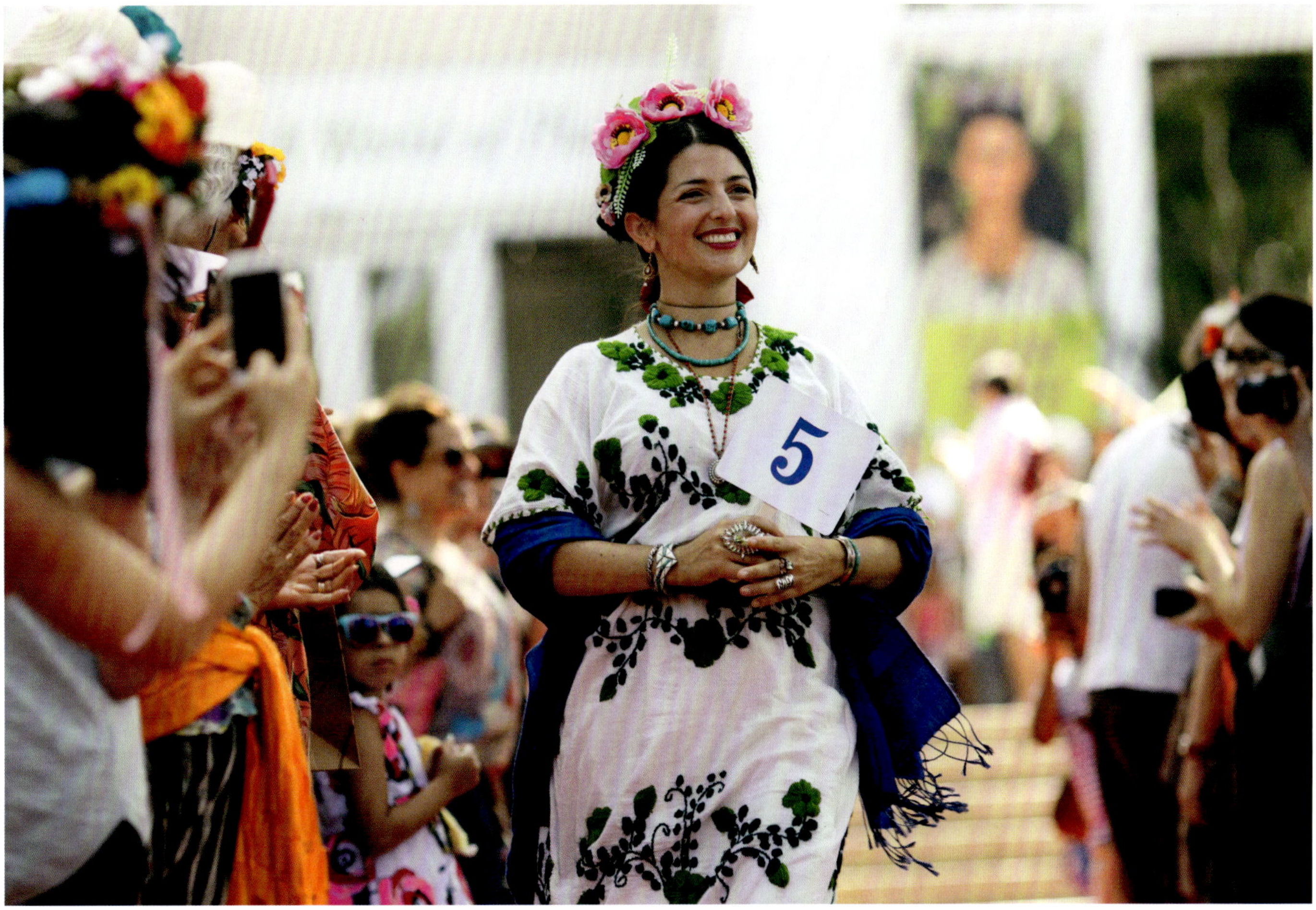

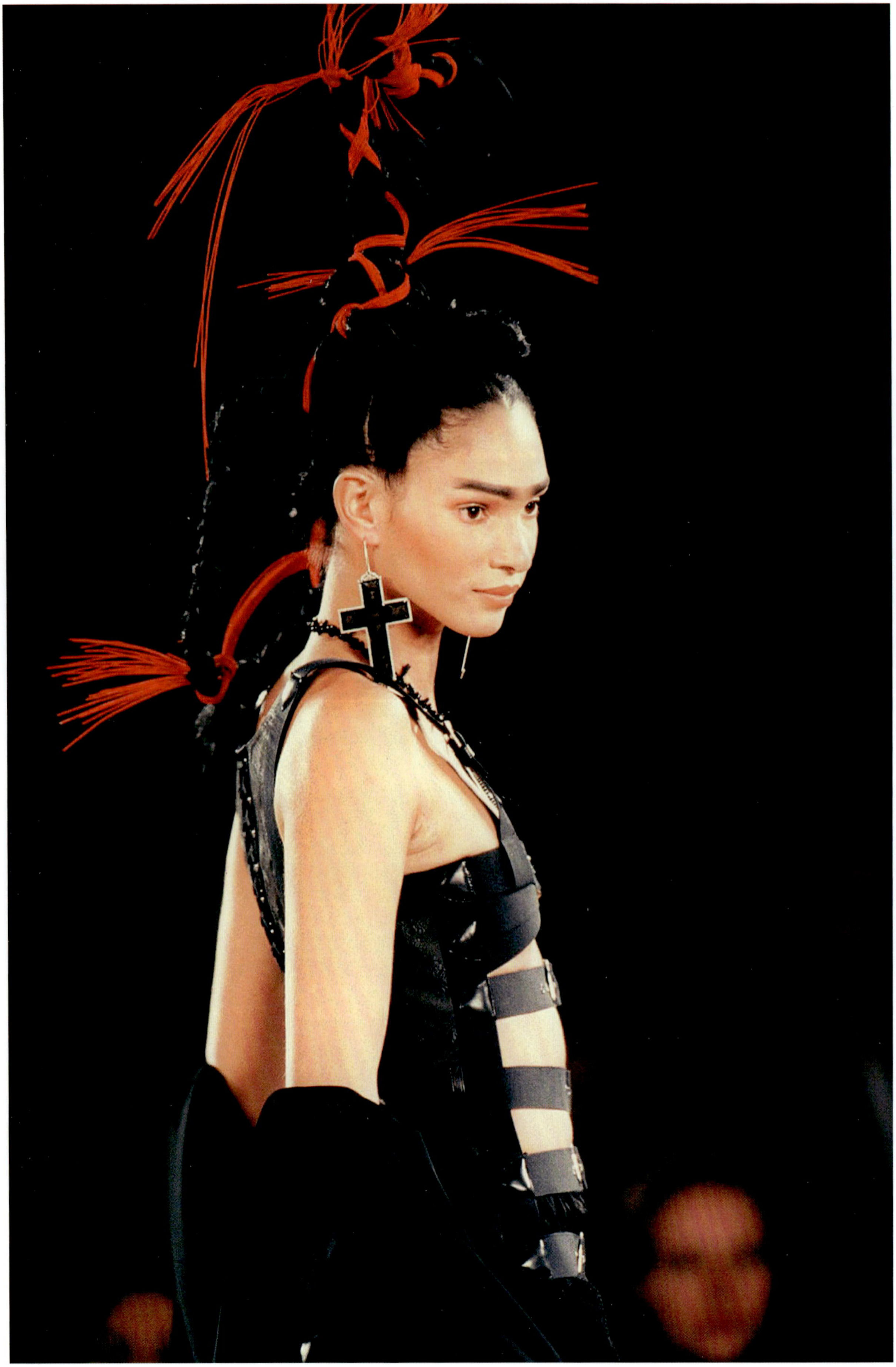

the Isthmus of Tehuantepec and ascribed to the matriarchal society of the region. In the anti-colonialist iconography of Mexico, the region represented a purer, more empowered, Indian culture. The legitimate mother was often used in opposition to the figure of the subjugated land of Mexico, as represented by the maligned figure of Malinche, the metaphorical mother of mestizo Mexico.[8] Within this gendered rhetoric of the region's colonial trauma, the phenomenon of the Tehuana woman was a long-accepted signifier of a strong unbowed Mexico. During the revolutionary period in Mexico, Spanish colonization was often characterized as the rape and dishonouring of the indigenous race through the allegory of Hernán Cortés taking the Indian woman Malinche as his mistress and then abandoning her. The Tehuana iconography, on the other hand, represented the indigenous woman resisting conquest and colonization.

As a protagonist during this era of polemical artistic rhetoric, Kahlo frequently used her body and biographical experiences to debate issues of colonial identity and sexual politics metaphorically. Her body is sometimes portrayed as the injured colonized territory or the empowered revolutionary state, but it is more often an amalgam of flesh and clothing designed to produce a hybrid embodiment of complex political histories. In some paintings, she finds strength by adopting clothing with references to redemption and hope even while she is presenting her body as injured, not only in her own personal reality, but also through the metaphorical pain and struggles of Mexico's past. The personal and the political are shown mirroring each other in explorations of her identity.

This is articulated most famously in *The Two Fridas*, originally painted in 1939, and exhibited at the International Exhibition of Surrealism held in Mexico City in 1940 [101]. The painting was one of her very few large-scale works aimed at a public audience and it depicts twin Fridas sitting impassively staring out at the spectator with a mixture of pride and despair. It is a work in which the figures' clothing takes precedence over the famous features of Kahlo's close-up self-portraits.

On the stretched canvas stage of the painting the protagonists are dressed in clear opposition. On the viewers' left is the colonial Frida in a demure European-style white lace dress, decorated with spots of blood

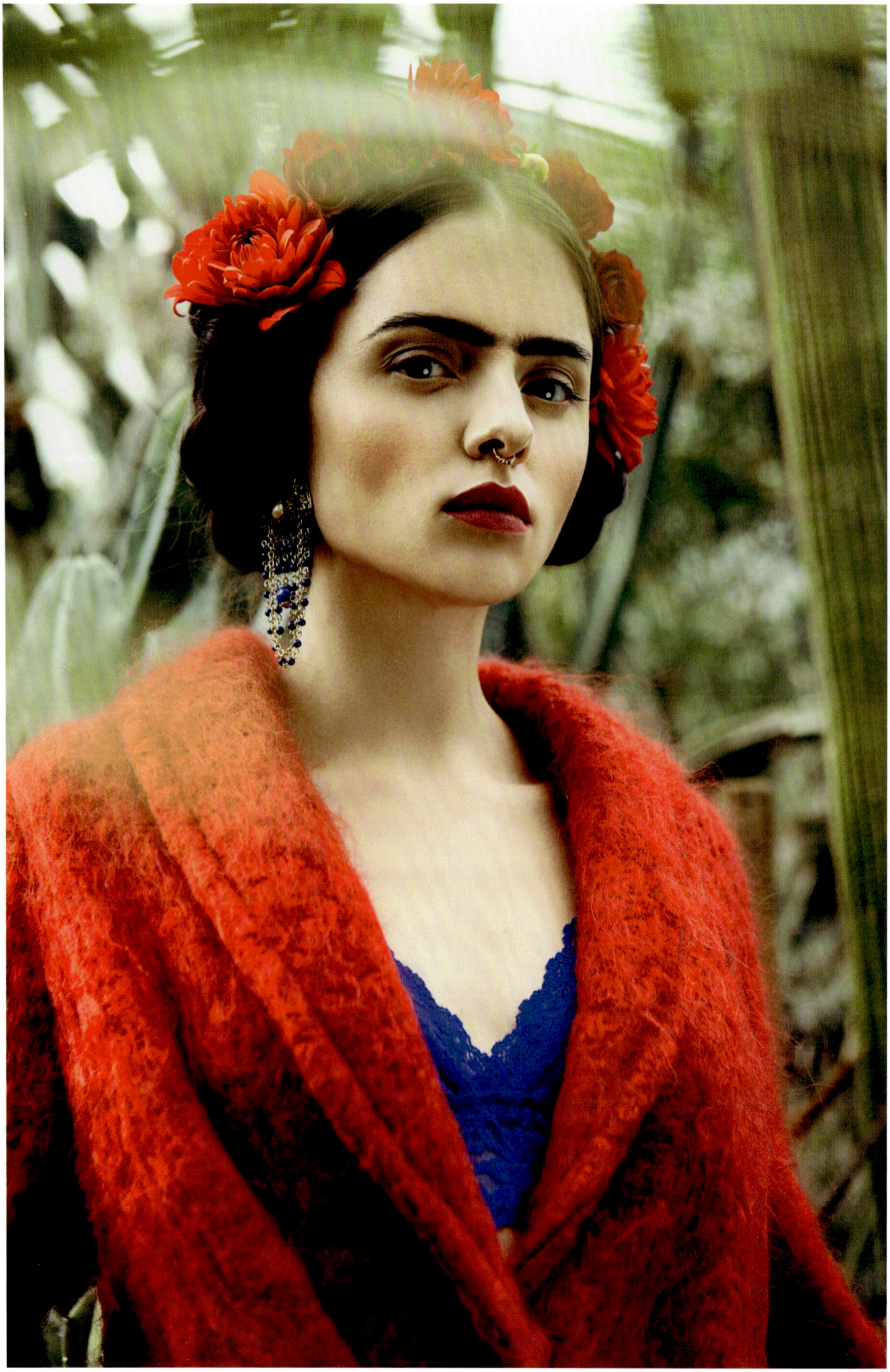

94. JENN WERNER
'FRIDA', VOGUE ITALIA, DECEMBER 2014
Stylist and Creative Director: Lisa-Marie Mewes; Model: Kate Heck @ Tune Models; Hair and Make-up: Claudia Astorino; Stylist Assistant: Tim Slotta

95. NICKOLAS MURAY
FRIDA KAHLO WITH OLMEC FIGURINE, 1939
Nickolas Muray Photo Archives

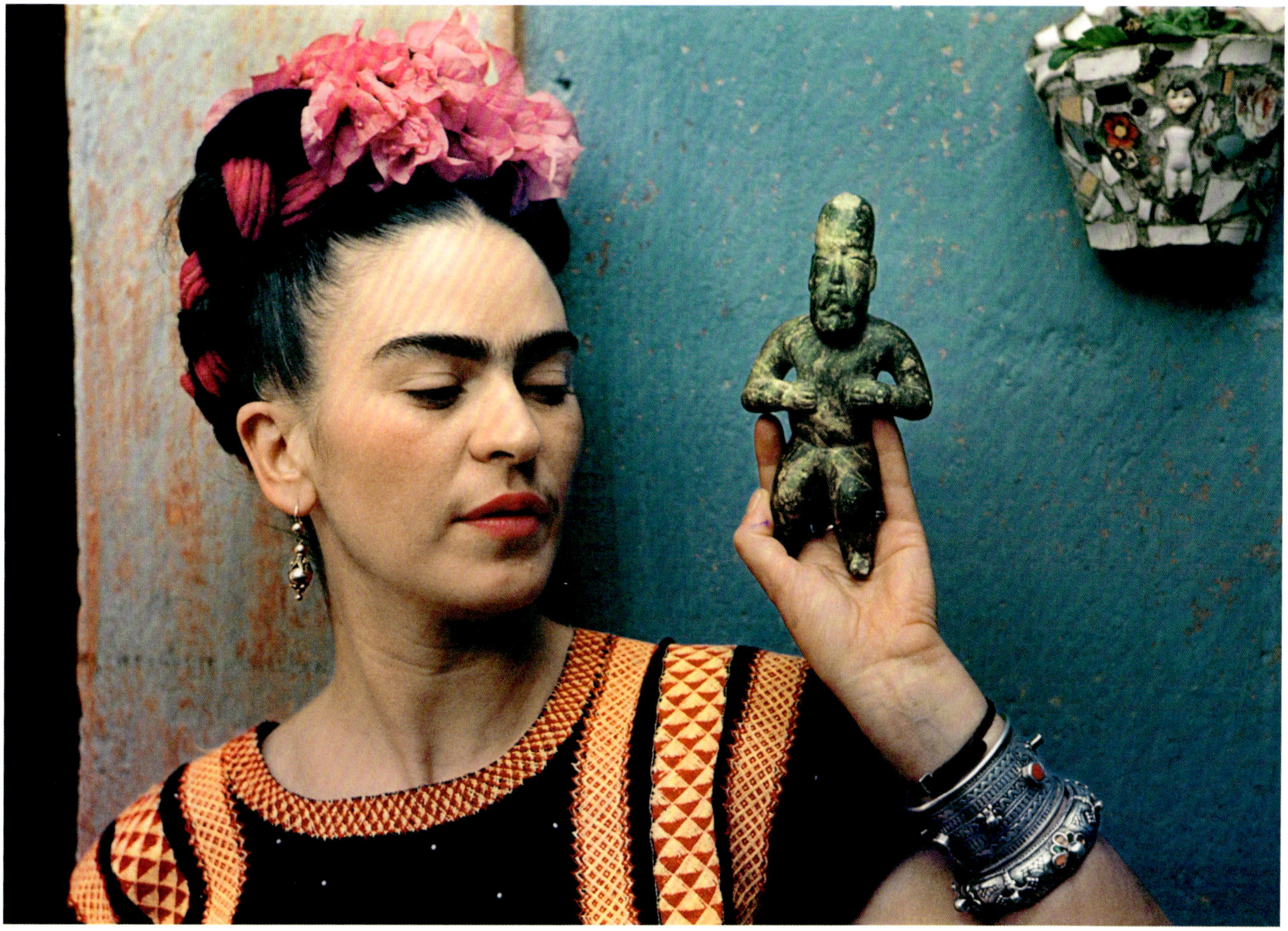

dripping from the vein of her other self, the recognizably Tehuana-clothed Frida. The subordinate colonized bride and the powerful unbowed matriarch – they are interdependent yet incompatible – doomed to a perpetually interwoven conflict. Within the iconography of Kahlo's art, the cluster of meanings symbolized by the Tehuana woman represents not just an unconquered native soil but the new, positively chosen, future of a post-colonial Mexican state. In the use of the analogy between the self and the nation, Kahlo characterizes her own physical and emotional problems as symptomatic of the post-colonial condition, with dress as the mechanism through which the individual can both change and heal.

The twin Fridas are the embodiment of the conflict implicit in a mestizo culture, never truly European but never truly Indian. On one level, the artist is proposing that it is the Tehuana Frida that Rivera purportedly loved, the colonial Frida his rejected wife. However, Kahlo also recognizes that she, and Mexico, are not one or other of these two identities but both, making the point that there is maybe no more one true Frida than there is one true Mexico.

In another key work to address these themes, *My Dress Hangs There* (1933) painted while unhappy and homesick in the United States, the artist makes it clear that the *Tehuana* dress means more to her than clothing [96]. In this work, the disembodied dress hangs in the very North American environment that for the artist represented a world antithetical to the values associated with the concept of the Tehuana. Her chosen clothing has lost its strength-giving powers, disconnected from the reality of Mexico, it becomes a ghost-like apparition evoking instead a sense of alienation and loss. The composition suggests that the dress and the body need to be in harmonious union or Kahlo's choice of clothing becomes meaningless.

It is this metaphor of dress as choice that makes the use of clothing in Kahlo's art so intriguing. Just as the ancient Greeks had the story of the mythological shirt of Nessus imbued with the poisoned blood of the Hydra [9], which kills the hero Hercules, Kahlo is clear that if clothing can redeem, it can also condemn. The theme of the poisoned dress is memorably evoked by Kahlo in her painting *The Suicide of Dorothy Hale*

96. FRIDA KAHLO
MY DRESS HANGS THERE, 1933
OIL AND COLLAGE ON HARDBOARD. 46 × 50 CM
Private collection

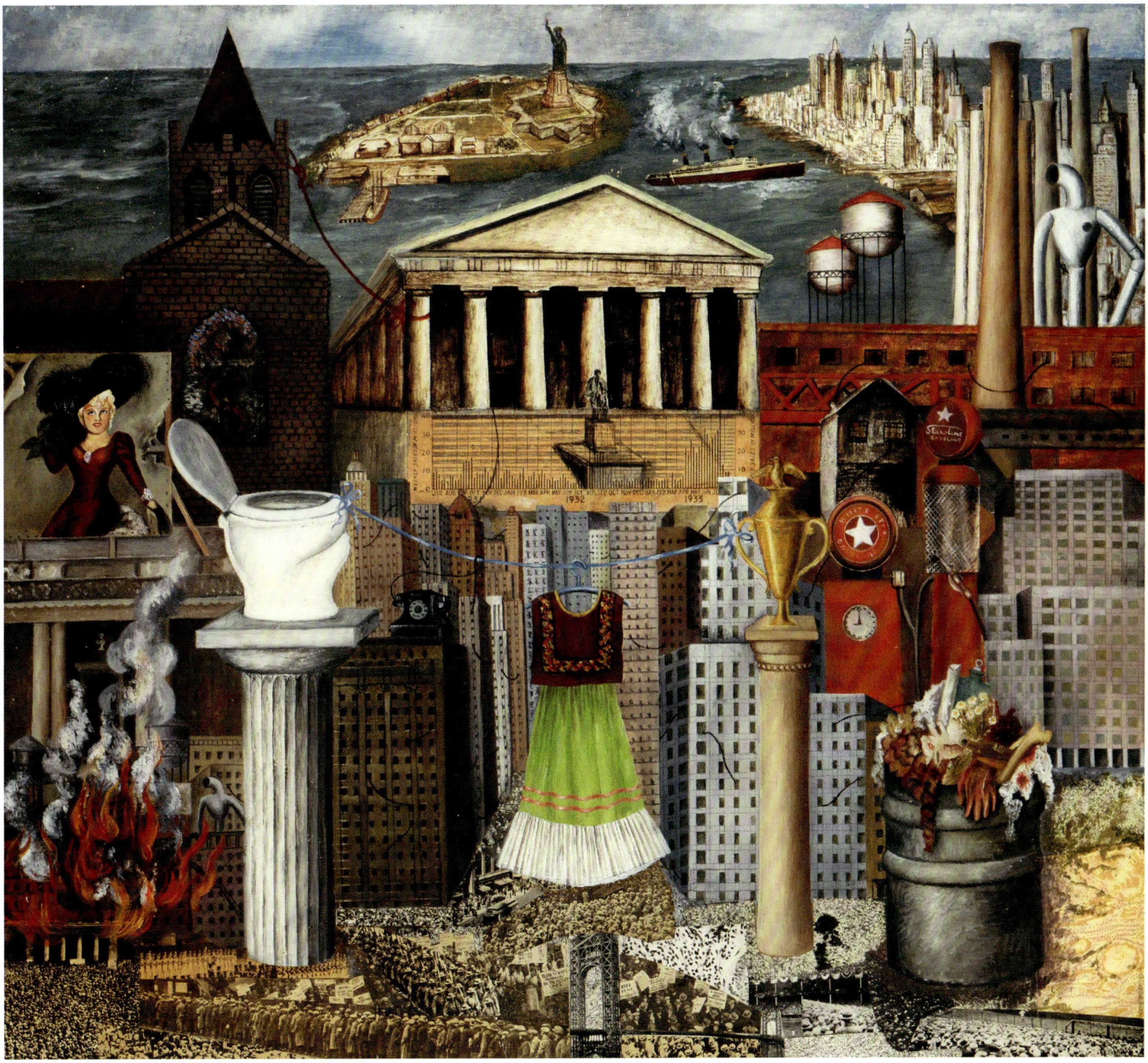

97. FRIDA KAHLO
THE SUICIDE OF DOROTHY HALE, 1939
OIL ON HARDBOARD WITH PAINTED FRAME.
50 × 40.6 CM
Phoenix Art Museum. 1960.2

(1938) [97]. In this small, disturbing painting commissioned by Hale's friend Clare Booth Luce,[10] Kahlo shows Hale falling from the window of her smart Central Park apartment in Hampshire House, New York.

The multiple versions of Dorothy within the painting show the unfolding tragedy, from the initial suicidal leap to the surprisingly alert corpse that lies awkwardly along the bottom of the composition. The blood seeping across the artist's dedication onto the picture frame adds a level of violence and threat otherwise lost in the misty clouds from which Hale's body descends. The tragedy of the young woman's death is turned into a cautionary moral tale through the emphasis on the black velvet dress and corsage. Here is a woman, hailed as a beauty, with the surface appearance of wealth and social success destroyed by the very society she represents. Dorothy Hale's despair and unhappiness at being unable to find success through a career, a husband or inherited wealth, was well documented in the gossip of the time.[11] Kahlo puts the blame clearly on the values of New York society for the needless loss of a woman with her life ahead of her. In her painting the black evening dress symbolizes all the things that Hale both yearned for and which ultimately proved her downfall. Hale's choice of dress was a political one, her inability to survive the values of the society within which she was trapped turns the dress into a little black shroud.

In the end, Kahlo leaves us with a proposition: inherit the world you are given or choose to change it. The appearance created by Frida Kahlo was not so much about who she was, it was about who she wanted to be; dress became a magical cloak of identity. In the Museum of Modern Art in New York, Kahlo's *Fulang Chang and I* (1937) is hung next to a mirror in a matching frame [98]. Through this very knowing curatorial device the museum visitor confronts their own role as a viewer of Kahlo's work.[12] You look at her, looking at a reflection of herself, and then turn to your own reflected appearance. The spectator is caught in an infinite process of identification; self-contemplation as self-contemplation. In this fascinating act of spectatorship, however, something is lost. Kahlo becomes a vehicle upon which to project a feminist dialogue, but her own intentionality is subsumed.

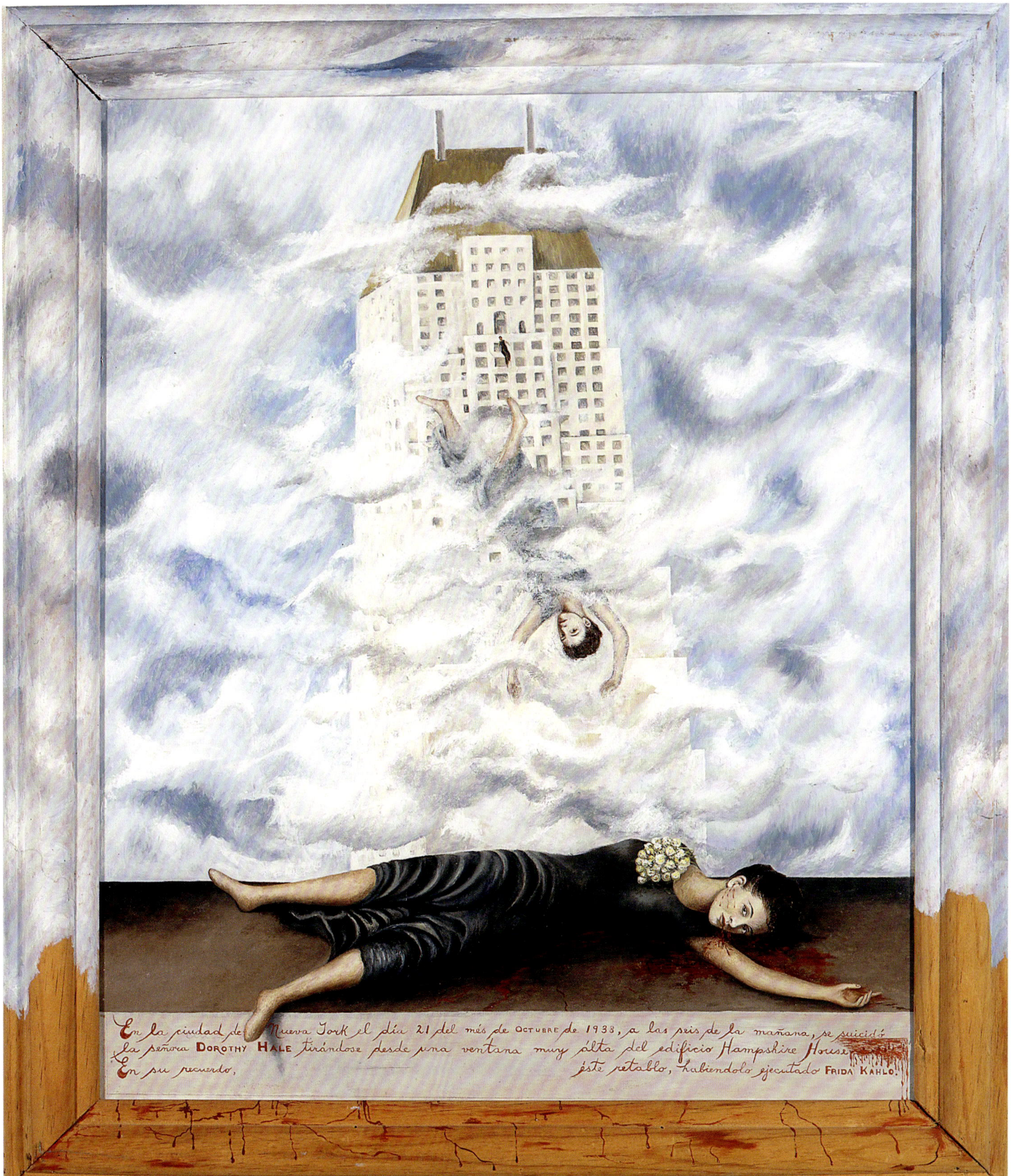
En la ciudad de Nueva Iork el día 21 del més de OCTUBRE de 1938, a las seis de la mañana, se suicidó
la señora DOROTHY HALE tirándose desde una ventana muy álta del edificio Hampshire House.
En su recuerdo, éste retablo, habiendolo ejecutado FRIDA KAHLO.

p.188

98. FRIDA KAHLO
FULANG-CHANG AND I, 1937
(ASSEMBLED AFTER 1939)
OIL ON COMPOSITION BOARD (1937) WITH PAINTED MIRROR FRAME (ADDED AFTER 1939); AND MIRROR WITH PAINTED MIRROR FRAME (AFTER 1939). 56.5 × 44.1 CM
Museum of Modern Art, New York. 277.1987.a-b

p.189

99. NICKOLAS MURAY
FRIDA KAHLO WITH PAINTED MIRROR FRAME, C.1939
Private collection

pp.190–1

100. LEO MATIZ
FRIDA KAHLO, C.1941
Leo Matiz Foundation

pp.192–3

DETAIL OF EUROPEAN SILK MANTILLA
Museo Frida Kahlo

It is that very intentionality, purpose and conscious action that is so frequently perceived as the key characteristic of the artist. In Kahlo's case there is the constant danger that the woman not the artist becomes the focus of audience attention. Gaultier's corset or Beyoncé's Halloween costume evoke the appearance of Frida, but not the artistic language of Kahlo. The cartoon characteristics of Frida-mania so easily become parody, obscuring the intelligence underpinning the work of one of the twentieth century's great artists. It remains important to remember that it was Kahlo who first created Frida [99].

101. NICKOLAS MURAY
FRIDA KAHLO PAINTING 'THE TWO FRIDAS' C.1939
Nickolas Muray Photo Archives

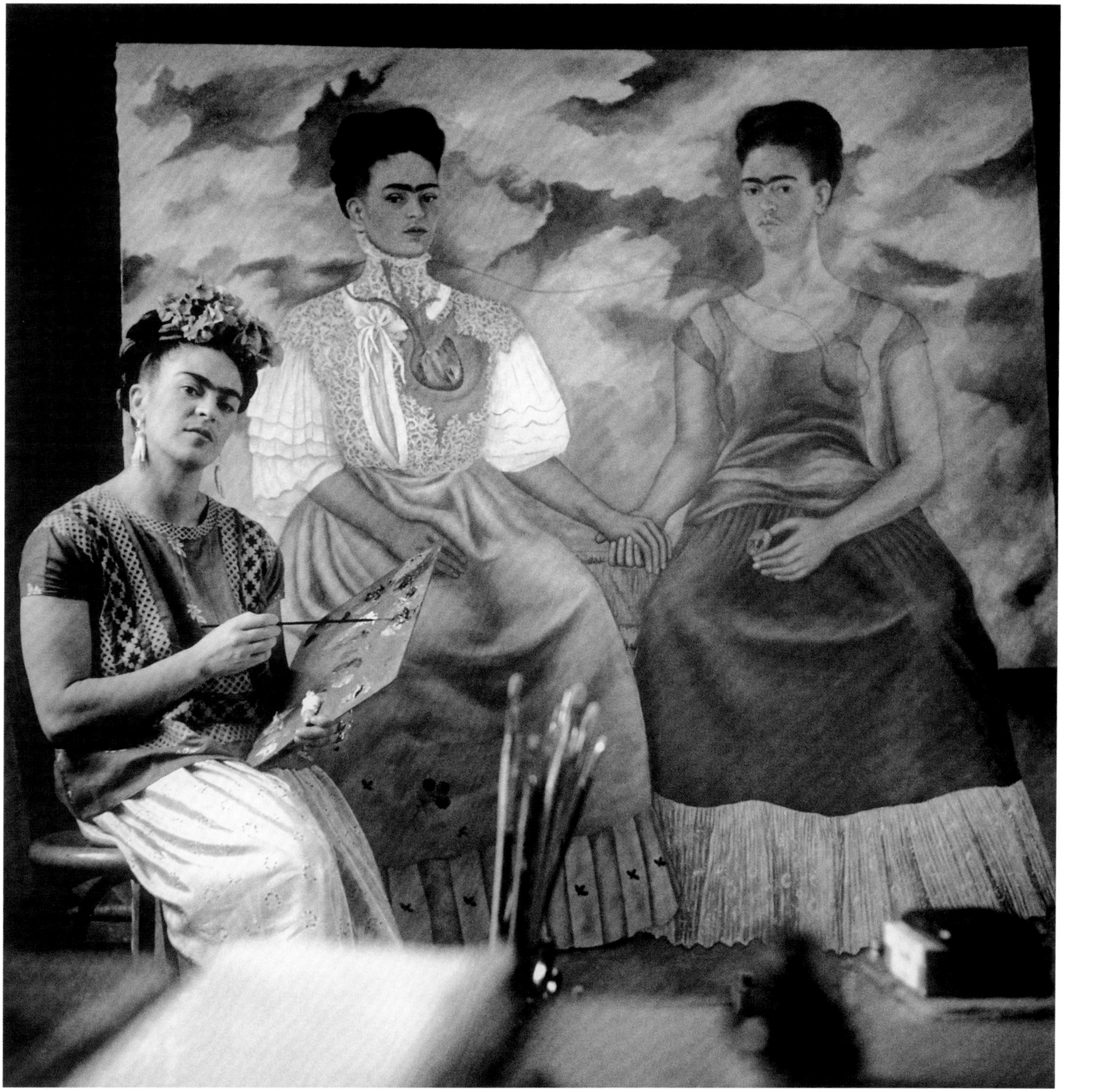

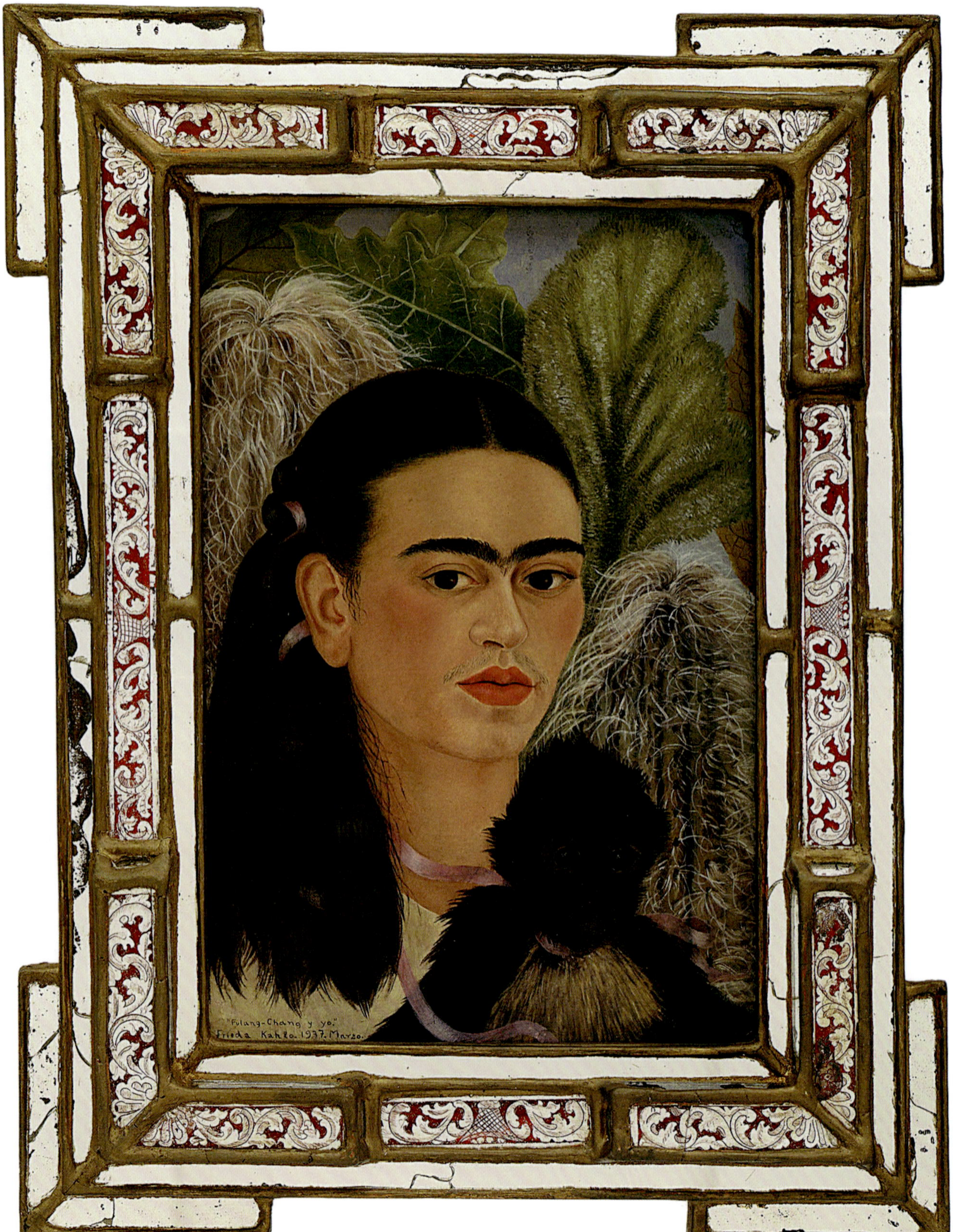
"Fulang-Chang y yo."
Frieda Kahlo. 1937. Marzo.

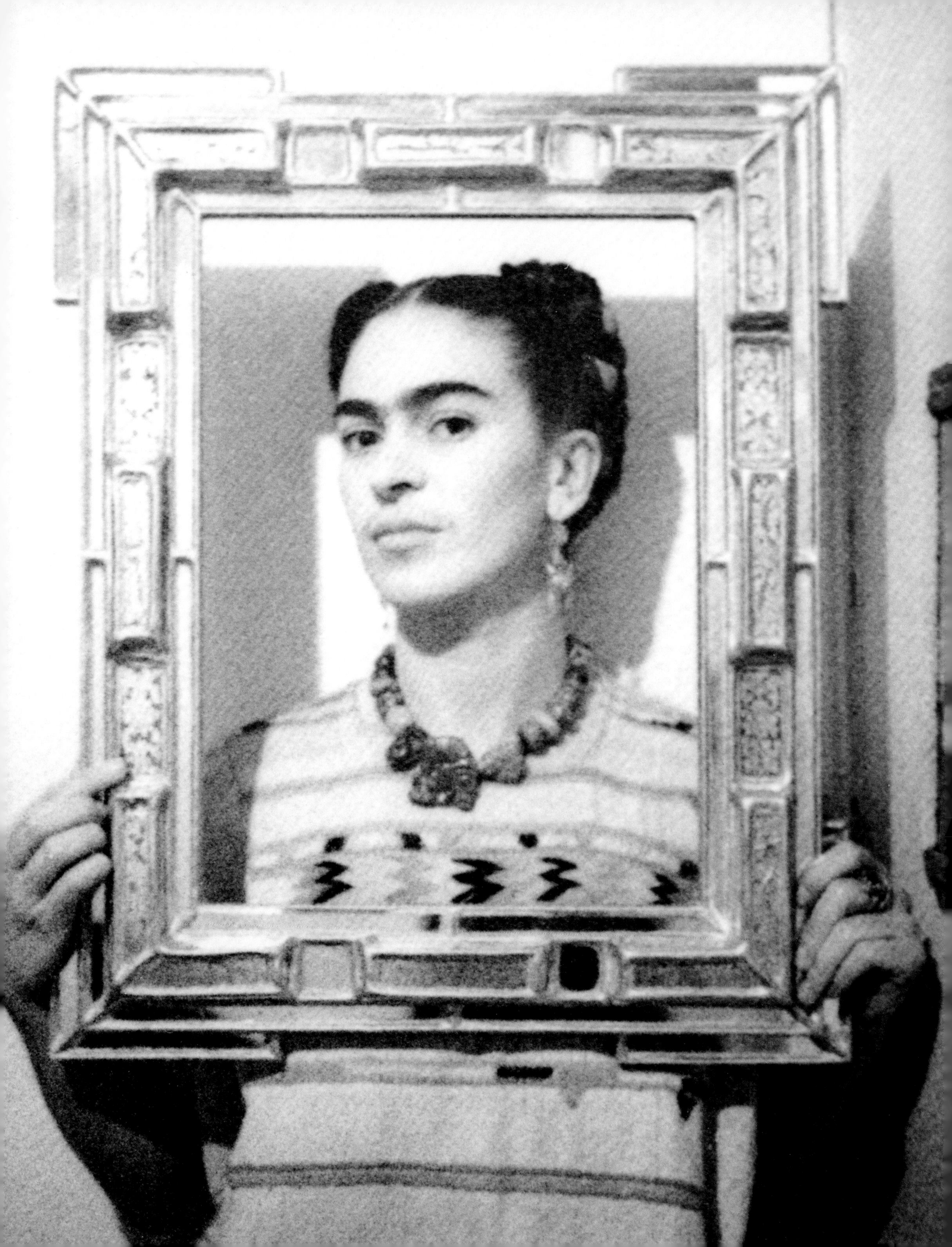

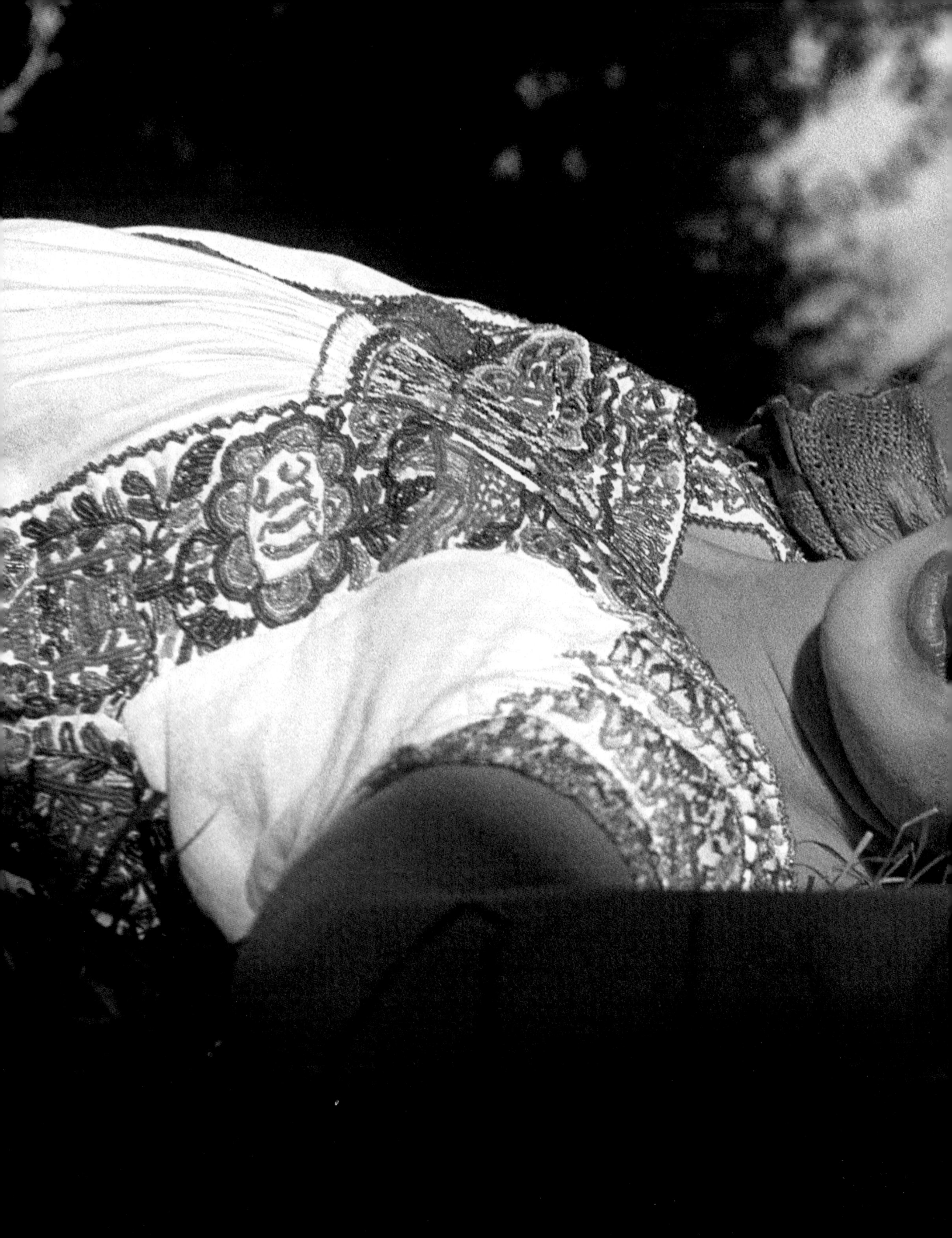

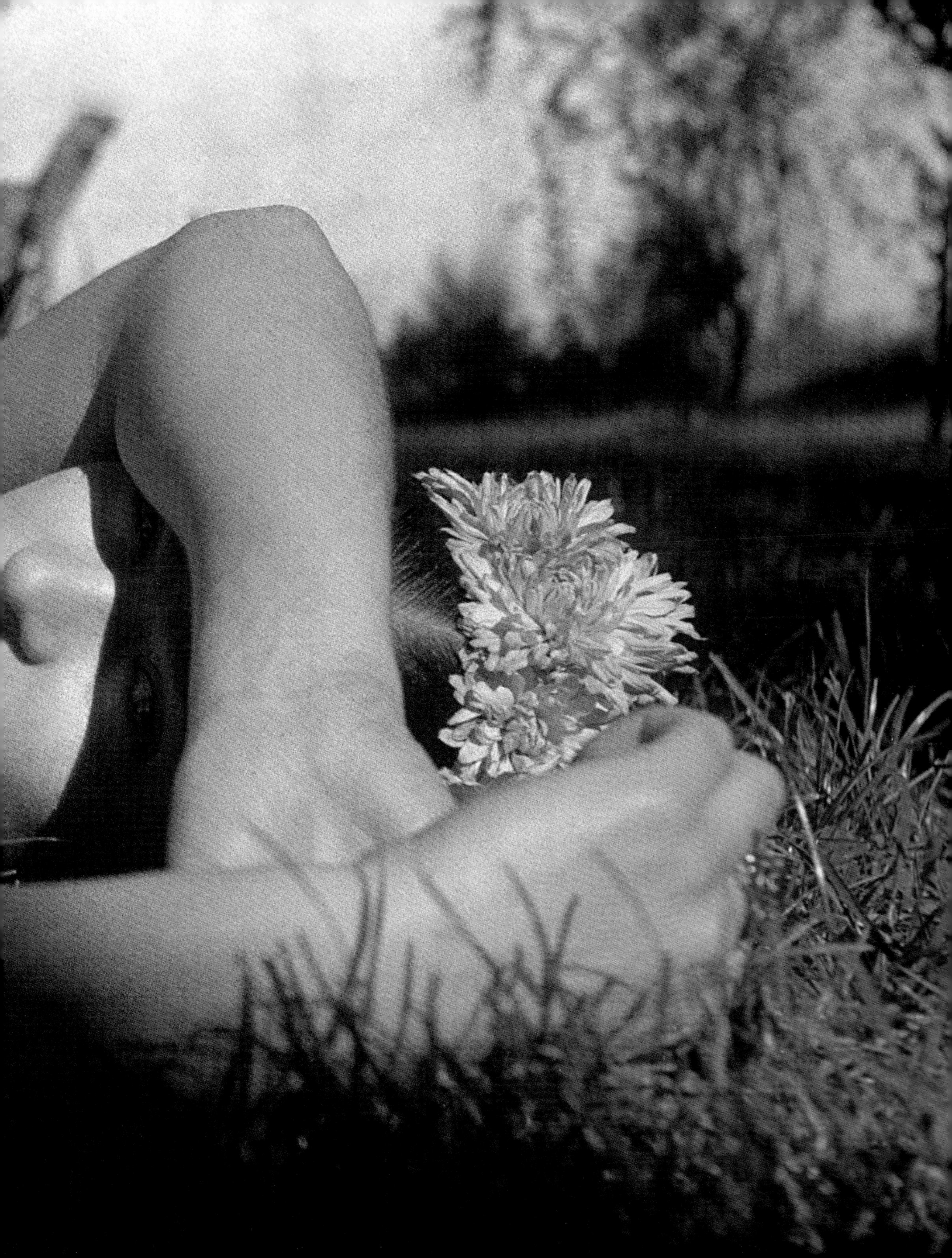

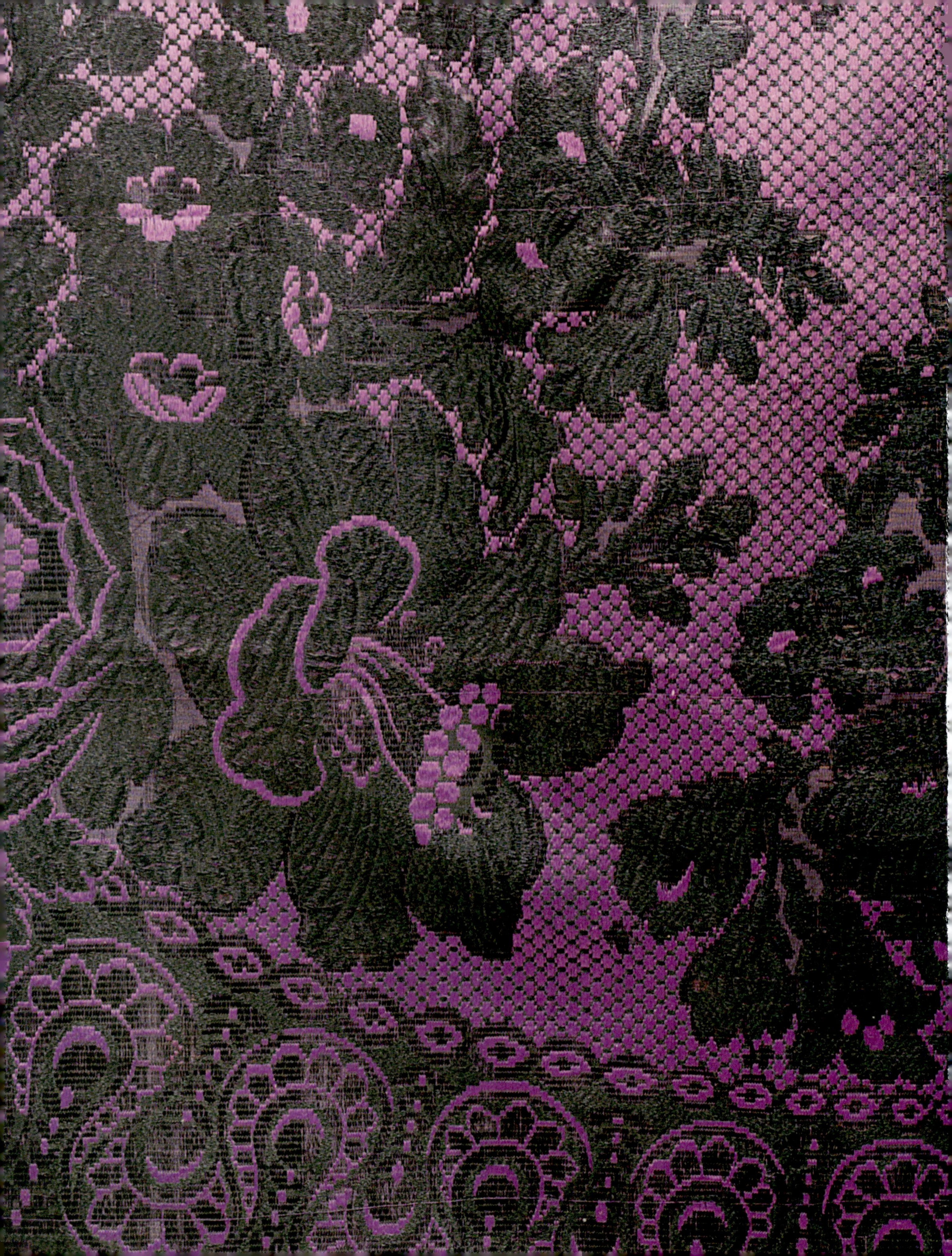

SALICATO DE SODIO (SODIUM SALICYLATE)
Museo Frida Kahlo

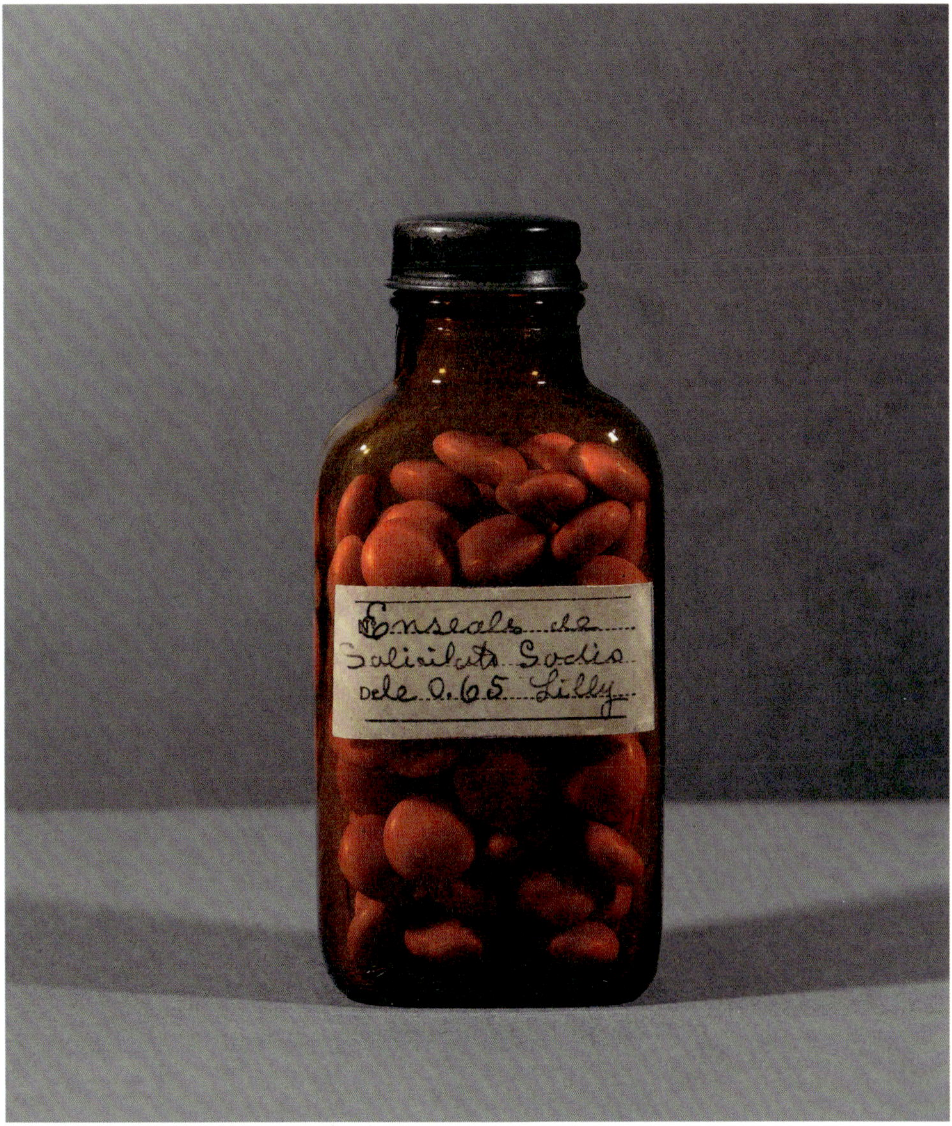

RIBOFLAVINA (RIBOFLAVIN)
Museo Frida Kahlo

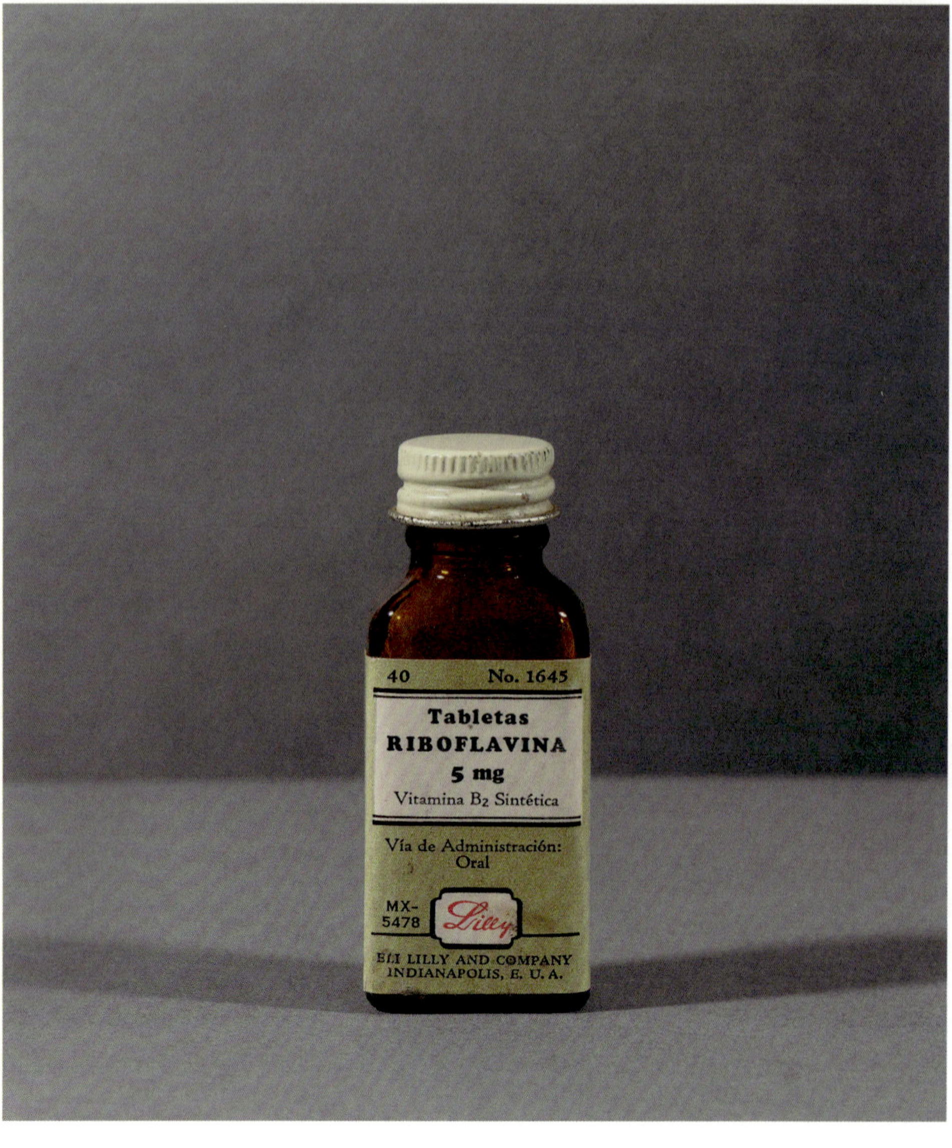

SALICATO DE SODIO (SODIUM SALICYLATE)
Museo Frida Kahlo

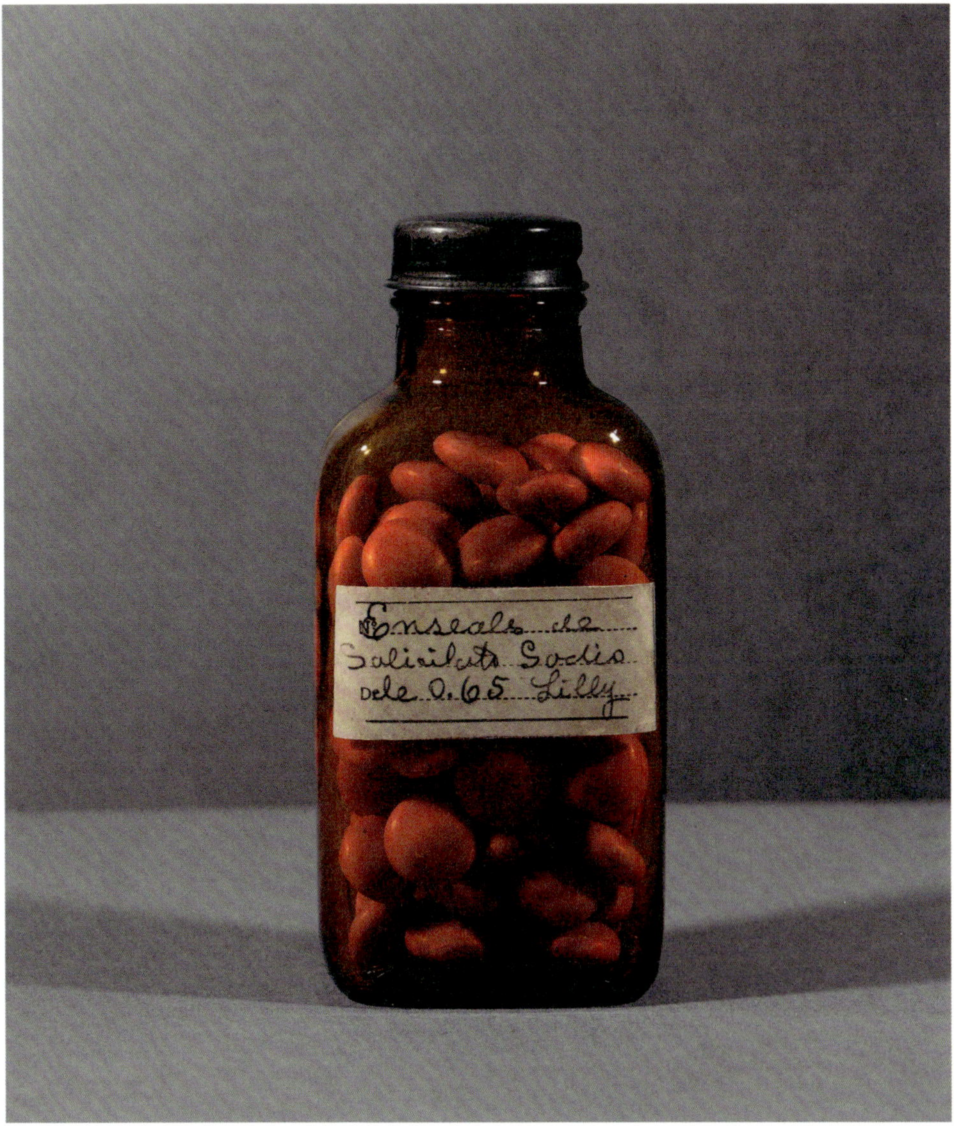

RIBOFLAVINA (RIBOFLAVIN)
Museo Frida Kahlo

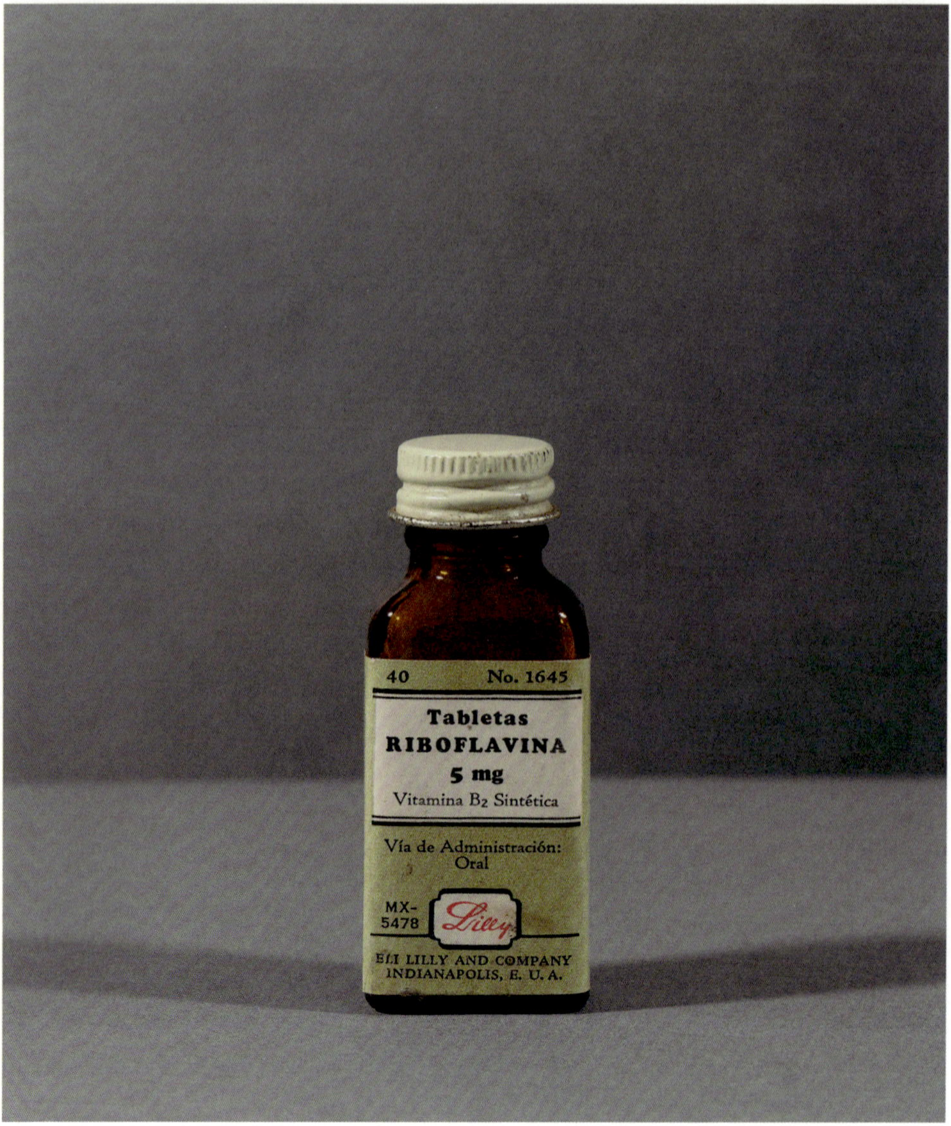

TIAMINA (THIAMIN)
Museo Frida Kahlo

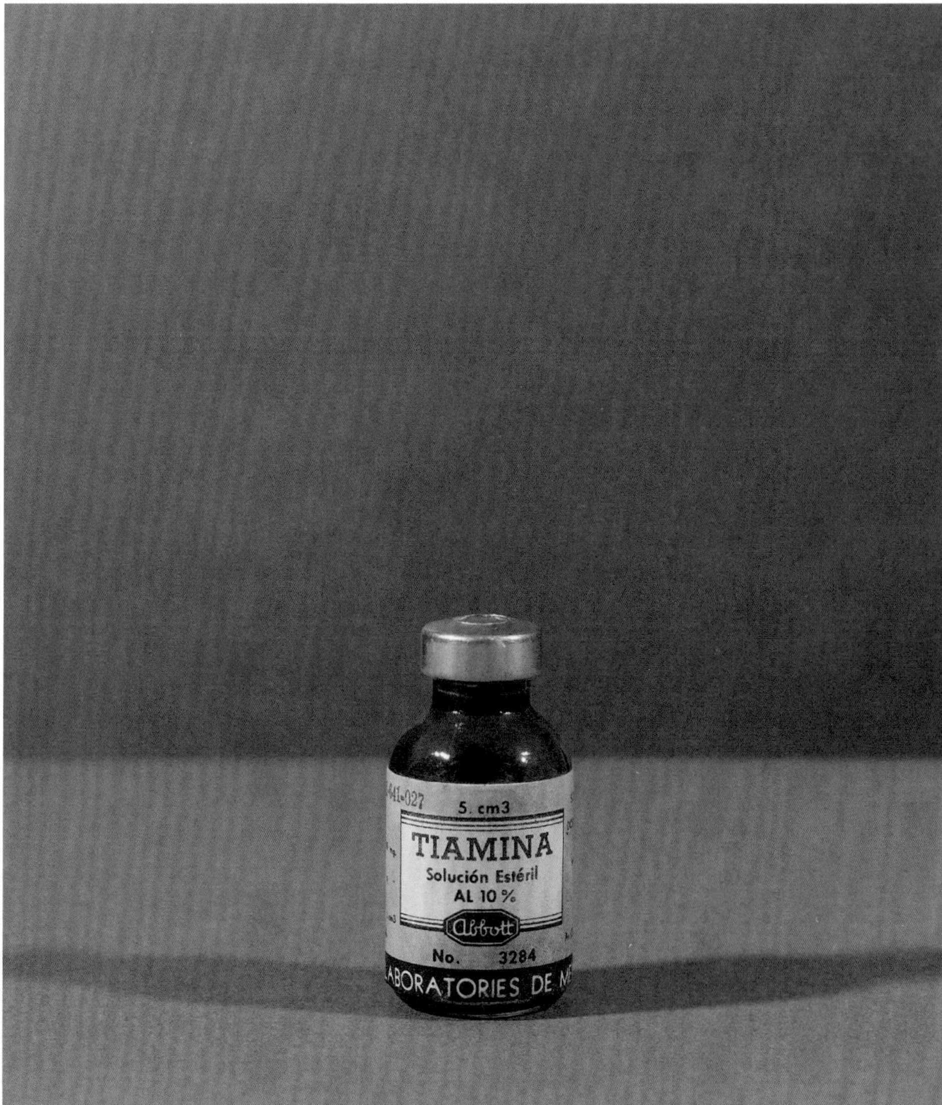

LECHE DE MAGNESIA DE PHILLIPS
(PHILLIPS' MILK OF MAGNESIA)
Museo Frida Kahlo

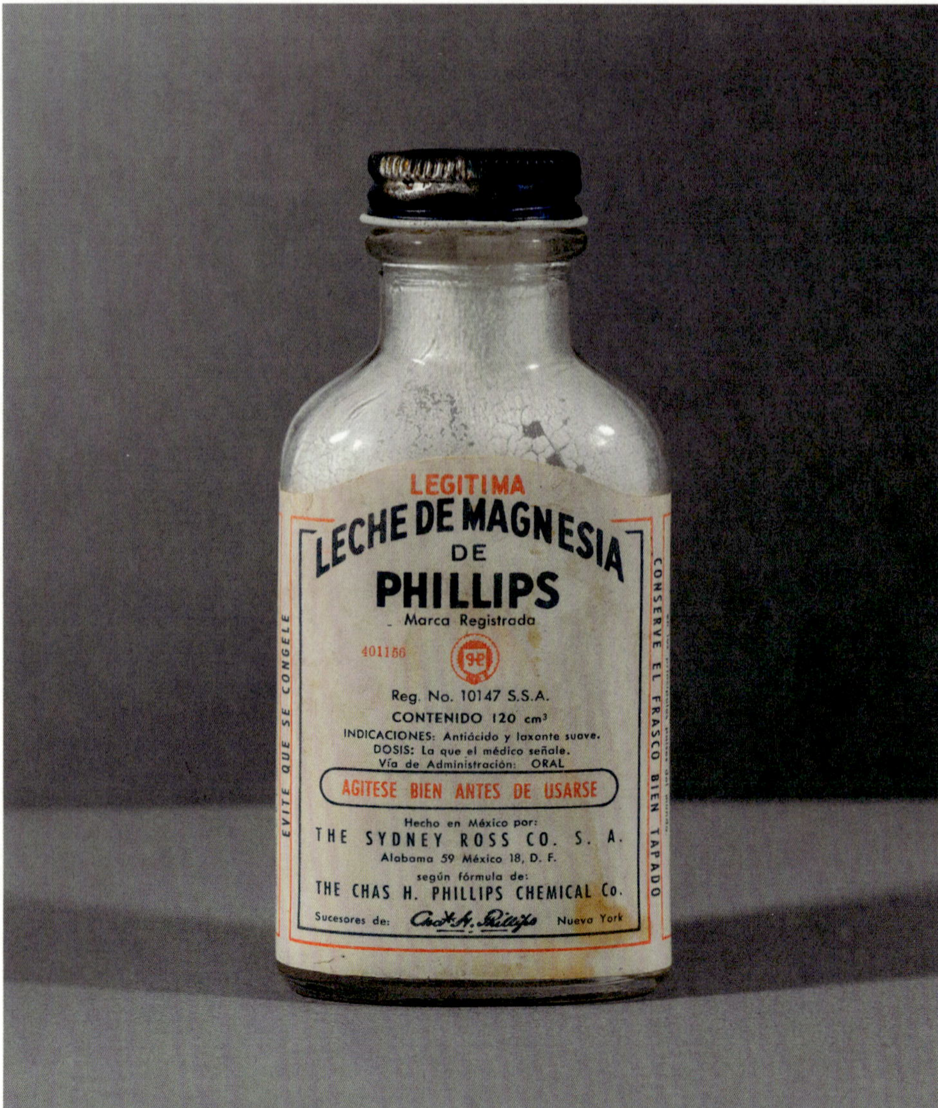

SOLUCION ADRENALINA STEIN
("STEIN" ADRENALINE SOLUTION)
Museo Frida Kahlo

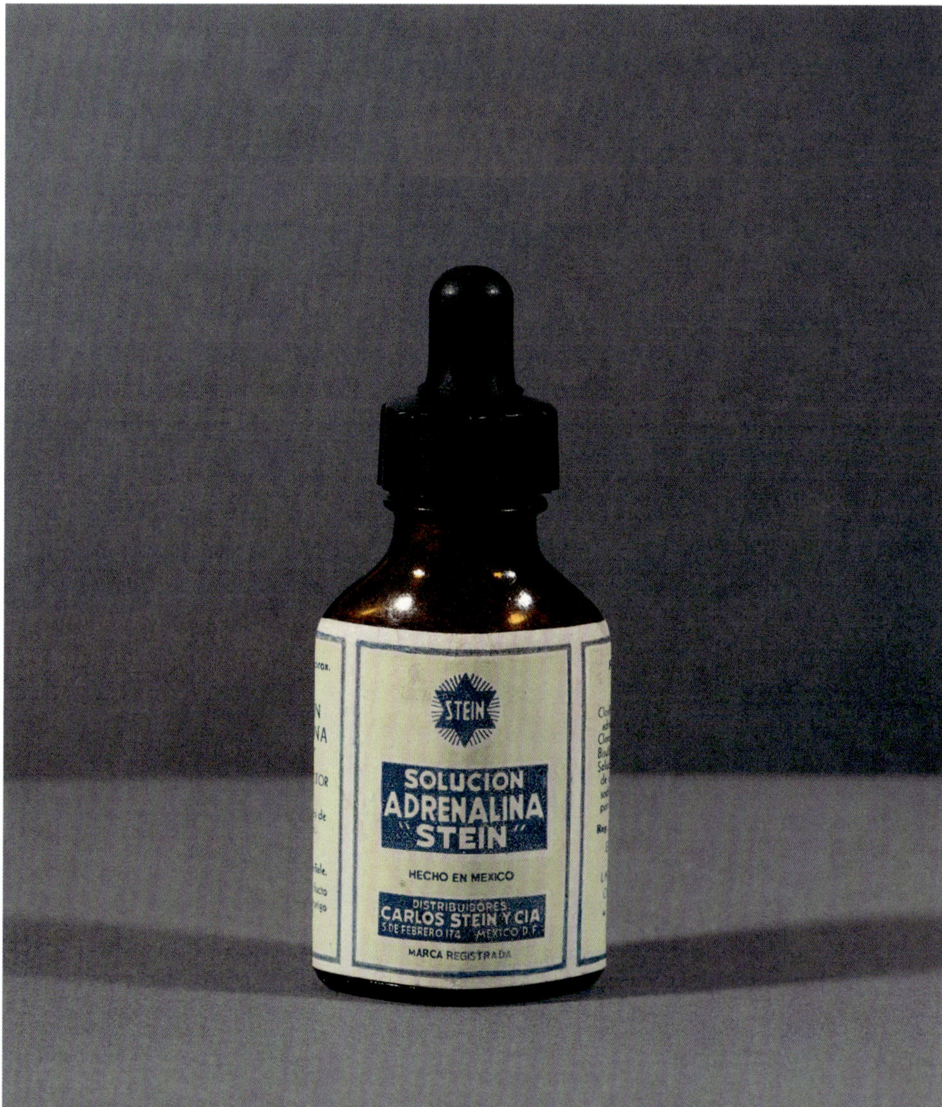

AMPOULES: LUTOCICLINA, NEURIBISMO,
LOBELINA DOSIS FUERTE
Museo Frida Kahlo

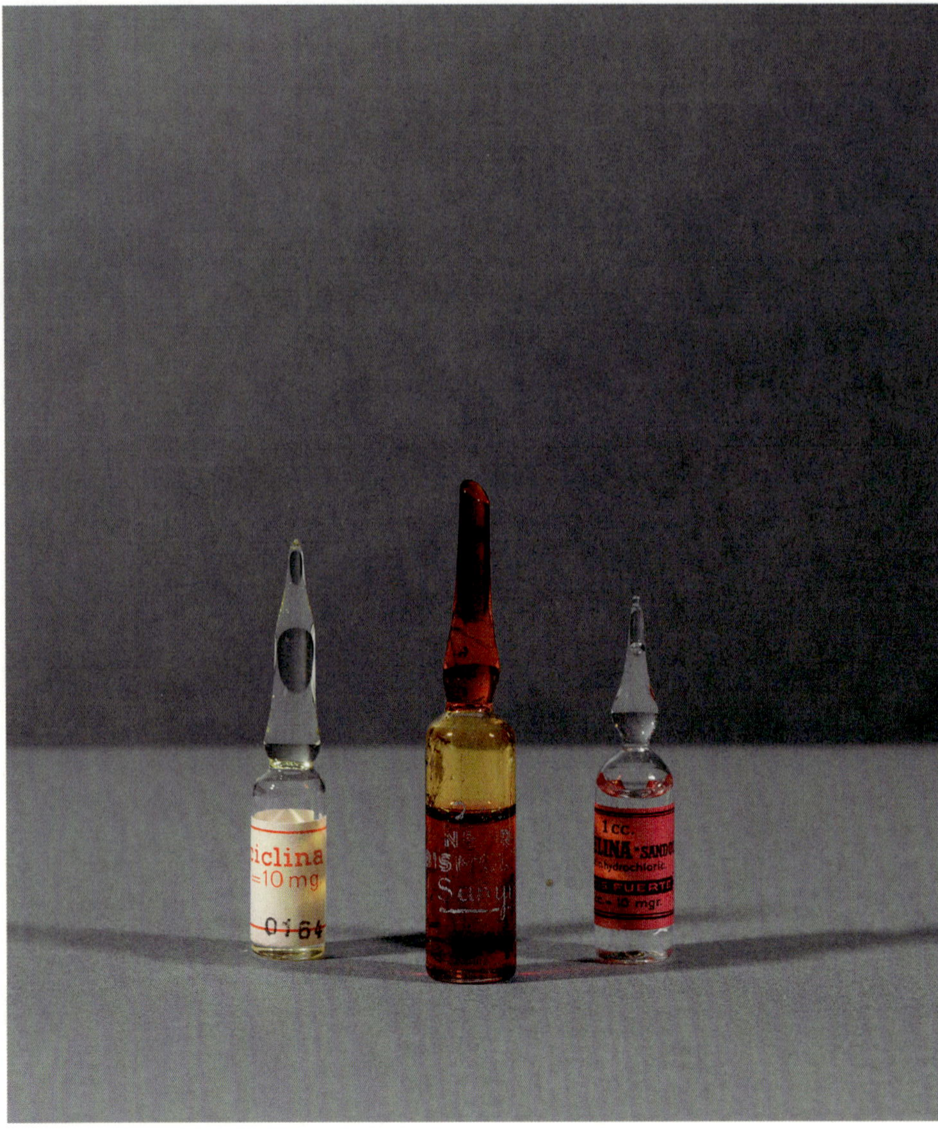

TERPIONYL. BOX OF 10 AMPOULES
Museo Frida Kahlo

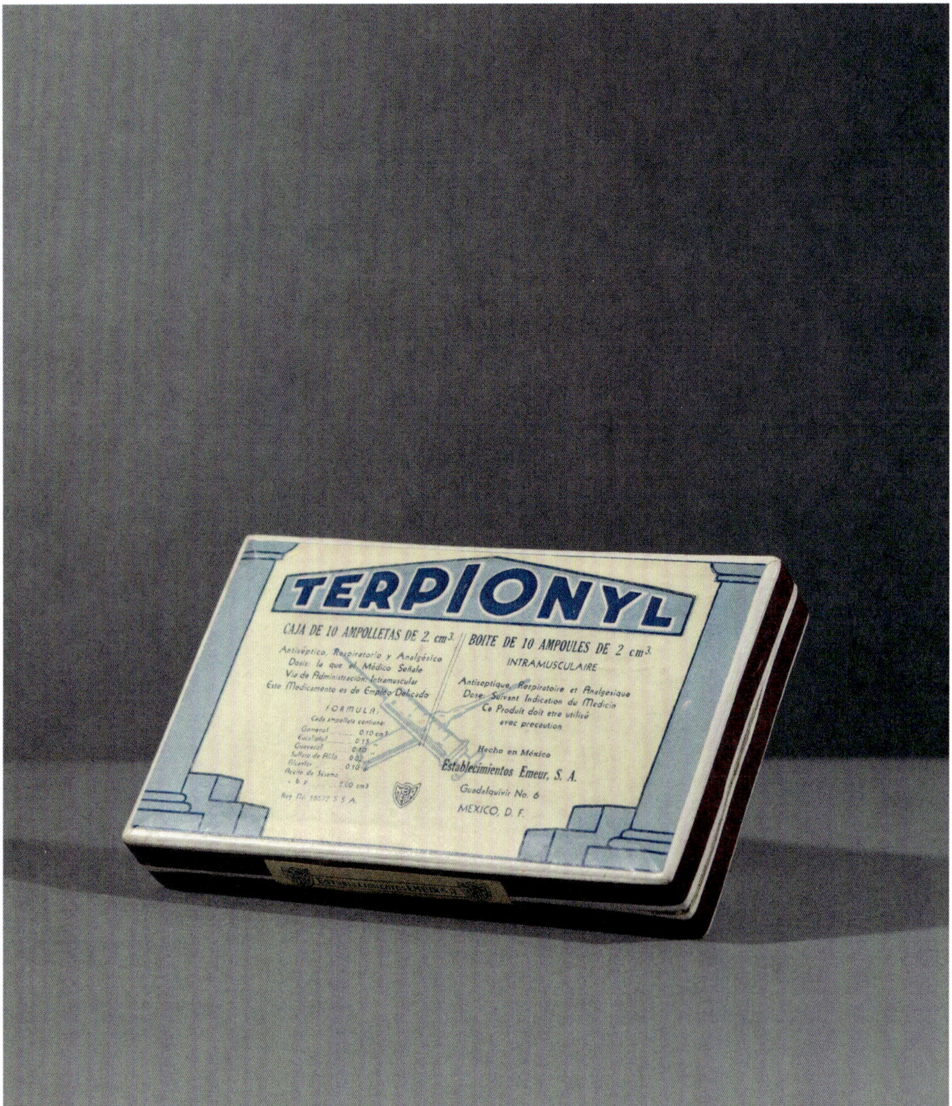

VI. 7

CHLOROFORMO (CHLOROFORM)
Museo Frida Kahlo

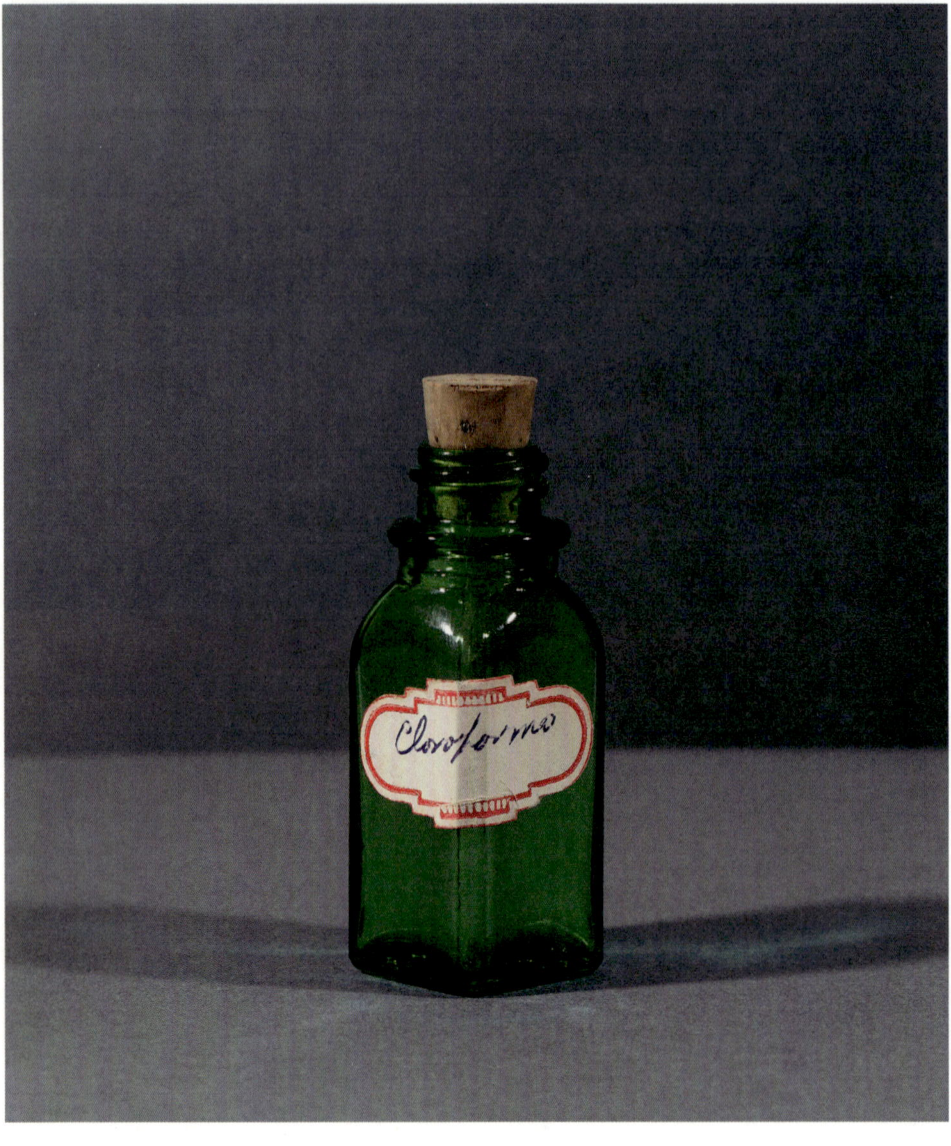

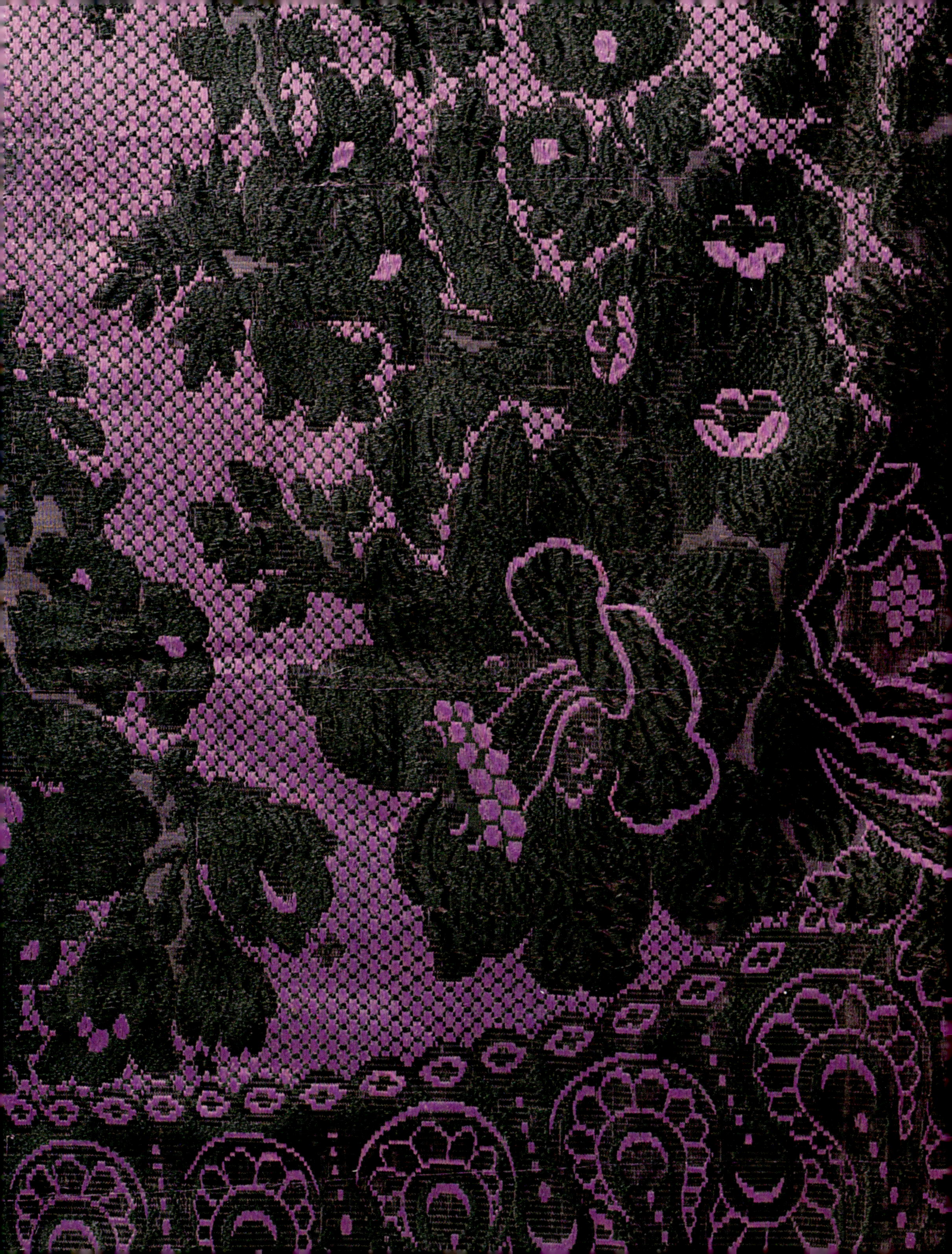

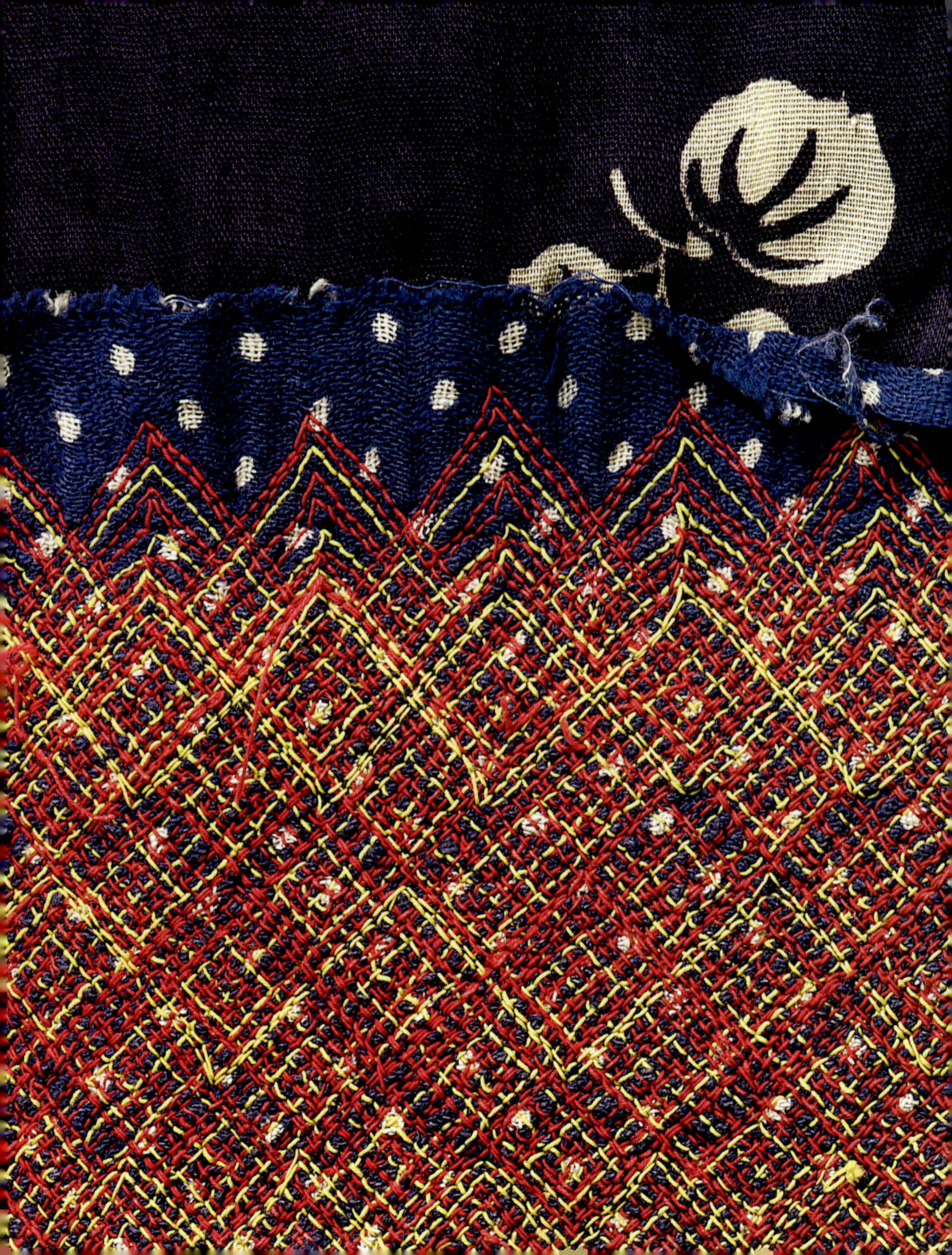

NOTES

INTRODUCTION: FASHIONING FRIDA
Claire Wilcox and Circe Henestrosa

1 A packet of American 'Lucky Strike' cigarettes is visible in Gisèle Freund's photograph of Kahlo sitting in front of her portrait of her father (1951). Kahlo's lover, Nickolas Muray, photographed the 1936 advertising campaign for 'Lucky Strike'.
2 This ancient breed of hairless dogs nearly died out in the 1950s, and was rescued by breeders of the Mexican Kennel Club. One of Kahlo's dogs was called *Señor Xolotl* and another *Señorita Xolotzin*, amongst others.
3 Kahlo kept spider monkeys (*Ateles*) that caused chaos in the Blue House. One was called *Fulang Chang*, another *Caimito de Guayabal*. The species is native to the tropical forests of Central and South America and is characterized by its long, prehensile tail.
4 Tibol 1993, p.324.
5 Personal correspondence, 2017.
6 *Ex-votos* were painted on small panels of wood, tin and copper and depicted the survival of a dangerous or life-threating event, thanks to the intercession of a sacred person. Their narrative structure had a profound impact on Kahlo's paintings, and many of her paintings are also painted onto metal.
7 According to the Mexican census of 1930, 97 per cent of the Mexican population were Catholic. Kahlo's mother was devoutly religious.

TREASURE IN THE BLUE HOUSE
Hilda Trujillo Soto

1 In 1957, Diego Rivera set up an irrevocable trust in the Bank of Mexico, ceding Frida Kahlo and Diego Rivera's estate including the *Casa Azul*, today the Museo Frida Kahlo, to the Mexican people. The museum opened on 12 July 1958 and included a small display of Kahlo's clothing and jewellery. The remainder of her wardrobe was sealed away until its rediscovery in 2004.
2 This discovery was made by Ricardo Pérez Escamilla, the then research administrator of the project and chief curator of the exhibition *Tesoros de la Casa Azul (Treasures of the Blue House)*.
3 As demonstrated in the recent exhibition *Las apariencias engañan: los vestidos de Frida Kahlo*, curated by Circe Henestrosa. The exhibition opened in November 2012.

QUETZALCOATL'S GRIN: THE CHANGING FACE OF ART AND CULTURE IN FRIDA KAHLO'S MEXICO
Adrian Locke

1 Taken from Sergei Eisenstein's 1935 description of José Clemente Orozco, 'The grin of Quetzalcoatl would be his smile.' Karetnikova 1991, p.164.
2 Meyer and Sherman 1979, p.511.
3 Knight 1986, p.2.
4 Brenner 1925, p.127. See also Charlot 1963.
5 Debroise 1997, p.44.
6 Twenty-third interview, 14 May 1971 taken from 'Jean Charlot: interviews with John Charlot, 14 September 1970–7 August 1971; 26–9 September 1975; 24 March–24 April 1978' edited by John Charlot and Janine Richardson, 1910. Published online at www.jeancharlot.org.
7 Rivera's Cubist period has been the subject of several exhibitions: Ramón Favela, *Diego Rivera: The Cubist Years*, exh. cat., Phoenix Art Museum, 1984; Jessica Stewart and Leah Dickerman, *The Cubist Paintings of Diego Rivera: Memory, Politics, Place*, exh. pamphlet, National Gallery of Art, Washington DC, 2004; Sylvia Navarrete (ed.), *Diego Rivera: The Cubist Portraits 1913–1917*, exh. cat., Meadows Museum, Dallas, 2009.
8 Stanton L. Catlin, 'Anfiteatro Bolívar' in Linda Downs and Ellen Sharp (eds), *Diego Rivera: A Retrospective*, exh. cat., Detroit Institute of Arts, 1986; Philadelphia Museum of Art; Museo del Palacio de Bellas Artes, Mexico City; Salas Pablo Ruiz Picasso, Madrid; Staatliche Kunsthalle, Berlin; Hayward Gallery, London, p.237.
9 Paz 1993, p.114.
10 See Oles 1993 and Locke 2013.
11 David Alfaro Siqueiros, 'A Declaration of Social, Political and Aesthetic Principles', 1922, reproduced in Siqueiros 1975, pp.24–5.
12 The journal was published between 1925 and 1937. A book, illustrated by Carlos Mérida, was also published: Frances Toor, *A Treasury of Mexican Folkways: The Customs, Myths, Folklore, Traditions, Beliefs, Fiestas, Dances and Songs of the Mexican People*, New York, 1947.
13 Brenner 1929. See Conger 1983, pp.47–9.
14 Charlot 1925, p.25.
15 See John Ittman (ed.), *Mexico and Modern Printmaking: A Revolution in the Graphic Arts, 1920 to 1950*, exh. cat., Philadelphia Museum of Art, 2006; Dawn Ades and Alison McClean, *Revolution on Paper: Mexican Prints, 1910–1960*, exh. cat., British Museum, London, 2009.
16 Locke 2013, p.166.
17 Ibid., p.61.
18 Charlot 1939, pp.62–3.

APPEARANCES CAN BE DECEIVING – FRIDA KAHLO'S CONSTRUCTION OF IDENTITY: DISABILITY, ETHNICITY AND DRESS
Circe Henestrosa

In this text, disability is defined according to the World Health Organisation's definition. 'Disabilities is an umbrella term, covering impairments, activity limitations, and participation restrictions. An impairment is a problem in body function or structure; an activity limitation is a difficulty encountered by an individual in executing a task or action; while a participation restriction is a problem experienced by an individual in involvement in life situations.' See www.who.int/topics/disabilities.

1 As a native from Ixhuatan, Oaxaca, Andrés Henestrosa could only speak indigenous languages until the age of 15. He later learnt and mastered the Spanish language, creating the first Zapotec–Spanish dictionary. He became

p.194
DETAIL OF PRINTED COTTON SKIRT WITH EMBROIDERY, SEE P.103
Museo Frida Kahlo

a member of the Mexican Academy of the Spanish Language in 1964.

2 Turok 2007, p.172, n.11, 12, 19; p.173, n.36.
3 Covarrubias 1946, p.246.
4 For a history of outsider's views and representations of the Tehuantepec Isthmus, see Campbell and Green 1996, pp.155–86.
5 de Laguna 1928, pp.196–270.
6 de Bourbourg 1981 [1861].
7 Henestrosa 1937, p.10.
8 Tibol 1993 [1983].
9 Del Conde 2007, pp.27–49.
10 An ethnographic description of the textiles is given in Turok 2007, pp.52–171.
11 de la Cueva, et al. 2007, p.36.
12 Herrera 2002 [1983], p.110.
13 Herrera 2002 [1983], p.x.
14 Herrera 1990, p.3.
15 Baddeley 1990, p.14.
16 Herrera 2002 [1983], p.111. This is also mentioned in Del Conde's and Turok's contributions to the book *El Ropero de Frida*, Mexico City, 2007.
17 Baddeley 1990, p.14.
18 Herrera 2002 [1983], pp.15–18.
19 Kahlo's right leg was amputated in August 1953, the year before she died.
20 Around 6,000 photographs were discovered at the Blue House in 2004. There are around 14 'mutilated' photographs in the collection.
21 Judith Clark, 'Five Rooms', unpublished essay, 2013.
22 Entwistle 2003, p.112.
23 Sennet 1977; Finkelstein 1991.
24 Rosemarie Garland Thomson has drawn enlightening parallels between feminist and disability theories. See Thomson 1997, pp.279–94.

FRIDA KAHLO'S JEWELLERY
Clare Phillips

1 Herrera 1983, p.163 (referring to 1933).
2 Ibid.
3 de Cortanze et al. 2013, p.26.
4 Herrera 1983, p.275 (referring to 1940, from a private interview, New York City, June 1978).
5 Fuentes 1995, p.7.
6 Carmen López Figueroa quoted in Williams 1994, p.138.
7 Parker Lesley quoted in Herrera 1983, p.275.
8 Herrera 1983, p.412 (quoting a private interview).
9 'Modern Mexican Silver: Reflections Across Time', http://unframed.lacma.org/2013/04/11/modern-mexican-silver-reflections-across-time (accessed 5 June 2017).
10 Herrera 1983, p.474, n.250, letter dated 3 May 1939 from Peggy Guggenheim.
11 Sotheby's New York, Latin American Art 19–20 May 1987, lot 139. My thanks to Maddie Sadofski and Ellen Dooley for bringing this to my attention.
12 Herrera 1983, p.111.
13 Gisèle Freund, 1991 quoted in de Cortanze et al. 2013, p.19.
14 Herrera 1983, p.438 (Adelina Zendejas, private interview).
15 Álvarez Bravo 1991, p.11.
16 Herrera 1983, p.275.
17 de Cortanze et al. 2013, p.26.

FRIDA KAHLO'S WARDROBE
Chloë Sayer

1 Elisa Speckman Guerra, 'Población y sociedad (1880–1930)', *México Contemporaneo*, vol. 3, Mexico City, 2015, pp.119–73.
2 In a letter written to the King of Spain in 1520, Hernán Cortés noted that Aztec textiles could not be surpassed 'for the variety and naturalness of the colours and handiwork'. Cortés 1986, p.101.
3 Weaving procedures are described with diagrams in Burnham 1980; Deuss 1981; Sayer 1985 and 2015.
4 For an analysis of woven designs and techniques, see Johnson 1976.
5 The European legacy is described in Sayer 1985, pp.76–95 and Sayer 2015, pp.40–61.
6 Sayer 2015, pp.116–18.

FRIDA KAHLO: MAKING HER SELF UP
Claire Wilcox

1 Grimberg 2008, pp.46–7. Olga Campos was a Mexican psychology student who conducted a series of psychological studies of Kahlo between 1949 and 1950. The longer description of Kahlo's cosmetic practice reads like a medical report: 'Her light-tan face was not pretty, perhaps, by established norms, but she possessed – and even radiated – a strange and alluring beauty. Her eyes were large and had a deep, questioning look. Her characteristic eyebrows were shaped like the wings of a bird in flight. She had a small, average nose. Her lips, though thin, were sensuous. She had a special skill for applying makeup and achieving a natural look, and spent a lot of time on this effect. She used blush and rice powder by Coty. Her lipstick and nail polish were always in a strong colour, and, for her eyebrows and lashes, which she carefully combed, she used Talika black powder. She used Trushay hand lotion. She was always made-up and well dressed, even when she did not expect visitors. There were only a few times I saw her without makeup.'
2 See also *Diego in My Mind* (1943) and *Diego and I* (1949).
3 Rivera 1960, p.102.
4 Gannit Ankori links the pervasiveness of images of flight, frustrated flight and identification with birds and other winged creatures to Kahlo's lifelong disability, beginning with her polio, deteriorating after the accident and culminating with the amputation of her leg shortly before her death. See Ankori 2002, pp.82–3; 99; 208–14.
5 The earring appears also in *Self-Portrait Dedicated to Dr Eloesser* (1940).
6 Campos wrote 'she customarily parted her hair in the middle and made two braids with ribbons or wool yarn woven through them. At home, she would let the braids fall down her back, but for dress-up she would raise them over her head, crowning them with a ribbon tiara, and adorning them with flowers or combs covered with rhinestones.' Grimberg 2008, pp.46–7.
7 Kahlo painted Natasha Gelman in 1943. Del Rio lived a few streets away from the Blue House.
8 Nor did Kahlo remove her underarm hair. See Julien Levy's photographs, *c.*1938 [77]. Hormone treatment in 1941 may have coarsened her facial hairs (see the later self-portraits).
9 Grimberg 2008, p.87.
10 Tibol 2003, p.31.
11 Details of eyebrow pencil packaging:
REG NO 226490 SSA
Made in Mexico by Revlon
Fray Servando Teresa de Mier No 92
Mexico City
12 Kahlo wore many different types of perfume, including Shalimar by Guerlain (1921), Emir by Dana (1935), Chanel No. 5 (1921) and Jean Marie

Farina by Roger & Gallet. Campos recalls kissing Kahlo's proffered cheek: 'For the first time, I noticed the beauty of her scent: Schiaparelli. Maybe other women I had met had worn it, but it smelled different on her.' Grimberg 2008.

13 Helena Rubinstein bought one of Kahlo's still lives on a visit to Mexico in 1941, and in a telegram to Julien Levy in the same year, Kahlo urged him to try to sell another to her, because of the expenses she had incurred following her father's death.

14 Moreno 2003, pp.137–9.

15 This was filmed in the Blue House in 1939. It shows Kahlo languorously inserting flowers into her hair and kissing Rivera, but unable to take her eyes away from the camera.

16 Bottles of nail varnish discovered among Kahlo's belongings in 2004 include Revlon's 'Frosted Snow Pink' and 'Raven Red Frosted' plus some varnish with an undecipherable name which has turned green over time.

17 Frida Kahlo, Paris, France letter to Nickolas Muray, New York, N.Y., 27 February 1939. Nickolas Muray papers, 1910–78. Archives of American Art, Smithsonian Institution.

18 Grimberg 2004, p.22.

19 Revlon was one of the first to introduce matching lipstick and nail varnish, sold as a boxed set.

20 Álvarez Bravo 1991, p.7. Kahlo called Emma Hurtado, Rivera's agent and fourth wife, whom he married in July 1955, one year after Kahlo's death, 'that stupid, overly made-up woman'.

21 Ankori 2002, pp.10–11.

22 Álvarez Bravo 1991, p.x.

23 Grimberg 2008, p.51.

24 'Faces', Walt Whitman, *Leaves of Grass*, 1855.

FRIDA KAHLO: POSING, COMPOSING, EXPOSING
Gannit Ankori

1 This essay explores the nexus between photographs of Frida Kahlo, her self-styled fashion and her paintings. The similarities and distinctions between these three modes of creativity will be highlighted with the help of select, pivotal images; the accompanying text will oscillate between Kahlo's formative childhood years and her accomplishment as a mature painter.

2 Frida Kahlo, cited by Hayden Herrera: Herrera 1983, p.99.

3 Romualdo Garcia's photographs of indigenous couples are perhaps the best examples of this genre. I am familiar with two photographs by Reyes from this photo session, one in black and white of the couple standing side by side; another in both black and white and a hand-coloured version of a seated Kahlo next to a standing Rivera that is in the collection of Boston's Museum of Fine Arts (accession number: 2016.112).

4 In addition to several photographs by an anonymous press photographer, a posed group photograph exists by Tina Modotti documenting participants of the 1 May march, including Rivera and Kahlo. Modotti is credited with introducing Kahlo to the communist party and to Rivera.

5 Rivera painted Kahlo in similar fashion in a Mexico City mural at the *Secretaría de Educación Pública*, see Ankori 2013, p.70 quoting Wolfe 1963, pp.244–5.

6 Kahlo's close lifelong friend, Alejandro Gómez Arias recalled how she became an expert at taking, developing and retouching photographs, skills that later influenced her practice as a painter, see Ankori 2013, p.172. Frida Kahlo's photographs, recently revealed by the Museo Frida Kahlo, confirm this assertion.

7 This section uses first names to distinguish between Frida Kahlo and Wilhelm (Guillermo) Kahlo. On his relationship with his daughter and a general overview of the family relations, see Ankori 2013, pp.20–43.

8 Kahlo developed a lifelong passion for dolls and even as a grown woman collected and played with dolls. See Ankori 2002, pp.83–4; 91; 101; 144. She also painted dolls in a self-portrait from 1937 [2] and in a still life from 1943, both on view in the exhibition *Frida Kahlo: Making Her Self Up*.

9 This observation appears in Grimberg 2015, pp.7–8. On Kahlo's experience following polio, see Ankori 2013, pp.44–51.

10 Elsewhere I have elaborated on Kahlo's affinities with photography and photographers, see Ankori 2013, pp.172–6; 229. Significant publications about Kahlo and photography include, Salomon Grimberg, *Lola Álvarez Bravo: The Frida Photographs*, Dallas, 1991; Carla Stellweg (ed.), *Frida Kahlo: The Camera Seduced*, San Francisco, 1992; Margaret Hooks, *Frida Kahlo: Portrait of an Icon*, New York, 2002; Salomon Grimberg, *I Will Never Forget You: Frida Kahlo to Nickolas Muray*, Munich, 2004; Pablo Ortiz Monasterio (ed.), *Frida Kahlo: Her Photos*, Mexico City, 2010; and Grimberg 2015.

11 A detailed examination of the shift in Kahlo's painting appears in Ankori 2005, pp.30–45.

12 On Kahlo's 'Childhood Series' see Ankori 2002, pp.25–92.

13 Ankori 2002, fig.16; Grimberg 2015, pp.40–1. Kahlo's alteration of her appearance coincided with Rivera's affair with her younger sister, Cristina. Hence, *Memory* has also been interpreted as a recollection of the heartbreak caused by this 'double betrayal'. See Ankori 2002, pp.84–90.

14 Gannit Ankori, interview with Alejandro Gómez Arias, March 1989; Ankori 2013, pp.58–60.

15 Elsewhere I have provided a comprehensive analysis and multi-layered interpretation of *Memory*, demonstrating how Kahlo aligns herself not only with the Tehuana 'persona' but also with mythical Mexican women who were marginalized and despised, like *La Llorona* (the weeping woman) and the 'screwed' *Chingada*, see Ankori 2002, pp.84–90; 91–2. For an analysis of Christian symbols embedded in the painting, see Grimberg 1990–1, pp.3–7. Kahlo often used mirrors to paint self-portraits, hence the mirror image of her atrophied right leg appears wounded in this painting.

16 I thank Circe Henestrosa for sharing photographs and written material regarding her exhibition 'Appearances Can Be Deceiving' on view since 2012 at the Museo Frida Kahlo.

17 Several photographs taken by Nickolas Muray in 1940 show Kahlo in traction (see Ankori 2013, p.156). These were not intended to be seen in public and were only recently revealed. Kahlo gave a signed copy of the photograph to Rivera in 1940, in order to elicit his sympathy during the time of their divorce. It worked. After receiving the photograph,

he remarried Kahlo in San Francisco. A number of additional photographs by Muray from 1946 show Kahlo preparing for her spinal fusion operation in New York. These too were not intended to be seen by the public were only discovered in 2004, among Kahlo's private papers in Coyoacán.

18 Ankori 2005.
19 Salomon Grimberg, 'Self-Portrait Drawing,' in *Christie's: New York, Latin American Sale, Important Paintings, Drawings, and Sculpture*, 24 and 25 November 1998, lot 2, p.8. Grimberg connects Kahlo's self-image with multiple arms to Hindu precedents.
20 The painting, which is known from a black and white photograph, was lost in a fire in the early twentieth century. Kahlo's right foot was her ailing limb; she paints her left foot as bandaged because she used a mirror to paint this work. See Ankori 2002, figs 19–22; pp.111–21.
21 Adelina Zendejas, interview with Karen and David Crommie, c.1960s; Also see Ankori 2002, pp.96–100. Kahlo's strategies for coping with the two physical traumas that framed her childhood – inventing an imaginary friend (or 'double') and 'splitting' – are discussed in detail in ibid, pp.93–121.
22 Kahlo's close friends, interviewed by Karen and David Crommie in the 1960s (among them Judith Ferretto and Ella Proenza) and scholars like Hayden Herrera and Salomon Grimberg, suggest that one reason Kahlo wore long skirts was to cover her disability.
23 In this section, I also use the given names – Frida and Guillermo – so as not to confuse the two artists named Kahlo.
24 See Ankori 2013, p.130.
25 See analysis in Ankori 2013, pp.29–43.
26 *Soldaderas* were women who followed the revolutionary troops during the Mexican Revolution. Although some participated in the actual fighting, most were camp followers who performed 'traditional' female roles: cooks, mothers, caretakers and lovers of the soldiers.
27 See Phillips et al. 2010, pp.42–7; 88–95. It seems puzzling that Kahlo never credited her mother with providing inspiration for the artist's own self-presentation as a Tehuana woman. One may speculate that a fraught mother and daughter relationship is related to this, but we may never know for sure.
28 See Ankori 2013, pp.44–57.
29 On the National Preparatory School and Kahlo's milieux, see Herrera 1983, pp.22–44; Ankori 2013, p.207, n.13 with reference to James Oles, 'At the Café de los Cachucahs: Frida Kahlo in the 1920s,' *Hispanic Research Journal*, vol. 8, no. 5, 2007, pp.467–589. See also Adrian Locke's essay in this volume.
30 Grimberg 2015, p.9.
31 The 1929 photograph is by Guillermo Dávila; the 1931 photographs are by Imogen Cunningham. The paintings are *Self-Portrait (Time Flies)* and *Frieda Kahlo and Diego Rivera* respectively.
32 Ankori 2002, pp.140–1; Ankori 2013, pp.70–3. On Nahui Olin see, Adriana Maldivo, *Nahui Olin: La Mujer del Sol*, Mexico, 1999.
33 Ankori 2013, pp.75–85.
34 Frida Kahlo, note to Guillermo Kahlo, on the last page of a letter to her mother dated 'November 1930', cited in Ankori 2013, p.76.
35 Rosenzweig 2008, e.g., pp.86–99.
36 Kahlo, letter to Matilde Calderón, 21 November 1930, cited in Ankori 2013, p.10.
37 Ibid.
38 Helen Appleton Read in *Boston Evening Transcript*, 22 October 1930, p.45. Although outside the scope of this essay, the gender and racial biases inscribed in the language used by the press about Kahlo must be noted.
39 Cited in Ankori 2013, pp.79–81.
40 Edward Weston, *The Daybooks of Edward Weston*, vol. II (New York, 1973), pp.198–9.
41 Ankori 2002, pp.84–90; 123–34; Ankori 2013, pp.102–7. Contemporary Japanese artist, Ishiushi Miyako's photographs of Kahlo's empty dresses illuminate Kahlo's paintings, see Gannit Ankori, 'A Poetics of Absence and Silence: Ishiushi Miyako's Frida Kahlo Photographs' in Miyako 2013, unpaginated.
42 Julien Levy, unpublished transcript of interview with Hayden Herrera, 1977. Julien Levy's photographs are in the Philadelphia Museum of Art collections and available online: www.philamuseum.org/collections (accessed 1 September 2017).
43 Bertram D. Wolfe, 'The Rise of Another Rivera', US *Vogue*, 1 November 1938, p.131.
44 Herrera 1983, pp.355–6; Ankori 2002, pp.116–7.
45 Cited in Ankori 2002, p.135.
46 Ankori 2002, 2005, 2013, passim.
47 Kahlo's letters to Rivera are sometimes signed '*la grad ocultadora*'. The term also appears in Kahlo's diary (*Diary*, p.145) in a copy of a letter that Kahlo identifying as 'the great concealer' addressed to Rivera, to whom she refers as 'her child'. Margaret Hooks also linked Kahlo's photographs and costumes with her self-description as '*la gran ocultadora*' See Hooks 2002, pp.16, 25.
48 Judith Ferretto, unpublished interviews with Karen and David Crommie, c.1960s and Judith Ferretto interviewed in David and Karen Crommie, *The Life and Death of Frida Kahlo*, San Francisco, 1966, film.

THE RESPLANDOR: CULTURAL AND SPIRITUAL SIGNIFICANCE IN TWO SELF-PORTRAITS

Kirstin Kennedy

1 Oles 2007, p.467.
2 Marta Turok, 'Frida's Attire: Eclectic and Ethnic' in Rosenzweig 2008, pp.170–1.
3 Dalton 2010, p.131.
4 Henestrosa 2013, pp.43–4.
5 See Circe Henestrosa's essay in this volume, pp.66–83.
6 Covarrubias 1947, p.263.
7 Photograph reproduced in Vidal 2016, after p.74.
8 See Banco de Mexico, 'The history of coins and banknotes in Mexico', 2017, p.32 available online: www.banxico.org.mx/billetes-y-monedas.pdf (accessed 27 June 2017). The current 500-peso banknote reproduces self-portraits by Rivera and Kahlo, together with an image of their paintings *Nude with Calla Flowers*, 1944 (Rivera) and *The Love Embrace of the Universe, Earth (Mexico), Me, Diego and Mr Xólotl*, 1949 (Kahlo).
9 Herrera 1989, pp.366–7.
10 Covarrubias 1947, p.263.
11 Bargellini 2004, p.85.
12 *The Diary of Frida Kahlo*, commentary to p.137 (Fuentes 1995, p.275); G. Salamanca Bautista et al., 'Especies

Ornamentales en las Iglesias de Cholula Durante las Fiestas', *Proceedings of the Interamerican Society for Tropical Horticulture*, vol. 45, 2001, pp.92–4 (at p.92).

13 Ankori 2005, p.34; Barson 2005, p.69.

14 Córdova 2014, p.2; Pernoud 1983, pp.47–8.

15 Córdova 2014, pp.91–2.

16 Luis G. Cabrera, *Plantas curativas de México*, 4th edn, Mexico City, 1950, pp.33–4 and 337–8. Kahlo owned a copy of this book: see Ankori 2005, p.40, n.30.

17 Herrera 1989, p.328.

18 *The Diary of Frida Kahlo*, p.23 and translation, p.216 (Fuentes 1995).

19 *The Diary of Frida Kahlo*, p.102: '*Siempre hay cosas nuevas. Siempre ligadas a las antiguas vivas*'. The author's translation.

FRIDA REDRESSED

Oriana Baddeley

1 The clipping from *San Francisco News*, January 1931 was preserved in an album belonging to Jean Wight, wife of Rivera's assistant Clifford Wight (collection of the author).

2 Diego Rivera was visiting San Francisco at the invitation of both William Gerstle, president of the San Francisco Art Institute, and architect Timothy Pflueger to paint the mural Allegory of California (1930–1).

3 Post by Lorena Muñoz-Alonso 'Beyoncé and Jay-Z Dressed as Frida Kahlo and Basquiat for Halloween' 3 November 2014: https://news.artnet.com/art-world/beyonce-and-jay-z-dressed-as-frida-kahlo-and-basquiat-for-halloween-152825.

4 *Frida Kahlo: Art-Garden-Life*, New York Botanical Gardens, 16 May to 1 November 2015.

5 Kahlo's famous statement 'I am not sick I am broken' was quoted in *Time* magazine 'Mexican Autobiography', 27 April 1953.

6 Baddeley 2005.

7 Baddeley 1991.

8 The Spanish conqueror Hernán Cortés' discarded Indian mistress Malinche has traditionally been used allegorically to represent the injured and colonized body of Mexico. The classic account of this narrative of identity is Octavio Paz's chapter 'The Sons of La Malinche' in his book *The Labyrinth of Solitude* first published in *Cuadernos Americanos* in 1950.

9 In Greek Mythology Hercules's wife Deianeira gives him the poisoned shirt to regain his love. Tricked into using it by the dying Centaur Nessus to ensure Hercules love for her it imparts an agonizing death for the hero, burning itself into his skin. See: Ovid *Metamorphoses* Book IX 'The Agony of Hercules'.

10 The New York writer, socialite and editor of *Vanity Fair*, Clare Boothe Luce (1903–1987), commissioned the work from Kahlo, though was horrified on the receipt of the actual picture and had to be stopped by friends from destroying it, see: Herrera 1983, p.173.

11 The narrative inscribed in the painting by Kahlo was suggested by New York gossip and even elements of the news at the time see: 'Dorothy Hale Dies in 16 Storey Plunge' *New York Times*, 22 October 1938.

12 *Fulang Chang & I* was repositioned alongside the mirror as part of the 2009 rehang at MoMA New York which for the first time included a gallery dedicated to Mexican Modernist art.

BIBLIOGRAPHY

ADES AND MCCLEAN 2009
Dawn Ades and Alison McClean, *Revolution on Paper: Mexican Prints, 1910–1960*, exh. cat., British Museum, London, 2009

ÁLVAREZ BRAVO 1991
Lola Álvarez Bravo, *The Frida Kahlo Photographs*, Dallas, 1991

ANKORI 2002
Gannit Ankori, *Imaging Her Selves: Frida Kahlo's Poetics of Identity and Fragmentation*, Wesport and London, 2002

ANKORI 2005
Gannit Ankori, 'Frida Kahlo: The Fabric of her Art', *Frida Kahlo*, exh. cat., Tate Modern, London, 2005, pp.31–45

ANKORI 2013
Gannit Ankori, *Frida Kahlo*, London, 2013

BADDELEY 1990
Oriana Baddeley, '"Her Dress Hangs Here": De-frocking the Kahlo Cult', *Oxford Art Journal*, vol. 14, no. 1, 1990

BADDELEY 2005
Oriana Baddeley, 'Reflecting on Kahlo: Mirrors, Masquerade and the Politics of Identification', *Frida Kahlo*, exh. cat., Tate Modern, London, 2005, pp.47–53

BARGELLINI 2004
Clara Bargellini, 'Originality and Invention in the Painting of New Spain', *Painting a New World: Mexican Art and Life 1521–1821*, exh. cat., Denver Art Museum, Denver, 2004, pp.78–92

BARSON 2005
Tanya Barson, '"All Art is at Once Surface and Symbol": A Frida Kahlo Glossary', *Frida Kahlo*, exh. cat., Tate Modern, London, 2005, pp.55–79

DE BOURBOURG 1981
Charles Etienne Brasseur de Bourbourg, *Viaje por el istmo de Tehuantepec*, Mexico City, 1981 [1861]

BRAUN 2010
Barbara Braun, 'Diego Rivera's Collection: Pre-Columbian Art as a Political and Artistic Legacy', Elizabeth Hill Boone (ed.), *Collecting the Pre-Columian Past*, Washington, 2010

BRENNER 1925
Anita Brenner, 'A Mexican Renascence', *The Arts*, vol. 8, no. 3, 1925

BRENNER 1929
Anita Brenner, *Idols Behind Altars*, New York, 1929

BURNHAM 1980
Dorothy K. Burnham, *Warp and Weft: a Textile Terminology*, Toronto, 1980

CAMPBELL AND GREEN 1996
Howard Campbell and Susanne Green, 'A History of Representations of Isthmus Zapotec women', *Identities*, vol. 3, nos 1–2, 1996

CHARLOT 1925
Jean Charlot, 'Un precursor del movimento de Arte Mexicano: El grabador Posada', *Revista de Revistas*, vol. 16, no. 799, 1925

CHARLOT 1939
Jean Charlot, *Art from the Mayans to Disney*, London, 1939

CHARLOT 1963
Jean Charlot, *The Mexican Mural Renaissance, 1920–1925*, New Haven, 1963

CONGER 1983
Amy Conger, *Edward Weston in Mexico, 1923–1926*, exh. cat., San Francisco Museum of Modern Art, 1983

DE CONTRERAS 1987
Chistobal Manso de Contreras, *La Rebelión de Tehuantepec*, Mexico, 1987

CÓRDOVA 2014
James M. Córdova, *Crowned Nun Portraits and Reform in the Convent*, Texas, 2014

CORDRY 1968
Donald and Dorothy Cordry, *Mexican Indian Costumes*, Austin, 1968

DE CORTANZE ET AL. 2013
Gérard de Cortanze et al., *Frida Kahlo: The Gisèle Freund Photographs*, New York, 2013

CORTÉS 1986
Hernán Cortés, *Letters from Mexico*, trans. and ed. by Anthony Pagden, New Haven and London, 1986

COVARRUBIAS 1947
Miguel Covarrubias, *Mexico South: The Isthmus of Tehuantepec*, London, 1947

DE LA CUEVA, ET AL. 2007
Alicia Azuela de la Cueva, et al., *Tesoros de la Casa Azul, Frida y Diego*, Mexico City, 2007

DALTON 2010
Margarita Dalton, *Mujeres: Género e identidad en el istmo de Tehuantepec, Oaxaca*, Mexico City, 2010

DAVIS AND PACK 1963
Mary L. Davis and Greta Pack, *Mexican Jewelry*, Austin, 1963

DEBROISE 1997
Olivier Debroise 'Action Art: David Alfaro Siqueiros and the Artistic and Ideological Strategies of the 1930s', *Portrait of a Decade: David Alfaro Siqueiros, 1930–1940*, exh. cat., Whitechapel Gallery, London, 1997

DEL CONDE 2007
Teresa Del Conde, 'Frida Kahlo: Her Look', in Denise and Magdalena Rosenzweig (eds), *El Ropero de Frida*, Mexico City, 2007, pp.27–49

DEUSS 1981
Krystyna Deuss, *Indian Costumes from Guatemala*, London, 1981

DIEZ 1989
Lourdes Suarz Diez, 'Conchas prehispánicas en México', *British Archaeological Reports International Series*, no. 514, 1989

DOWNS AND SHARP 1986
Linda Downs and Ellen Sharp (eds), *Diego Rivera: A Retrospective*, exh. cat., Detroit Institute of Arts, 1986

ENTWISTLE 2003
Joanne Entwistle, *The Fashioned Body: Fashion, Dress and Modern Social Theory*, Cambridge, 2003

FAVELA 1984
Ramón Favela, *Diego Rivera: The Cubist Years*, exh. cat., Phoenix Art Museum, 1984

FINKELSTEIN 1991
Joanne Finkelstein, *The Fashioned Self*, Cambridge, 1991

FUENTES 1995
Carlos Fuentes (ed.), *The Diary of Frida Kahlo. An Intimate Self-Portrait*, New York, 1995

GRIMBERG 1990
Salomon Grimberg, 'Frida Kahlo's *Memory*', *Woman's Art Journal*, vol. 11, no. 2, 1990–1

GRIMBERG 2004
Salomon Grimberg, *I Will Never Forget You: Frida Kahlo and Nickolas Muray*, San Francisco, 2006

GRIMBERG 2008
Salomon Grimberg, *Frida Kahlo: Song of Herself*, London, 2008

GRIMBERG 2015
Salomon Grimberg, 'Frida Kahlo: Before She Discovered Mirrors', *Mirror Mirror ... Portraits of Frida Kahlo*, exh. cat., Throckmorton Fine Art, New York, 2015

HECHT 2002
Ann Hecht, *Textiles from Guatemala*, London, 2002

HENESTROSA 1937
Andrés Henestrosa, *El Retrato de mi Madre*, New Orleans, 1937

HENESTROSA 2013
Circe Henestrosa, 'Las apariencias engañan: los vestidos de Frida Kahlo', *Todo el Universo: Frida Kahlo. El Mundo* México, Mexico City, 2013, pp.39–69

HERRERA 1983
Hayden Herrera, *Frida: A Biography of Frida Kahlo*, New York, 1983

HERRERA 1989
Hayden Herrera, *Frida: A Biography of Frida Kahlo*, London, 1989 (first published 1983)

HERRERA 1990
Hayden Herrera, 'Why Frida Kahlo Speaks to the 90's', *New York Times*, 28 October 1990

HOOKS 2002
Margaret Hooks, *Frida Kahlo: Portrait of an Icon*, New York, 2002

JOHNSON 1976
Irmgard Weitlaner Johnson, *Design Motifs on Mexican Indian Textiles* (2 vols.), Graz, 1976

ITTMAN 2009
John Ittman (ed.), *Mexico and Modern Printmaking: A Revolution in the Graphic Arts, 1920 to 1950*, exh. cat., Philadelphia Museum of Art, 2006

KARETNIKOVA 1991
Inga Karetnikova, *Mexico According to Eisenstein*, Albuquerque, 1991

KETTENMANN 2015
Andrea Kettenmann, *Frida Kahlo 1907–1954: Pain and Passion*, Köln, 2015

KNIGHT 1986
Alan Knight, *The Mexican Revolution. Vol. 1: Porfirians, Liberals and Peasants*, Cambridge, 1986

DE LAGUNA 1928
Juan de Torres de Laguna, 'Descripción de Tehuantepec', *Revista Mexicana de Estudios Históricos, Apéndice II*, 1928

LECHUGA 1982
Ruth D. Lechuga, *El traje indígena de México: su evolución desde la época prehispánica hasta la actualidad*, Mexico City, 1982

LINATTI 1956
Claudio Linatti, *Trajes civiles, militates y religiosos de Mexico*, Mexico, 1956

LOCKE 2013
Adrian Locke, *Mexico: A Revolution in Art, 1910–1940*, exh. cat., Royal Academy of Arts, London, 2013

MAPELLI MOZZI 1965–8
Carlota Mapelli Mozzi and Teresa Castelló Yturbide, *El traje indígena en México*, (2 vols), Mexico City, 1965–8

MEYER AND SHERMAN 1979
Michael C. Meyer and William L. Sherman, *The Course of Mexican History*, New York, 1979

MIYAKO 2013
Ishiuchi Miyako, *Frida by Ishiushi*, Mexico City, 2013

MORENO 2003
Julio Moreno, *Yankee Don't Go Home!: Mexican Nationalism, American Business Culture, and the Shaping of Modern Mexico, 1920–1950*, North Carolina, 2003

NAVARRETE 2009
Sylvia Navarrete (ed.), *Diego Rivera: The Cubist Portraits 1913–1917*, exh. cat., Meadows Museum, Dallas, 2009

OLES 1993
James Oles, *South of the Border*, exh. cat., Yale University Art Gallery, New Haven, 1993

OLES 2007
James Oles, 'At the Café de los Cachuchas: Frida Kahlo in the 1920s', *Hispanic Research Journal*, vol. 8, no. 5, 2007, pp.467–89

PAZ 1993
Octavio Paz, 'Re/Visions: Mural Painting', in Octavio Paz, *Essays on Mexican Art*, New York, 1993, pp.113–68

PERNOUD 1983
Emmanuel Pernoud, 'Une Autobiographie Mystique', *Gazette des Beaux Arts*, vol. 101, 1983, pp.43–8

PHILLIPS ET AL. 2010
Carlos Phillips et al., *Frida Kahlo: Her Photos*, Mexico City, 2010

RIVERA 1960
Diego Rivera (with Gladys March), *My Art, My Life: An Autobiography*, New York, 1960

ROSENZWEIG 2008
Denise and Magdalena Rosenzweig (eds), *Self-portrait in a Velvet Dress: Frida's Wardrobe: Fashion from the Museo Frida Kahlo*, San Francisco, 2008

ROWE 1981
Ann Pollard Rowe, *A Century of Change in Guatemalan Textiles*, Washington DC, 1981

SAYER 1985
Chloë Sayer, *Mexican Costume*, London, 1985

SAYER 1990
Chloë Sayer, *Mexican Patterns: A Design Sourcebook*, London, 1990

SAYER 2002
Chloë Sayer, *Textiles from Mexico*, London, 2002

SAYER 2015
Chloë Sayer with Alexandra Palmer, *Mexico: Clothing & Culture*, Toronto, 2015

SCHEVILL 1993
Margot Blum Schevill, *Maya Textiles of Guatemala: The Gustavus A. Eisen Collection 1902*, Austin 1993

SENNET 1977
Richard Sennet, *The Fall of Public Man*, Cambridge, 1977

SHAUGHNESSY, 2013
Roxane Shaughnessy et al, *Ancestry and Artistry: Maya Textiles from Guatemala*, exh. cat., Textile Museum of Canada, Toronto, 2013

SIQUEIROS 1975
David Alfaro Siqueiros, *Art and Revolution*, London, 1975

START 1980
Laura E. Start, *The McDougall Collection of Indian Textiles from Guatemala and Mexico*, Oxford, 1980

STEWART AND DICKERMAN, 2004
Jessica Stewart and Leah Dickerman, *The Cubist Paintings of Diego Rivera: Memory, Politics, Place*, exh. pamphlet, National Gallery of Art, Washington DC, 2004

TAIT 1986
Hugh Tait (ed.), *Seven Thousand Years of Jewellery*, London, 1986

THOMSON 1997
Rosemarie Garland Thomson, 'Feminist Theory, the Body, and the Disabled Figure' in Lennard J. Davis (ed.), *Disability Studies Reader*, New York, 1997

TIBOL 1993
Raquel Tibol, *Frida Kahlo. An Open Life*, Albuquerque, 1993 [1983]

TIBOL 2003
Raquel Tibol, *Frida by Frida: Selection of Letters and Texts*, Mexico City, 2003

TOOR 1947
Frances Toor, *A Treasury of Mexican Folkways: The Customs, Myths, Folklore, Traditions, Beliefs, Fiestas, Dances and Songs of the Mexican People*, New York, 1947

TUROK 2007
Marta Turok, 'Los Ajuares de Frida: Eclectisismo y Etnicidad' in Denise and Magdalena Rosenzweig (eds), *El Ropero de Frida*, Mexico City, 2007

VIDAL 2016
Susana Martinez Vidal, *Frida Kahlo: Fashion as the Art of Being*, New York, 2016

WILLIAMS 1994
Adriana Williams, *Covarrubias*, Austin, 1994

WOLFE 1939
Bertram D. Wolfe, *Diego Rivera: His Life and Times*, London, 1939

WOLFE 1963
Bertram D. Wolfe, *The Fabulous Life of Diego Rivera* (1963), New York, 1984

INDEX

Page numbers in *italic* refer to the illustrations. Roman numbers refer to the booklets.

PHOTOGRAPHY CREDITS

BY PLATE NUMBER, UNLESS OTHERWISE STATED.

AKG-IMAGES/ALBUM/ORONOZ: 89

ARCHIVART/ALAMY STOCK PHOTO: 80

DIGITAL IMAGE AKG-IMAGES © DACS 2017: 15

© ALEJANDRA MATIZ. LEO MATIZ FOUNDATION: 45, 71, 100

© ARCHIVES OF AMERICAN ART SMITHSONIAN INSTITUTION: P.8

© ARCHIVO MIGUEL COVARRUBIAS, UNIVERSIDAD DE LAS AMERICAS PUEBLA (UDLAP): 14, 29

© ARIZONA BOARD OF REGENTS, CENTER FOR CREATIVE PHOTOGRAPHY: 75

© 2017. PHOTO ART RESOURCE/BOB SCHALKWIJK/SCALA, FLORENCE: 78, 82

© BEN HIDER/THE NEW YORK BOTANICAL GARDEN: 92

© CENTER FOR CREATIVE PHOTOGRAPHY, THE UNIVERSITY OF ARIZONA FOUNDATION: 19, 21, 22, 24, 66

© CENTER FOR CREATIVE PHOTOGRAPHY, THE UNIVERSITY OF ARIZONA FOUNDATION/ DACS 2017: 30

© CENTER FOR CREATIVE PHOTOGRAPHY, THE UNIVERSITY OF ARIZONA FOUNDATION/ VICENTE WOLF PHOTOGRAPHY COLLECTION: 18

© 2017. CHRISTIE'S IMAGES, LONDON/SCALA, FLORENCE: 70

CINCINNATI ART MUSEUM, OHIO, USA/GIFT OF THE ARTIST/BRIDGEMAN IMAGES: 84

COLLECTION EDUARDO F. COSTANTINI, BUENOS AIRES © BANCO DE MÉXICO DIEGO RIVERA FRIDA KAHLO MUSEUMS TRUST, MEXICO, D.F./DACS 2017: 9

COURTESY OF ORIANA BADDELEY. PHOTOGRAPH © VICTORIA AND ALBERT MUSEUM, LONDON: 91

COURTESY OF RAFAEL DONIZ: 60

COURTESY OF THROCKMORTON FINE ART, INC., NEW YORK: II.3, II.4

© D.R. RUFINO TAMAYO/HEREDEROS/MÉXICO/ FUNDACIÓN OLGA Y RUFINO TAMAYO, A.C. 2017/ DACS 2017: 12

© DACS 2017: 8, 16

© DANIELA ROCHA: PP.20, 34, 66, 84, 98, 114, 130, 162, 174

DEGOLYER LIBRARY, SOUTHERN METHODIST UNIVERSITY: 40

DIEGO RIVERA AND FRIDA KAHLO ARCHIVES, BANCO DE MÉXICO, FIDUCIARY OF THE TRUST OF THE DIEGO RIVERA AND FRIDA KAHLO MUSEUMS: 4, 5, I.1, I.2, I.3, I.5, I.7, I.8, II.1, II.7, II.8, 31, 35, 36, 37, 38, 41, 44, 64, 74, 79

© DIGITAL IMAGE MUSEUM ASSOCIATES/LACMA/ ART RESOURCE NY/SCALA, FLORENCE: 85

FIRSTVIEW: 93

© FLORENCE ARQUIN PAPERS/ARCHIVES OF AMERICAN ART, SMITHSONIAN INSTITUTION: 87

© FLORENCE ARQUIN/COURTESY OF THROCKMORTON FINE ART, INC., NEW YORK: 33

© FRITZ HENLE ESTATE: 1

IMAGE COURTESY OF GANNIT ANKORI: 73

© GERARDO SUTER/THE JACQUES AND NATASHA GELMAN COLLECTION OF 20TH CENTURY MEXICAN ART AND THE VERGEL FOUNDATION: PP.15, 16; 2, 58, 59, 61, 88

© GISÈLE FREUND: 3, 6

© GRANGER/REX/SHUTTERSTOCK: P.2

© GUILLERMO DÁVILA. COURTESY OF THROCKMORTON FINE ART, INC., NEW YORK: II.5

© JENN WERNER: 94

© LIBRARY OF CONGRESS PRINTS AND PHOTOGRAPHS DIVISION, WASHINGTON DC: P.12; 17

© MODERN ART INTERNATIONAL FOUNDATION, COURTESY MARÍA AND MANUEL REYERO: P.5

© MUSEUM OF FINE ARTS, BOSTON: 67

© 2017. DIGITAL IMAGE, THE MUSEUM OF MODERN ART, NEW YORK/SCALA, FLORENCE: 11, 13, 62, 81, 98

© 2017. DIGITAL IMAGE, THE MUSEUM OF MODERN ART, NEW YORK/SCALA, FLORENCE/ DACS 2017: 7

© NICKOLAS MURAY PHOTO ARCHIVES: P.6; 27, 34, 39, 65, 79, 95, 99, 101

© PHILADELPHIA MUSEUM OF ART: 76, 77

PHOENIX ART MUSEUM, ARIZONA, USA/GIFT OF AN ANONYMOUS DONOR/BRIDGEMAN IMAGES: 97

PHOTOGRAPH: JAVIER HINOJOSA. DIEGO RIVERA AND FRIDA KAHLO ARCHIVES, BANCO DE MÉXICO, FIDUCIARY OF THE TRUST OF THE DIEGO RIVERA AND FRIDA KAHLO MUSEUMS: PP.19, 32–3, 64–5, 96–7, 128–9, 160–1, 192–3, 194; 20, 23, 25, 26, 32, 43, 46, 47, 48, 49, 50, 51, 52, 53, 54, 55, 56, 57, 90; III.1, III.2, III.3, III.4, III.5, III.6, III.7, III.8, IV.1, IV.2, IV.3, IV.4, IV.5, IV.6, IV.7, IV.8, V.1, V.2, V.3, V.4, V.5, V.6, V.7, V.8, VI.1, VI.2, VI.3, VI.4, VI.5, VI.6, VI.7, VI.8

PRIVATE COLLECTION: 28, 63, 83, 86

PRIVATE COLLECTION/PHOTO © CHRISTIE'S IMAGES/BRIDGEMAN IMAGES: 96

IMAGE COURTESY OF SALOMON GRIMBERG: 69, 72

© 2017. PHOTO SCHALKWIJK/ART RESOURCE/ SCALA, FLORENCE: 10

© SPENCER THROCKMORTON, NEW YORK/ ARCHIVES OF AMERICAN ART, SMITHSONIAN INSTITUTION: 42

© TONI FRISSELL/LIBRARY OF CONGRESS: P.1

ACKNOWLEDGEMENTS

[Text correct at time of first publication.] *Frida Kahlo: Making Her Self Up* has been the result of a collective effort and we would like to thank everyone who has made this exhibition and book possible. Above all, we are grateful to Carlos Phillips Olmedo, Director General, Museos Dolores Olmedo, Frida Kahlo y Diego Rivera Anahuacalli and Hilda Trujillo Soto, Director, Museo Frida Kahlo who has worked tirelessly to support the exhibition. Her colleagues at the Blue House: Perla Labarthe Álvarez, Claudia Romo Tobón and Luanda López Herrera, have worked closely with Circe Henestrosa, originator of *Frida Kahlo: Appearances Can Be Deceiving* (2012), upon which the V&A exhibition has been based. At the V&A, Ana Baeza Ruiz, Research Assistant, has worked assiduously to bring the project to fruition alongside Natalia Ferreiro, Exhibition Manager, and Manuela Buttiglione, Exhibition Assistant. They have been instrumental to the exhibition. In addition, we wish to acknowledge Robyn Earl, Claire Everitt and Sarah Scott of the V&A Exhibitions department. We are grateful to Linda Lloyd-Jones and Christopher Wilk who, along with Susan Chapman and Stephen Smith of the Anglo Mexican Foundation, championed and supported this project from the start. We also extend grateful thanks to the Mexican Ambassador to the United Kingdom H.E. Mr Julián Ventura.

We are immensely grateful to all the institutional and private lenders to the exhibition for their generosity and good will. Thanks to Eva Ayala Canseco, Amanda Bock, Magda Carranza, Megan Clancy, Ángeles Cortés, Tely Duarte, Estefanny Esquivel Magdaleno, Salomon Grimberg, Xavier Guzmán Urbiola, Jan Hendrickx, Cibeles Henestrosa, Nancy Leeman, Robert Littman, Alejandra Matiz, Teresa Nutter, José Enrique Ortiz Lanz, María and Manuel Reyero, Mélina Reynaud, Norberto L. Rivera, Christine Rosenlund, Mariana Sainz Pacheco, Spencer Throckmorton, Dimitri Treantafilos, Magdalena Zavala Bonachea. In particular, we would like to thank the staff of the Fideicomiso Museos Diego Rivera y Frida Kahlo: Luis Urrutia Corral, Luis Rodrigo Saldaña Arellano, Luis Alberto Salgado Rodríguez, Dolores Moreno Cruz and Carla Barri Rosendo and Museo Frida Kahlo, especially José María Aguilar Suárez, Berenice Ángeles Correa, Mariana Arellano Cadena, María Luisa Cárdenas Aburto, Xochiquetzal González Gómez, Ximena Jordán Poblete, Daniela Rivera Soriano, Karen Sandoval Arellano and Laura Zavala Hernández.

The exhibition design has transported us to Frida Kahlo's world, and we owe thanks to Tom Scutt, Lead Designer, Patrick Berning and Matt Thornley, architects, Mireille Burckhardt, 2D Design, Tupac Matir, AV Design, and also to Florence Andrews, Ellie Clarke, Izzie Farr and Duncan Green from Focus who have steered this project.

This publication would not have been possible without the dedication of its contributors, many of whom have also advised on the content of the exhibition, and we are hugely grateful for their expertise and fresh insights. Many thanks to Oriana Baddeley, Kirstin Kennedy, Adrian Locke, Clare Phillips, Chloë Sayer and Hilda Trujillo Soto. A special thanks to Gannit Ankori, who as content advisor has been hugely supportive of this project and always astounded us with her knowledge of Kahlo's life and art. For many, their first encounter with Frida Kahlo was through Hayden Herrera's biography *Frida*. First published in 1983, it remains the source for much of our understanding of this remarkable artist.

For the book, we want to especially thank editor Sophie Sheldrake for her vision and patience, as well as Coralie Hepburn, Emma Woodiwiss and Tom Windross of V&A Publishing; Fred Caws and Liz Edmunds for picture research; Javier Hinojosa and his assistant Dulce Sánchez Cruz for the wonderful new photography and Rebeka Cohen for meticulously proofreading the text. We would also like to extend thanks to Maria Blyzinsky for her skilful copyediting of the exhibition text. Immense thanks to Daniela Rocha, who designed this beautiful book.

Numerous colleagues from the UK and abroad, among them scholars, curators, conservators and collectors, have generously given their time, support and invaluable advice, and we would especially like to thank Muriel Altchek Mercier, Aurelia Álvarez Urbajtel, Sofía Arévalo, Rocío Bermejo, Claudia Bermúdez, Daniel Bish, Dinu Bodiciu, Walter Boelsterly Urrutia, Martin Bonney, Patricia Brambila Gómez, Sarah Bryan, Rosana Calderón Martín del Campo, Nahún Calleros Carriles, Renato Camarillo, Ginette Chittick, Harah Chon, Carina Cruz Fuentes, Anna Dannemann, Emma Dick, Steve Dixon,

Tely Duarte, Dave Ellison, Tania Estrada, Rocío Gamiño Ochoa, Rocío Gaona, Carlos García Ponce, Roberto Gavaldón Arbide, Juan Pablo Gómez Morín Rivera, Laura González Flores, Jan Grenci, Gabriel Gutiérrez, Lesley Hall, Karen E. Heisler, Karl F. Heisler, Aleph Henestrosa, Cassandra Henestrosa, Claudio Hernández, Roxana Hernández, Nur Hidayah Abu Bakar, Stine Høholt, Adrian Huang, Eva Hughes, Kate Jarvis, Ingrid Jiménez, Cristina Kahlo Alcalá, Francisco Kochen, Vera Kwok, Lidia Lavín, Lucinda Law, Erika Lepe, Ramón López Quiroga, Diego López Rivera, Sophia Lorent, Gustavo Lozano, Susana Lucio, Olivia Ludlow, Luis Mancera de Arrigunaga, Rafael Matos Moctezuma, Sean McCallion, Leticia Medina, Mayra Mendoza, Silvia Mesa Dávila, Daniela Monasterios Tan, Mimi Muray, Pablo Ortíz Monasterio, Fernando Osorio Alarcón, Roderick Palacios, Alberto Mario Palma, Mariana Palma, Ariadna Patiño Guadarrama, Ernesto Peñaloza, James Peto, Guadalupe Phillips Margain, Irene Phillips Olmedo, Ana Julia Poncelis, Kate Pourshariati, Christopher Purnawan, Venka Purushothaman, Charles Rezandi, Trinidad Rico, Miguel Rivera, Guadalupe Rivera Marín, Ana Isabel Rivero Borrell, Ariadna Rodríguez, Rodolfo Rodríguez Castañeda, Brett Rogers, Patricia Ruiz, Bridget Rutherford, Alexandra Samkova, Paola Santos Coy, Wai Kit Seetoh, Juan Solís, Brodie Standen, Marina Straulino, Kelly Talamas, Jeremiah Tan, Natsuko Teruya, Miguel Ángel Trinidad, Marta Turok, Ted Utoft, Allan René Velázquez Hernández, Nadya Wang, Edénida Webster Henestrosa, Helen Wolfe, Jo Wright, Agnes Wan and Ling Wu.

At London College of Fashion, University of the Arts London, we would like to thank Judith Clark, designer of the original exhibition *Frida Kahlo: Appearances Can Be Deceiving*, which remains the foundation of this project, Head of College Frances Corner, Jane Harris, Amy de la Haye, Ben Whyman, Bre Stitt, and Dai Rees. Thanks also to MA Fashion Curation students Wen Bi, Annabel Hoyng, Xinyi Li, Jessica Taylor, Natalie Tilbury and Matthew Whaley for their enthusiasm. To Anusha Mistry and Suet May special thanks for their invaluable help. We are very grateful to LASALLE College of the Arts, Singapore, which has supported Circe Henestrosa's travel and research.

We are immensely grateful for the expertise and support of colleagues across all departments of the V&A, but would especially like to thank Rachael Lee, Lead Conservator, for her creativity and commitment, along with Sophie Manhire, Technician and Mount Maker. We would also like to thank in Conservation Lauren Ashley-Irvine, Clair Battison, Alan Derbyshire, Louise Egan, Lara Flecker, Chris Gingell, Joanne Hackett, Frances Hartog, Charlotte Hubbard, Fiona Jordon, Lilia Prier Tisdall, Sandra Smith, Joanna Whalley, Gesa Werner; in Technical Services Richard Ashbridge, Allen Irvine, and Robert Lambeth. Across other departments, we wish to express our thanks to Sophie Brendel, Veronika Tarasidis and Jane Rosier; Zoe Franklin, Kate Morais and Catherine Poust; Julia Bailey, David Judd and Faunsia Tucker; Hannah Geddes, Holly Hyams, Asha McLoughlin and Bryony Shepherd; Barry Ginley and Laura Jones. We are also very grateful to curators across the V&A for their knowledge, encouragement and support. We wish to thank Martin Barnes, Susanna Brown, Ana Cabrera-Lafuente, Oriole Cullen, Edwina Ehrman, Anna Jackson, Elizabeth James, Kirstin Kennedy, Jenny Lister, Lesley Miller, Joanna Norman, Clare Phillips, Bill Sherman, Sonnet Stanfill, Salma Tuqan and Catherine Yvard. Lastly, we thank colleagues in the Research Department, especially Joanna Norman, Tao Chang and Alice Bailey, and from Word & Image, Juliet Ceresole and Catherine Troiano, for their help with our research. Finally, we extend our special thanks to Tristram Hunt and Tim Reeve.

Lastly, we thank our friends and families, for their encouragement and support.

In memory of William Stair (1960–2015) who loved Mexico, and Noris Henestrosa (1944–2015) who always encouraged women to voice and defend their ideas.

CLAIRE WILCOX AND CIRCE HENESTROSA